COMMUNICATING FACTS AND IDEAS IN BUSINESS

Second Edition

COMMUNICATING FACTS AND IDEAS IN BUSINESS

LELAND BROWN

Professor of Business Communication
Eastern Michigan University

PRENTICE-HALL, INC., *Englewood Cliffs, New Jersey*

13–152876–9
Library of Congress Catalog Card Number 71–107964

Current printing (last digit)

10 9 8 7 6 5 4 3 2 1

PRINTED IN THE UNITED STATES OF AMERICA

PRENTICE-HALL INTERNATIONAL, INC., London
PRENTICE-HALL OF AUSTRALIA PTY. LTD., Sydney
PRENTICE-HALL OF CANADA, LTD., Toronto
PRENTICE-HALL OF INDIA PRIVATE LIMITED, New Delhi
PRENTICE-HALL OF JAPAN, INC., Tokyo

To my children,
Marshall Jonathan and Cindra Lee

PREFACE

Autumn 1970

Dear Reader:

Like the first edition, *Communicating Facts and Ideas In Business,* 2nd edition, seeks to present to you a broad, general foundation on which to build and to help you develop your ability to apply the principles of communication to any situation. Similarly, it explores the relationship of creative, logical, and critical thinking to the problem-solving nature of business communication; yet its major emphasis is on developing your ability to think and express yourself effectively, especially in written form, for business purposes.

At the time the first edition was conceived and published, the whole area of business communication was in a state of flux, and traditional courses were being dropped or changed, partly as a result of the influence of the Gordon and Howell report and the Pierson report. At that time, there was a trend toward general, integrated courses covering the entire field of communication. The first edition was designed to meet the new trends and needs.

Since then, courses in business communication have staged a comeback. Businessmen have recognized that college students need to be able to think and express themselves effectively. Consequently, most schools offer a one-semester course in business communication in which the major emphasis is on developing a student's ability to communicate in general, and specifically in writing letters, memos, and reports. Also, since the first edition of *Communicating Facts and Ideas in Business,* there has been an upsurge in junior and community colleges, and there is a need for good communication textbooks to meet the needs of the junior college student and instructor. This second edition is designed to meet these challenges. Its arrangement and sequence of topics will help the student progress from less complicated situations, routine in nature, to more advanced problems of persuasion and report writing. For the instructor, the course is thus organized; a separate teacher's manual is also available.

To aid both instructor and student, a summary and a list of references for further reading have been placed at the end of each chapter. Problems, exercises, and case studies have also been included, for as the reader works at solving these, he will gain further insights and knowledge, develop more effective use of communicating skills and principles, and acquire an increased appreciation of the art of communication. Appendix C will encourage the reader to check the rules as the need arises, because of the ease of finding them.

You will notice as you look through this book that following certain topics, specific lists are preceded by a small black square. These suggest ways of thinking about the ideas raised in the material and reacting to them by associating them with your previous knowledge and experience, and by applying the principles in various situations. They will also serve as a basis for class discussion that will make the facts and ideas meaningful and give you practice in oral communication. Further oral communication is provided for in several of the problems at the ends of chapters; specifically, interviewing is discussed in the chapter on applying for a job, and Appendixes A and B give helpful hints for dictation and improving telephoning techniques.

Through some twenty years of working with students, the key to my success has been *involvement.* The student involved in the give and take of his classmates in discussion, in criticizing and evaluating illustrations and his own work, in exchanging facts and ideas about problems and issues, is indeed in a learning environment and situation. The student who is confronted with communication problems in which he has to think through the situation, use known information, and create ideas and new ways for presenting his messages is developing his ability to think and to express himself effectively.

To you, the student, and to your instructor, I wish you much success in your study and involvement in reading and using *Communicating Facts and Ideas in Business.* I thoroughly enjoyed writing it. Communication can be fun, for you are exchanging facts, ideas, attitudes, and courses of action with others.

No author can write in a vacuum, and I am certainly no exception. It is through the interchange of ideas and working with students to improve their communication effectiveness that I am able to write. I am grateful to all the students I have taught, for I have learned much from them, and I like to think I have helped some along the way. It is also through association with others that we keep abreast of what is going on in the colleges and universities. I am grateful for my longtime association with members of the American Business Communication Association and with other authors and publishers of communication texts.

To my communication-teaching colleagues at Eastern Michigan University, John F. Fisher, Robert Westfall, and especially James Wrixon (my office mate while I was writing the manuscript), I am grateful for their ideas and for their service as a sounding board for mine, and for their trying out some of the materials and problems. To Professors Eugene Logan of Diablo Valley College, and George Nelson of Brigham Young University, who reviewed the manuscript, I am appreciative of their time, effort, and suggestions. Thanks also to Dr. W. Oscar Collins, head of the General Business Department, and Dr. Earl Roth, Dean of the College of Business, Eastern Michigan University, for their encouragement and assistance in finding time for writing and providing secretarial and typing aid for me. I am also appreciative of my wife's help in proofreading and to her and my children for their interest and patience, and for just putting up with me during troublesome periods.

In addition, many others have contributed illustrative materials, problem materials, examples, and comments. Among them have been former students at both Tulane University and EMU, businessmen and companies from all over the United States, authors, educators, publishers' representatives, etc. Although there are too many to list, special credit has been given in a number of footnotes. I am thankful for all this cooperation and help.

Sincerely,

LELAND BROWN

CONTENTS

COMMUNICATING FACTS AND IDEAS IN BUSINESS

Chapter One

ORIENTATION FOR YOUR STUDY OF BUSINESS COMMUNICATION

Communication began early in your life, and all your life you will continue to exchange facts, ideas, feelings, and experiences with others. The need to communicate effectively will always be present, for each opportunity to communicate may be met with success or failure. This book seeks primarily to help you develop communicative power and to serve as a basis for your further professional development. It presents the basic elements, principles, and practices underlying all business communication. The book considers not only skills and techniques, but also ways of thinking and of understanding others so that you can communicate effectively with them. Particular attention is given to the thinking and creative processes involved in writing letters, memorandums, and reports. Practice gained in these activities will help you to improve your skills and abilities and to increase your understanding of human relations and communicating situations. This book should thus stimulate you into thinking creatively, logically, and critically, and should help you to express yourself clearly, interestingly, and persuasively.

OBJECTIVES

At the beginning of any study it is a good idea to take stock of your goals and what you will need to do to accomplish them. This gives direction to your effort and more satisfaction in your results. Consider the following objectives:

1. To understand the communication process, its importance, and its role in a business enterprise
2. To learn how to apply the principles underlying all communication, especially how to handle problem situations with letters, memorandums, and reports
3. To develop the power to inform and persuade others through the use of language
4. To understand human nature and the role of communication in human relations
5. To develop the ability to gather, organize, and evaluate facts and ideas in order to reach conclusions and make recommendations
6. To understand form, style, and tone, and to use them for more effective letters and reports

This list represents the author's objectives for you in writing this book; the numerical order corresponds with the sequence in which the topics are covered.

- At this point it might be well for you, your instructor, and the other class members to discuss your objectives, which may or may not be the same as those given here. You may decide to concentrate more on some than on others, depending upon your own present stage of development, or you may wish to add to the list to suit the individual needs of your class.
- It will also be helpful for you and your instructor to become acquainted so that he can help you develop your skills and abilities. Write him a letter telling him about yourself. Include any factual details about your education, work experience, family background, and activities that will help him to see you as an individual student. He may also be interested in having you analyze your present communicative ability and skills, asking you to point up areas where improvement should be made. Check Chapter 2 for the appropriate form to follow.
- A slightly different twist to writing a get-acquainted letter to your instructor might be to assume that the class section is filled and to write a letter persuading him to admit one more student to his class (this may well be the true situation).

DEFINITION OF COMMUNICATION

As Lee Thayer has indicated, there are more than twenty-five conceptually different definitions of *communication* in the literature.[1] Yet when

[1]Lee O. Thayer, "On Theory Building in Communication: Some Conceptual Issues," *The Journal of Communication*, Vol. XIII, No. 4 (December 1963), 219.

one examines them, as Professor Robert L. Minter did,[2] some common elements and characteristics are found. Communication is the transmission and interchange of facts, ideas, feelings, or courses of action. It is an event or happening that takes place; when it is perceived, it influences and changes the information and behavior of an individual. Mental or emotional concepts are conveyed by means of symbols from one person to another, each being compelled to think in terms of who says what, how, to whom, and with what effect, for good communication is the result of clear thinking.

There is always a communicator, a message, and a receiver. Something happens that stimulates the communicator. He sees a friend, he hears a loud noise, he smells a rose, he reads a business letter. The telephone rings, his boss enters the room, production is down, sales are up. An event or condition stimulates the communicator through his eyes, ears, or other sensory organs, which send nervous impulses to his brain and from there to muscles and glands. These in turn produce feelings and preverbal tensions, which he translates into words according to his accustomed verbal patterns. Thus the "meaning" of the event becomes known to him. Out

[2]Robert L. Minter, "A Denotative and Connotative Study in Communication," *The Journal of Communication*, Vol. XVIII, No. 1 (March 1968), 26–36. The five most commonly acceptable definitions Professor Minter found, in rank order, are as follows:

a. Jurgen Ruesch and Gregory Bateson, "Communication does not refer to verbal, explicit, and internal transmissions of messages alone. . . . The concept of communication would include all those processes by which people influence one another. . . . This definition is based upon the premise that all actions and events have communicative aspects, as soon as they are perceived by a human being; it implies, furthermore, that such perception changes the information which an individual possesses and therefore influences him." *Communication: The Social Matrix of Psychiatry* (New York: W. W. Norton & Company, Inc., 1961), pp. 5–6.

b. Claude Shannon and Warren Weaver, "The word *communication* will be used here in a very broad sense to include all of the procedures by which *one mind* may affect another. This, of course, involves not only written and oral speech, but also music, the pictorial arts, the theatre, the ballet, and in fact all human behavior." *The Mathematical Theory of Communication* (Urbana: University of Illinois Press, 1949), p. 95.

c. Lee O. Thayer, "In its broadest perspective, *communication occurs whenever an individual assigns significance or meaning* to an internal or external stimulus." *Administrative Communication* (Homewood, Ill.: Richard D. Irwin, Inc., 1961), p. 43.

d. S. S. Stevens, "This definition (communication is the discriminatory response of an organism to a stimulus) says the communication occurs when some environmental disturbance (the stimulus) impinges on an organism and the organism does something about it (makes a discriminatory response). If the stimulus is ignored by the organism, there has been no communication. The test is differential action of some sort. The message that gets no response is not a communication." "Introduction: A Definition of Communication," *The Journal of the Acoustical Society of America*, Vol. XXII (1950), 689.

e. Carl Howland, "[Communication is] the process by which an individual (the communicator) *transmits* stimuli (usually verbal symbols) to *modify* the behavior of other individuals (communicatees)." "Social Communication," *Proceedings of the American Philosophical Society*, Vol. 92 (1948), 371.

of this he recognizes the need for transmitting his feelings and ideas to someone. Stimulation creates a desire to communicate and helps provide a need or purpose for communicating.

Once he recognizes the need, the communicator decides what to say to accomplish his purpose. From the possible points that he might include in a message, he selects certain ones that will fulfill his need and then arranges them in some meaningful sequence. At the same time, he has to think not only of what he is going to say, but also how he is going to present the message, for he is seeking, after all, a favorable response from the recipient. The message is adapted to the level of understanding and interest of the reader or listener. Then, by means of sound waves and light waves, the communicator speaks and his message is transmitted. The recipient's eyes, ears, or other sensory organs are stimulated by the sound waves and light waves. The resulting nervous impulses travel to his brain and from there to his muscles and glands, which in turn produce feelings and tensions. These are translated into words according to the accustomed verbal patterns of the receiver. Thus "meaning" becomes known to him, he is stimulated by the message he has received, and he desires to respond. Next he selects a message to satisfy his desire, arranges and adapts it, then speaks, thereby stimulating the original communicator or someone else. The process of communication thus continues and never ends, for each time a person communicates, another person responds by further communicating facts, ideas, feelings, or attitudes.

CHARACTERISTICS OF COMMUNICATION

Communication is a two-way, continuing process, as indicated in the statement: "Mr. A communicates with Mr. B." It is also a social process and a symbolic process.

A Two-Way Continuing Process

It takes two or more people to complete the communication cycle. When Mrs. Smithson calls her husband and asks him to stop and pick up a quart of ice cream or a loaf of bread on his way home from work, the cycle is not completed until Mr. Smithson understands what his wife is saying and completes his response. His immediate answer will be a promise: "Yes, darling, I will." Although this may end their telephone conversation, Mrs. Smithson's purpose in calling will not be accomplished until he stops, buys the ice cream, and arrives home with it. In the meantime, other communication cycles have started. He sees a friend in the store; they exchange pleasantries. He may ask for a certain flavor of ice cream; the clerk may ask for the money. Two or more people become involved.

1. To the darkness of Mr. A's brain there comes a vague feeling.

2. Something has happened to stimulate Mr. A through his eyes, ears or other sensory organs that carry impulses to his brain. Mr. A then, according to his customary verbal patterns, translates the feeling into words.

3. From the maze of possible meanings of those words, Mr. A arrives at a purpose or feels a need or desire to say something to someone else.

4. Mr. A in the meantime has soaked up ideas and bits of information from which he selects or abstracts certain ones that he decides pertinent to accomplish his purpose, and thus determines <u>what</u> he is going to say.

5. He decides <u>how</u> he can best say what he has to say - written report or letter, conference or speech.

6. The message is then transmitted from Mr. A to Mr. B, whose mind is in darkness at first.

7. But Mr. B is stimulated by what <u>he</u> hears. Nervous impulses carry messages to <u>his</u> brain and he translates them . . . Then Mr. B responds by communicating to Mr. A or to Mr. C or by doing what A has asked him to do.

Mr. A communicates with Mr. B

Time magazine sends out a direct-mail letter offering a subscription at introductory rates. Robert Jefferson, a senior at UCLA, receives it and throws it unread in the wastebasket. Ward Kelley, a senior at Boston University, receives a copy of the same letter and reads it, but likewise throws it in the wastebasket. John Brooks, a young accountant in Chicago, reads the letter and mails a check for the subscription. *Time* therefore receives a favorable response from Mr. Brooks and unfavorable ones from the other two men. Communication is immediately effective in the one instance; the purpose is accomplished when the receiver responds favorably. However, Robert Jefferson may order *Time* later, partially as a result of his having seen *Time*'s return address on the envelope he threw away. Likewise Ward Kelley may order *Time* later, partially as a result of his having read *Time*'s letter before he threw it away. In the latter instances Kelley and Jefferson would be acting from a dormant stimulus or from an accumulation of stimuli.

Management might distribute a policy bulletin to a group of supervisory personnel, but not until there is some response in the form of comments, or until a check has been run on whether or not the policy is being followed, does management know how effective the statement is. Communication is an exchange; for it to be successful, information must flow back to the originator or he must have some knowledge of the reaction of the receiver. The flow back to the originator is known as *feedback*. It enables him to change his communication so that it will be more effective (when his purpose was not accomplished), or to communicate again. This makes communication cyclic in nature rather than linear.

A Social Process

Communication is a social process, because two or more people are involved. Every letter requires a reader; every conversation requires a listener, who may respond to the message he receives by reporting it to someone or by taking some action that will influence others. A musical composition or a painting may result from the work of one person, but it is not completed until an audience has reacted to it. You have heard people speak of communing with nature; the beauties of nature have a message. The recipient of the message from nature may try to tell it to someone else, or he may respond by taking some action. A look at the majestic Grand Canyon, for instance, or a glorious sunset or beautiful rainbow may cause you to exclaim how great God is.

Communication as a social process affects all society. It enables us to satisfy our basic needs and desires and to get along with our fellowmen. This social process is also the means of recording knowledge and passing it on to succeeding generations. Without it a business enterprise cannot operate. Communication is the means of individual and group progress.

A Symbolic Process

Communication is a process that uses a set of symbols, such as language, to convey ideas from one person to another. Symbols challenge the user to select them with an awareness of what they will mean to the listener or reader. For an artist the color red used in a painting may convey boldness or violence; the soft shades of green and blue, calmness and serenity. For a musician the beat of the drums might indicate turmoil in the emotions of the composer. For a schoolboy H_2O means water. For a mathematician $a = \sqrt{b + c}$ is significant. The noises of animals are important in indicating their wants or needs. In each instance a pattern has been formed that is recognized, clearly understood, and accepted by members of the group.

Language results from men's living together. Early man used picture writing as symbols; American Indians used smoke signals. Different countries have developed different languages. As the need arose to communicate with someone, language was developed as a means of transmitting ideas, feelings, and attitudes. Just as man cannot live alone, so language cannot exist with a single individual. A clearly recognized and understood set of language symbols is accepted by each generation and is modified to meet its particular needs.

A word is a symbol for an idea or object. A desk is called a *desk* because people have agreed that the word, *desk,* shall represent the particular object. Although words refer to things, they are not themselves things. The word *table* symbolizes the object; it is not the object itself. Likewise, verbal accounts are merely symbols for the situations or conditions they represent. The concepts reccived from a verbal account of an automobile accident may or may not correspond to reality, depending upon whether or not the communicants agree on the meanings of the words used and on their relationship to reality. A child's concept of hot and cold is based on his experiences, which determine meaning and reality for him. A word means something because it calls to mind an object, action, experience, sensation, concept, or attitude met previously. Through association and experience one understands the meaning of a message.

Whenever a businessman dictates a letter, compiles a set of figures, creates a new product or improves an old one, solves a problem, or writes a report, he is using a set of symbols to communicate. He will select those he uses for what they will mean to the listener or reader. The effective communicator thus needs to understand human nature and develop sensitivity not only to the meanings of words but also to their effect on people.

- Discuss communication as a stimulus–message–response theory.
- Read Shannon and Weaver's book, *The Mathematical Theory of Communication.*[3] Check the summary in the latter part of the book, as it is less technical and easier to understand. Discuss how it is applicable to the use of machines in communication. Explain *noise* as it affects the message and the receiver.
- Read Berlo's *The Process of Communication,*[4] especially the background

[3]Shannon and Weaver, *The Mathematical Theory of Communication,* p. 95.

[4]David K. Berlo, *The Process of Communication* (New York: Holt, Rinehart & Winston, Inc., 1960).

material in the first few chapters. Discuss how his theory relates to a human relations theory of communication.

- Devise a linear model and a circular model of the communication process. You might use the references given in footnote 2.
- Develop your definition of *communication* in terms of your personal experiences. This could be expanded into a written essay, making use of additional reading material. (Follow correct footnote and bibliography forms as given in Appendix C.)
- Bring a business letter to class. Discuss its purpose and its effect on the reader.

IMPLICATIONS FOR THE BUSINESS WRITER

The aspect of communication theory that is the most applicable for business writers is recognition of the two events that occur at the beginning and end of the cycle: *stimulus* and *response*. All communication affects the receiver. It either adds to his information or store of knowledge, or (through his response) changes his behavior, for it results in action. Whenever the action is favorable and coincides with the communicator's purpose, then the communication has been effective.

Sitting at the breakfast table, Bill said to his roommate, "Please pass the butter, John." Why? He wanted butter to spread on his toast because he enjoyed eating it that way. He said "please" instead of yelling, "Give me the butter!" because he knew that the polite, courteous request would secure the necessary response quickly and at the same time preserve harmonious relations. He asked John because the butter dish was closest to him and thus he was the logical one to do the passing. In this simple request are the elements of all communication: desire or need, something to say, and someone to say it to. The communication was initiated for the purpose of securing a definite response.

Although no advance preparation was necessary in order to ask that the butter be passed, there are times when careful preparation is needed. Three basic steps are involved in preparing any kind of communication:

1. Determine its exact purpose in terms of audience response.
2. Plan the content of the message with this purpose in mind and develop your ideas to obtain the desired effect on the audience.
3. Strive for easy, effective expression to secure the desired reaction.

Purposes of Business Letters

The purpose of a business letter may be to provide a record, make a request or inquiry, sell, build goodwill, collect money, serve the customer's needs, or in some way perform any other business function, thus contributing toward making a profit and serving the public.

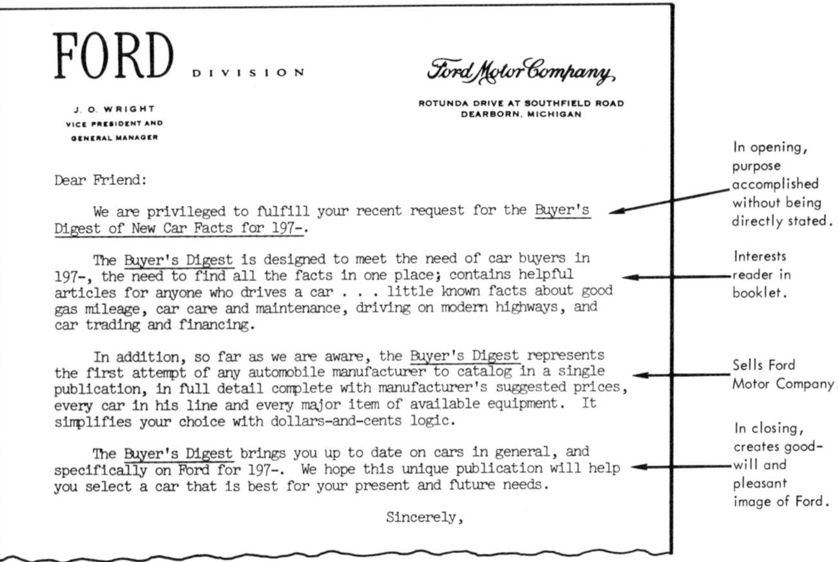
FORD DIVISION

J. O. WRIGHT
VICE PRESIDENT AND
GENERAL MANAGER

Ford Motor Company
ROTUNDA DRIVE AT SOUTHFIELD ROAD
DEARBORN, MICHIGAN

Dear Friend:

We are privileged to fulfill your recent request for the Buyer's Digest of New Car Facts for 197-.

The Buyer's Digest is designed to meet the need of car buyers in 197-, the need to find all the facts in one place; contains helpful articles for anyone who drives a car . . . little known facts about good gas mileage, car care and maintenance, driving on modern highways, and car trading and financing.

In addition, so far as we are aware, the Buyer's Digest represents the first attempt of any automobile manufacturer to catalog in a single publication, in full detail complete with manufacturer's suggested prices, every car in his line and every major item of available equipment. It simplifies your choice with dollars-and-cents logic.

The Buyer's Digest brings you up to date on cars in general, and specifically on Ford for 197-. We hope this unique publication will help you select a car that is best for your present and future needs.

Sincerely,

In opening, purpose accomplished without being directly stated.
Interests reader in booklet.
Sells Ford Motor Company.
In closing, creates good-will and pleasant image of Ford.

Courtesy Ford Motor Company

Note the letter from the Ford Motor Company above, which accompanied a booklet used for promoting sales. It answers a request and obviously fulfills its purpose of transmitting the *Buyer's Digest;* however, it does more than just that. Observe how it sells the reader by interesting him in reading the booklet to obtain information he can readily use. Both the content and the sequence of ideas help the reader perceive a favorable image of Ford. He received the booklet he requested but also is interested in using the material it contains. Perhaps sometime he will consider buying a Ford (should he not already own one).

The next letter, which received an award for the credit manager who wrote it, brought in 70 percent of the collections within two weeks. For

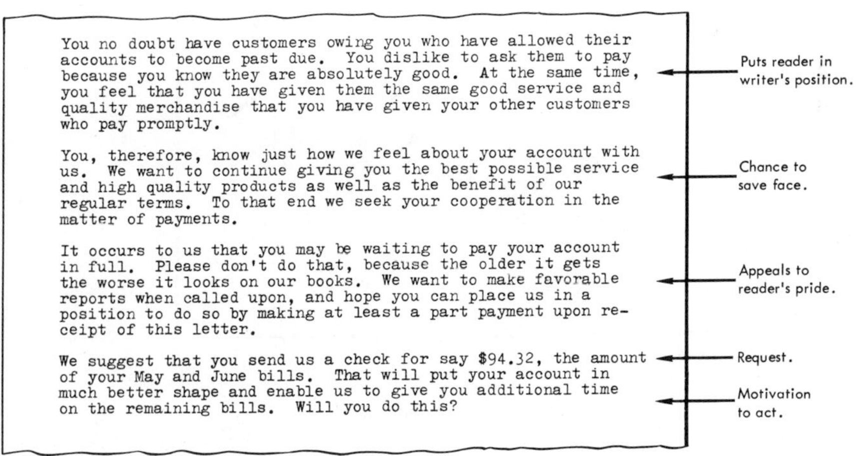
You no doubt have customers owing you who have allowed their accounts to become past due. You dislike to ask them to pay because you know they are absolutely good. At the same time, you feel that you have given them the same good service and quality merchandise that you have given your other customers who pay promptly.

You, therefore, know just how we feel about your account with us. We want to continue giving you the best possible service and high quality products as well as the benefit of our regular terms. To that end we seek your cooperation in the matter of payments.

It occurs to us that you may be waiting to pay your account in full. Please don't do that, because the older it gets the worse it looks on our books. We want to make favorable reports when called upon, and hope you can place us in a position to do so by making at least a part payment upon receipt of this letter.

We suggest that you send us a check for say $94.32, the amount of your May and June bills. That will put your account in much better shape and enable us to give you additional time on the remaining bills. Will you do this?

Puts reader in writer's position.
Chance to save face.
Appeals to reader's pride.
Request.
Motivation to act.

the writer the letter collected past-due accounts. For the reader it provided the opportunity to save face. The letter effectively combines two approaches, the "put yourself in my position" suggestion and the request for a partial payment immediately. As the response proved, many customers reacted very favorably.

Holiday magazine was confronted with the problem of saying no to a reader while at the same time maintaining customer goodwill for the magazine.[5] The letter, reproduced below, shows appreciation to the reader, avoids an opening refusal, and explains why the booklet could not be sent.

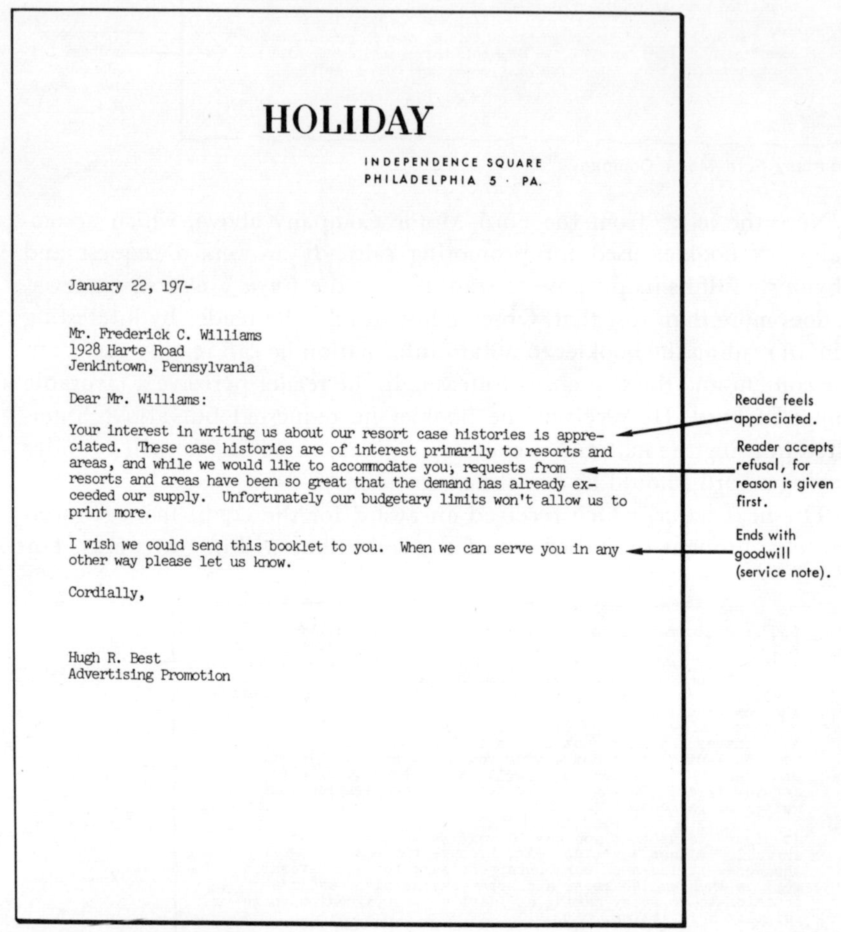

HOLIDAY

INDEPENDENCE SQUARE
PHILADELPHIA 5 · PA.

January 22, 197-

Mr. Frederick C. Williams
1928 Harte Road
Jenkintown, Pennsylvania

Dear Mr. Williams:

Your interest in writing us about our resort case histories is appreciated. These case histories are of interest primarily to resorts and areas, and while we would like to accommodate you, requests from resorts and areas have been so great that the demand has already exceeded our supply. Unfortunately our budgetary limits won't allow us to print more.

I wish we could send this booklet to you. When we can serve you in any other way please let us know.

Cordially,

Hugh R. Best
Advertising Promotion

Reader feels appreciated.
Reader accepts refusal, for reason is given first.
Ends with goodwill (service note).

Courtesy *Holiday* magazine

[5]For further information concerning refusal letters, see Chapter 4, pp. 105–7. For information on reflecting a pleasing personality and attitudes, see also Chapter 5, pp. 156–58.

When a letter builds goodwill or sells an idea or product, and when it also contains elements of effective style and tone and presents a favorable appearance, it will be successful. The content of the letter should be selected and arranged with a purpose in mind, and ideas should be developed and expressed so that they will secure the desired reaction from the reader.

Analysis of the Reader or Listener

The better the communicator's understanding of the receiver, the more effective his presentation can be, and the more likely it is to accomplish its purpose. For the reader or listener, what is said and how it is said become important motivating forces. Effective messages are always presented from the recipient's point of view, and understanding his makeup makes it possible to adapt material to his needs and interests. Recall the last speech you heard. Listen to one of your favorite television programs tonight. Read an article from one of the magazines you read regularly. How does each of these meet the needs and interests of the audience?

Note the following letter from a department store to one of its delinquent customers. This letter was effective because it succeeded in col-

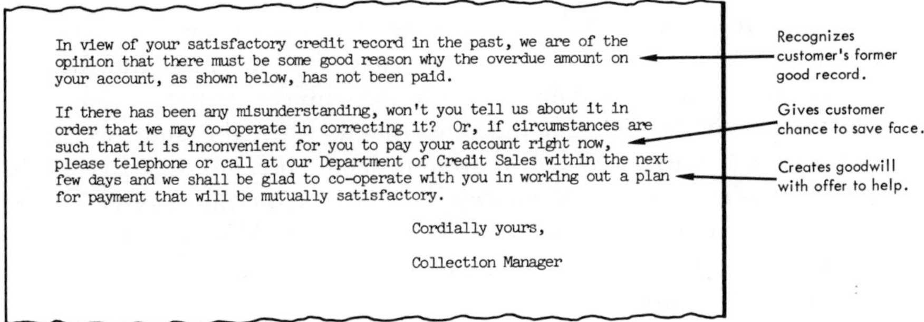

In view of your satisfactory credit record in the past, we are of the opinion that there must be some good reason why the overdue amount on your account, as shown below, has not been paid.

If there has been any misunderstanding, won't you tell us about it in order that we may co-operate in correcting it? Or, if circumstances are such that it is inconvenient for you to pay your account right now, please telephone or call at our Department of Credit Sales within the next few days and we shall be glad to co-operate with you in working out a plan for payment that will be mutually satisfactory.

Cordially yours,

Collection Manager

Recognizes customer's former good record.
Gives customer chance to save face.
Creates goodwill with offer to help.

Letter from a department store

lecting over 80 percent of its accounts from customers falling in this classification. It is a form letter, but it recognizes the customer as an individual with a previous good payment record and gives him a chance to pay and maintain his good rating. Not all letters are perfect, however, and this one is no exception. Can you see what weakens its impact? It is the negative and hackneyed words used throughout its content. A negative word is one that contains a "no" or a "not" or that has an unfavorable connotation. There are five here. A hackneyed expression is one that is overused and thus no longer has a definite meaning. There are also five of these. Eliminating these words would make the letter more concise and direct. We will discuss these issues further in Chapter 3; here we simply wish to call attention to the fact that not every letter is perfect and to mention how this particular one can be improved.

Some factors to consider in analyzing an audience include:

age	social position	other recreational interests
sex	language level	organizations
educational background	personality traits	community activities
job experience	habits	religion and church activities
occupation	likes and dislikes	politics
type of business	prejudices	
family	sports	
location of residence	hobbies	

Not all of these would be known or usable in every communication situation. In each case apply what is appropriate and adaptive to your purpose.

When a message is clearly understood, the audience should be interested and receptive. Interest and acceptance, however, depend on the relation and rapport established between the communicator and his audience. He should accept his reader or listener as an equal in the total communication process, and should try to meet individual needs and wants. The more he knows about his audience the more harmonious a relationship he can establish. Individual differences in the experience and personality makeup of the receivers vitally affect their acceptance of the message. For an audience familiar with the subject matter, explanatory details are not needed. On the other hand, when the audience is unfamiliar with the material, background details become necessary at the very beginning. Every consideration must be given to the receiver because the message must reach *him* and serve *his* purpose. Otherwise the communication process cannot be completed, and the communicator cannot accomplish *his* purpose.

- Examine the four letters on pages 14 and 15, then:
  1. State the purpose and explain its relationship in this situation to the writer and the reader.
  2. Explain how the arrangement of ideas contributes to accomplishing the purpose.
  3. Visualize the reader as an individual. What do you know about him? What might his reaction be to the ideas? To the sequence? Why?
  4. What action is the reader to take?
- Are there any weak spots in the four letters? What changes can you suggest to improve them?
- Discuss the effect of humor, appreciation, repetition of a brand name, curiosity, a free gift, etc., on the reader of a business letter.

- Start collecting a file of letters. You might begin by bringing one to class and discussing it, using the factors mentioned above. As you continue your collection you will need to classify the letters. This may be done by purpose, business function, reader, principles illustrated, or ideas.

Much emphasis has been placed upon the writing of a business letter here and rightfully so, for it is the best vehicle for developing your communicative abilities, and the medium most frequently used by business firms. You should, however, understand the functioning of communication in a broader perspective than just in letters.

THE FUNCTIONING OF COMMUNICATION IN A BUSINESS ENTERPRISE

A very important function of management is developing and maintaining a system of communication. For example, Mr. Philip Jones, an enlightened, modern business executive and president of the Asteck Company, has much to learn about understanding and being understood by other people. The Asteck Company is expanding by opening a new plant near Shreveport, Louisiana. Machines and tools from the old plant in New Orleans are being shipped to Shreveport, and new, modern equipment is to be installed in the New Orleans plant to replace the old. The employees who have manned the home plant are to be retained and given salary increases. Mr. Jones is living through an exciting, happy time, for he expects that through this expansion his company will take the lead in the industry. But some of his employees are not at all happy. They have been told nothing of Mr. Jones's plans, but they have watched machinery being packed and moved out. One of the employees, whose wife does not want to leave New Orleans and move to Shreveport, has obtained a job with another company. Another employee plans to sell his house in New Orleans; he and his family even looked at homes in Shreveport one weekend.

Seeing no need to tell the employees the company's plans, Mr. Jones intends to surprise them later with the good news. In the meantime, the men have been left to draw their own conclusions, however erroneous they might be.

Employee Communication

A system of communication developed and maintained in a company should keep employees informed. Management can build attitudes, develop rapport, and influence productive, cooperative action by keeping employees informed. A worker who understands his job, who feels like a part of the company, and who has a sense of loyalty will work harmoniously with management as part of the company team.

Dear Subscriber:

In Oklahoma City recently cafe owners opened a school to teach their waitresses to smile pleasantly.

And before you laugh, you might admit that smiling waitresses have a lot to recommend them.

Here at TIME, we've always felt the same way about "collection" letters.

We just smile pleasantly and say: "Our bill for your current subscription is enclosed."

Wonder if you wouldn't like to substantiate our faith in smiles by sending us your check, please, today?

Cordially,

Charles Mason
Credit Manager

Reprinted by permission from *Time*, The Weekly Newsmagazine

Letter from Time

Letter about plastic plants

Dear Friend:

Has someone ever given you something for nothing?

All of us know that nowadays a business concern doesn't give something away unless there is a catch to it.

There are a lot of ways to handle a decorating problem. . . With Kendra Vinyl Foliage and Flowers the possibilities are as unlimited as your imagination. . .

Just a touch of true-to-life Kendra adds a "custom design" look to any home or office.

But best of all, Kendra is so economical . . . does so much for so little and it fits every taste . . . every decor. Makes every room and office as garden fresh as the cool crisp outdoors.

Now, Craig Plastic Plants is offering you a free gift . . . .

> An attractive plastic plant for your home planter just for bringing this letter to our store.

Is there a catch to it? Frankly there is . . . .

We are anxious to show you the solution to dying house plants . . . The solution . . . Kendra Plastic Plants . . . There is no care . . . Heat and cold resistant, fireproof and completely washable and their permanent beauty is unexcelled . . . Kendra is the trademark of these attractive home beautifiers . . .

This offer is good till June only . . . Take advantage of it TODAY . . .

Cordially yours,

Collection Manager

Dear Mr. Johnson:

There is a poem, which you probably had to recite when you were a boy, which begins - "I shot an arrow into the air, it fell to earth I know not where."

Recently we "shot" you a copy of "J. J. Letterhead, Salesman," the new letterhead folio. Where it landed and what it did, we know not.

We'd certainly like having some report on this "lost arrow."

Very cordially,

Letter from a printing company

Dear Friend:

Thank you for completion of your Club Plan Account. We like your patronage. Your account will be kept active, and we are very eager to have you return.

Surely there must be other furnishing or appliances needed for your home . . . Danish modern furniture . . . smart sectional sofas . . . attractive wrought-iron dinette suites . . . charming bedroom groups in many styles.

See everything that is new in appliances . . . color television sets . . . washers . . . electric refrigerators. Air-conditioners and dryers are a "must" these days.

Do you want to work wonders with the decorating of your home, and save time and money besides? Then avail yourself of our Interior Decorating Service, which includes floor covering, draperies, slip covers, furniture of different periods and styles, as well as all the accessories, in furnishing a beautiful home. Telephone Mr. Robert at JA 2-9261 as this service is free for the asking.

A visit to our "Maple House," the most complete in the South, is well worthwhile.

Come in at your leisure
and browse around.

Vice President & General Manager

Letter from a furniture store

There are four broad areas about which information should be communicated in an industrial plant:

1. Information about the company—employees and management need to know about company operations, products, and prospects.
2. Information about company policies and practices affecting people and their jobs—employees need to know these things to feel secure and happy on the job.
3. Information relating to special situations arising in the plant—employees and management need to have an understanding of problem situations.

4. Information about the relationship of the employees to the economic system—employees need to have an understanding of the economic system in terms of their experience and the company for which they work.

Employees have many questions about the company for which they work. They want to know how the company got started, how it grew to its present position, and the outlook for the future. They want to know the company products, how they are made, how they are used, and by whom. Many operating problems, once they are known and understood, will call forth from the workers cooperation and extra effort toward a solution. Some companies give employees information about personnel and labor policies. When employees understand the "what" and "why" of policies affecting them, many difficulties can be avoided. Workers want to know where they stand and what their chances are for advancement. They want to be recognized and treated as individuals.

Sometimes a special situation arises, such as a necessary layoff of workers, the need for a new policy, or a demand for increased output or quality. When there is a layoff, it is important that the employer let the workers have the facts they need to know. Alert employers retain goodwill by explaining the reasons that made the layoff necessary and by attempting to secure other employment for laid-off workers. This eases the pain for both employer and employee. With established, accepted information channels functioning regularly, management has an effective voice when it is needed to secure understanding and cooperation on a particular problem. Keeping employees informed about the business reaps dividends in terms of loyalty, cooperation, and productivity. Planning and getting out the work also calls for communication among members of the firm; every company has its own pattern of communication built around the operation of the business.

A system of communication developed and maintained in a company should also provide channels through which operational and technical information can be disseminated to the people concerned. A retail store in Indiana once planned a special mattress promotion, but failed to communicate information about the promotion to the sales and supporting departments. The mattress promotion was planned by the home furnishings divisional merchandise manager and the furniture buyer. The shipment of mattresses arrived, but the receiving, marking, warehousing, and delivery departments had not been informed of the delivery date, much less the promotion itself. Chaos was the result. Extra help had to be called in to clear space in the warehouse for receiving and storing the merchandise. Another store planned a sale of ready-to-wear clothes that required alterations. The alterations department was not informed about the sale until after the advertisement appeared in the newspapers. The result here was that the uninformed alterations department was unable to handle the extra load of work from the sale. Also, alterations on regularly priced merchandise sold prior to the sale were not completed as promised.

In another incident, customers read an advertisement saying that there would be a sale of merchandise at a main store and that the merchandise could also be purchased at a branch store. The branch manager, however, had not been notified of the event or of the scheduled advertisement. When the merchandise arrived, selling space at the branch store had to be provided and extra selling personnel called in. There was no time, however, for the branch manager to have a meeting prior to the sale to give the salesclerks special sales facts about the merchandise. There are many examples of lost sales and customer dissatisfaction resulting from lack of communication within department stores. For any type of business to operate efficiently, communication is necessary. Orders and instructions must be given and received. They must be clear and accurate and must include enough facts to motivate action.

Intramanagement Communication

A system of communication developed and maintained in a company should provide opportunities for intramanagement communication. In carrying out the executive functions of planning, organization, and control, management must communicate with management. There are times when each member of the management team needs to know what other members are doing. The plans made by the advertising manager may be influenced by his knowledge of what the sales manager is planning. An overall policy for all company personnel will have to be considered in order to devise a policy applicable to only one department, and vice versa. Otherwise, the two policies might run counter to each other.

Management, which is concerned largely with policy making and decision making, must have enough information and data to formulate workable policies and to make wise decisions. These must be communicated to others and then put into action. Here communication functions as a valuable tool of management; as such,

1. It serves as an instrument of control that operates within and outside the company.
2. It provides information needed to coordinate the activities of management.
3. It provides data as a basis for intelligent management decisions.
4. It makes possible the delegation of authority and responsibility through a system of records and reports.
5. It functions as the essential element in cooperation.

Management is also concerned with problem solving. Top executives are constantly faced with problems that call for solutions and action.

They have to predict and reach growth goals, handle public and private finances, win cooperation from a union, build a management staff, and meet scores of other problems with solid, imaginative solutions.

Customer and Public Communication

Communication is the means of contact a company has with people on the outside. As an integrating force within the company it brings together the parts of the business into a working organization. It also helps establish a relationship with labor, with suppliers of equipment and materials, and with buyers and sources of products; it promotes business activity; and, through its relation to government control and public opinion, it is the link with society in general. A firm is established to serve people in some particular way and to make a profit. Contacts with customers and the public in general are provided through communication opportunities, for customers must be "sold." They must be satisfied and kept happy, and they should feel that they are dealing with a friendly and reliable organization. The company story must be told to the public to help build attitudes and loyalties that will result in favorable impressions and responses.

The proper public image must be created for the company and its products. The idea of a superior, thoroughly reliable, and desirable product or service must be communicated, as well as the idea of a company firmly rooted in know-how and sound business sense. A positive, favorable disposition must be produced in the customer and the general public by helping them develop friendly, confident feelings toward the firm and its products. Correspondence of all types, direct mail, sales promotions, advertising, news items, and annual reports are a few of the many media used to accomplish these purposes.

METHODS OF COMMUNICATION

Communication in a business organization moves in four directions—down, up, across, and out, according to the lines of organization and authority. It is the function of management to create and use communicative channels effectively.

The downward flow of communication consists largely of giving orders, providing oral and written instructions, transmitting information needed to run the business, and informing the employees of what they want to know and need to be told. But in order to make decisions and give orders, executives need to know what is going on in their organization. The upward flow of communication provides data and reports needed by management. It also includes suggestions and complaints which, when considered,

Management Levels Provide Communication Channels

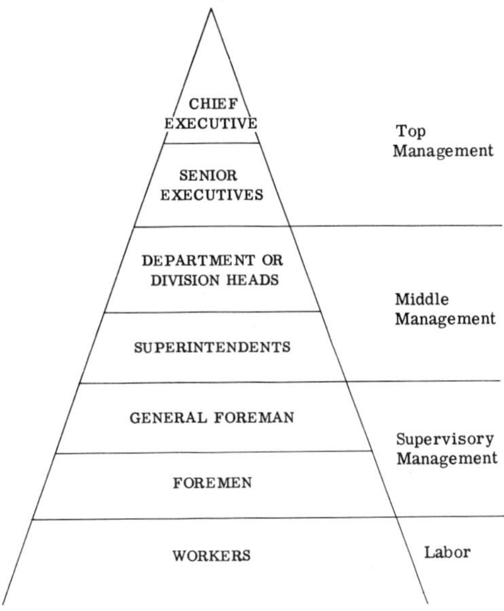

will cause the business to be run more smoothly than would otherwise be the case. Not only must management have data from an upward flow, but it must also constantly check up on attitudes, reactions, and opinions through interviews, polls, surveys, and observation. There should also be a crossing and even a crisscrossing of channels as operations and expediency demand. Whatever channels are used, there are three basic methods of communication—oral, written, and visual. It is also possible to combine any of these, resulting in audiovisual, written-pictorial, or some similar classification.

Oral Communication

Communication methods involving person-to-person, verbal communication, participated in by all levels of management, generate interest, acceptance, and influence. The man-to-man, personal approach offers a real opportunity for two-way discussion. It also has the advantage of being rapid, and it can instantly be changed to meet the listener's mood and understanding. In addition, personal contact is a convincing guarantee of the sincerity and honesty of the company and results in employee support and endorsement. Naturally the chief executive cannot continually engage in oral communication with rank-and-file workers. Department heads and foremen, however, are key communicators.

Not all oral communication is from one person to another. Many are the instances in which employee meetings are utilized.[6] These may be mass informational meetings, group discussions, conferences, interviews, or committee meetings. At a group meeting the Kirsten Pipe Company laid out its advertising plans to its employees, in detail and in advance. Workers saw sales curves and buying trends as well as exhibits showing layouts, art, and copy, and learned how money would be spent on advertising. At Vermont Foundries, one of the vice-presidents reviewed directly at an employees' meeting a market situation that made it necessary to reduce costs to meet competition. Workers were given ample opportunity to ask questions and make suggestions. The company presented its plan to cope with the situation and, in carrying it out, received excellent cooperation from the employees. At a metals refining company in New Jersey, any one of the employees can pick up his phone, dial the number 8, and get a tape-recorded message telling him what's going on around the plant. Each morning a new tape is prepared to dispense company news. One day it may be a talk on safety; another day, a talk on new machinery or the retirement fund. This phone communication system is credited with producing a friendly and informal atmosphere for the company's employees. These are but a few of many situations in which oral methods of communication can be used with successful results.

Written Communication

Written communication methods provide recorded information and data for use at the moment and for later reference. These methods derive a lot of their effectiveness from the interest the reader has in learning about happenings in his company and from the fact that written material can be utilized to deal with special situations, problems, and happenings that are of particular interest as they occur or at some future time. A new plant being built by the company can be described in a letter to employees, an article in the company newspaper, or a notice on the bulletin board. The story of new machinery, the explanation of a layoff, a statement of management's views with respect to an election for a bargaining agent, or the launching of a new product can likewise be explained in a letter or in an article in the magazine or newspaper. Any of these may be described in a company bulletin, a memorandum report, or some other written medium. Instructions, orders, policies, and procedures can all be given in manuals, handbooks, bulletins, or reports. Announcements can be inserted in pay envelopes or sent in personal letters to the employee's home address. A system for presenting data and other

[6]The three company examples given here are from *Case Book of Employee Communications in Action*, published by the National Association of Manufacturers, New York, 1950, and are typical of what companies are doing.

material in report form, to be used in reaching conclusions, solving problems, or making decisions and taking action, is a necessary part of any company's operations.

Visual Communication

During the past few years, increased emphasis has been placed upon visual methods of communicating ideas and factual information. "A picture is worth a thousand words" has been taken at face value. Material on the bulletin board can augment information supplied in company magazines. Posters, charts, graphs, and other pictorial media attract attention and interest or convince the observer to act. The Westinghouse Electric plant at Lansdowne, Pennsylvania, stimulates worker interest by placarding big jobs. Attached signs a foot or more in width tell employees whether they are assembling an FM transmitter for stock, a 5-kilowatt transmitter for a radio station, or a 100-kilowatt induction heater for the Firestone Rubber Company.

Visual techniques are adaptable to a variety of situations and are often used in employee publications, annual reports, mass meetings, conferences, bulletins, and training activities. Realizing that employees of very large companies often have misconceptions about their company profits, and aiming to present the profit-and-loss picture on a personal, individual basis, a large oil corporation a few years ago used a double-page spread in chart form in its publication of highlights of the year. Beginning with the premise, "If you owned a business equal to one employee's portion of the company, it would be worth $28,000," the explanation goes on: "Now, assume you had run your business last year as we did. Here's how it would look." An explanation follows of dollar amounts of products and services, subtracting the cost of buying and processing crude oil plus other operating and administrative expenses. The resulting figure is the dollar profit, from which federal income taxes are subtracted, leaving the net profit. At the end the chart comments: "This is typical of what is happening in the average business today. . . ." The whole thing is a clear, concise picture, cleverly done through the use of blue for profit figures and red for money spent and the final total. The use of the single chart was an impressive way of getting the subject across to employees in a simple manner.

Demonstrations, community open houses, and plant visits are likewise visual methods of communicating with the public. They show the plant at work and, in a very effective manner, tell the company story.

The results achieved by various media of communication must be checked, and the media used must be evaluated in relation to the communicative process. Does the process accomplish the objectives that are being sought? Does it challenge interest? Does it promote understanding?

Does it produce cooperation? These are several of the questions that should be answered. The total results and overall effectiveness of communication can be appraised by individual reactions, objective records, opinion surveys, and other methods of letting management know whether it is getting its messages across to employees, customers, and the public.

- Recall situations in which you have participated when ineffective communication resulted in some embarrassing or dire consequence. Discuss what brought about the barrier and what should have been done for the communication to have been effective.
- Recall a business situation involving either employee, customer, public, or management communication that was not effective. Analyze what went astray and why, then discuss what should have been done.
- Organize your class for a panel discussion on the functioning of communication in a business enterprise. Let each of three speakers prepare a talk concerning one of the three methods of communication, and let the other class members participate in a discussion led by the moderator. Read further into the three areas. Think of problems that might arise and how they may be solved or prevented.

SUMMARY

Communication is a vital part of everyone's life. Although not everyone agrees on a common definition, authorities in defining communication do agree on common elements in the process. Communication is the transmission and interchange of facts, ideas, feelings, or courses of action. It is persuasive. It requires a sender, a message, and a receiver, and must add to the knowledge of the receiver or change (influence) his behavior in some way. It is a two-way, continuing process, a symbolic process, and a social process.

Some important suggestions growing out of the body of theory concerning a definition for communication are that the communicator should always begin with an analysis of the situation, arrive at a purpose or need for the communication, plan his message to include material that will accomplish his purpose, and state it so that the receiver will perceive it as was intended and act favorably upon it. All communication is purposeful; when its purpose is accomplished, it is effective. Business letters may provide a record, make a sale, build goodwill, seek or make an adjustment, collect money, or in some other way perform a business function.

An effective communicator selects, arranges, and presents material with a purpose and a reader in mind. Ideas are developed and expressed to secure the desired reaction. The better understanding the communicator has of his audience, the more effective his presentation can be. The reader or listener must become interested in what is being said before he will be motivated to act favorably. Every consideration must be given to adapting the message to his needs and interests; it must reach *him* and serve *him* to accomplish the communicator's purpose.

A very important function of management is developing and maintaining a system of communication. In a business enterprise, communication functions in three major areas: employee communication, intramanagement communication, and customer and public communication. Communication moves up, down, across, and out for a company; all channels must be used. Oral, written, and visual methods are all-important. The more personal the message is, the more likely it is to get the desired action. Good human relations are necessary for any effective communication.

FURTHER READING

Aurner, Robert R., and M. Philip Wolf, *Effective Communication in Business,* 5th ed. Cincinnati: South-Western Publishing Co., 1967, pp. 1–19.

Berlo, David K., *The Process of Communication.* New York: Holt, Rinehart & Winston, Inc., 1960, pp. 1–70.

Campbell, James H., and Hal W. Hepler, eds., *Dimensions in Communication.* Belmont, Calif.: Wadsworth Publishing Company, Inc., 1970.

Cherry, Colin, *On Human Communication,* 2nd ed. Cambridge: MIT Press, 1966, pp. 2–29, 40–52.

Dance, F. E. X., ed., *Human Communication Theory: Original Essays.* New York: Holt, Rinehart & Winston, Inc., 1967.

Dawe, Jessamon, and William J. Lord, Jr., *Functional Business Communication.* Englewood Cliffs, N. J.: Prentice-Hall, Inc., 1968, pp. 1–21, 80–91.

Fabun, Don, *Communications: The Transfer of Meaning.* Beverly Hills, Calif.: Glencoe Press, 1968.

Haney, William V., *Communication and Organizational Behavior.* Homewood, Ill.: Richard D. Irwin, Inc., 1967, pp. 153–82.

Korzybski, Alfred, *Science and Sanity: An Introduction to Non-Aristotelian Systems and General Semantics,* 4th ed. Lakeville, Conn.: Institute of General Semantics, 1962.

Menning, J. H., and C. W. Wilkinson, *Communicating Through Letters and Reports,* 4th ed. Homewood, Ill.: Richard D. Irwin, Inc., 1967, pp. 1–8, 661–73.

Scholz, William, *Communication in the Business Organization.* Englewood Cliffs, N. J.: Prentice-Hall, Inc., 1962.

Thayer, Lee O., ed., *Communication: Concepts and Perspectives.* Washington, D. C.: Spartan Books, Inc., 1967, pp. 9–28, 51–60.

QUESTIONS AND PROBLEMS

1. Your former high school principal has written you for information concerning your college and your activities. He wants to use it in counseling high school seniors who plan to attend your college. Answer his letter. Be as specific and helpful as you can.

2. Discuss what you would do, write, or say in each of the following communicating situations. What effect on the receiver should you consider?
   a. You have just recently moved into a new home in the suburbs and want to invite your colleagues to an open house.
   b. An employee in the maintenance department tells you that the showers are inadequate. Assume that you are the personnel director.
   c. Your boss has been hospitalized for two weeks.
   d. You want to impress the need for safety upon the employees under you on the production line.

3. Your older brother, who has just been graduated from college and has started working in an advertising agency in Chicago, has written you for advice on whether or not he should take a course in business communication. He knows that you are taking one this semester, and he could take one from the evening division of Northwestern University.

4. Assume that you are Mr. Fisher, an instructor at Eastern Michigan University, and you have just received the following invoice for payment. Write a letter correcting the error. Try to give the company a chance to "save face."

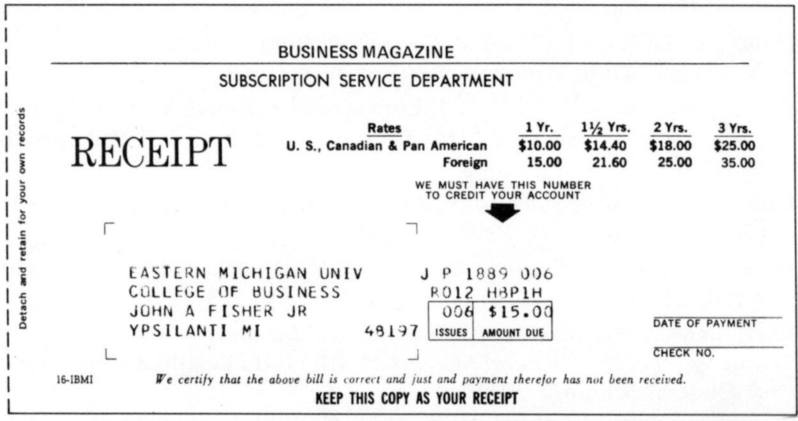

Detach and retain for your own records

BUSINESS MAGAZINE

SUBSCRIPTION SERVICE DEPARTMENT

RECEIPT

Rates	1 Yr.	1½ Yrs.	2 Yrs.	3 Yrs.
U. S., Canadian & Pan American	$10.00	$14.40	$18.00	$25.00
Foreign	15.00	21.60	25.00	35.00

WE MUST HAVE THIS NUMBER TO CREDIT YOUR ACCOUNT

EASTERN MICHIGAN UNIV
COLLEGE OF BUSINESS
JOHN A FISHER JR
YPSILANTI MI 48197

J P 1889 006
R012 H8P1H
006 ISSUES $15.00 AMOUNT DUE

DATE OF PAYMENT

CHECK NO.

16-IBMI *We certify that the above bill is correct and just and payment therefor has not been received.*

KEEP THIS COPY AS YOUR RECEIPT

5. Write a letter in answer to the following one. *Better Letters* is a service for business organizations and is priced accordingly. There are forty-one bulletins in the set, costing $2 each. Additional copies are 50 cents each. Over 10,000 business executives have subscribed to this service. The publishers, however, cannot offer the bulletins for free educational use. This would amount to giving away something to the very people (students) they hope to add later to their list of subscribers.

Gentlemen:

The promotional invitation I received for a *free* trial subscription to *Better Letters* was misleading. It did not seem too definite whether it would be a free service or whether I would be billed six months hence.

The material about *Better Letters,* however, seems interesting and practical. Therefore I would like to receive four complimentary copies for use in the classroom. There are five of us who teach business communication at EMU and letter writing is about one-half of the basic course. I feel that our using *Better Letters* will serve as advertising for you.

May we have them, please? Thank you.

6. As an economist for the Gulf Oil Company, you were attracted to these excerpts from the *Wall Street Journal*:

   In a lucid new book, *Great Myths of Economics,* Don Paarlberg says a large share of the populace holds some strange notions about the economy. Mr. Paarlberg, who was economic adviser to President Eisenhower and now teaches economics at Purdue University, sets out to slay most of the economic myths and to set up more reasonable principles in their place. . . . An example [of businessmen's folklore] is the protectionist myth which holds it's possible for trade to be a one-way street, with the U.S. selling goods abroad and buying only home-produced items. . . . Among the more widespread of economic myths is the idea that if someone gains in a transaction someone must lose.

   Write a letter requesting a complimentary copy. The book was published by New American Library in 1968.

7. As secretary to the faculty teaching business communication in your school, write to the Sheraton-Chicago Motor Hotel to make reservations for three of the faculty to attend the national meeting of the American Business Communication Association on August 28–30. Two of the men will room together and will want a room with twin beds. The other man will want a single room. The hotel has quoted convention prices as: single, $10, $13, and $15; double (twin beds), $14, $17, and $19. Although they will be reimbursed for expenses, the men want the lowest-priced rooms available. Request confirmation. The arrival time will be late on the night of August 27.

8. You are a member of the staff of the Bank of America, San Francisco. The morning mail brought you a letter from one of your clients, who is sending in checks totaling $675.75, $575 for deposit to his checking account and the rest for his savings account. He has asked for an acknowledgment by letter. Write your reply. Ordinarily you would not write a letter, but he has requested it—so here goes. You'll want to keep it short and direct but at the same time to include a preventive measure for the future.

9. Read the following letter. Wouldn't you prefer to go out, check the fan, repair it as good as new, and sell the customer on keeping the Hunter fan, rather than give the money back so that he can buy a Reed fan at Smith's? How would you answer the letter?

Dear Sir:

The Hunter fan I bought from you April 27 made a loud noise when I turned it on today. It ran at top speed and then conked out. I don't want it. Yesterday my wife saw a Reed fan at Smith's Store and wants me to buy it.

Since I've paid you only the down payment, let me have my money back to go to Smith's. Do this at once, for my wife has very little patience.

Truly yours,

Chapter Two

CREATING THAT FAVORABLE IMPRESSION

Effective letters are a key area of communication for most business firms, because the quality of their letters plays a vital role in their success. Letters are the basic means of business communication and serve as a worthy substitute for personal contact. To be effective, a business letter must have an appealing form and appearance to create that first favorable impression on the reader; it must create goodwill that will help the reader to become receptive; it must be easily understood; and it must interest and persuade so that the reader will respond favorably and thus accomplish the writer's purpose. These characteristics are the subjects of this and the next four chapters; they should prove valuable for increasing your skills in writing letters and for developing your communicative and thinking abilities.

LETTER APPEARANCE AND FORM

The trend today is to present a pleasant, attractive letter that will be simple and hence timesaving as well as clean-cut. Business letters are costly (most estimated cost figures are close to $2.50 each);[1] they should therefore be produced without waste of time and effort for both the writer or dictator and the reader.

[1]New York Life Insurance Company cited $2.44 in *Effective Letters Bulletin*, Spring 1968; the IBM Corp. also cited $2.44 on a TV program in June 1968; and the *ABCA Bulletin*, May 1969, cited $2.74 from the Dartnell Institute of Business Research.

Stationery and Letterhead

The first things that impress a reader of a business letter are the stationery and letterhead. Common use has standardized 8½ by 11 inches as the most practical size for business purposes. Files, machines, and envelopes are all geared to this size. For specific purposes, however, variations in length may be selected; for instance, the short sheet (8½ by 7¼ inches) and half-sheets (8½ by 5½ inches) are used for acknowledgments, requests, and other short or routine messages and intracompany notes. For messages of a semibusiness nature and for executive use, the off-standard size (7½ by 10½ or 11 inches) is frequently used.

Generally, 20-weight plain white bond is used. For prestige, some executives and companies use heavier bond (24-weight). Carbon copies are done on lighter-weight paper to lower costs and to produce more and clearer copies on the typewriter.

Although pure white is the color generally used, you can run the gamut of the rainbow. Some colors produce a certain psychological effect, and you must consider this as well as their appropriateness to your company image and type of business in determining which color to select. Color may also be used for printing the letterhead: for instance, blue on gray, green on white, or brown on yellow.

Buff indicates conservatism and dignity.
Blue instills confidence and harmony.
Brown suggests strength and utility.
Gray is associated with age, wisdom, and judgment.
Green suggests life, growth, coolness, and restfulness.
Pink is for daintiness and refinement.
Purple denotes tradition and stateliness.
Yellow creates cheerfulness and an atmosphere of brightness.
Red suggests intense activity and excitement.

Most color tests have found that yellow has more pulling power than any other color but white.

Designing a letterhead is an important job that combines good planning, good printing, and good paper; it has become a task for specialists. Most paper companies provide this service. The basic elements of a letterhead are:

1. The name of the company, organization, or individual
2. The street and number
3. The city, state, and zip code number
4. The telephone number

The trend for years has been toward a simple, straightforward arrangement of these essential elements, as:

```
Telephone Number

                    NAME OF COMPANY
                    Street and Number
                    City, State, Zip Code
```

Dressing up a letterhead makes it distinctive. The nature of the business should be added. Other added elements may include:

1. A trademark, emblem, or seal
2. A trade name or founding date
3. Products, services, or committees
4. Illustrations
5. Color

Firms doing an international business should give a code address for cablegrams. A pleasing and attractive arrangement of these parts lends distinction to a letterhead and identifies it more closely with the firm, its products, or its services. (See next page.)

Parts of a Business Letter

The standard conventional practice of form for good business letters is easily understood and followed. Most business letters contain seven basic parts: letterhead or heading, inside address, salutation, body, complimentary close, signature, and signature identification.

When there is no *letterhead,* use a *heading* to indicate the address of the sender:

```
                                        3409 Haring Road
                                        Miami Beach, Florida  33139
                                        June 19, 19 --
```

Telephone No. 529-5333

The ROYAL ORLEANS

ROYAL AND ST. LOUIS STREETS • NEW ORLEANS, LOUISIANA 70140

Burroughs Corporation

SECOND AVENUE AT BURROUGHS · DETROIT, MICHIGAN 48232

CORPORATE COMMUNICATIONS SERVICES

TULANE UNIVERSITY

Graduate School of Business Administration

NEW ORLEANS, LA. 70118

Office of the Dean

communication / information inc

5163 Lee Highway / Arlington Virginia 22207 / Phone 536-7231

Attractive letterheads win favorable attention

Letterhead
COLLINS BUSINESS SCHOOL
1412 EAST LONG STREET MINNEAPOLIS, MINNESOTA 55400

Date line (part of heading)
July 10, 19—

Inside Address
Professor Paul P. Fullmer
School of Business Administration
Tulane University
New Orleans, Louisiana

Salutation
Dear Professor Fullmer:

Body
You will find it easy to follow the arrangement of the basic elements illustrated in this letter.

The body is single spaced with a blank line between paragraphs. Between the other elements there should be at least one blank line. Space may be increased as necessary for attractive page balance.

Complimentary Close
Sincerely yours,

Signature

Signature Identification
Fred K. Jones
Director of Placement

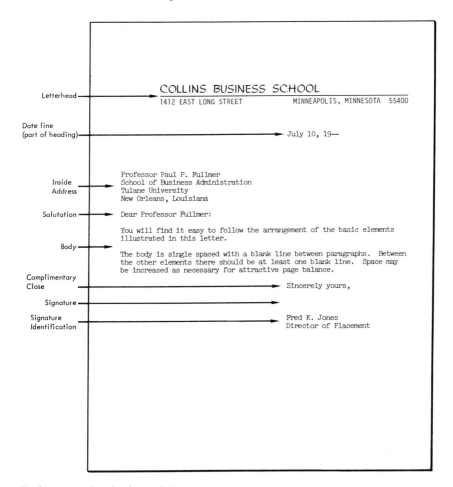

Basic parts of a business letter

Generally the heading is typed as shown here, with the *date line* considered one of its parts. However, sometimes the heading is centered and the date line separated, as:

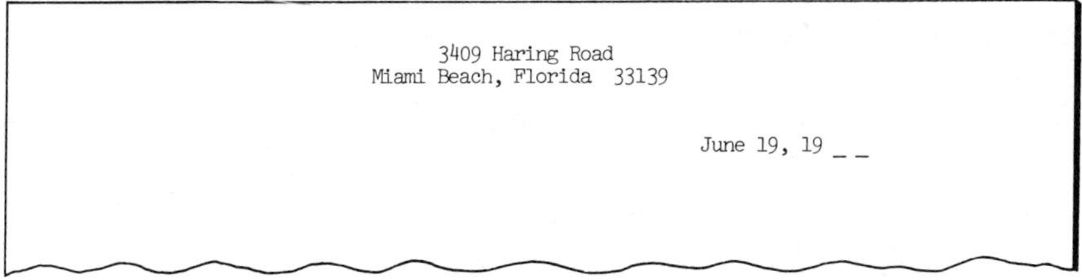

3409 Haring Road
Miami Beach, Florida 33139

June 19, 19 _ _

When there is a letterhead, the date line is separated from it by spacing; you may select one of three positions for placement:

1. Center it with the letterhead:

```
MONROE STATE BANK
Fifth and National Avenue
Springfield, Ohio 45500

November 11, 19 _ _
```

2. Place it even with the right-hand margin:

```
                MONROE STATE BANK
            Fifth and National Avenue
             Springfield, Ohio 45500

                                      November 11, 19 _ _
```

3. Type it below the letterhead and to the right, but start just to the right of center:

```
                MONROE STATE BANK
            Fifth and National Avenue
             Springfield, Ohio 45500

                          November 11, 19 _ _
```

Spaces above and below the date line are increased or decreased according to the length of the letter.

The *inside address* is the same as that on the envelope; it must agree in person with the *salutation*:

1. A letter addressed to a company, a department, or a group has *Gentlemen* as its salutation, since it is plural in form:

    American Can Company
    100 Park Avenue
    New York, N.Y. 10017

    Gentlemen:

or

Public Relations Department
American Can Company
100 Park Avenue
New York, N.Y. 10017

Gentlemen:

If the group is composed entirely of women, *Ladies* is used:

_______ Chapter
Phi Gamma Nu
University of Southern California
Los Angeles, Calif. 90000

Ladies:

2. A letter addressed to a single office or job title is singular in form and takes *Dear Sir*; the title may also be used when it can be substituted for the person's name:

Director of Public Relations
American Can Company
100 Park Avenue
New York, N.Y. 10017

Dear Sir:

or

Dean of Men
Syracuse University
Syracuse, N.Y. 13208

Dear Dean:

3. A letter addressed to a person may have as its salutation either *Dear Sir* or the person's name, depending upon the degree of formality of the relationship between the writer and the reader:

Mr. Samuel Winestein, Personnel Director
The Detroit Edison Company
200 Second Avenue
Detroit, Mich. 48226

Dear Sir: (formal)

or

Dear Mr. Winestein: (informal)

or

Dear Sam: (personal)

The *salutation* is a greeting that conveys the varying degrees of formality existing in the writer–reader relationship; it must agree with the degree of formality expressed in the *complimentary close*. The following list is arranged in descending order of formality:

Salutation	*Complimentary Close*
Sir:	Respectfully,
My dear Sir:	Yours respectfully,
Dear Sir:	Respectfully yours,
My dear Mr. Blank:	Yours sincerely,
Dear Mr. Blank:	Sincerely yours,
My dear John:	Cordially yours,
Dear John:	Faithfully yours,

Forms of *truly* are impersonal and hence are used with both formal and informal salutations:

Yours truly,
Yours very truly,
Very truly yours,

Some novel expressions may be used to convey a special meaning. They are informal and relate to the letter's content and purpose as well as to the informality of the salutation:

Persistently yours,
Yours for more profits,
Yours with appreciation,
Thank you!
Yours for progress,
Smilingly,

Expressions such as the following ones are hackneyed and old-fashioned. Whether they are part of the ending sentence or are used as a complimentary close, they have no place in today's letters:

Obligingly yours,
I beg to remain,
Hoping this meets with your approval,
Trusting this is satisfactory, I remain,

The *signature* indicates the writer of the letter, the company, or both. Unless the writer's official position, department, and company are included in the letterhead, they may appear in the signature block as the *signature identification*:

```
Sincerely yours,

James Wrixon
```

```
Sincerely yours,

James Wrixon
Advertising Manager
Northland Steel Corporation
```

To indicate company responsibility for the letter:

```
Very truly yours,

CENTRAL LIFE ASSURANCE COMPANY

James Wrixon
Director of Public Relations
```

To indicate individual responsibility for the letter:

```
Very truly yours,

James Wrixon
Director of Public Relations
Central Life Assurance Company
```

A woman indicates her marital status in the signature so that the reader will know how to address her in his reply:

Single

```
Cordially yours,

(Miss) Betty Lou Johnson
```

Divorced

```
Cordially yours,

(Mrs.) Betty Lou Johnson
```

Married or Widowed

```
Sincerely yours,

(Mrs. John R. Day)
```

Relatively large firms, government agencies, and people who handle large quantities of correspondence find it necessary to use additional parts in their letters, such as file numbers, attention lines, subject lines, initials of the dictator and typist, indications of the number of enclosures and distribution of copies, and postcripts. Each part should be used only when it serves a particular function. The figure below shows the positions of these additional parts in relation to the basic elements of a business letter.

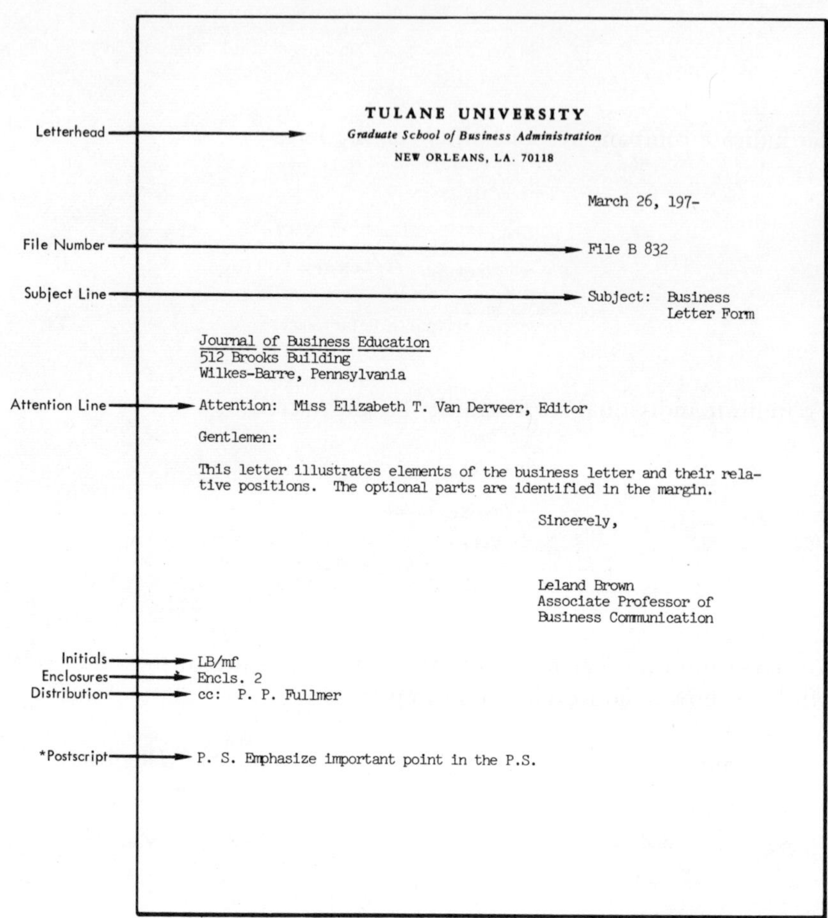

TULANE UNIVERSITY
Graduate School of Business Administration
NEW ORLEANS, LA. 70118

March 26, 197-

File B 832

Subject: Business
Letter Form

Journal of Business Education
512 Brooks Building
Wilkes-Barre, Pennsylvania

Attention: Miss Elizabeth T. Van Derveer, Editor

Gentlemen:

This letter illustrates elements of the business letter and their relative positions. The optional parts are identified in the margin.

Sincerely,

Leland Brown
Associate Professor of
Business Communication

LB/mf
Encls. 2
cc: P. P. Fullmer

P. S. Emphasize important point in the P.S.

*The postscript is often handwritten to add a personal or individual touch to the letter.

Additional parts of a business letter

Although it is shown opposite the inside address in the figure, the *subject line* is more often typed in the space indicated for the *file number* or *attention line,* whenever neither of them is used. The subject line calls the reader's attention to the subject of the letter, arouses his interest, and helps get the letter routed to the proper person when it is addressed to the company and not to an individual. The attention line is used when the letter is addressed to the company but the writer wants a particular person to handle the situation or to be informed. The salutation, however, must still agree with the inside address, as indicated in the model letter on page 36.

Whenever there is a second page to a letter it should carry identification information:

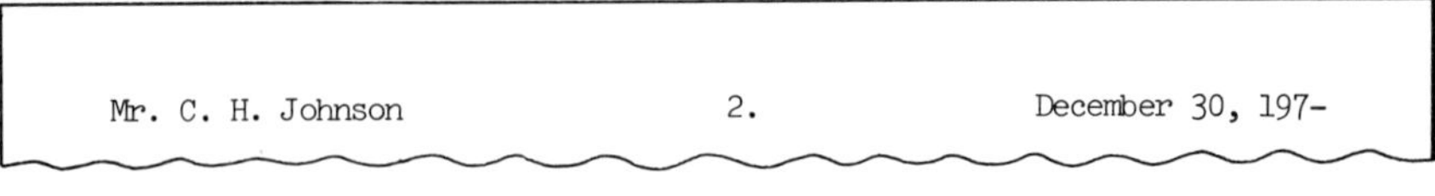
Mr. C. H. Johnson 2. December 30, 197-

or

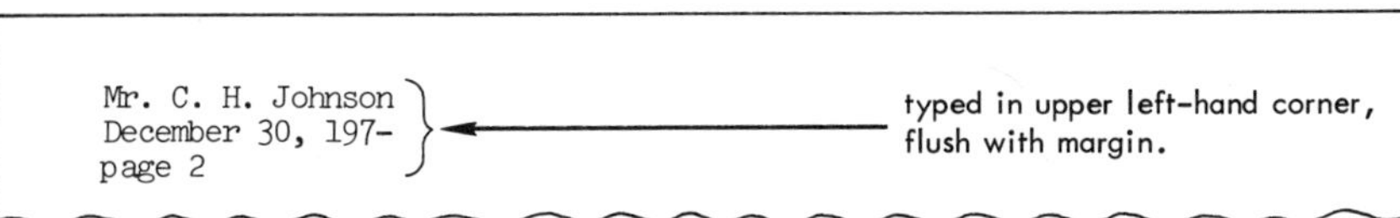
Mr. C. H. Johnson
December 30, 197-
page 2

Sometimes the subject line is repeated on the second page instead of using the name of the person to whom the letter is addressed. When there are two or more pages to a letter, they are never stapled or fastened for mailing, although the carbon copy may be secured for filing purposes or use within the company.

Business Letter Forms

The two most commonly used forms for business letters are the *fully blocked form* and the *modified block form,* as shown in the letters on page 38. Of the two, the modified block is the more widely used.

By using his creative imagination, the letter writer can vary the standard forms and still come up with an appealing format and attractive appearance in his letters. The letter on page 39 shows one way of changing the modified block form. A further change in arrangement could be made by simply indenting entire paragraphs for added emphasis or display purposes.

For years the Administrative Management Association (formerly the National Office Management Association) has advocated a simplified letter form that is basically a modification of the fully blocked letter. It was devised to save time and effort for the secretary who types the letter and for the reader. Every time a secretary shifts a typewriter carriage or makes a keystroke or space for position, she consumes working seconds. Every time she does one of these things needlessly, she reduces production and adds to fatigue.

3409 Haring Road
Metairie, Louisiana 70003

December 2, 19--

Mr. C. R. Lawrenceville
10 West 52nd Street
New York, New York

Dear Mr. Lawrenceville:

This letter illustrates the completely blocked form. Every letter part begins flush with the margin on the left-hand side of the page.

Sincerely,

John Kickerson

Encl.

3409 Haring Road
Metairie, Louisiana 70003
December 2, 19—

Mr. C. R. Lawrenceville
10 West 52nd Street
New York, New York

Dear Mr. Lawrenceville

In the modified block form, the heading, complimentary close, and signature lines are on the right instead of on the left, and the paragraphs may be indented or blocked.

Sincerely

John Kickerson

Encl.

Fully blocked form of a business letter (top) and modified form of a business letter (bottom). Note that the standard colon after the salutation and the comma after the close may be omitted when done consistently in both places.

MONROE STATE BANK
FIFTH AND NATIONAL AVENUE
SPRINGFIELD, OHIO 45500

March 11, 19--

Mr. Brooks Walkerson
672 North Hampton Street
Albany, New York

Dear Mr. Walkerson:

This is a form that emphasizes the hanging paragraph.
It can be used for long or short letters by merely
indenting more or fewer spaces.

It lends variety to the layout of a letter on the
page.

Cordially,

Leon Simpson
Vice President

LS:mf

Varied form of a business letter

There is more to the simplified letter than simply dropping the *Dear Sir* and *Yours truly*. The form is important, but most important is the improvement in the content of the letter; the philosophy behind the form is to reduce slow starting and to minimize the often stodgy results of production-line letter writing. The association offers these suggestions for improving the content of letters:

1. Maintain a normal, friendly, relaxed type of attitude. Be conversational.
2. Instead of linking thoughts with clichés, seek a fresh, orderly flow of ideas, directed to the person to whom you are writing.
3. Avoid fumbling around trying to decide whether to begin *Dear Sir, Dear Mr. X,* or *Dear Bob.*
4. State the problem or point of the letter at the outset, in the subject line.
5. Make the first sentence firm and convincing. Make it different and pertinent.
6. Be friendly. Warmth and friendliness dispersed with an intelligent and courteous touch make the reader receptive to the message.

ADMINISTRATIVE MANAGEMENT ASSOCIATION

WILLOW GROVE, PENNSYLVANIA

Philadelphia: HAncock 4-6703 Willow Grove: OLdfield 9-4300

this is a *SIMPLIFIED* letter

Dated Today

Ms. Office Secretary
Better Business Letters, Inc.
1 Main Street
Busytown, U. S. A.

SIMPLIFIED LETTER

There's a new movement under way to take some of the monotony out of letters given you to type, Ms. Secretary. The movement is symbolized by the Simplified Letter being sponsored by AMA.

What is it? You're reading a sample.

Notice the left block format and the general positioning of the letter. We didn't write "Dear Miss-----," nor will we write "Yours truly" or "Sincerely yours." Are they really important? We feel just as friendly toward you without them.

Notice the following points:

1. Date location
2. The address
3. The subject
4. The name of the writer

Now take a look at the Suggestions prepared for you. Talk them over with your boss. But don't form a final opinion until you've really tried out The Letter. That's what our secretary did. As a matter of fact, she finally wrote most of the Suggestions herself.

She says she's sold--and hopes you'll have good luck with better (Simplified) letters.

Arthur H. Gager - Staff Director, Technical Division

cc: R. P. Brecht, W. H. Evans, H. F. Grebe

By permission of the Administrative Management Association

Simplified letter

Folding Letters and Addressing Envelopes

Since the envelope and folded letter are seen first, pay careful attention to folding and addressing. Standard business envelopes are of two sizes: No. 6¾ (3⅝ by 6½ inches) and No. 10 (4⅓ by 9½ inches).

1. For the longer, official size, fold from the bottom of the page, typed side inward, with the fold approximately one-third up, then fold

"We don't put 'sealed with a kiss' on business correspondence, Miss Jones."

down from the top with the fold about one-third of the way from the top, overlapping the folded-up portion so that the edge of the last fold falls just short of meeting the other edge.

2. For the short, commercial size, fold the letter upward almost halfway, with the edge about 1/4 or 1/2 inch from the top, and with the typed side inward. Then fold from right to left one-third the width and from left to right one-third the width, so that the last fold overlaps and falls just short of meeting the other edge.
3. In either case, insert the letter into the envelope with the last fold to the back and the open edge up so that the recipient can open and unfold the letter easily and quickly.

The advent of the U.S. Post Office Department's zip code system and the installation of optical scanners to read the address electronically and sort the letters into appropriate bins have brought increased pressure for typing addresses according to postal regulations. Because the line scanned optically is the one with the state on it, the city, state, and zip code should all be on that line. Abbreviations are used for the states; they are all two letters, both capitalized, have no period or other punctuation, as:

Cincinnati, OH 45200

There is a 2½-inch-high "read zone" 8 inches long; it starts ½ inch from the bottom of the envelope and extends to 1 inch from each side.

Postal regulations include the following:

1. Use only block form, with a uniform left margin.
2. Double-space three-line addresses.

3. Either double-space or single-space four-line addresses. Single-space addresses of more than four lines.
4. Type and space the optically scanned line no lower than ½ inch and no higher than 3 inches from the bottom of the envelope.
5. When apartment numbers and the like are on the same line as the street, they should be placed after the street number, not before it. If they are on a separate line, the line should precede rather than follow the street line.

The two-letter state abbreviations that have been authorized for use in conjunction with the zip code appear opposite.

(Return address) (Stamp)

Mr. James R. Oxen
Personnel Director
Inland Steel Corporation
Gary, IN 46400

(Postal directions)

Mrs. Henry Oxen

274 Coleman Street, Apt. 10

Dallas, TX 75204

Model addressed envelopes

Alabama	AL	Montana	MT
Alaska	AK	Nebraska	NB
Arizona	AZ	Nevada	NV
Arkansas	AR	New Hampshire	NH
California	CA	New Jersey	NJ
Canal Zone	CZ	New Mexico	NM
Colorado	CO	New York	NY
Connecticut	CT	North Carolina	NC
Delaware	DE	North Dakota	ND
District of Columbia	DC	Ohio	OH
Florida	FL	Oklahoma	OK
Georgia	GA	Oregon	OR
Guam	GU	Pennsylvania	PA
Hawaii	HI	Puerto Rico	PR
Idaho	ID	Rhode Island	RI
Illinois	IL	South Carolina	SC
Indiana	IN	South Dakota	SD
Iowa	IA	Tennessee	TN
Kansas	KS	Texas	TX
Kentucky	KY	Utah	UT
Louisiana	LA	Vermont	VT
Maine	ME	Virginia	VA
Maryland	MD	Virgin Islands	VI
Massachusetts	MA	Washington	WA
Michigan	MI	West Virginia	WV
Minnesota	MN	Wisconsin	WI
Mississippi	MS	Wyoming	WY
Missouri	MO		

■ To test yourself on the mechanics of letter parts, make corrections as needed in the following:

1.

9/21/75

United States Steel Corporation
159 Drew Street
Chicago, Ill.

Dear Mr. Gafferty,

Cordially yours,

Miss June Nix

2.

J. L. Hudson & Co.
510 Woodward Avenue
Detroit, Mich. 48200

Dear Mr. Talbot:

Attention: A. C. Talbot, Personnel.

Yours Truley

3.

Beta Gamma Sigma Fraternity
101 North Skinker Boulevarde
St. Louis Mo 63130

Dear Gentlemen,

Cordially,

John Lee
Smith and Adams
Public Relations Director

4.

Dear Sirs:

Sincerely

Ruth Joneson (Mrs.)

- For discussion, select five to ten letterheads from letters you have received or from business acquaintances. Evaluate them according to criteria you might set up after reading the section on letterheads, then, in class, reach conclusions concerning current practice and trends in letterheads.
- Select and bring to class several letters to illustrate different forms, then judge them on the basis of that favorable first impression. What factors contributed to good appearance and form? What detracted from a good first impression?

MEMORANDUM FORM AND USE

The memorandum is used internally in the company, usually for business of a routine nature. Often it presents data relating to a special problem or pertinent information needed for decision making or problem solving. It also may be used to speed up the flow of information from one department or office to another. The information is generally of current, temporary interest. For example, it may give sales figures for a particular period, for the information of the sales manager. Because it provides figures used in compiling statistics and because it records what is going on within a company, it coordinates the work of various men and departments.

Observe details of form from the model memorandum below. Its parts parallel those of a business letter. Although a letterhead may be used, usually there is merely the heading *Memorandum* or *Interoffice Communication.* There is no inside address or salutation as there is in a business letter. Instead there are simple *TO, FROM,* and *SUBJECT*

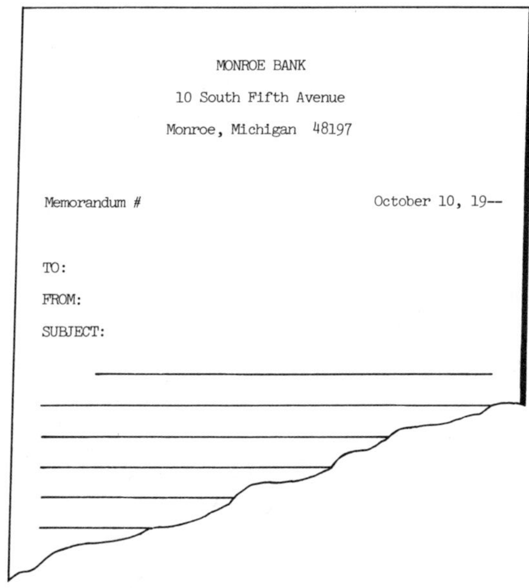
MONROE BANK
10 South Fifth Avenue
Monroe, Michigan 48197

Memorandum # October 10, 19--

TO:
FROM:
SUBJECT:

Model memorandum (interoffice communication)

lines that convey the needed information. The data line is used, and a reference line connects the memorandum, when necessary, to previous ones. However, memorandums are usually referred to by numbers or subjects rather than by dates. There is no complimentary close or signature, although sometimes memorandums are signed or initialed at the end. At other times they are signed beside the name on the *FROM* line. The *TO, FROM,* and *SUBJECT* are printed and the lines are filled in as the paper is used. If printed paper is not available, the headings are typed at the top of the page.

Standard-size paper (8½ by 11 inches) is used for memos of several paragraphs or pages, although a memo would rarely exceed three pages. For brief notes small-size paper is used, usually the half-sheet (8½ by 5½ inches). Memorandums may be folded and inserted into envelopes for intercompany distribution; often, however, their pages are stapled and distributed flat and unenveloped. When more than one page is used, the heading at the top of additional pages is as follows:

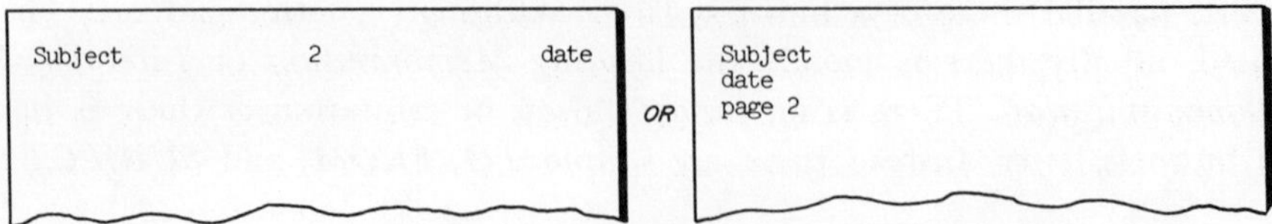
Subject 2 date

OR

Subject
date
page 2

Sometimes the memorandum form is used as a cover to route a longer or more formal report or informational material through specific channels. It may then contain a request for each reader to initial the report and send it on its way to the next person, as:

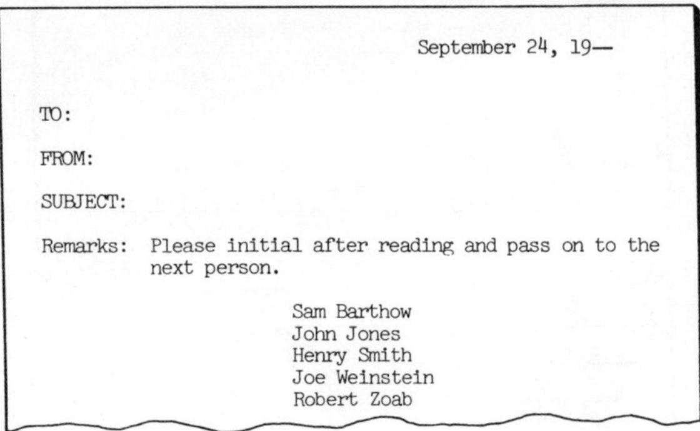
September 24, 19—

TO:

FROM:

SUBJECT:

Remarks: Please initial after reading and pass on to the next person.

Sam Barthow
John Jones
Henry Smith
Joe Weinstein
Robert Zoab

- Discuss the similarities and differences between a business letter and a memorandum.
- As office manager of a large office consisting of twenty-five people, largely secretaries and stenographers, get out a memorandum about the postal regulations they are to follow in addressing envelopes. What would you do about attaching the list of two-letter state abbreviations? How would you organize it?

The form of letters and memorandums serves as a means to an end and not as an end in itself. It helps the letter or memo make that favorable first impression on the reader. However, he becomes interested and motivated through the message and the goodwill, interest, and persuasiveness presented there. Here goodwill is a prime factor in creating a first favorable impression and also in making the reader receptive to whatever else the letter contains.

GOODWILL-BUILDING LETTERS

An accountant's definition of goodwill is the same as the third definition listed in *Webster's New World Dictionary*: "the value of a business in patronage, reputation, etc., over and beyond its tangible assets." The same dictionary also gives as definitions of goodwill,

> "a friendly or kindly attitude; benevolence."

and

> "cheerful consent; willingness; readiness."

The two latter listings are significant for our use in business writing because they consider the human elements. A letter creates goodwill when it produces a favorable, positive reaction from the reader by developing in him a friendly, confident feeling toward the writer and the products or services of the firm. People are human and should be treated as such.

Millions of dollars in business are lost each year and thousands of good customers and prospects are antagonized and take their business to other companies, all because proper application of the goodwill concept is not followed. The favorable effect of a letter is important, as is the feeling of warmth the reader has for the writer and for the company's product or service.

Look at the two letters on page 48. Both answered a letter requesting correspondence and communication manuals to be placed in a university library for student and faculty use. Yet the first one creates an unfavorable image and the second one a favorable image. How is the company put in a favorable or unfavorable light here?

Next take a look at the two cards on page 49. The first card does not create the goodwill that the second one does, although the initial impression obtained from the appearance of the two was equal. Both messages were on four-fold informal social note stationery of high quality with matching envelopes and no business return address identification, thus giving the recipients the idea that they were social or personal notes. On the first note, the emblem of a steering wheel and the expression "Thanks for coming in" were on the outside. On the second note, the imprint "Thank you" was faintly made. So far each note has created goodwill in a friendly, personal way; everyone likes to be told "Thank you." The first note also added a special touch by being signed personally. The sender of the second note handled this by inserting a business card in the inside front fold. The difference lies in the messages and the way they were written. Note number one is more formal and generally evasive, seeking to promote sales rather than goodwill in its specifics. Note number two is simple, direct, and sincere, conveying appreciation and a willingness to serve.

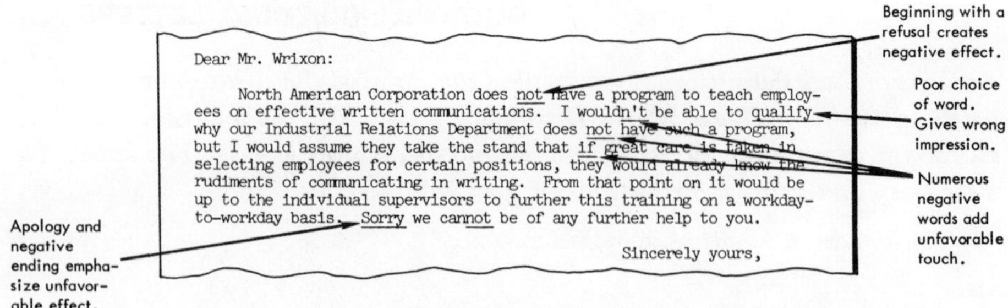
Dear Mr. Wrixon:

North American Corporation does not have a program to teach employees on effective written communications. I wouldn't be able to qualify why our Industrial Relations Department does not have such a program, but I would assume they take the stand that if great care is taken in selecting employees for certain positions, they would already know the rudiments of communicating in writing. From that point on it would be up to the individual supervisors to further this training on a workday-to-workday basis. Sorry we cannot be of any further help to you.

Sincerely yours,

Beginning with a refusal creates negative effect.
Poor choice of word. Gives wrong impression.
Numerous negative words add unfavorable touch.
Apology and negative ending emphasize unfavorable effect.

Goodwill letter #1: Creates unfavorable reaction for the reader and a poor image of the company

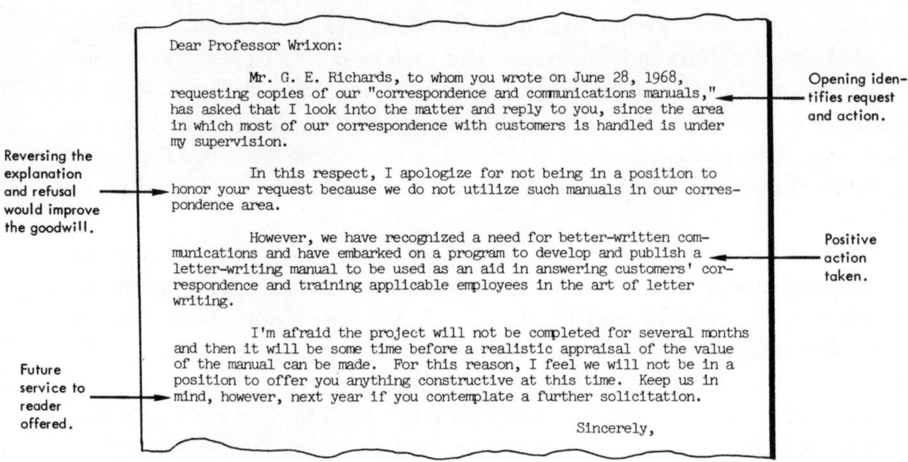
Dear Professor Wrixon:

Mr. G. E. Richards, to whom you wrote on June 28, 1968, requesting copies of our "correspondence and communications manuals," has asked that I look into the matter and reply to you, since the area in which most of our correspondence with customers is handled is under my supervision.

In this respect, I apologize for not being in a position to honor your request because we do not utilize such manuals in our correspondence area.

However, we have recognized a need for better-written communications and have embarked on a program to develop and publish a letter-writing manual to be used as an aid in answering customers' correspondence and training applicable employees in the art of letter writing.

I'm afraid the project will not be completed for several months and then it will be some time before a realistic appraisal of the value of the manual can be made. For this reason, I feel we will not be in a position to offer you anything constructive at this time. Keep us in mind, however, next year if you contemplate a further solicitation.

Sincerely,

Opening identifies request and action.
Reversing the explanation and refusal would improve the goodwill.
Positive action taken.
Future service to reader offered.

Goodwill letter #2: Creates favorable impression toward the writer and the company

OPPORTUNITIES FOR WRITING GOODWILL LETTERS

Although all letters should contain several elements of goodwill, a number of occasions arise in which goodwill is the major function of the letter. It is written solely for building goodwill and accomplishes no other purpose. Anyone can win friends and boost morale by writing letters that are not necessary but that will create a favorable impression and build harmonious human relations. It does not make any difference what kind of business is involved. Simply sending a friendly, personal message on some occasion when nobody would have thought very much about it if the letter hadn't been sent at all will build goodwill.

It was a pleasure to have you visit our showroom and to talk with you about your automotive needs.

Please call me if you have any questions regarding our products, our service or the trade allowance.

I will do everything possible to make you my customer.

Emphasis on sales

Emphasis on appreciation and service

Thank you for the opportunity to serve you.
I trust that your transaction
was handled to your complete satisfaction,
and I am looking forward
to serving you in the future.
Again my sincere thanks.

On the special occasions when one might write to a personal friend, he can also write business friends. These communications could include thank-you notes, congratulatory notes, sympathy notes, invitations, greetings for special holidays, and announcements. There might be an opportunity for a goodwill-building letter in any of the following business situations:

1. Thank a faithful employee for special cooperation.
2. Congratulate an energetic business acquaintance who has been elected president of his professional association.
3. Encourage a valued customer to continue shopping in the store.
4. Show sympathy to a worker who has been hurt in the factory.
5. Send an associate to a friend for advice.
6. Keep in touch with a business friend not seen for a while.
7. Send seasonal good wishes to clients.
8. Send thanks for some product or special service rendered.
9. Send a customer a newspaper clipping concerning him.
10. Show appreciation for a customer.

Guayaquil, Ecuador

Dear Dr. Keller:

Happy Birthday and thanks a lot for your past patronage.

We hope that you have many more birthdays and that we may serve you soon again.

MARS

International Airways

In each of these situations a letter can indicate a sincere interest or concern for the other person and will create goodwill. It will pay off in the long run, too—in friends, more business, more profits, being better liked—for it will indicate that one is a human being treating other people as human beings. Note in each of the examples on these pages how goodwill has been accomplished.

Sanger-Harris

DALLAS, TEXAS 75222 PHONE RI 8-3611

April 17, 1969

Mr. S____ R________
The Fieldcrest Company
New York, N. Y.

Dear Mr. R________ :

We are delighted that the Fieldcrest meeting will be in Dallas this year.

Please join us for a cocktail hour in our Carnation Room, Third Level, Downtown Sanger-Harris, Friday, May 16, beginning at 5:45 PM. If you should arrive after that time, please use the Federal Street entrance, since the store will be closed.

We want to show off our beautiful store to you, and especially the new Fieldcrest Bed and Bath Shop, which we think is a new and exciting concept of display technique.

Just in case you're tempted with our unusual, fun and distinctive 'take-me-home' dazzlers while touring the store, we enclose a VIP Charge Card for your convenience!

A temporary account has already been opened for you, and you have only to present the card for VIP service. You will also find it helpful in cashing personal checks.

If you need special assistance of any kind, please call me or my secretary, Mrs. Joy Wood, RI 8-3611, Ext. 320.

A Texas size welcome awaits you in Dallas and at Sanger-Harris!

Sincerely,

Richard Silk
Vice President

A DIVISION OF FEDERATED DEPARTMENT STORES, INC.

Courtesy Sanger-Harris department store

The sales letter shown[2] motivated the recipient to visit the Sanger-Harris department store when he attended a convention in Dallas.

The next letter not only created goodwill but facilitated the adjustment:[3]

[2]Used by permission of Sanger-Harris, Dallas, Tex.
[3]Used by permission of Mirro Aluminum Goods, Manitowoc, Wis.

Dear Mr. Standard:

Thank you for your prompt reply to our itemized statement of September 14.

For your comparison, we are sending you duplicate copies of our July 25, July 27 and August 23 credit memos, each for $6.18.

Perhaps upon examination, you will be able to adjust your records and deduct the credit memo which apparently you do not have.

When we can be of further help, please let me know.

Sincerely,

M. L. Knutson
Credit

Courtesy Mirro Aluminum Goods

The next example is typical of messages sincerely expressed on specially designed Christmas stationery:

CHRISTMAS
197–
It is a genuine pleasure
at the Holiday Season
to depart from the usual routine
of business and wish you and yours
A Merry Christmas.
May the New Year bring you much Happiness
and a full measure of Prosperity
(FIRM NAME HERE)

Long known for their "effective letters" improvement program, the New York Life Insurance Company (NYLIC) devoted a whole issue of their *Effective Letters Bulletin* (Winter 1967) to treating goodwill used as an extra measure. NYLIC believes that a letter to which the writer might not expect a reply, but gets one, maintains and enhances goodwill; several occasions demonstrating this were cited:

Dear Sir:

I received the notice of the termination of my certificate on October 12 this year. It is needless to say that I will miss this income, but I want to commend you on the wonderful service you have given this contract.

I could always depend on receiving my check right on the 12th of each month. When the 12th fell on a Sunday or holiday, I received it the day before.

Having received this check for 10 years, I miss it. However, I do appreciate the way it was taken care of all that time.

Sincerely,

Effective Letter Bulletin, New York Life Insurance Company, Winter 1967

If this letter had not been answered, NYLIC would still have had a satisfied customer, but their correspondent helped build an "extra measure" of goodwill with this reply:

Dear Mrs. --------

Thank you for your kind comments about our service.

We consider it a primary obligation to see that our payees receive their checks promptly on the due date, and we make it a point to see that this is done. It is very gratifying when we learn that our efforts have been successful.

I appreciate your writing to us, and if there is any way in which New York Life may be of service to you in the future, please let us know.

Sincerely yours,

Effective Letter Bulletin, New York Life Insurance Company, Winter 1967

In looking for exchanges of correspondence to demonstrate their "extra measure" theme, NYLIC came across this other good example:

Dear Sir:

I received your check for $7,074.03. Thank you for being so cooperative.

It may interest you to know that the money will be put to good use, as I have 2 grandsons whom I intend to help through college. One is a student already, and the other will be entering college next year. They are both good boys and their parents are happy with them.

I am certainly glad my husband joined your company.

Very truly yours,

Effective Letter Bulletin, New York Life Insurance Company, Winter 1967

NYLIC's correspondent's reply was as follows:

Dear Mrs. ---------

Thank you for acknowledging receipt of our check for $7,074.03 with such a nice letter.

Your plan to use this money to aid your grandsons in getting their college degrees, would, I feel sure, have met with your late husband's warm approval. It was a pleasure to have had him as a policy owner for the many years since 1927, and it is gratifying that our service can help you accomplish so much at this time.

Sincerely,

Effective Letter Bulletin, New York Life Insurance Company, Winter 1967

By acknowledging the writer's kindness and evidencing an interest in her plans for the education of her grandsons, the correspondent contributed an "extra measure" toward the enhancement of goodwill.

TECHNIQUES FOR CREATING GOODWILL

The following pointers are given as suggestions for writing letters that will create goodwill, either as an element of the letter or per se.

Creating a Friendly Atmosphere

A sincere letter will be conversational; it should be written as though it were being spoken to the reader over the writer's desk. It will mention points of interest to him, agreeing with him where possible. It will exhibit a friendly, courteous attitude and some human warmth. Notice the difference in the following two opening sentences:

> The receipt of your check in the amount of $50.55 is hereby acknowledged and duly credited to your account.
>
> Thank you for your prompt remittance of $50.55. We take pleasure in crediting it to your account.

The first sentence is cold, impersonal; it lacks any element of warmth. The second is courteous, indicates favorable action taken for the reader, and exhibits a friendly attitude on the part of the writer. It is warm, conversational, and easygoing. People like that.

Using a Personal Greeting

The salutation in a letter is the greeting to the reader. Call him by name. Say "Dear Mr. Johnson," not "Dear Sir." If you are on a first-name basis, write "Dear Tom." Use the person's name at least once in the body of the letter by directing a particular point to him. It will give added emphasis to what is said and will cause him to notice it. Try omitting the salutation and incorporating the reader's name in the first sentence:

> We are happy, Mr. Smith, to forward your refund check for $65.
>
> Your order of duck towels, Mrs. Jones, is on its way.

Showing Appreciation

Everyone likes to feel that he is appreciated. The customer is no exception. Tell him so:

> Doing business with friendly folks like you makes our work a pleasure.
>
> Our success depends entirely on your satisfaction with our merchandise.
>
> Thank you for the partial payment on your account.

We appreciate your business.

We were glad to see you last week.

The customer likes to be treated as an individual; he likes to feel recognized as a person and not as just another customer or name on the account ledger.

Taking a Personal Interest

Whenever the occasion arises, show awareness of the customer as an individual. Show an interest in what he is doing and in helping him:

I'm happy to learn you are recovering so quickly from your operation. You'll soon be back in the swing of things.

Now that you are enjoying your new home and have recovered from the trials of moving, I'd appreciate the chance to call when things are squared away and show you our line of . . .

Opening with a Smile

A happy frame of mind when writing letters means that pleasantness and friendliness will permeate what is written. Especially when taking any favorable action, let your happy attitude be apparent from the very beginning:

It was good of you to stop in the other day. Come back often.

We'll gladly show you the layout of our office.

It's a pleasure to fill your order for . . .

Making the Reader Feel Important

By showing the customer that you appreciate his business and by taking a personal interest in him and his needs, you make him feel important. Writing from his point of view and mentioning advantages and benefits to him are other ways of making him feel important:

To show appreciation for your prompt payments in the past, we are enclosing your 197– credit card.

We are holding a cash reserve of $500 open for you.

An investment in . . . can save you 50 percent.

When you mail the postage-free card in the window above, you will receive, without obligation, a genuine cowhide memo book and card case with your name embossed in gold.

Please visit us often, even though you may not wish to buy at the time of your call. It will be a pleasure to have you inspect our displays of fine furniture and quality electrical appliances to be seen at all times at. . . . Our courteous sales force will be happy to serve you.

Encouraging Future Business

Whenever a promise is made, explicitly or implicitly, good communication requires a follow-up to make sure that the promise is satisfactorily kept. Find out whether the customer is satisfied and whether service has been prompt. Whenever a complaint comes in, give it prompt, courteous attention. Failure to back up promises may lose the customer, not merely his goodwill.

Remembering Customer Goodwill

Customer goodwill is one major aim of business communication. Following the suggestions set forth here will go a long way toward creating customer goodwill. Such practices will produce positive, favorable reactions from readers. They will create a friendly, confident feeling toward the writer, his products or services, and his firm. Results can't always be measured in terms of dollars and cents, but creating goodwill will mean increased business and profits in the long run.

- Discuss the meaning and basis of goodwill in business. Illustrate carryover of personal goodwill to business transactions.
- Collect and bring to class for discussion various examples of goodwill letters. Point out phrases and words that are especially good at expressing ideas for creating goodwill. You might make a display of the better letters brought in and discussed.
- Dr. Kathy Sanderson, a charming, gracious lady, is associate professor of business education at a large California university where she has taught for the last fifteen years. She has achieved recognition and prominence in her field, has been an excellent teacher, and is a national officer of Pi Omega Pi, the business educational professional society.

  Since she is so well known and well liked, and is an interesting, stimulating speaker, she is often called upon to be guest speaker at various sorority, university, and business meetings. Last night she spoke at a society chapter meeting at Hall University in San Francisco. This was a dinner meeting following the installation of new officers for the following year. It was well attended, with about twenty faculty members and thirty-five students. Her subject, "Business Teaching as a Profession," was well received, and she was asked several questions afterward.

  After adjournment, the faculty advisor and the chapter president said to her informally, "In appreciation for the stimulating message, we want you to have the centerpiece [a lovely spring bouquet of pink, rose, and white carnations]. Please take it with you." Miss Sanderson graciously accepted their kindness and moved away to answer a question from someone standing nearby.

  Just then the dean of the college and his wife moved toward the center of the head table and the dean's wife remarked how beautiful the arrangement was. The dean said to her, "Honey, why don't we take it home with us? You'll enjoy having it on the coffee table." He then turned and, facing the faculty advisor and the chapter president, said, "We'll take this home with us."

Since nothing was said to prevent it, the dean and his wife took the centerpiece home.

1. What should have been said to the dean? By whom? Why?
2. What should the faculty advisor say to Dr. Sanderson?
3. Should Dr. Sanderson say anything to the dean? What? Why?
4. As the chapter president, write a letter to Dr. Sanderson, maintaining goodwill and explaining the situation.
5. Would you send flowers to her at her office? Why? What message would you send with them?

- Collect Christmas greeting letters sent to customers; compare and evaluate them. What is good practice? To what extent are the companies following goodwill concepts in their practice?
- Point out how the following two messages on postcards accomplished their purposes and created a tremendous amount of goodwill:

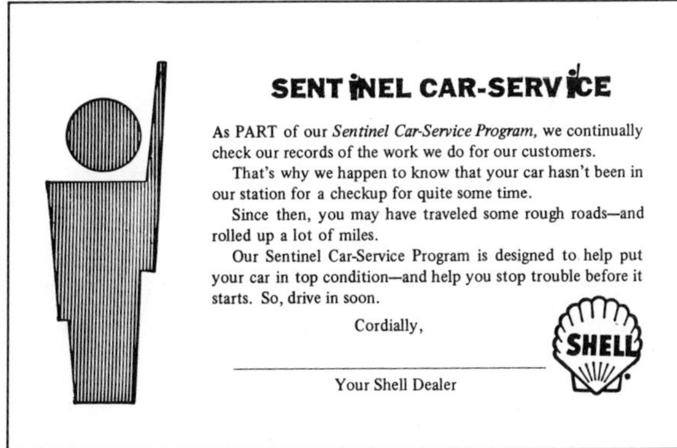

SENTINEL CAR-SERVICE

As PART of our *Sentinel Car-Service Program*, we continually check our records of the work we do for our customers.

That's why we happen to know that your car hasn't been in our station for a checkup for quite some time.

Since then, you may have traveled some rough roads—and rolled up a lot of miles.

Our Sentinel Car-Service Program is designed to help put your car in top condition—and help you stop trouble before it starts. So, drive in soon.

Cordially,

Your Shell Dealer

Dear Customer:

Thank you for your order, just received. It has been sent to our Order Department for prompt handling. Normally, the shipment should reach you within ten to fifteen days.

We are sure you will be pleased with the attractiveness and quality of this merchandise. Satisfied customers have contributed greatly to the growth of our company. Many refer their friends to us. We hope you will, too.

If you have occasion to write us about this transaction, be sure to mention the record number shown on the address side of this card.

Cordially

FF:UAC

Courtesy Shell Oil Company

SUMMARY

To create a favorable first impression and make the reader receptive to its message, a business letter should have an appealing form and appearance, and should create goodwill. The form and appearance of the letter make a favorable first impression; the goodwill created by the letter will interest the reader and influence his actions.

The modified block form is generally followed, although the simplified letter is slowly gaining in popularity—especially for routine and form letters. The trend in today's letterheads is toward simplicity, clearness in the information given, readability, and attractiveness. Emphasis should be given to addressing envelopes according to the postal regulations, including those for the zip code.

The techniques of creating a friendly atmosphere, using a personal greeting, showing appreciation, taking a personal interest, opening with a smile, making the reader feel important, encouraging future business—these will produce positive, favorable reader reaction. They will create a friendly, confident feeling toward the writer, the firm, and its products and services. Goodwill begets goodwill; its principles can be applied in all business letters as well as in those whose sole purpose is goodwill.

FURTHER READING

All the texts on business letter writing and basic business communication treat the letter's appearance and form and goodwill. The ones cited here simply provide some of the better treatments; the material is typical of that in other books. (The first set of pages cited treats letter appearance and form; the second set treats goodwill.)

Aurner, Robert R., and M. Philip Wolf, *Effective Communication in Business,* 5th ed. Cincinnati: South-Western Publishing Co., 1967, pp. 127–45, 247–65.

Dawe, Jessamon, and William J. Lord, Jr., *Functional Business Communication.* Englewood Cliffs, N. J.: Prentice-Hall, Inc., 1968, pp. 25–35, 35–62.

Devlin, Frank J., *Business Communication.* Homewood, Ill.: Richard D. Irwin, Inc., 1968, pp. 116–53, 221–40.

Menning, J. H., and C. W. Wilkinson, *Communicating Through Letters and Reports,* 4th ed. Homewood, Ill.: Richard D. Irwin, Inc., 1967, pp. 13–31, 77–95.

Wells, Walter, *Communications in Business.* Belmont, Calif.: Wadsworth Publishing Company, Inc., 1968, pp. 22–44, 194–214.

QUESTIONS AND PROBLEMS

1. For the following situations, set up and type the correct parts of the letter in good form. (Do not type the body of the letter.)
   a. A letter from the General Appliance Store, 110 South Main Street, your city and state, dictated by James Lee Johnson and typed by Mrs. Bertha Aries, his secretary, to Mrs. Barry Lee (Leona) Nunce, your city and state, 5509 Washington Avenue, S. W., Apartment 10. Date the letter October 5.
   b. A letter, attention line Mr. Michael Monsoon, Director of Public Relations, Elliott Oil Corporation, 3907 North Michigan Boulevard, 77004 Houston, Texas. From you, your address, current date.
   c. A letter, subject a railroad ticket refund, from you, your address, current date, to Monon Railroad, Indianapolis 47306 Indiana, North Lee Avenue 1054.
2. Design suitable letterheads for the three businesses mentioned in problem 1 above.
3. Arrange the following material in standard modified block letter form: General Life Insurance Agency, 300 North Stauton Avenue, Brookhaven, Illinois, December 8, 197–. Attention Mr. Andrew Collender, Personnel Manager, Ranther Manufacturing Company, 9563 South Gate Street, Chicago, Illinois, subject Group Accident Insurance, Gentlemen. This is the season of the year when the Christmas spirit of goodwill is evident in many ways, in the expression on the faces of the people, in their actions toward each other, and in the good deeds they perform for the more unfortunate. For all this we can be thankful. At this season of the year, too, I am not unmindful of the fact that I appreciate the business of your company's group accident insurance that you have entrusted to my care. It is my sincere desire to render the best possible service in connection with the policies I have sold, and I hope that I shall be able to measure up to this responsibility. For the year 197–, I wish you not only a Happy New Year, but good health and the fullest measure of success. KHW, Yours cordially, Kenneth Henry Wholsum, general agent.
4. Clip an article from a newspaper regarding some personal honor and write the person involved a letter, enclosing the clipping.
5. Select two of the situations from page 50 and write the letters called for.
6. Design Christmas or other seasonal stationery and write greetings or thank-you notes to customers.
7. You were in an automobile accident in which the driver of the other car, Mr. Samuel Snoop, was killed. The accident, although unavoidable, was considered your fault by the insurance company that paid liabilities. The deceased was the executive vice-president of the Snoop Fastener Corporation. The president of the Snoop Fastener Corporation is Mr. Bertrand Snoop III, the deceased's father. Write a letter expressing your sorrow to Mr. Snoop. You are the president of the General Fastener Corporation, a competitor.

8. Analyze the letter below and the one opposite. Discuss how they accomplish goodwill in what they say and do. How is goodwill related to a secondary purpose in each situation?
9. As the president of a large furniture store in your community, write a letter thanking a new customer for cash purchases made recently in your store. You handle quality furniture and home furnishings, sell on credit terms, offer free interior decorator services, and have been in business over sixty-five years.

PROPERTY MANAGEMENT — INSURANCE 215 CENTRAL AVE. TEMPE, ARIZONA

WE ARE PROUD TO
ANNOUNCE

YOUR NEW NEIGHBOR

We have just sold a home at:

3509 Welcome Road

It is a pleasure to introduce your new neighbor:

Mr. and Mrs. Joseph C. Watson

In selling this property, we contacted a number of families who wish to buy in this locality. If you are interested in selling your property, or would just like to know today's market value of your property, we would be happy to appraise it at no obligation to you. SUBURBAN has become the byword of local property owners.

Sincerely yours,

SUBURBAN REAL ESTATE, INC.

EJT/cr

Ve 4-7535
Ve 4-7536

E R BRADLEY
Vice President—Marketing

MARKETING DEPARTMENT **SUN OIL COMPANY** 1608 WALNUT STREET, PHILADELPHIA, PENNSYLVANIA 19103

Announcing a Special Privilege

for Educators . . .

You will be pleased to learn that we have made arrangements to issue Sunoco Credit Cards to certain members of your school. Simply complete the Educators Courtesy Signature Card and mail it in the enclosed prepaid reply envelope today. If you accepted our offer last year, may we suggest the use of another card for an additional member of your family.

The Sunoco Credit Card buys gasoline, tires, batteries, just about any automotive product or service. It is a priceless convenience on vacations, trips and in fact all the time.

Naturally, there is no obligation to use it, but you will find it handy to charge your motoring needs at the thousands of friendly Sunoco Service Stations where your gas is Custom Blended to make your car run best while you pay less.

The famous Sunoco Custom Blending Pump gives you the right gasoline for your car at savings of 1¢ or 2¢ a gallon for four out of five car owners. It offers eight different gasolines starting with Blend 190, priced below regular, up to Blend 260, the world's most powerful premium.

We will appreciate your friendship and patronage and will do our best to deserve it. One way of showing that appreciation is to make it easy for you to enjoy credit without the bother of filling out a burdensome application form.

Sincerely yours,

E. R. Bradley

E. R. Bradley

Enclosures

Courtesy Sun Oil Company, Sunoco Division

10. Correct and improve the following letter:

Dear Customer

In appreciation of your past patronage, we are enclosing a new calender for the year 19--. We sincerely hope our services will continue to be as satisfactory to you through this coming New Year, as it has been in the past. We have built our business on serving you our customer, offering only Quality Shoe Products and maintaining a good Customer Relationship. To sum it all up "Good Customers are hard to find and we aim to please".

Very Truly Your's

Al Greensteen

11. *The perfect runaround: a letter from a disenchanted customer.*[4] What happens when a businessman complains about a carrier's treatment? Here is an actual letter, with names fictionalized, written to an airline by the public relations manager of a large corporation.

Obviously the writer of the letter was either angry, sarcastic, facetious, or desirous of helping the recipient; also obviously, the person answering

July 6, 19--
Mr. J. F. Jones, President
Acme Airlines, Inc.
363 Fifth Avenue
New York, N. Y.

Dear Mr. Jones:

You have just lost a customer and I have decided to take the trouble to tell you why. I should add that I have considerable travel experience, as I have done much traveling in the past years.

On June 14, I called your reservations department and spoke with a Miss Cross. I asked her to figure out a routing for me leaving New York for Detroit on Monday morning, June 18, then from Detroit to Dallas on June 28, and flight from Dallas to New York on July 1--all coach. While I waited, she figured this out and put me on a 9:00 a.m. jet flight from New York to Detroit, then a flight leaving Detroit on June 28 at 4:20 p.m., connecting at Chicago with your nonstop flight to Dallas, arriving there at 6:57. She quoted me a price of $197 and some odd cents for the whole package. Miss Cross insisted on mailing me the tickets, as I was using an air travel card. I told her I would much rather have the tickets picked up since the time was short. However, she assured me that I would get the tickets in time. At my request she also checked the service on the Chicago-Dallas flight and told me it would be possible for coach passengers to purchase cocktails and that they would be served a complimentary dinner.

As of Sunday 17, the eve of departure, I had not received the tickets. I called the night supervisor of your New York reservations department and explained my predicament, and was assured that my tickets would be made up and waiting for me at the will-call desk at Kennedy Airport at 8:30 a.m. Monday, a half-hour prior to departure.

I arrived at Kennedy at 8:30, waited for 20 minutes in the will-call line while the young lady laboriously went through schedules figuring out a round-the-world trip for a prospective passenger. When I finally got waited on there were no tickets in the file, as I had been promised.

The young lady called reservations and was told that they planned to have my tickets there at 9:00 a.m., which was the time of departure. She quickly made up a new set of tickets, overcharging me by $8. Although I was aware of this, there wasn't time to complain, so I boarded the plane, strapped myself in and waited. At 9:15 the captain advised us that there was a delay. At 9:30 he suggested that we get off the plane and have a smoke since there were fueling problems. We finally took off at 10:45. The explanation was that someone had put in 1,000 extra gallons of fuel and it had taken that long to locate the problem, drain it out and rebalance the plane. We were one hour and 45 minutes late in Detroit for no good reason.

On Saturday, June 23, I decided to advance my departure for Dallas by one day. I walked to your reservations office in downtown Detroit

[4]Adapted from *Printer's Ink.*

and requested that my reservations be switched to the 27th. The young lady at the counter consulted a mimeographed sheet and advised me that these flights were all sold out and cautioned me to hold on to my present reservations. I returned to my hotel, but thinking there must be a mistake that the Wednesday afternoon tickets would be sold out so far in advance, I telephoned your reservations department and was told that these flights were wide open and they would be glad to make the change. They also advised me that I would have to walk back to the reservations office and have the tickets validated, which I did.

The next incident occurred shortly after I boarded the plane in Chicago. I rang for the hostess about 6:15 p.m. and ordered a martini. I was informed that coach passengers were not permitted any liquor on the flight, contrary to what Miss Cross told me when making my reservations. There is no excuse for misinforming passengers on such matters.

I realize that there are many factors over which airline management have no control. However, it seems to me that you could do a much better job of eliminating stupid mistakes such as these I have recounted.

Very sincerely,

David E. Harper

DEH:cjp

P.S. The overcharge was corrected during the fueling repair at Kennedy.

the letter cannot make any adjustments, since he had no control over what happened.

a. Analyze the situation and the writer of the letter. Use your analysis as a basis for arriving at a purpose to accomplish in a reply.
b. What attitudes can you indicate to Mr. Harper in your reply? Can you give any "real" explanation? What action can you take?
c. How can you create goodwill in your reply? What techniques are applicable? What effect do you want to produce?

12. Answer Mr. Harper's letter.

Chapter Three

ADAPTING LANGUAGE

Did you ever get into an argument with someone only to realize later that you were in agreement?

Did you ever listen to a thirty-minute lecture and not understand what the speaker was talking about?

Have you had one of your letters termed unacceptable by your instructor this semester because you did not fully understand the assignment?

You may feel that you are a fairly good communicator. So often we take our ability to communicate with others for granted, perhaps taking the attitude that having learned the English language, we should be able to understand one another. But occasionally we may find ourselves in a situation in which we become aware that something has gone astray. Most of our failures in communication result from misunderstanding the role that symbols play in the process or from inadequacies in the way we think, transfer, or perceive language symbols. This brings us to the purposes of this chapter: to understand the nature of language and its uses in communication and to increase our language power in applying these concepts by selecting and using words for their meaning and tone. This holds true for writing business letters in particular as well as for all communicating situations.

In the drugstore the other day three students were arguing about milk shakes. One of them said, "I've been gypped; mine has no ice cream."

The second said, "No, you got just what you asked for—if you wanted ice cream, you should have asked for a frosted. Milk shakes just have milk and flavoring."

The third one began to grin: "Now who's mixed up? That's called a frappé, not a frosted." At this point, being college students, they began an argument about the essentials of a milk shake.

What is a milk shake? What is a frosted? What is a frappé? Are they always described by one of the terms the students in the drugstore used? Who was right? This incident tells us several things about the nature of language.[1]

THE NATURE OF LANGUAGE

A Set of Symbols

Language is a set of symbols used to communicate ideas. The symbols must be used uniformly in ways agreed upon by a group of people who are thus able to communicate with each other. The term *milk shake* is used to represent the object for which it stands. A word has meaning because a number of people have agreed that it shall represent a particular object or idea, yet, as the student in the drugstore found, not everyone will attach exactly the same meaning to the same word. A speaker has to know the person or group with whom he is communicating. Words have meaning only when they are within the experience of the listener or reader, for verbal accounts are made up of symbols of situations or conditions they represent. Concepts derived from an account may or may not correspond to reality, depending in part on whether or not the communicator and the receiver agree on the meanings of the words used.

Let us consider the statement: "When I see Mike, I see red." Does this mean that Mike is red-haired? Does it mean that he is a Communist? Or does it mean that he makes you angry? It may even mean that Mike and his pal, Red, are inseparable companions. One projects meaning to the word *red* depending upon his acquaintance with the speaker and Mike, his experiences with how words are used, and the context in which the words are used. Calling a person dishonest does not necessarily mean that he is actually dishonest. Someone else may call the same person honest. Each is right because of the experience and knowledge he has of the person; what one believes to be true is true, as far as he is concerned.

A child learns the concepts of hot and cold from his experience. Parents tell him not to touch the hot stove or furnace; yet he has to touch it to feel the sensation of heat before he really understands its meaning. Touch-

[1]The idea for this story was suggested in David P. French, "A Class in Definition," *College English*, April 1956, pp. 405–7.

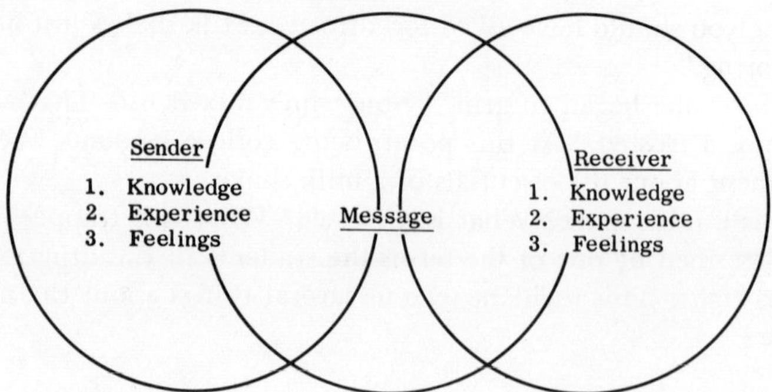

The larger the overlap, the more effective the message to be drawn

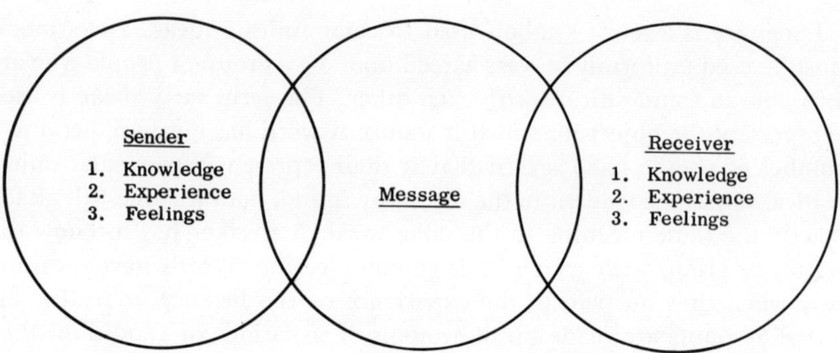

The smaller the overlap, the less effective the message to be drawn

ing an ice cube, feeling a piece of ice put down his back, or going out into the cold wind give him the meaning of cold. From these basic experiences he learns to distinguish between hot and cold. Then he has to learn gradually through further experiences: how hot is hot? and how cold is cold? For words also have various degrees or shades of meaning, depending upon their context. A word will call to mind a sensation, concept, attitude, action, or object because of association and because of one's own experiences.

The word *word,* for example, can be used many ways with different meanings. Some of the uses of *word,* with their meanings, follow:

What's the word?	(Decision or authority)
Give me your word.	(Promise)
I'd like a word with you.	(Short talk)
That's the last word in dresses.	(Style)
I received word from Bill.	(News)
Sunday I read "The Word."	(Scripture)

By permission of Johnny Hart and Field Enterprises, Inc.

How language is formed

Mother's word is law. (Authority)
My word! That's a bright red shirt! (Affirmation)

A word has meaning because people have agreed upon it; the meaning is conveyed when it is used appropriately within a human situation.

A Common Language

The meaning of a word depends upon the situation and circumstances in which it is used. For example, you might try your hand at describing the geometric figures that follow:

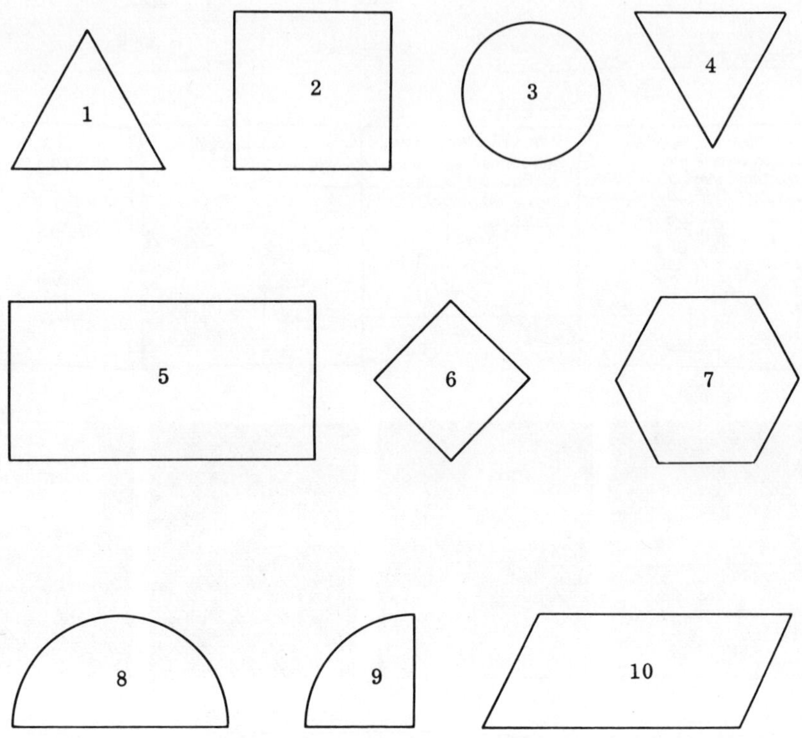

Next, have a friend describe the same figures. Were the descriptions the same? They probably were different, because you did not use the same language. This experiment indicates the misunderstandings that might result from a situation in which the people involved do not use a common language.

Go out of the room or behind a screen and describe the following figures, having a friend draw them from your description without speaking to you:

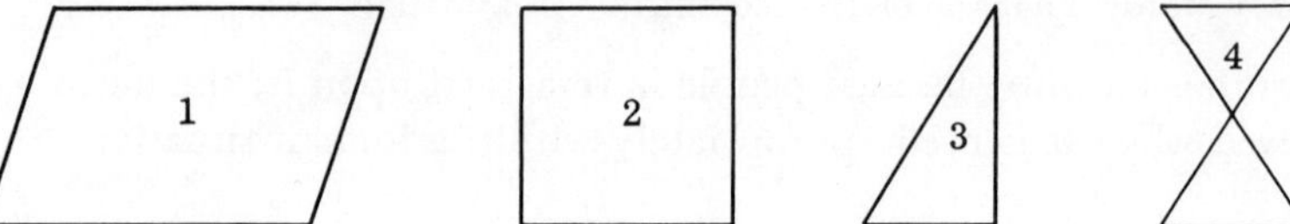

Now have a friend draw the same figures while you remain in his sight and describe them.

The two sets of drawings were probably different. Those made while you were in sight of your friend were probably more accurately drawn because you could react to his facial expression and adjust your language when you saw that he didn't understand fully. Such an experiment points out an important difference between making a speech and writing a report or letter. A speaker can see his audience and react to its apparent needs. A writer has to visualize how the reader will react and write what he thinks will receive the desired effect, but he may not be quite sure. In any event, he seeks to use a language common to himself and his audience.

How do you choose the proper language? Language must suit the communicator, his audience, and the situation. To be understandable, it must be common to the people concerned—speaker and listener, writer and reader—and it must be common to the locale or area in which it is used. It also must agree with standard usage.

There are three levels of language usage, as indicated by the following figure. Most of the language used in communicating for business purposes

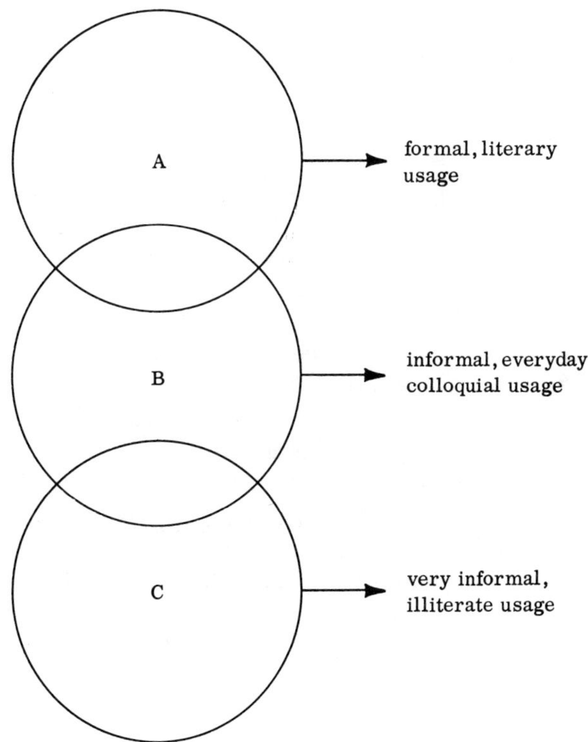

Levels of language usage

is the informal, everyday language indicated in circle *B*. To suit the needs of his audience, however, the communicator will reach upward when communicating to people who have had the experience and education to understand at that level and will reach downward as it becomes necessary. In writing a letter to be sent to a mass readership or in speaking to a mass audience, he will direct his group with informal colloquial language, recognizing that his audience also includes a few people belonging to the other two levels. If he occasionally dips downward and rises upward, he lends variety to his speech and reaches the two extremes of his audience.

Using a common language also means using technical terminology only when it is understood by both communicator and audience. Nontechnical language is generally acceptable to all persons. To the average businessman, for instance, the following sentences from a report, intended for an experienced chemist only, would have little if any meaning:

> The anhydroamenobenzyl-alcohols are characterized by their insolubility in water and in the usual organic solvents. They are soluble in dilute hydrochloric or other mineral acid, with formation of the corresponding salt. . . .

A chemist would readily understand the technical terminology because it is within his realm of experience.

Meanings Are in People

Individual experiences are never identical, for no two people can be in the same spot at the same time. The meanings people get out of words are dependent upon their experiences, knowledge, and feelings. Even when several people look at the same thing, they still do not experience it in the same way, for each one selects some of what he sees and rejects the rest. For instance, the three photographs opposite are the same picture, but three different people have seen it in three different ways.

Meaning is in the eye of the beholder. The fable about the blind men and the elephant (see pages 72–73) illustrates very well that words cannot have meanings in themselves. Meanings are in people and words are the symbols used to express them.

Our discussion thus far in this chapter has been concerned primarily with the *semantic* meanings of words and not their *syntactic* meanings. *Syntax* refers to the standardized relationships among words established in our language system over a period of years. Consider these simple sentences:

1. The boy met the girl.
2. The ball is round.
3. John threw the ball.

Each contains a subject, a verb, and a predicate noun or adjective; these describe the syntactic relationships of the sentence elements. Semantically the word *and* always indicates a connection of two equal ideas, and *but* shows a contrast of ideas. Syntactic values of *and* and *but* are conditioned by their use within sentences. *And,* for instance, may connect a series of words or two clauses. Using a common language means meeting syntactical as well as semantic requirements of standard usage. Our language is in a constant state of change. A linguist studies the history of words (etymology) and their syntactic forms and meanings. A semanticist studies word meanings (semantics) according to the idea, attitude, or emotion conveyed. Both aid us in using language to convey meaning and to get things done.

A young man "on the town"

A person needing to cash a check

Someone who is late for an appointment

- Discuss the topic: "What is language and how does it operate in the communicative process?" Define language. Read some reference books on the subject and report your findings to the class. (Stuart Chase, S. I. Hayakawa, and Irving Lee would be good authors to use.)

- Discuss "What language means to me." Relate personal experiences to illustrate your statements.

- Try the experiment suggested on pages 68 and 69. Discuss why it turned out as it did. What implications has this demonstration?

- Recall incidents in your personal experience and in business that will show that "meanings are in people."

- If it is available, have your instructor obtain and show the film *The Eye of the Beholder*. Discuss its concepts.

Courtesy Kaiser Aluminum News, 1965

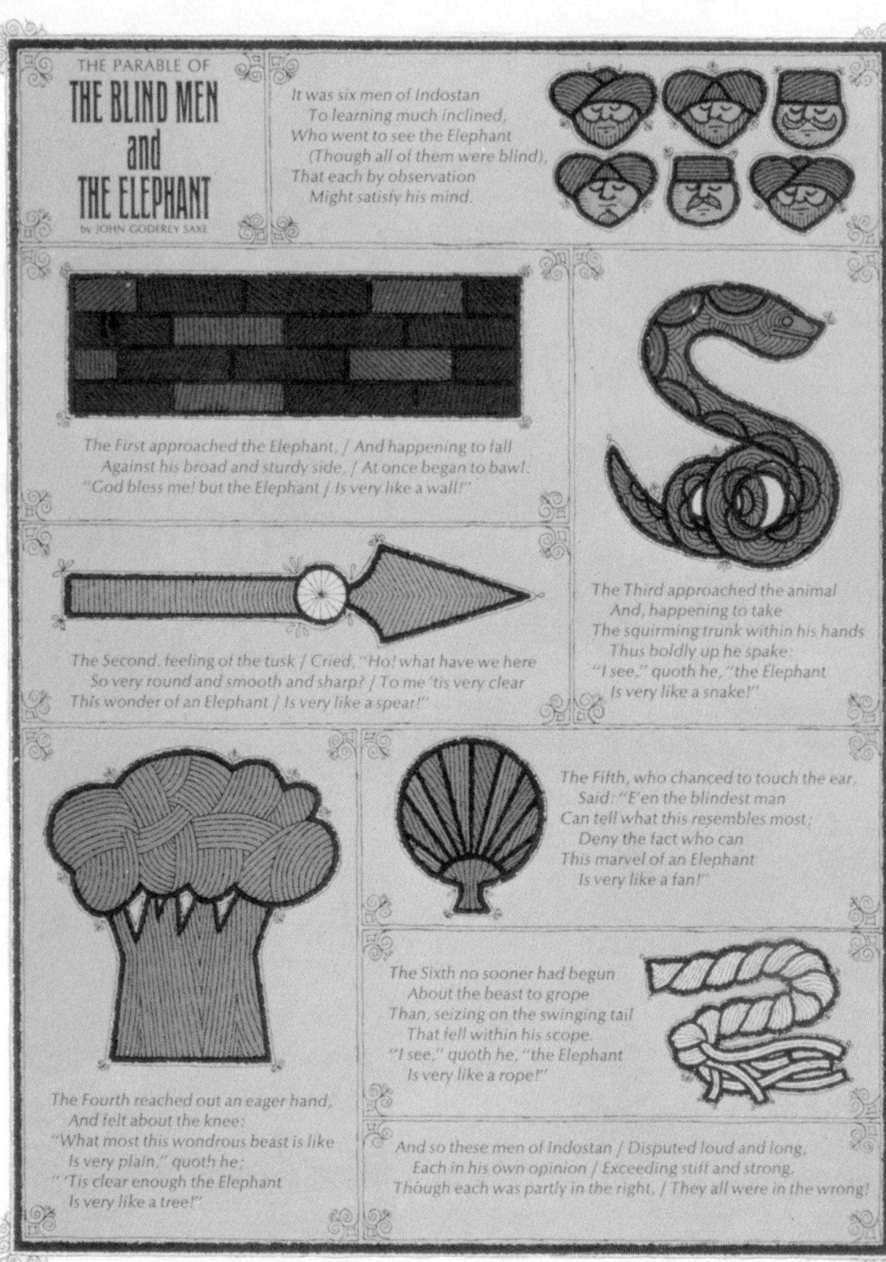

THE PARABLE OF
THE BLIND MEN and THE ELEPHANT
by JOHN GODFREY SAXE
It was six men of Indostan
To learning much inclined,
Who went to see the Elephant
(Though all of them were blind),
That each by observation
Might satisfy his mind.
The First approached the Elephant, / And happening to fall
Against his broad and sturdy side, / At once began to bawl:
"God bless me! but the Elephant / Is very like a wall!"
The Second, feeling of the tusk / Cried, "Ho! what have we here
So very round and smooth and sharp? / To me 'tis very clear
This wonder of an Elephant / Is very like a spear!"
The Third approached the animal
And, happening to take
The squirming trunk within his hands
Thus boldly up he spake:
"I see," quoth he, "the Elephant
Is very like a snake!"
The Fourth reached out an eager hand,
And felt about the knee:
"What most this wondrous beast is like
Is very plain," quoth he;
"'Tis clear enough the Elephant
Is very like a tree!"
The Fifth, who chanced to touch the ear,
Said: "E'en the blindest man
Can tell what this resembles most;
Deny the fact who can
This marvel of an Elephant
Is very like a fan!"
The Sixth no sooner had begun
About the beast to grope
Than, seizing on the swinging tail
That fell within his scope,
"I see," quoth he, "the Elephant
Is very like a rope!"
And so these men of Indostan / Disputed loud and long,
Each in his own opinion / Exceeding stiff and strong,
Though each was partly in the right, / They all were in the wrong!

Courtesy Kaiser Aluminum News, 1965

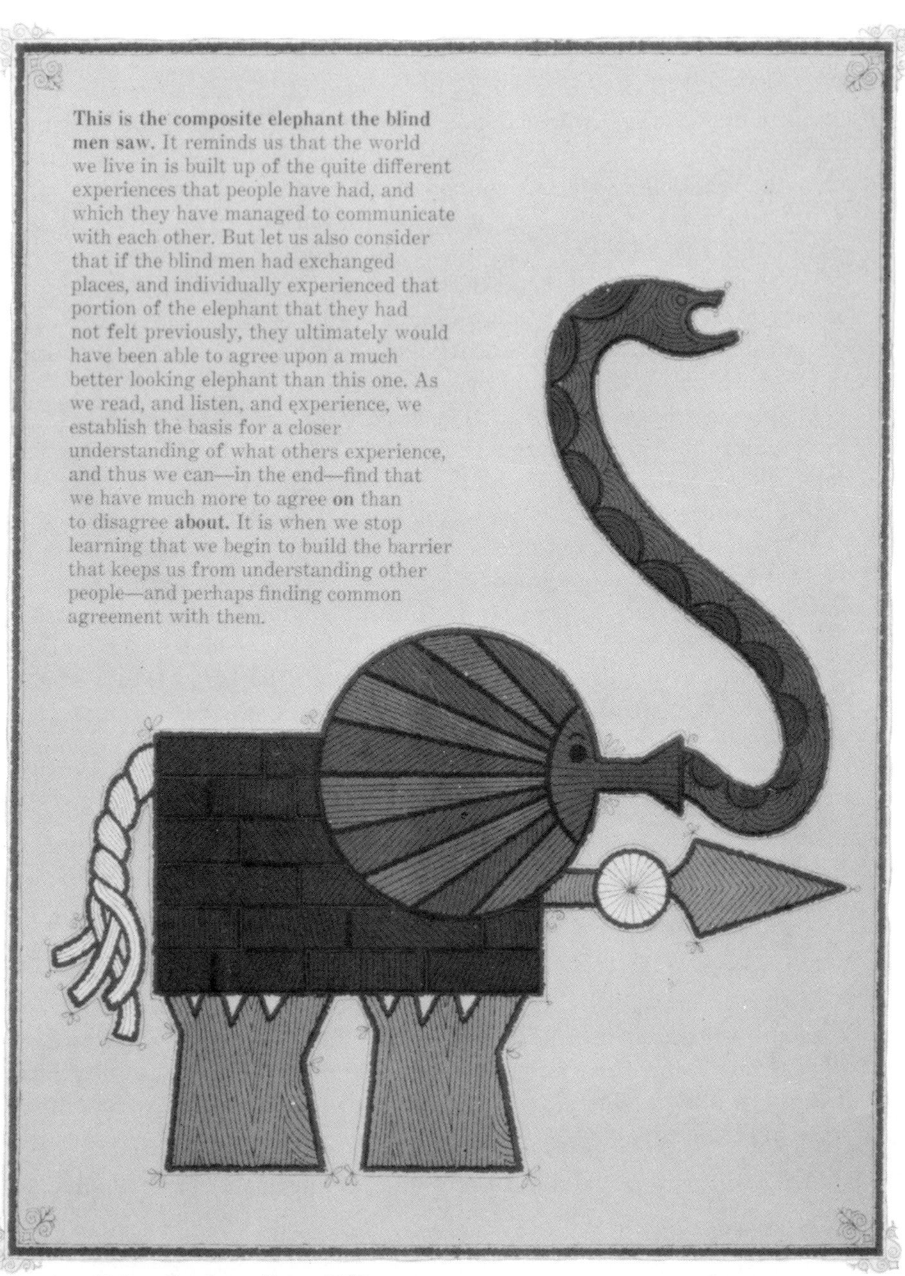

This is the composite elephant the blind men saw. It reminds us that the world we live in is built up of the quite different experiences that people have had, and which they have managed to communicate with each other. But let us also consider that if the blind men had exchanged places, and individually experienced that portion of the elephant that they had not felt previously, they ultimately would have been able to agree upon a much better looking elephant than this one. As we read, and listen, and experience, we establish the basis for a closer understanding of what others experience, and thus we can—in the end—find that we have much more to agree **on** than to disagree **about.** It is when we stop learning that we begin to build the barrier that keeps us from understanding other people—and perhaps finding common agreement with them.

Courtesy Kaiser Aluminum News, 1965

THE RIGHT WORD FOR MEANING

The relationship of the meaning of a word to the circumstances and situation in which it is used is called *context* and is a basis for recognizing differences in meanings of words. From a word's context, meanings are either explicitly given or connoted. The explicit meaning of a word is its recognized, standardized meaning (or meanings) as given in the dictionary. This meaning has been agreed upon by usage and has stood a test of time. Connotation, on the other hand, is the impression, feeling, or emotional overtone that a word calls forth. It is the effect the word has because of a hearer's experience and association with it; thus connotative meaning may vary from person to person.

A store advertises a sale on nylon hosiery for ladies, offering for $3.98 three pairs that would normally sell for $1.75 per pair. The advertising copy speaks of the *bargain* the women will receive, and says that the hose are *cheap*—three pairs for little more than the price of two. The explicit meaning of both words, *cheap* and *bargain,* in this context is *low-priced.* The connotation of *cheap,* however, is that the hose are of low-quality material or poor workmanship. A woman reading the newspaper ad will probably not bother to go to the store to look at the hosiery.

Suppose, on the other hand, that the advertising copy speaks of the *economical budget price* of the hosiery, three pairs for $3.98. The reader still receives the explicit meaning of *low price,* but *economical budget price* does not carry the connotations that *cheap* might.[2] In all communicating situations the connotative effect of the word has to be considered, as does its explicit meaning. Although exact, precise words are useful because they prevent confusion, the connotation of a word is also important for the vividness it conveys and the impact it makes in motivating action.

The choice of the right word is not always an easy matter. Almost every word has several possible meanings, so that potential misunderstanding constantly threatens to interfere with thought. One of the chief misuses of language stems from failure to recognize the variety of meanings that words can convey. Here are several guiding principles that are helpful in selecting and using words:

1. Avoid general, abstract words and use specific, definite words.

General:	*Specific:*
product	electric blanket
commodity	butter
service	eight-hour delivery

[2]Remember, however, that the connotations of a word like *cheap,* apparently clearly negative, could change considerably during a period of general financial hardship.

"I have a pet at home"
"Oh, what kind of a pet?"
"It is a dog."
"What kind of a dog?"
"It is a St. Bernard."
"Grown up or a puppy?"
"It is full grown."
"What color is it?"
"It is brown and white."
"Why didn't you say you had a full-grown, brown and white St. Bernard as a pet in the first place?"

"Why doesn't anybody understand me?"

When we communicate with each other, it is useful to keep in mind that our common words may not evoke the same image in someone else's mind as they do in ours . . .

Knowing this, we can help improve our communications by being as specific as possible in the way we use words . . .

And, if you are on the receiving end, it often helps to ask questions.

Assuming that "everyone knows what you are talking about" . . .

and assuming you know what others are talking about without asking questions to make "sure" . . .

. . . are two common causes of communications failure. *Be specific!*

Courtesy Kaiser Aluminum News, 1965

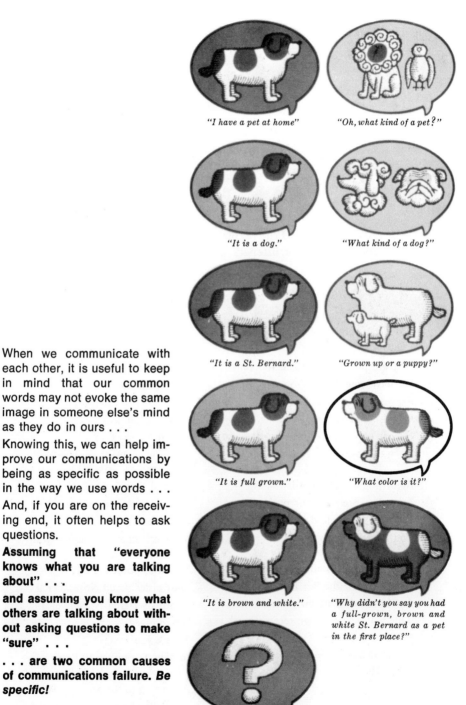

General:	*Specific:*
thing	table
factor	cost
crowd	troop
fragrance	gardenia
light	candle
great	adventurous
speak	squeak
work	spade
say	mutter
send	mail

2. Avoid clichés. Trite expressions frequently consume extra time for the reader or listener.

Do not say:	*Do say:*
Your letter was duly received.	We were glad to receive . . .
We are in receipt of . . .	Thank you for your check.
I beg to advise . . .	Your refund has been approved.
You will please find attached hereto . . .	Please find . . .
We have your kind favor of . . .	Thank you for . . .
For your information . . .	(State the information)
Please be advised that . . .	(State the advice)
We are happy to inform you that . . .	We are happy that . . .
Take this opportunity to . . .	Mail the enclosed application form.
According to our records . . .	We find that . . .
In accordance with our policy that . . .	According to our policy . . .
Enclosed please find . . .	Please find . . .
We beg to acknowledge . . .	We received and deposited your check.
Thanking you in advance . . .	We will appreciate . . .
Your letter of the 9th Inst . . .	Your order dated November 9 . . .
As of even date herewith . . .	(Omit) *or* Dated November 10 . . .
This will acknowledge receipt of . . .	We received . . .
We would like to . . .	Thank you!
I have before me your letter of December 10.	In your December 10 letter . . .
As per statement attached herewith . . .	According to the attached statement . . .
Hoping this will be satisfactory . . .	This should be satisfactory for . . .

Note the differences in the following:

Dear Mr. Roberts:

We want to acknowledge your kindness in returning to us, signed, our letter of February 2nd, outlining the understanding we have with your company in connection with your activities as a distributor of our ______ brands.

Appreciating the courtesy you have shown us, and with kindest wishes, I remain

Yours sincerely,

Dear Mr. Roberts:

Thank you for signing and returning our letter outlining your activities as a distributor of our ________ brands.

We appreciate your courtesy.

Sincerely,

The next letter also points up the overuse of *happy, sorry,* and *glad.* The boss had just dictated another of his "we are happy . . . we are sorry . . . we are glad" masterpieces to his overworked secretary. Twenty years of typing trite phrases was too much; the poor gal snapped under the strain.

Here is the letter she put on the boss's desk:

Ball, Bill, Bell & Bull
1010 Cornacre Street
Hometown

Gentlemen:

We are happy (the entire staff is wearing six-inch grins, the chairman of the board is organizing a game of tag to be played over the desk tops, and the treasurer is tearing up the petty cash) to have your letter. We are sorry (the stenographers are softly tapping out Chopin's Funeral March on their typewriters and everyone is bowed low with grief) we cannot fill your order for Model ZZ Whatzits. However, we are glad (the executives have shut off the brine, are drop-kicking inkwells through the windows; laughter runs through the place until it sounds like a convention hall--pardon while I do a handstand) to offer Model XX Whatzits as substitutes.

Cordially, cheerfully, and gleefully yours,

WHATZITS MFG. COMPANY

3. Reduce groups of words to single words.

Do not say:	*Do say:*
at all times	always
at the present time	now
along the lines of	like
costs the sum of	costs
we would ask that	please
in the nature of	like
for the purpose of	for
in order to	to
prior to	before
subsequent to	after
until such time as	until
due to the fact that	because
with regard to	about
with reference to	about
in connection with	by, in, for (or other appropriate word)
report to the effect that	report that
under date of	on
for the period of a year	for a year
in the amount of	for
in the event that	if
first of all	first
on occasion of	when, on
in view of the fact that	since
for the reason that	because
give consideration to	consider
is of the opinion that	believes

4. Avoid negative, unfavorable words. Use positive, pleasant words.

A negative reaction may result from the use of any of these words:

must	authoritative	hesitant
death	defeat	suspicion
disagreement	regret	careless
fault	refusal	blunt
fear	trickery	curt
neglect	not	selfish
dislike	reject	lazy
never	unfortunate	sorry
disaster	apology	trust
negligence	weak	prohibit
complaint	biased	wrong
unfair	untimely	blame
failure	inconvenient	if
hope	uncomfortable	

A positive reaction may result from the use of any of these words:

ability	distinction	accuracy
fair	assurance	ambition
adjustment	admirable	glad
right	benefit	happy
commendable	confidence	pleasure
cooperation	diplomacy	wise
courtesy	tact	useful
calm	understanding	willing
desire to serve	thoughtful	generous
substantial	loyalty	faith
effective	good	

Select words for their meaning and for their effect on those to whom they are directed. Language is the primary means by which human beings get things done, and it is probably the most essential activity involving human beings. Therefore it is very important to understand the ideas, attitudes, and emotions words convey, for they help to set the tone of our messages, especially in business letters.

THE RIGHT WORDS FOR TONE

Tone in a letter is an expression of the writer's attitude toward the reader. The recipient reacts to the tone the letter projects; like most things in a letter, the tone must be based on its effect on the reader. To obtain the desired reaction, a letter should be courteous, sincere, and written naturally.

Being Courteous

Following the Golden Rule, "Do unto others as you would have others do unto you," requires that you be courteous. This principle is fundamental to good communication and good human relations. Courtesy consists of putting yourself in the other person's place and showing him every consideration, as well as showing good common sense in daily living and getting along with other people. It is an attitude of mind based on kindness, respect, and understanding. It comes naturally to people who are considerate of the other person and of his feelings, needs, and reactions; this impresses the other person favorably.

It is important to show good manners and actions, to do what you should even if you are not obligated to do it. Take no unfair advantage; avoid words that hurt people or ruffle their feelings; and never be intentionally impolite. Being tactful means doing things in a pleasant way without neglecting others, and letters can reveal whether or not you have this quality.

Would you like to do business with a company whose letters sound like this?

Dear Mrs. Winsor:

We regret to inform you that the check for $10.00 representing your husband's disability benefit, which we released January 5, is not payable, as the Insured was dead on the date payment was due.

Please return the check. Enclosed find a self-addressed envelope toward that purpose.

Sincerely,

Or would you prefer to deal with one whose letters sound like this?

Dear Mrs. Winsor:

Please accept our deepest sympathy on the death of Mr. Winsor. This is a difficult time, we know, and we hope this letter does not intrude on your privacy.

Mr. Winsor's last monthly disability check of $10 was sent to him automatically, before we learned of his death. Unfortunately, since he died before payment was actually due, the check must be returned.

As you can see, this situation was unavoidable. I am truly sorry if this caused you even the slightest inconvenience.

Sincerely,

A letter similar to the first one was actually (and unfortunately) sent to the newly widowed wife of a policyholder.[3] The widow was so offended that she threatened to stop doing business with NYLIC. What is wrong with its tone? It is abrupt and curt, it lacks human warmth, and it fails to show concern for the reader or to recognize her as a human personality.

The second letter, on the other hand, recognizes and shows concern for Mrs. Winsor and her needs in her present situation. She is not treated impersonally, nor are her feelings hurt by the explanation. It is a friendly, constructive letter, showing understanding and "feeling" for the reader.

Ways of showing courtesy in writing letters include:

1. Getting off to a friendly start
2. Being helpful and constructive
3. Respecting the other person's point of view
4. Listening to the other person
5. Indicating appreciation
6. Showing confidence

[3]See NYLIC's *Effective Letters Bulletin,* Winter–Spring 1968.

7. Being genuinely polite, cheerful, and sincere
8. Boosting morale
9. Writing promptly

Ways of being discourteous in writing letters include:

1. Being verbose
2. Showing lack of interest
3. Expressing anger or sarcasm
4. Being impolite
5. Blaming the other person
6. Losing respect and self-control
7. Taking up the other person's time unnecessarily
8. Showing lack of poise
9. Using stereotyped language
10. Being unsympathetic
11. Failing to consider the feelings of others

Courtesy genuinely expressed by the manner assumed toward others, by a generous attitude toward others, and by the language and tone used in expressing that attitude pays off when others are convinced to listen, understand, and react favorably.

Being Sincere

Like courtesy, sincerity is an individual personality trait that is expressed naturally by the people who possess it. A sincere person is without deceit, pretense, or hypocrisy; he is honest, straightforward, and unaffected in his relations with other people.

As he reads your letter, the receiver must feel that its message, its tone, and its writer are genuine. Which of the following two letters seems sincere?

Dear Mrs. Wilson:

I am extremely sorry that you did not telephone me immediately that the flowers for Sue's wedding were terribly wilted. I am sure that I would have been so happy to come out personally and see they were replaced with fresh ones.

You have always been so very lovely and good in your dealings with us that I'm very sorry you didn't even give me a chance to explain nor to correct the error which I would have made every effort imaginable to do so very promptly.

Sue was such a very beautiful bride! As I read the glowing account of the wedding in the paper I could just visualize her extreme loveliness she presented as she so very gracefully walked down the aisle to the wonderful strains of Mendelssohn's Wedding March. . . .

```
Dear Mrs. Wilson:

     Had you telephoned me about the flowers for Sue's wedding, I would
have had them replaced.  Obviously, you should not pay for the flowers,
so we are enclosing our check for the full amount of the order.  Please
accept, also, our sincere apology.

     The flowers were made up just before our closing time at 6:00 p.m.
and should have been fresh for the wedding the next morning.

     I saw the pictures of the wedding in the Sunday Times.  It was in-
deed one of the loveliest of the season.

     The next time, Mrs. Wilson, I shall make every effort to give you
the very best flowers and service.
```

What keeps the first letter from being sincere? The overuse of adjectives and superlatives simply does not ring true. The writer creates an image of affectation, hypocrisy, and exaggeration. She appears gushy, overenthusiastic, and thus insincere. The second letter, however, shows a sincere willingness to do something about the situation, and it does! It also expresses an apology without placing undue emphasis on it, attempts an explanation without placing any blame on the customer or telling her what she should have done, presents an honest simple compliment, and leaves the door open for further service.

Ways of showing sincerity in writing letters include:

1. Being a genuine person
2. Reflecting an honest interest in the other person
3. Using personal pronouns and references
4. Writing in the active voice
5. Admitting mistakes
6. Apologizing briefly and quickly
7. Showing friendliness
8. Placing emphasis on constructive, positive action
9. Keying the tone to simple dignity

Ways of showing insincerity in writing letters include:

1. Overusing adjectives and superlatives
2. Being gushy or overenthusiastic
3. Blaming the other person
4. Being arrogant or overbearing
5. Making high-handed statements

Write a prompt, pleasant, direct letter and your sincerity will show through. Write a delayed, overapologetic, overenthusiastic letter and the reader will need to be convinced of your sincerity.

Writing Naturally

The best business letters are simple and relaxed. They get to the point, like one person talking to another. "Write the way you talk" is advice that is given repeatedly; it means that you should try to capture the originality and warmth of expressions used in ordinary conversation. The easy simplicity of language used in conversation is friendlier and more natural than the stiff, formal language that sometimes creeps into our letters. This means that we must avoid the trite, hackneyed phrases mentioned earlier and the pompous, stuffed-shirt expressions that make dull, confusing reading. Instead the words should flow naturally and informally to set the general overall tone. NYLIC[4] offers these illustrations:

We are most grateful for the promptness shown in forwarding to this office the information requested on the new policy forms. It will do much to expedite our operations here.	(Polite, friendly, but not an easy natural flow. Expressions used have a stiff, formal tone.)
Thank you for sending the information on the new policy forms so promptly. It will be very helpful to us.	(Simple, clear, natural flow. Informal, sincere tone.)

Why write like this?

> In reference to your letter of November 21, in connection with our account, we are remitting our check herewith in the amount of $110 as per your request.

You could more simply and naturally say:

> Here is our check for $110, requested in your November 21 letter.

NYLIC also cautions against becoming too familiar or casual, as:

> Thanks loads for the info on the new policy form. It'll sure come in handy in helping us get the ball rolling at this end.

This language detracts from the message, causing you to question its appropriateness and to doubt its sincerity. Use the language of conversation, but not at the risk of flippancy.

Other points to follow in writing naturally include:

1. Using your own language
2. Letting your personality show
3. Talking with, not at, your reader
4. Being cheerful

[4]*Effective Letters Bulletin*, Fall 1967.

■ Now that we have discussed, illustrated, and shown examples of the right words for meaning and tone, try your skill in the following exercises:

1. Distinguish between the explicit and connotative meanings of these words:

cheap	no	delightful
blame	hope	happy
unfortunate	inexpensive	sorry
yes	high-priced	trust

2. Which words in the foregoing list produce positive effects? Negative? Why?
3. For picturesque and concise speech, compounds are helpful. Form compounds from these phrases. Remember that a compound adjective preceding a noun is hyphenated.

   a survey over the whole school
   the pace that kills men
   a chairman whose mind is open
   atomic warfare conducted by push buttons
   an account by a witness
   water the color of the blue sky

■ Consider these three meanings of the word *true*:

1. A statement is *true* because it can be verified by data or observation.
2. A statement is *true* because we feel it is true.
3. A statement is *true* because it has been declared true (the directive language concept).

Explain how one of the three meanings can be applied to each of the following statements so that the reader or listener will accept them as true:

1. The atomic age began in the twentieth century.
2. Scientists should be objective.
3. The possibility of an atomic war is very frightening.
4. A good command of English is important.
5. The Soviet Union is trying to cut our throats in the world trade markets.

■ Rewrite the following sentences to avoid wordiness and improve tone:

1. Modern practice is to deviate from the system of accepting a letter of recommendation as very important.
2. According to our records, a check was mailed you September 15.
3. If you will either return the book or send us the $5, as the case may be, we will set our records straight.
4. In reply to your letter of January 15th, I wish to state that your order will be shipped January 25th.
5. We have duly considered your kind offer.
6. He wrote us under date of November 14.
7. The copy is herewith enclosed for your perusal.
8. On referring to our files, we found that your account was in error.
9. We wish to thank you for your order.
10. We would like to ask you to pay promptly.

11. Let me take this opportunity to inform you of the change in our policy.

- Discuss the relationship of *tone* to *goodwill* in writing business letters. Why are most of the techniques that are applied the same for both concepts?

- Evaluate the following letter for the meaning and tone in its language. Why is its meaning obscure? Why is its tone insincere and discourteous? Is it written naturally? Does it create goodwill?

Dear Sir:

I have just received your letter inst. November 1st. In it you complained that we did not allow you a refund for your first class, reserved seat, airplane ticket from San Francisco, California, to Houston, Texas, which was sold to you through the Acme Travel Agency in San Luis Obispo, California, on September 29.

You should know by now, my well-travelled friend, that we cannot make refunds unless space is relinquished in time for reassignment. Unfortunately you made no mention in your letter that this had or had not been done. Luckily for you, I have also just received in this morning's mail a letter from the Customer Service Division in San Francisco, informing me that you had telephoned them at your hotel to the airport that morning when your plane was due to leave at 6:30 p.m. This of course was in plenty of time to allow cancellation and reassignment of your seat.

For these various and sundry reasons we had no alternative but to deny your refund. You surely understand that we would have been only too happy to do so had we known the full story from you with substantial evidence to back it up.

We are most grievous and sorry for this so we are now only too happy to inform you we have asked our treasurer to write and mail you our check for the full amount of your ticket from San Francisco to Houston via AMA airlines. There will be a delay of two weeks, for he is on a late vacation trip and we are short of help currently at present. You should, however, receive the price of your one-way ticket in the amount of $105.98 plus 10% tax.

Yours for better service,

- The above letter also calls for a different opening and organization of its points. Rewrite it with the proper meaning, tone, and organization.

Selecting and using the right words for meaning and tone help get the message across to the reader. However, this is only part of the larger problem of adaptation that gives every consideration to the reader and the effect language has on him, in order that the writer may accomplish his purpose.

ADAPTATION OF LANGUAGE

There are two major reasons for adapting language: to gain understanding and to secure interest leading to motivation. Both purposes encompass the role that language plays in the communicating process.

Knowledge of human nature in general and understanding of the person with whom you are communicating are requisite to effective adaptation of language. By considering factors such as education, age, sex, position, and experience, you can adapt ideas, language, and style to help the reader or listener comprehend easily and react favorably. Give emphasis to your important points. Adjust your choice of words and expression of ideas to the mental level of your audience. The Prudential Insurance Company's letter writers, when writing to policyholders, maintain an average sentence length of seventeen words and an average word length of two syllables—a practice that helps the reader economize his effort and time.

The principle of adaptation further indicates the use of short words, simple sentences, short sentences, and short paragraphs when writing to readers whose education has been limited. It prohibits their use with people who would take such writing as an insult or feel that they were being "talked down to."

The principle of adaptation also means using a wide range in style—from the informal and conversational to the dignified and conservative. Put what you have to say in terms that will interest the reader. A woman who dresses on a low-income budget will buy a pair of $1.25 hose because they are good-looking, inexpensive, or long-wearing. A teenager will buy the same hose for their "sheer silken quality" or "sheer loveliness." Make the reader think well of himself by treating him courteously. Meet him on his level. Be serious, sincere, and confident. Be interested in the things he is interested in. Being courteous to and interested in the other person are also personality attributes that help make a person likable and aid him every day in getting along with other people.

To adapt language for ease of comprehension and motivation, we need to remember that words in our language not only represent logical relationships, but also provoke emotional responses. We use them not only to *express* what we want to say but also to *impress* our audience, to move them to action. Influencing people to react favorably demands that we select words for their emotional effect, use vivid expressions, emphasize the positive aspect, and be specific. These are all important aspects of adapting our language to our audience; they will be discussed at length in subsequent chapters.

The first letter reprinted here was mailed to all faculty members at Tulane University from the owner–manager of a New Orleans restaurant. A credit card and guest check were enclosed with the letter. Because of its effective adaptation of language, the letter brought a good response. It is clear, easily understood, interesting, and motivating. It further illustrates a clever adaptation of language to interest the reader.

A policyholder wrote his insurance company that he wanted to take a

Dear Mr. Reed:

For an education in fine foods you should dine at T. Pittari's.

Tom Pittari has his master's degree in the preparation of French and Italian Cuisine. He has his Ph.D. in the selection of fine wines and liquors.

His thesis -- "The Satisfaction of the Most Discriminating Tastes."

Won't you and your guests visit us and have a complimentary cocktail with Tom Pittari at 4200 South Claiborne Avenue at Milan.

For your convenience, attached is your Credit Card. Please sign. Keep one for yourself and return the other to us in the enclosed stamped envelope.

We are anticipating your visit.

Very sincerely yours,

T. PITTARI'S

Encls.
Credit Card
Guest Check

Courtesy Mr. Tom Pittari, President, Pittari's Restaurant, New Orleans, La.

health conservation examination because he had not been feeling well lately and wanted to find out what was wrong. The company wrote back:

Dear Mr. Oakland:

We are always pleased to be of service to our policyholders. People like yourself, however, who desire health conservation examinations naturally expect diagnosis and advice. This falls within the medical field and for your protection, by law, can only be given by a medical organization. I suggest, therefore, that you see your family doctor.

Whenever you have any questions concerning the insurance field, please write me personally, and I shall forward the available information as soon as possible.

Sincerely yours,

Here language that is clear, concise, and direct tells the reader in a positive, constructive manner what he does not want to hear, for it is a refusal of a request. The effect, nevertheless, is a favorable one because the service attitude is emphasized, and comprehension is easy because the explanation is clear and definite. Negative words and hackneyed expressions are eliminated; definite, short words, short sentences, and positive words build up to a single favorable impression.

The following opening was used in a letter sent to personnel directors:

> A Timely
> "Check Chart" for
> The Personnel Director -
>
> "But I tell, you, Bill, he's a 'Square Peg' in a 'Round Hole' - he's the Bottleneck in my department!"
>
> A situation like that is typical of the problems that are being avoided today by the use of a new technique in personnel administration.

The language here captures the reader's attention and interest, for it tells of a problem common to its group of readers.

The two major purposes for adapting language—to gain understanding and to secure interest leading to motivation—are accomplished in the sales promotion letter and enclosure reproduced on these pages. The homey, informal language is especially appropriate to the type of product it is offering and to the business it represents. The sentence, "Yep, ever since I talked Mom into baking fruitcakes for me to sell to our neighbors so that I could make some extra money, and later on to make money to put myself through college, we've been stormed with orders, and oh boy, how we love it," not only tells the story of the business, but its informal,

FRUITCAKE MINIATURES

. . . are individually home-baked, perfect little fruitcakes, just the right size for serving. Ready to eat . . . like candy . . . each one is a titillating tidbit of sheer ambrosia! Every package includes a container of rum sauce which is served hot or cold, buttered on the fruitcakes. All packages include an assortment of Mrs. Carver's delicious LIGHT and DARK fruitcake miniatures.

#31—Attractive, long woodlike mailer contains 10 miniatures and rum sauce.

13½ ozs. $1.99

#34—(not illustrated). Beautiful bronze-colored revolving Lazy Susan contains 26 miniatures and rum sauce.

2 lbs., 5¾ ozs. . . . $7.65

Courtesy Gerald H. Carver, President, Mrs. Carver's Kitchen

personal words convey friendliness, sincerity, and pride, and the reader is convinced that the cakes are good.

In the enclosure, the copy reading, "Ready to eat . . . like candy . . . each one is a titillating tidbit of sheer ambrosia!" creates a desire to eat one of the fruitcake miniatures. The reader is influenced into ordering.

'The World's Finest Fruit Cake and Fruit Cake Miniatures

MRS. CARVER'S KITCHEN
P. O. Box 2101, Houston 1, Texas
2000 Dorsett Street Phone OR 2-8247

Gift Givin' and Good Eatin' Time

Dear Friend,

My Mom would like to bake your fruitcake . . .

She is already out in the kitchen baking up a storm . . . baking for the thousands of her customers who annually say to her "Bake me another fruitcake just like the one you baked for me last year".

Yep, ever since I talked Mom into baking fruitcakes for me to sell to our neighbors so that I could make some extra money, and later on to make money to put myself through college, we've been stormed with orders, and oh boy, how we love it.

Mom loves to bake her cakes and I love to sell them. Mom even thought up the revolutionary new FRUITCAKE MINIATURES that have been acclaimed all over the world by the most discriminating gourmets, and even royalty.

Mom's fruitcake is ultra quality . . . nothin' but the best. Not only that, her cakes are so beautiful, all hand decorated. Also, our service is complete . . . all we need is your gift list. We sign your greeting card, beautifully gift pack, and prepay each shipment.

But it's late, and Mom says to please send your order today. Thanks!

Sincerely,

Jerry Carver

Courtesy Gerald H. Carver, President, Mrs. Carver's Kitchen

"PACING" FOR THE READER OR LISTENER

Pacing refers to the rate of speed at which a listener or reader understands most readily what is being presented. The rate of speech is naturally very important. Slow, measured speaking and rapid-fire talk indicate opposing moods and attitudes. The amount of time given to the formation of words and to the production of sentences may have much to do with the interest you create in your audience. The optimum rate of speaking will vary with the situation in which you are communicating, with the ideas communicated, and with the listeners. A good average rate of delivery, suitable to most audiences, is 100 to 120 words per minute, but the same rate does not, of course, suit all situations, and even in any one situation the rate of speech would vary. A too-rapid rate will overstimulate or overtax the listeners and thus lose them. A too-slow rate will cause them to become uninterested and to cease listening. An occasional pause is very valuable as a means of changing pace and placing emphasis on what has been said. One idea must be understood before a new one is introduced.

In writing, help set the pace for the reader by using short sentences, short words, punctuation, and other stylistic elements. Punctuation marks indicate pauses between ideas and thoughts. Short words and short sentences hurry the reader up; longer sentences slow him down. Specific, concrete words and vivid action words help him to grasp quickly what is written. Padding, repeating, and spreading out ideas slow the pace. Presenting too many facts and ideas in a short space makes reading difficult. Generally, one idea or major fact to a sentence is enough for most readers to grasp. For a change of pace, however, several ideas in one sentence can produce effective variety. The last five sentences in the preceding paragraph, for example, might be combined thus:

> If, however, the rate is varied too greatly and too quickly, ideas may be lost, for a too-rapid rate will overstimulate or overtax the listeners and thus lose them, and a too-slow rate will cause them to become uninterested and to cease listening. Furthermore, in speaking, a pause is a valuable means of changing pace and placing emphasis on what is said, but one should always be sure that one idea has been understood before going on to the next one.

For easier reading, however, several shorter sentences express the separate ideas better and give emphasis to each one.

STARTING ON THE RIGHT PATH AND ENDING EFFECTIVELY

The beginning of a letter should start the reader on the right path so that it will be easy for him to keep going in the direction in which he is intended to go. The beginning should be vital. It should get an immediate favorable reaction. It should attract attention, introduce the subject, and put the reader or listener in the right frame of mind.

Too often the beginning wastes time and effort with meaningless generalities and unnecessary words that say little or nothing. It fails to interest people because the writer has neglected the fundamentals of attention-getting. Nearly every situation has elements of vital interest to look for and utilize. The beginning of a letter should cause the reader to react favorably. It should catch immediate attention and should be vivid and specific. Note how attention is obtained in the following letter openings:

Want $10,000 more income in 197–?	(Monetary appeal)
Why incur extra costs?	(Savings appeal)
Wouldn't you like a book containing all the correct and graceful answers to your children's embarrassing questions?	(Benefit stressed)
Take pictures and see them completely finished in only 1 minute—if it isn't the way you want you can shoot another immediately.	(Advantage of special feature emphasized)
What form of health protection could be more beneficial, more valuable, and more enjoyable than taking an annual vacation?	(Health and pleasure)
Would you like to prepare dinner tonight in only 20 minutes?	(Timesaving)
Recently a girl came to me and she was embarrassed over having purchased an expensive suit to wear to a tea on campus and . . .	(Curiosity aroused)
Joe Jones was just another average, intelligent young man; he was no more immune to making mistakes than you and I.	(Narration of human interest)
Thanks for your congratulations.	(Appreciation)

In each of these illustrations consideration has been given to getting the reader to react favorably. He becomes involved personally in what he is reading and thus reads further. Knowledge of the reader and the reader–message–writer relationship are the determining factors in composing the beginning.

The question, "What does the reader want or need to know first?" provides a good clue to follow. Whenever favorable action is being taken, present the good news first. When negative action is necessary, find a common ground with the reader and present an explanation or reasons before the refusal. Most people like praise and like to be appreciated; they do not like criticism. The right note at the beginning can often be centered around points characterized by courtesy, helpfulness, and sincerity, as shown in the following examples:

Here is the information you wanted on our training program.	(Good news first)
Yes, Mr. Smith, we agree with you that . . .	(Common ground)
You certainly showed foresight in increasing your order. Demand for the new . . .	(Complimentary)
Your shipment of work gloves is on its way, and you . . .	(Positive action taken)
Please accept our deepest sympathy on the death of . . .	(Sincere personal concern)
We are always pleased to serve our policyholders.	(Courtesy "with a smile")
My mom would like to bake your fruitcake . . .	(Personal helpfulness)
We will be happy to replace the crystal cake set that was broken in delivery.	(Pleasant attitude toward action)
Thank you for your promptness in . . .	(Appreciation)

The opening sentence can also be used to tie down the reference:

The gross of ladies' black kid gloves you ordered September 20 is being shipped today.	(Date identification)
We appreciate your telephoning us yesterday about the ticket refund.	(Event association)
The items, your order #1095, are being shipped "Rush" as you requested.	(Order number reference)
The items, order #1095, dated November 5, are being shipped "Rush" as you requested.	(Both order and date reference)
The booklet, "How to Write Better Letters," which you sent November 10, has proved very helpful.	(Specific name and date identification)

The foregoing principles and techniques, used singly or in combination, will strengthen your letter openings and stamp them with character and originality. They will start the reader on the right path, providing tone and direction for the rest of the letter.

It is just as important to end a letter effectively as it is to start the reader on the right path. A good ending follows through. If the function of the letter is to get the reader to take a particular course of action, the letter should have led up to the ending, which then clearly states the action, seeks to motivate the reader, and makes it easy for him to act. For instance:

Fill in the enclosed card and drop it in the mail today.	(Clear and easy action)
Our attractive booklet and full information will be sent promptly.	(Prompt service as motivation)
Remember, ______ is one gift you can give with confidence to everyone on your list . . .	(Quality advantage as motivation)

Often a special inducement such as a sample, free trial, premium, or introductory price is offered to the reader. A time limit might also be placed on the offer to get the reader to act immediately. Stressing what the reader will gain, restating the central point of the letter, and using a special appeal are good motivating techniques:

> Let me know how many gallons of paint you want, and our truck will make delivery the same day.
>
> We will gladly provide free estimates for your building plans.

When the function of the letter is to give information or to do something other than persuading the reader to act in a specific way, then the ending might repeat or summarize the main thought, show appreciation for serving the reader, or state an interest in continuing to serve him:

> It will be a real pleasure to serve you and have you say "Charge it" again.
>
> We shall be interested in knowing how your new car air conditioner works.
>
> It will be a pleasure to see you and serve you again.
>
> After you have read the booklet, should there be any specific question, please let me know.

Being courteous, friendly, and sincere will help to leave a good taste with the reader and will make a favorable impression as well as accomplishing the desired purpose, which is action.

- ■ Why is it important in a business letter to adapt one's language to the reader's level of comprehension and interests?

- ■ Discuss the statement, "The beginning is the reader's; the ending belongs to the writer." Explain its applicability to writing letter openings and endings.

- ■ Point out what is weak in the following opening sentences and rewrite for effectiveness:
  1. We cannot comply with your request for a copy of our training manual.

2. Thank you for your remittance in the amount of $5.97 enclosed in your letter dated October 30. We are glad to be able to credit it to your account.
3. Your letter of November 5 is hereby acknowledged.
4. We wish to point out to you that you will agree that courtesy pays off in the long run.
5. Before we can consider granting you a loan, we must make a thorough investigation.

■ Point out what is weak in the following endings and rewrite for effectiveness:

1. Trusting that this will prove to be satisfactory for your purposes, we are . . .
2. Hoping to be of further service to you . . .
3. I wish we were able to supply you with the booklet you requested.
4. I regret the necessity of this action and trust you will understand our position.
5. Won't you please complete the information on the enclosed self-addressed postcard and mail it today without delay so we can fill your order?
6. Why not drop into the store tomorrow? Browse around all you want to; we don't mind. Perhaps you will find something of interest which we can in turn sell to you?

SUMMARY

Language is a set of symbols used in communicating ideas. When people agree on uniform ways for the symbols to be used and on the meanings they convey, standardization is created; however, not everyone attaches the same meaning to the same word. Understanding is dependent upon the receiver and the communicator's agreeing on the same meaning. Meanings are in people.

Language is common when it suits the communicator, his audience, and the occasion. It must be understood, within the knowledge and experience of the sender and the receiver, and it must agree with standard usage. Most language used for business purposes falls into the informal, everyday colloquial classification.

The relationship of the meaning of a word to the circumstances in which it is used is a basis for recognizing differences in word meanings. The explicit meaning of a word is its standardized meaning as given in the dictionary; its connotation is the impression, feeling, or implied meaning that it calls forth from the reader or listener. The choice of the right word is highly important. Avoid general, abstract words and use specific, definite ones. Avoid clichés and trite expressions that consume extra time and say little or nothing. Reduce groups of words to single words. Avoid negative, unfavorable words, and use positive, pleasant ones in their place.

Tone in a letter is an expression of the writer's attitude toward the reader. Because the recipient reacts to the tone, the writer must always adapt his language to get a favorable reaction from the reader. To do this he must be courteous and sincere and must write naturally. Courtesy and sincerity are personality traits, but expressed naturally and genuinely, they can set the tone for the letter; by expressing the writer's attitude toward the message, the reader, and the situation, they pay off in getting the reader to understand and react favorably.

When we give every consideration to the meaning and effect language can have on the reader to accomplish a purpose, we adapt our language to gain understanding and to secure interest leading to motivation, for words not only express but impress, and often it is the impression that motivates.

Pacing refers to the rate of speed followed by the receiver to understand most easily what is being presented. The rate varies with the situation, ideas, and listener or reader, but a good average for most speaking occasions is 100 to 120 words per minute; for most written letters and reports, the average sentence length should be 17 to 23 words per sentence. An occasional change of pace is helpful, and a variety of paces helps make material interesting.

Starting the reader on the right path makes it easy for him to keep going in the right direction. The beginning of a letter should attract attention, introduce the subject, and put the reader in the right frame of mind. Good openings include presenting good news first, finding a common ground with the reader, emphasizing positive action, and being complimentary. There are times when the opening should be used to tie down the reference. This may be done by date, event, or specific subject identification.

It is just as important to end a letter effectively. If a particular course of action is the purpose, state it clearly, make action easy for the reader, and motivate him to act. When giving information, you might summarize or restate the major point, show appreciation, or indicate continued interest in serving the reader.

CHECKLIST FOR LETTER WRITERS

The purposes of Chapter 3 have been to understand the nature of language and its uses in communication and to increase your language power in applying these concepts to select and use words for meaning and tone in writing business letters. It might be well to discuss the following checklist of items covered thus far and to use it in evaluating your own letters.

Rate yourself on what you have mastered from this chapter by answering what is applicable to a given letter-writing situation. To measure your degree of effectiveness in the letter, simply ask yourself two questions:

1. What degree of effectiveness will this have on the reader?
2. To what degree does this accomplish the purpose of the letter?

Not all points apply to every letter.

Letter Openings	*Not Applicable*	*Average Effectiveness*	*Highly Effective*
1. Have I attracted the reader's attention?			
2. Have I introduced the subject?			
3. Did I find a common ground with the reader?			
4. Have I emphasized a benefit or advantage for the reader?			
5. Does the good news come first?			
6. Has positive action been taken?			
7. Have I been pleasant and appreciative?			
8. Did I tie down the reference by date, event, or specific idea?			
Letter Endings			
1. Have I led the reader to a definite course of action?			
2. Did I request action clearly and make it easy?			
3. Have I motivated action?			
4. Did I use an appropriate appeal?			
5. Did I offer a special inducement?			
6. Did I summarize or repeat the main point?			
7. Did I show appreciation?			
8. Have I indicated an interest or concern in serving the reader further?			
Wording and Phrasing for Meaning			
1. Have I used familiar terms?			
2. Have I omitted nonessential technical terminology?			
3. Have I avoided hackneyed words and expressions?			
4. Did I use specific words?			
5. Did I adapt my language to the level and interest of the reader?			
6. Have I avoided negative, unfavorable words and used positive, pleasant ones?			
7. Have I reduced groups of words to single words?			

Tone Considerations	*Not Applicable*	*Average Effectiveness*	*Highly Effective*
1. Have I put myself in the reader's place and shown him consideration?			
2. Was I helpful and constructive?			
3. Was I polite, appreciative, and cheerful?			
4. Did I show concern for the reader's problems?			
5. Did I exhibit friendliness and warmth of personality?			
6. Was I honest, straightforward, and unaffected?			
7. Did I avoid an overuse of adjectives and superlatives?			
8. Did I use personal pronouns and references?			
9. Did I admit mistakes?			
10. Was I overapologetic or overenthusiastic?			
11. Does the letter read like conversation?			
12. Does the letter have a simple, natural flow?			
Other Stylistic Considerations			
1. Have I paced the material for the reader?			
2. Are sentences clearly and easily grasped?			
3. Is the average sentence length seventeen to twenty words?			
4. Have I adapted language for understanding and interest?			
5. Did I always consider the effect on the reader?			
6. Does the letter effectively accomplish its purpose?			

You might want to review Chapter 2 by making out your own checklist for evaluating the appearance of letters and the goodwill principles.

GRAMMAR REVIEW TEST

At this point in your semester's work it would be well to check up on your skill in using grammar, punctuation, and spelling correctly. The following grammatical exercise is presented to be used at your instructor's discretion. It may serve as a review or a diagnostic test, or to increase grammatical effectiveness. A similar test on punctuation and spelling has been added at the end of Chapter 4. You could also simply test yourself, checking your answers with the principles in Appendix C. Appendix C may be used in preparing for the test, or you may be skillful enough not to need a grammar review. The test will help prove you right.

Correct the following sentences:

1. Your order of red roses were delivered at 10:00 a.m. July 15.
2. Roses goes a long way to cheering up a sick room.
3. The public relations director of General Electric and the Advertising Manager of General Motors is to attend the ABCA annual meeting.
4. All our services are guaranteed, and our twenty years of experience stands behind us.
5. The price for the one-day shirt services are . . .
6. We feel that the workmanship on your mower will be very precise, with the extra winter months to work on it, so all services will be guaranteed for one year.
7. All kinds of equipment is available for minimum-price rental.
8. The committee on profit improvement have approved the suggestion to purchase a new opaque projector for the training director to use at their discretion.
9. Try and send him his order today, at once.
10. Did you see the Waysides Theatres new show?
11. You know these facts as well as her or me, now don't you?
12. She, not the company should stand the loss.
13. The reports on production figures came in faster from you than he.
14. For management wants to make a profit and so does the workers.
15. Its merely a difference of opinion between him and I.
16. The secretarys pen was misplaced temporarily.
17. Who did you mail the refund check to?
18. Free pick up and delivery is also available.
19. Neither the sales manager nor the training director intends to attend the convention in Atlanta.
20. Everyone but she realized how costly the error had been.
21. Every young man should try to determine the vocation they are suited for.
22. He looked suspicious at the customer.
23. I shall write to them soon to inform them the error has being corrected.
24. The television set is equiped with a color changer which add to it's appearance.

25. We only have $10 left in the checking account.
26. He entered the office just as the price of the stock jumped two points and walked aimlessly about the room.
27. The snow was very deep, and we could not make deliveries.
28. I like the new department head much more than Jim.
29. On the menu was two kinds of pie and three kinds of drink.
30. She entered the office, waving her promotion notice in her hand and shouting excitedly about it.
31. He dictated very rapid the 10 letters needing to be answered on his desk.
32. The accountant took the letter from George because he wanted to tear it up.
33. Who is the oldest of the two girls who you hired last week?
34. I shall reply to his letter soon.
35. Its incorrect either way you wrote it.
36. In her purse was Mary's billfold and also her lipstick which she had forgot to return as she promished.
37. The school board owes her a days substitute pay.
38. In a company the employees must have a feeling of status. For this will make him feel important and management will obtain a better job from them.
39. I was very impressed by his promptness in payment of his bills balance.
40. We haven't no more of those sox in stock.
41. The company sent their deposits to the National Bank of California by mail.
42. Mr. Wilson wrote him that his record on his books showed he owed $25 more.
43. Walking up the aisle, the woman's skirt was caught and torn by a nail.
44. Mr. Grayson was not on the plane apparently, and I took a taxi back to the office.
45. Being a past customer, we are letting you in on our special winter prices.
46. There is plenty of sunshine and activities at the "Desert Isle" for one and all.
47. Or perhaps you were one of the fortunate ones who got their mower into the repair shop before the "sorry, no vacancy" sign was put out, only to find that your mower could not be repaired until a month later.
48. In every case the persons opinion of the new secretary depended upon their experience with her.
49. "You can't tell a book by it's cover" applies also in the business world.
50. A businessman must communicate on his clients level.

FURTHER READING

The references cited below are for further reading in the area of meaning and expression in language. For information on the specific adaptation of language in business letter writing situations, consult the references presented at the end of Chapter 2, which specifically treat such topics as the right word, tone, letter openings, and endings.

Berlo, David K., *The Process of Communication.* New York: Holt, Rinehart & Winston, Inc., 1960, pp. 168–88, 190–215.

Chase, Stuart, *Power of Words.* New York: Harcourt, Brace & World, Inc., 1954, pp. 49–55, 100–109.

Cherry, Colin, *On Human Communication,* 2nd ed. Cambridge: MIT Press, 1966, Chap. 2.

Flesch, Rudolf, *The Art of Plain Talk.* New York: Harper & Row, Publishers, 1946.

Gunning, Robert, *The Technique of Clear Writing.* New York: McGraw-Hill Book Company, 1952, pp. 43–180.

Hayakawa, S. I., *Language in Thought and Action,* 2nd ed. New York: Harcourt, Brace & World, Inc., 1964.

QUESTIONS AND PROBLEMS

1. To find out how some of the magazines have adapted to changing times, readers, etc., read John Tebell's article, "A New Look at Curtis," in the *Saturday Review,* June 11, 1966, pp. 94, 95, and 102. This may be done as your instructor directs: as a special report, a written summary, or a class discussion. Otherwise read it for your own enlightenment.
2. Rate the letter on page 101 by applying the "Checklist for Letter Writers" on pages 95–97. After you have done this and are aware of all its weaknesses, rewrite it; then rate it again. The comparison of ratings should prove revealing.
3. Assume that your father is being transferred by his company to a city in another state. This means a promotion for him and creates the need to sell his house. There is quite a shakeup going on in the firm and a number of other people will be moving into your city. One of the newcomers is a prospect for buying the house. He has heard of your father's promotion and has written for information about the house. Answer his inquiry, but first sit down and think through what a person in this situation would want to know. Then plan your letter to give him descriptive details that will fit his desires and needs.

Dear Professor Wrixon:

Your letter of June 28 addressed to Mr. G. E. Olds, Vice President of Communications, __________ Corporation, has been directed to me for reply. We apologize for the delay in answering your letter, but the vacation season has interfered with our usual promptness.

Unfortunately we are not in a position to send you our manuals and style sheets concerning written communications. Currently, we are up-dating our policy manuals and when these are complete they may be of interest to you. We will pend your request and as soon as possible will contact you concerning what we have available. We are certainly interested in your efforts, and wish you all success.

Sincerely,

Daniel Gendon, Director
Corporate Communication Services

DG:cb

4. Mr. "Mike" Baugh sent you a drawing that he did and one that his six-year-old sister Sue drew. (Mike is ten years old.) You are editor of a children's magazine, *Childhood Arts and Crafts.* Mike sent the drawings for you to consider for publication. You will use his but not Sue's, since hers is neither good enough nor appropriate for your use. Write a letter to Mike. You will need to adapt your language to his level, but don't talk down to him.
5. Write a memorandum to be mimeographed and distributed among your office workers announcing the beginning of a campaign to improve their letters. Your job is to get the staff to recognize that their letters are not as effective as they should be and to get their cooperation in raising letter-writing standards.

Chapter Four

WRITING FOR UNDERSTANDING

The first test of the effectiveness of a business letter or of any communication is that it be understood by the recipient. The reader can become neither interested nor motivated to respond favorably unless he has comprehended the message. Afterward he can take the action necessary for accomplishing the purpose of the communication. What is said and how it is said contribute toward making the message understood. Skill at getting ideas across is essential and can be developed by anyone who takes the time and effort to practice its techniques. The purpose of this chapter is to discuss principles and techniques that will enable you to get your message across to the reader—in other words, to develop your ability to write for understanding.

PLANNING AND ORGANIZING AS AIDS TO UNDERSTANDING

Careful planning involves logical and creative thinking that results in writing for understanding. In planning your letters you should work through successive steps, progressing toward your goal. This means determining your purpose in advance in terms of reader response; planning your content with the purpose and the reader in mind; and striving for easy, original expression to secure the desired reaction. Planning will take you through several stages of thinking and of developing ideas; this will culminate in a final outline from which your message can be expressed and understood.

In planning a letter, always begin with the situation and circumstances in which it is being written:

1. *Analyze the situation giving rise to the letter.* This means analyzing the reader, the need, and the facts. Why is the letter necessary? Are you answering a request, sending information, taking action, or initiating the correspondence? What does the reader need or want to know? What is the reader like? What are his age, educational level, occupation, and interests?
2. *Determine the purpose.* This means drawing conclusions from your situation analysis as to what you seek to accomplish. Is there a long-range goal? An immediate objective? What action is the reader to take? How should he react?
3. *Select the contents.* This follows from the first two steps, for contents are determined by your purpose and your reader's need or interest. What questions are to be answered, whether they are asked directly by the reader or anticipated by the writer? What must be included to fulfill the purpose? What must be added to interest and motivate the reader?
4. *Plan for unity, coherence, and emphasis. Unity* is oneness, a single purpose or central idea. Everything supports it or centers the reader's mind on it. *Coherence* is relatedness and clearness, a logical flow of ideas. *Emphasis* brings out the main points and adds a spark of enthusiasm or feeling in the right place.
5. *Arrange the sequence of ideas or outline the contents.* The beginning and ending of a letter are emphatic positions and should be decided upon before arranging the ideas (which will generally fall into place) between them. Organization will usually follow one of four basic patterns according to the nature of the message, the letter's purpose, and its effect on the reader. These are commonly referred to as the *"yes" pattern,* the *"no" pattern,* the *psychological effect,* and *relationship of ideas.*
6. *Write the letter.* In writing, follow all the principles and techniques applicable to the given situation, seeking a logical flow of ideas and effective expression.

As a student or novice letter writer, you will need to consciously work through these six steps. With practice, however, you can establish them as a habit and reduce your time and effort in applying them.

Saying "Yes" in Letters

A letter that tells the reader "yes" to what he wants to hear or have done accomplishes its purpose and receives a favorable response in spite of anything else that may be weak or ineffective about it. For this reason, always present good news first. This type of letter is direct, positive, and is always received favorably.

Your refund check of $10 is on its way.	(Adjustment given)
Your order #1009 is being shipped "Rush."	(Order acknowledged)
We are happy for you that you have been promoted.	(Personal interest)
A complimentary copy of the book you requested, *Creative Thinking*, is being sent to you.	(Action taken)
I shall be glad to speak at your fraternity banquet November 17.	(Request answered)
Your silver cup damaged in the mail is being replaced.	(Adjustment made)
Your credit card is enclosed, ready for your immediate use.	(Credit accepted)

The "good news first" arrangement calls for following up with whatever details or facts are needed to fit the situation and purpose, and ending with a positive expression of appreciation, continued service, or action, as:

> We appreciate your interest in our air-conditioning systems, and will send our representative Monday to discuss them with you.
>
> As soon as you let us know the size of the boy's jacket, we will ship it "Rush."
>
> We are looking forward to meeting and talking with you personally.

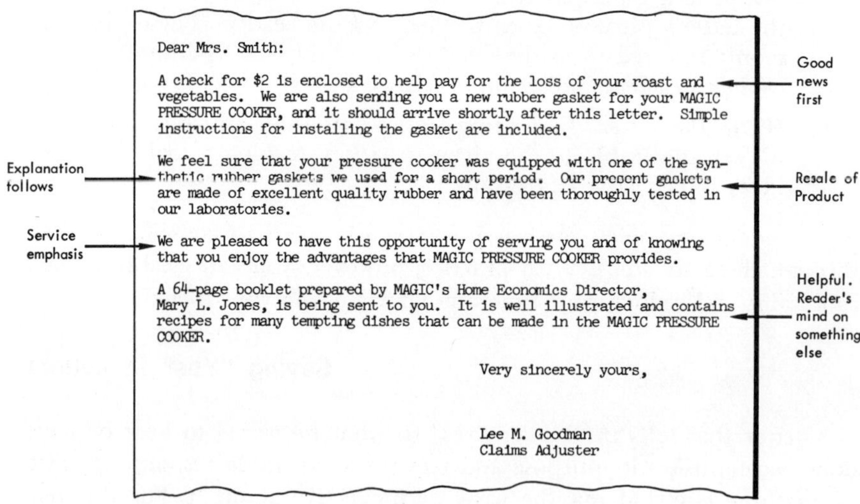

Dear Mrs. Smith:

A check for $2 is enclosed to help pay for the loss of your roast and vegetables. We are also sending you a new rubber gasket for your MAGIC PRESSURE COOKER, and it should arrive shortly after this letter. Simple instructions for installing the gasket are included.

We feel sure that your pressure cooker was equipped with one of the synthetic rubber gaskets we used for a short period. Our present gaskets are made of excellent quality rubber and have been thoroughly tested in our laboratories.

We are pleased to have this opportunity of serving you and of knowing that you enjoy the advantages that MAGIC PRESSURE COOKER provides.

A 64-page booklet prepared by MAGIC's Home Economics Director, Mary L. Jones, is being sent to you. It is well illustrated and contains recipes for many tempting dishes that can be made in the MAGIC PRESSURE COOKER.

Very sincerely yours,

Lee M. Goodman
Claims Adjuster

Example of adjustment letter saying "yes"

Saying "No" Tactfully

The reader never wants to hear "no" in a letter, for he desires and expects a "yes" answer to his request. For this reason, never begin the "no" letter with the refusal. Bury it later in the middle of the letter, even imply rather than state it, or subordinate it to a positive feeling or constructive action. Begin by expressing a favorable feeling or attitude toward the reader or toward what he has written about to you, by showing appreciation, by indicating an interest or concern in the reader and what he is doing, or by establishing a common ground in some other way:

We agree with you, Mrs. Jones, that you have every right to expect satisfactory service from your electric fan.	(Agreement)
We appreciate your writing us about the china damaged in transit.	(Appreciation)
We would like to send you a complimentary copy of ________.	(Attitude)
Your putting on the League Follies as a charity benefit for the Orphan's Home is indeed commendable.	(Interest or concern)

Before presenting a refusal, give the explanation or reason so that the reader can understand it. He is then psychologically prepared to accept the "no" and is less likely to feel ill will toward you. Afterward, be constructive by emphasizing anything you may be able to do or by helping him to get his request fulfilled somewhere else. End by getting his mind on something else or by showing continued interest or service for him. The various situations in which refusals are made may call for some differences in the points presented, but the basic pattern of the "no" letter is fairly standardized.

In refusing an order:

1. Thank the customer for his interest in the company and its products.
2. Explain why the order is being refused.
3. Give directions on how he can obtain the article elsewhere.
4. Emphasize resale, sales, or service—whichever is appropriate.
5. When delay or a back order is necessary, use resale to keep the customer interested and explain the reasons for the delay.

In refusing a request:

1. Express appreciation or establish a common ground.
2. Let the reasons precede the refusal.
3. Stress any positive or favorable action.
4. Be patient, courteous, and considerate.

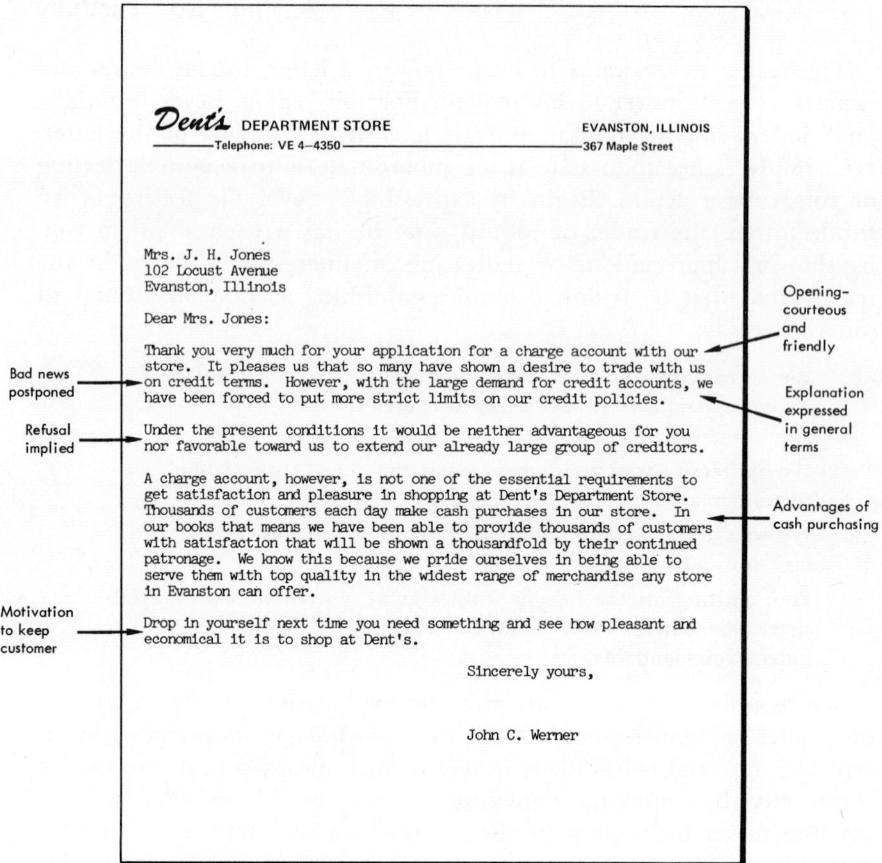

Dent's DEPARTMENT STORE EVANSTON, ILLINOIS
Telephone: VE 4–4350 367 Maple Street

Mrs. J. H. Jones
102 Locust Avenue
Evanston, Illinois

Dear Mrs. Jones:

Thank you very much for your application for a charge account with our store. It pleases us that so many have shown a desire to trade with us on credit terms. However, with the large demand for credit accounts, we have been forced to put more strict limits on our credit policies.

Under the present conditions it would be neither advantageous for you nor favorable toward us to extend our already large group of creditors.

A charge account, however, is not one of the essential requirements to get satisfaction and pleasure in shopping at Dent's Department Store. Thousands of customers each day make cash purchases in our store. In our books that means we have been able to provide thousands of customers with satisfaction that will be shown a thousandfold by their continued patronage. We know this because we pride ourselves in being able to serve them with top quality in the widest range of merchandise any store in Evanston can offer.

Drop in yourself next time you need something and see how pleasant and economical it is to shop at Dent's.

Sincerely yours,

John C. Werner

Example of credit refusal letter

In refusing an adjustment:

1. Establish a common ground.
2. Give reasons or an explanation (follow a logical sequence of details and show evidence).
3. State your decision.
4. If possible, make a counteroffer.
5. Emphasize what you can do.
6. Give a motive for accepting the decision.
7. Close on a positive note (resale, service, goodwill, or continued interest).

In refusing credit:

1. Postpone the bad news.

2. Establish a common ground.
3. Explain in general and impersonal terms.
4. Point out the advantage of a cash purchase.
5. Try to keep the customer as a cash customer.

Organizing for Psychological Effect

Most letters that do not fall into a "yes" or "no" pattern of organization have persuasiveness as their function. A bill is to be collected, a product is to be sold or promoted, information is to be given to bring about a change in attitude or behavior, etc. Here the basis for organizing the letter is its psychological effect on the reader. Thus the writer takes the reader through the four psychological sales steps: *attention, interest, conviction,* and *action.* These steps are also widely used in preparing advertising material and other messages aimed at persuading the reader to act.

Note how the four steps are applied in the following letter:

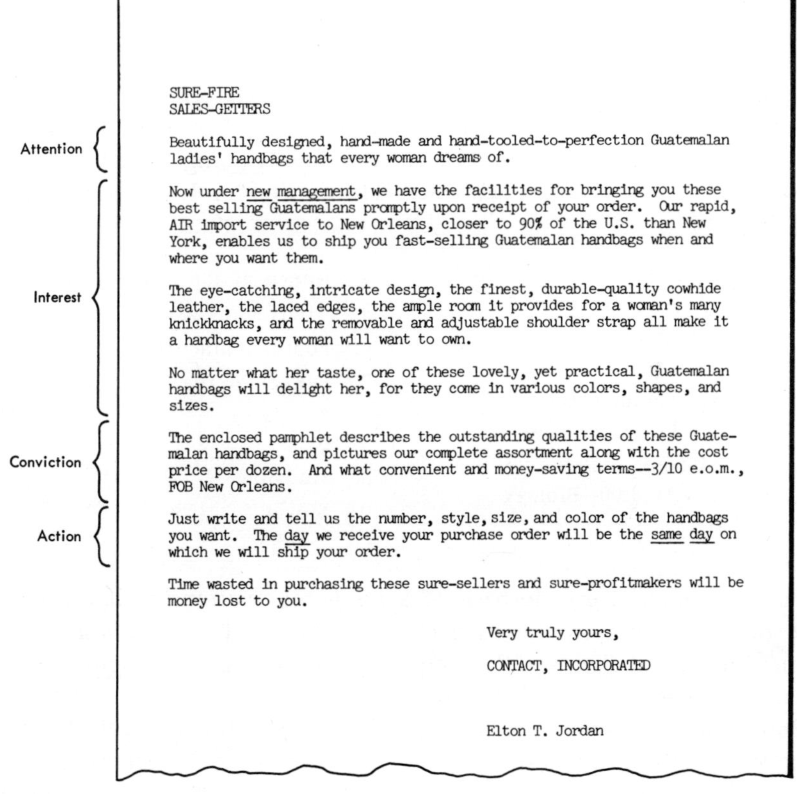

SURE-FIRE
SALES-GETTERS

Beautifully designed, hand-made and hand-tooled-to-perfection Guatemalan ladies' handbags that every woman dreams of.

Now under new management, we have the facilities for bringing you these best selling Guatemalans promptly upon receipt of your order. Our rapid, AIR import service to New Orleans, closer to 90% of the U.S. than New York, enables us to ship you fast-selling Guatemalan handbags when and where you want them.

The eye-catching, intricate design, the finest, durable-quality cowhide leather, the laced edges, the ample room it provides for a woman's many knickknacks, and the removable and adjustable shoulder strap all make it a handbag every woman will want to own.

No matter what her taste, one of these lovely, yet practical, Guatemalan handbags will delight her, for they come in various colors, shapes, and sizes.

The enclosed pamphlet describes the outstanding qualities of these Guatemalan handbags, and pictures our complete assortment along with the cost price per dozen. And what convenient and money-saving terms--3/10 e.o.m., FOB New Orleans.

Just write and tell us the number, style, size, and color of the handbags you want. The day we receive your purchase order will be the same day on which we will ship your order.

Time wasted in purchasing these sure-sellers and sure-profitmakers will be money lost to you.

Very truly yours,

CONTACT, INCORPORATED

Elton T. Jordan

The writer was concerned with his customer's needs and sought a reaction as the letter progressed to its action ending. Because of its effect, the reader is probably prepared to stock Guatemalan handbags. Because this method of organizing is so pertinent in writing persuasive letters and especially sales letters, a fuller treatment will be presented in Chapter 6. Another method, however, is worthy of attention here, for it also is a direct aid to securing unity, coherence, and emphasis in the flow of ideas in a letter. This method is organization by the relationship of facts and ideas.

Organizing by the Relationship of Ideas

Consider the case of four college students, Jim, Bob, Don, and Sam, who wrote letters home to their parents. Jim, a new student at the school, wrote in great detail what he did during the day. He began: "After I get up at 7:00 in the morning, I hurriedly shave and dress, for we eat breakfast at 7:30. My roommate and I share the bath with two other students. Breakfast this morning consisted of. . . . I had to skip it, however, because I. . . ." Then he continued: "My first class is Biology 203 at 8:00. This morning during class. . . ." and later: "Instead of eating lunch at the fraternity house today, Sam and I ate at the new cafeteria on the campus." Then, still later in the letter: "After my last class, which was over at 3:00, Sam and I went to watch the football team practice. Our first home game will be on Saturday." Jim wrote further about the evening meal at the fraternity house, his studying for an hour afterward, then going to a movie, and finally going to bed. He thus arranged his ideas in a time sequence. The outline for Jim's letter would look like this:

1. At 7:00
   a. Awaken
   b. Dress
2. At 7:30
   a. Eat breakfast
   b. Leave for class
3. Morning classes
   a. At 8:00—Biology
   b.
   c.
4. Lunch at the cafeteria
5. Afternoon classes
6. Football practice
7. Dinner at the fraternity house
   a.
   b.
8. Studying
9. Movie

Arranging material on the basis of a *temporal relationship* lends a degree of importance to the time element. Although it emphasizes the points mentioned first and last, equal emphasis may be given to each item. A time sequence is useful for relating events or steps in a process.

Bob wrote first about his classes: "Here is my class schedule for the semester. It will show you what I'm taking and when. . . . I believe biology will be particularly interesting. Students tell me that business communications will be time-consuming and a lot of hard work. . . . Because I've always made good grades in English, I should be able to write with very few mistakes."

Bob had just pledged a fraternity, so he discussed next the house and facilities and some of the boys there, giving his impressions and letting his folks know that he was thoroughly enjoying his new friends and fraternity life. Then he discussed the upcoming football game and gave the season's schedule and his predictions for a good year for the team. He ended by saying that he was going to a movie with Sam and Jim.

In his letter, Bob arranged his material by a *topical relationship:* classes, fraternity, and football. Under classes he discussed his schedule, biology, and business communications. Facilities, members, and activities pertained to the fraternity and were discussed together. Generally, topics are related by being a part of the same whole or by having a common denominator.

Don's letter was written to motivate his parents to send him additional money. He organized his attack by using facts to show a need for money; then he made his request and projected the possible results if he received it. His points were arranged to show a cause-and-effect relationship:

1. Reasons for running out of money, leading to
2. a need for additional money, which if sent will provide
3. good effects as a result of receiving additional money.

A *causal relationship* emphasizes the need for a change and is very useful in presenting recommendations for improvements or a problem and its solution. Highly persuasive, it helps the reader or listener to visualize what has happened or what might take place. Sometimes the result or effect is given first, followed by a discussion of the causes. The order would depend largely upon the relationship between the audience and the material used.

Sam arranged his ideas by a *spatial relationship.* (*Spatial* comes from the Latin root *spatium,* meaning *space,* and is used to refer to position, direction, or location.) Sam grouped the ideas in his letter by placing together those that pertained to a particular location or place, such as the school, the fraternity house, or the church. When a sales supervisor who has several states in his territory sends in his weekly or monthly report, he usually groups his sales by state. A study of exports from Boston or San Francisco might group these exports according to the country to which they are being sent. Arrangement according to a spatial relationship always facilitates comparisons. Tying the fact or event to a definite location also serves as an aid to memory.

Whether you organize your ideas and facts by temporal, topical, causal, or spatial relationships, you make your letters more easily and quickly understood. A logical, natural flow aids understanding.

- Why not write a letter home to your parents or to some other relative or family friend? Use some of the ideas and suggestions given here while they are still fresh in your mind.
- The following letter-writing situations are presented for analysis and discussion. As a result of class discussions, see if you can't agree on one of the basic letter plans for organizing a reply. Outline the points to be included and point out where various relationships of ideas occur. Your instructor may ask in addition that you write the letter.

1. As dean of administration at Tulane University, you received a request this morning from the Junior League of Women Voters for the use of McAlister Auditorium. The League wants it for two performances of its Junior Follies, a variety show featuring local citizens as performers. This is a benefit show, of course. All stage scenery is either donated or loaned by local business houses. The programs are donated by a local printer, and the actors provide their own costumes. Everything, in fact, is donated, so that the entire proceeds can go toward maintaining the Crippled Children's Clinic. The chairman (Mrs. Amy Body) blandly adds that the group is sure the university will want to do its share by contributing the use of the auditorium for the two nights, three months from now. From your point of view, it isn't that simple. Tulane runs on a limited budget, though of course many local people have given generously to its support. Costs for heating or air conditioning, lights, water, a watchman and electrician, clean-up details, and depreciation add up to a figure that your auditor has fixed at $150 a night and that has consistently been charged to any nonuniversity group. You'll be glad to schedule the auditorium for the Follies and waive the usual requirement of payment in advance. Both nights happen to be open. The League's address is 207 Common Street.
2. The following complaint was sent to the Box of Jewels, Winchester, Virginia:

Attention: Watch Repair Department

Gentlemen:

A few days ago, my wife, Mrs. R. G. Mills, left a lady's Bulova watch to have tomato juice cleaned from the crystal. When she called for this watch, Friday, August 15th, imagine her surprise at being charged $15.00 for what was described as "cleaning and replacing a new main spring."

Needless to say, we are not in accord with such procedures when the watch was originally left for one specific reason--cleaning dark stain from the crystal.

Since moving to Winchester from Harrisonburg, we have been bringing the Box of Jewels all our watch repair business. There are three watches in our family--two of them ladies'. We assume from the above procedure that you are desiring to weed out some of your customers, and you can rest assured that our family for one has been "weeded out."

When you examined this watch and found that more needed to be done than was requested, we feel the proper thing to have done would be to call our residence and discuss the matter before proceeding to run up a $15.00 charge.

As stated above, you have certainly shown us one Watch Repair Department that will get no more of our business and we, of course, expect to advise our friends likewise.

Very truly yours,

■ Analyze the weaknesses in the following letter, then rewrite it so that it will be effective. Which organizational pattern will you follow? Why?

Dear Mr. Monlife:

We have completed our investigation and review of the file in connection with your pending claim but regret to advise you that we cannot assume liability.

Information contained in the file indicates that you had considerable insurance and medical history prior to the time our policy was applied for, which was not mentioned in the application and which would have materially affected the underwriting of the case. Under the circumstances, we do not feel that it would be fair to retain the premiums you have paid and so we are enclosing our draft in the sum of $38.00 as a full refund of these premiums and are marking our records to show policy #374-231 void as of Nov. 25th, 197-, its date of issue.

Regretting the necessity for this action, but trusting you will understand our position, we remain

Very truly yours,

ESSENTIALS OF STYLE FOR UNDERSTANDING

Style is the method the writer uses to convey his ideas in order to win the response he desires. It expresses what is in his mind in a way that will accomplish his purpose. The style should fit the subject matter and purpose and be suitable for the reader. Style is said to have the "C" qualities of letter writing (so-called because each begins with a letter *C*)—clearness, completeness, conciseness, correctness, concreteness, and courtesy—which have always been essential for understanding the message in any type of communication. The U. S. government calls these the "S's" of correspondence, maintaining that every letter should be characterized by shortness, simplicity, strength, and sincerity; these qualities are just as essential today as they were hundreds of years ago.

Courtesy has already been discussed as part of both tone and goodwill. The other "C" qualities will be discussed in this section with the exception of concreteness. This is treated as a part of clearness and is also discussed under strength, which we have added to the "C's." There is a direct relationship among clearness, conciseness, and completeness; between clearness and correctness; and between strength and all the other qualities—for the techniques applicable in securing one quality also result in another quality being established.

Clearness

Communicating clearly simply means speaking or writing to be understood rather than misunderstood. It depends at the outset on careful, efficient planning that produces a logical, easy-to-follow arrangement of material in which ideas flow smoothly from beginning to end.

To make letters clear, plan them carefully. What is to be accomplished in this letter and how can it best be done? One of the most important things to think about in planning a letter is the reader. What are his interests? What are his needs? What kind of a letter would he like to receive? Consider the reader's position, his convenience, and his comfort; have a mental picture of him while you are writing. Plan what to put into the letter and how you will arrange its contents. Decide on what the central thought will be, then make sure there is a sequential flow of ideas.

Writing a policy owner about an outstanding loan on his policy calls for a chronological statement of facts:

> On June 14, 1958, a loan of $237.65 was taken to pay the premium due May 14, 1958. On June 14, 1959, the loan was increased to $487.14 to pay the premium due May 14, 1959.
>
> On June 31, 1959, a loan repayment of $248.49 was made, with a resulting loan balance outstanding of $238.65. The interest of $11.93 due on the outstanding loan was not paid and was added to the outstanding loan, making a total of $250.58 outstanding.[1]

The facts are here in chronological order as they should be, but consideration has not been given to the reader, who cannot easily grasp what is said. We can create a natural flow of ideas for the reader by putting in some guideposts:

> On June 14, 1958, you made a loan of $237.65 to pay the premium due May 14, 1958. A year later, on June 14, 1959, you increased this loan to $487.14 to pay the premium and interest due May 14, 1959.
>
> Then on July 31, 1959, you made a loan repayment of $248.49. This left a balance outstanding of $238.65, but since the interest of $11.93 wasn't paid, we added it to the loan. This makes, therefore, a total of $250.58 outstanding.

The second example is more readable. It helps the reader to shift from one fact to another because it indicates the passage of time. It is also clearer because the active voice is used instead of the passive voice, and forms of *you* involve the reader in what is being said.

Because it points out relationships and thus keeps the flow of ideas running smoothly, effective transition is an important aid to clearness. Thoughts should be linked together either by words, phrases, sentences, and paragraphs, or by a natural flow of ideas. *And, but, or,* and *for* are connecting words used to join ideas of equal importance; they are known as coordinate conjunctions. Ideas of unequal rank are connected by subordinate conjunctions.

[1]This example and the following one are taken from NYLIC's *Effective Letters Bulletin,* November–December 1959.

The following conjunctions show particular subordinate relationships:

Conjunction	*Relationship*
because, since	cause
as, more than, rather than	comparison
although, even if, though	concession
if, in case, except	condition
where, whence, wherever	place
to, so that, in order that	purpose
so that, so . . . as, such . . . that	result
after, when, ever since, now, when, until, while	time

Link sentences together by arranging them to form a close relationship of ideas. The same point of view should also be maintained among sentences making up a paragraph. Repetition of key words and the use of significant phrases such as "in addition" and "on the other hand" show the relationships between sentences. It must be remembered, however, that a too-liberal use of connectives may slow down comprehension.

Let us look at another example:

> Thank you for your check for $1,516.21, representing payment of the annual premium in advance on this policy. We are enclosing our check for $26.54. You will become 60 years old on December 6, 1970. The Waiver of Premium Benefit contained in your policy will accordingly be discontinued as of June 24, 1971, and the annual premium thus reduced. The enclosed check represents the refund due you on account of the discontinuance of this benefit.[2]

Surely it is much clearer to say:

> Thank you for your check for $1,516.21, which you sent us to pay the annual premium in advance on your policy. But since you will become 60 years old on December 6, 1970, your premium will, as a result, be less.
>
> You see, when you attain this age, the Waiver of Premium Benefit contained in your policy expires as of June 24, 1971. This benefit costs you $26.54 a year, and we are pleased to enclose our check to you, refunding this amount.[3]

In this last example the writer first put his facts in order, then linked them together. The word *benefit* at the beginning of the second sentence, second paragraph, shows good use of repetition. Beginning a sentence with a key word from a previous sentence is also an effective way to make a transition.

[2]NYLIC *Effective Letters Bulletin.*
[3]*Ibid.*

To make letters clear, make them easy to read. All the formulas that have been developed for measuring readability are based on sentence length and syllable count. For easy, quick comprehension of letters, write predominantly short sentences and use simple, short words. An average sentence length of seventeen words is quickly understood. This does not mean, however, that you must always use short sentences, for that would result in a childish and monotonous letter. Vary the sentence length, using some long sentences and some short ones, but maintain an average of seventeen words.

Words are powerful when properly chosen and arranged. The rule of choosing short words over long ones works well for most occasions. But the longer word should not be rejected just because it is long. It may have a more precise meaning than a specific shorter one, and it may be within the realm of the reader's experience. Use words that the reader will understand and that will convey exactly what is to be said. Simplicity, accuracy, and clarity should help to govern the choice of words. It is important that the reader get the same meaning out of the word that the writer had in mind.

Using words that have many meanings confuses the reader and hides the writer's thoughts. The recipient does not know which meaning was intended, so he takes a guess and may very well find he was wrong. The statement, "Experience proved the procedure successful," tells less than the concrete, "Seventy-five percent of our salesmen reported that they increased sales 20 percent by using pre-approach direct mail letters for compiling a selected prospect list."

Specific words, qualifying statements, and exact language clarify meaning. Concrete, simple language can be readily understood by all readers. In a message intended for a technician, special and technical terms may be used; in one intended for a layman, terms must be made clear through definition or common terms must be used. Aristotle once made the statement, "Think as the wise men do; write as the common people talk." This practice will help in getting people to understand a message, for as La Bruyère put it, "The greatest things gain by being said simply." Talking the other person's language, being conversational, writing simply and naturally, and using little words to express big ideas will all go a long way toward achieving understanding.

Economy of words is a great aid to writing clear letters. Letters should contain what the writer needs to say and what the recipient wants to read. Include in a letter all that belongs there, but no more. Avoid stale, trite expressions that say nothing. A short, well-thought-out letter may take more time to write, for the writer must spend time marshaling his ideas and eliminating all unnecessary words. But the reader will be more likely to read the letter with understanding and to do what the writer asks.

Careful attention should also be given to layout and display possibilities, such as the spacing of headings or captions, charts, tables, and other graphic forms. Alignment and indentation as used in lists indicate the subordination of ideas and facts. In addition, principles of parallelism should be applied. If a sentence is used for one item in a list, sentences should be used for all; if a participial phrase is used for one, participial phrases should be used for all. For instance:

1. Prompt acknowledgment *is* desirable. 2. A short letter *is* more sincere than a long letter.	(Parallel construction)
1. Always *acknowledge* a letter promptly. 2. A short letter *is* more sincere than a long letter.	(Unparallel construction)
1. *Acknowledging* a letter promptly. 2. A short letter *is* more . . .	(Unparallel construction)

In the unparallel sentences the verb forms do not have the same grammatical construction: the second person imperative and the participial *-ing* form are used.

Completeness

Completeness means comprehensive treatment of the subject at hand; it results in clear, motivating messages. Specific, pertinent details aid clearness, whereas nonessential details, overuse of quotations, long descriptions, and tedious introductions sidetrack the listener or reader and result in a lack of clarity. Evidence can be stated precisely; the significance of facts and their relationships can be shown. Messages must be complete enough so that the reader will have an understanding of what is being said.

In working for completeness, one always considers the reader. For one familiar with the subject, few details are needed; for the uninformed person, complete explanations and interpretations become necessary. The reader should find answers to any questions he might have about the material presented.

Conciseness

Often conciseness is confused with brevity. Brevity refers to length; a letter or report is brief when it is less than a page long. A letter less than a page long, however, may not be concise, for writing concisely requires that every thought be expressed in the fewest words that are consistent with writing completely and clearly. The same principle applies to speaking situations.

The Royal Bank of Canada's *Monthly Letter* for July 1956 states:

> To use too many words to communicate one's thoughts is a sign of mediocrity, while to gather much thought into few words, clearly and accurately, stamps the person of executive genius. . . . The thing needed . . . is to have something to pass along, and to use words the reader will understand, put up in packages small enough for him to grasp.

One necessary principle of conciseness is: be precise. Words that are definite, concrete, and common create directness and simplicity of expression, which contribute greatly to forcefulness. The successful communicator will resolve his thoughts into exact, concrete, concise expression. He will avoid superlatives, for they are often unnecessary and can mislead the reader or listener. He will avoid exaggeration, for it is confusing. His appeal will be through the effective use of facts, stated so that they will be readily comprehended. He will avoid overuse of adjectives, for they make for affectation, but he will use them where they can make the meaning more precise and concrete. Conciseness becomes a matter of choosing the right words to convey meaning clearly.

Whenever possible, a word should be used instead of a phrase, a phrase instead of a clause, a clause instead of a sentence, and a sentence instead of a paragraph. The process of condensing, however, should not be carried so far that the message becomes general and loses its meaning. Words should not be wasted; irrelevant and repetitious details should be omitted, and hackneyed words and phrases should be eliminated. Passive construction requires more words than the active voice and may obscure meaning. Long, rambling sentences use words needlessly and should be recast. There are instances, though, when long, well-knit sentences lend variety and move the message along. Most of the popular magazines have an average sentence length of eighteen words. Conciseness conserves the reader's or listener's time and effort. The shorter, simpler word and the shorter sentence can be grasped quickly and easily.

Correctness

Correctness is accuracy; it is the result of good judgment and conformity to an accepted conventional standard. Correctness applies to both the subject matter and the manner in which it is expressed. It involves careful checking to insure that there is freedom from error. Data not only must be accurate but must be stated exactly and used to show reasoning and how conclusions were reached. Figures, facts, quotations, and such must be checked with their sources for verification and accuracy because they are the basis for sound judgment and therefore must be reliable.

ONCE UPON A TIME, a fish dealer was planning a new sign for his store. It was to read "FRESH FISH FOR SALE HERE TODAY." A critical friend, however, had some suggestions:

"You don't need the word 'HERE,'" he said. "People can see where the store is. And you don't need 'FOR SALE' either. They know you're not giving things away."

The friend continued: "And how about 'FRESH FISH' and 'TODAY'? Do you want customers to think this is the only day you have fresh fish? that you sell old fish on other days? Take out 'FRESH.' And while you're at it, take out 'TODAY.' People know you wouldn't be open if you weren't selling something today.

"You might as well drop 'FISH' too. Anyone within half a mile can tell what you're selling."

The moral of our fish story? Write concisely and say everything you have to say in the fewest possible words. But don't destroy your message.

You can't chop so many words that you lose clarity — or courtesy. When you do eliminate words at the expense of either of these qualities, your writing is not concise but merely brief and often — discourteous.

Reproduced by permission of New York Life Insurance Company, from *Effective Letters Bulletin*, Spring 1967

Correctness demands conformity to good usage in all matters of form and language. Spacing, erasures, strikeovers, and misspellings detract and destroy understanding. Faulty grammar, incorrect punctuation, the wrong choice of words, and faulty construction of sentences distract the reader from the thought. Grammar is a systematic and responsible way of dealing with language, but it is a living and changing thing. Grammatical standards are based on usefulness and usage. Incorrect usage may arouse contempt for the speaker or writer and cause the listener or reader to put him down as careless or ignorant. When this happens, the message not only may be misunderstood, but also may lack persuasiveness, so that the communicator's purpose cannot be achieved.

Strength

A letter that has strength is forceful and direct, and has *language power*—the capacity to stand up and produce a potent reaction or effect. What gives it this power? All the other qualities mentioned contribute their share to the total effect of the letter. Clarity gives the letter strength by letting it be understood easily and quickly; conciseness gives it directness. Completeness and correctness, too, add strength to what is being said. Otherwise, even if the message were understood, it would not be very credible.

For strength in your writing, follow these steps:

1. *Use concrete, specific words.* Much has already been said about using concrete, specific words. The weak writer deals in abstract nouns, which do not give the reader a clear idea of what is being said. Note the difference:

He expressed the opinion that the amount of money spent on the road construction project appears to compare favorably with costs of similar undertakings.	(Weak)
The engineer told me that the cost of blacktopping the two-mile strip of road just south of Mecca, Indiana, is no more than similar costs have been for blacktopping roads in that area.	(Strong)

The weak sentence contains *opinion, amount of, construction, undertakings*—all general and abstract words whose meanings are not discerned readily. Abstract nouns name qualities, conditions, or relations. Often, changing them to verbs or adjectives gives more force to the message.

Do not say:	*Do say:*
He is a man of honesty.	He is an honest man.
I am of the opinion that the typewriter is efficient.	The typewriter has a light touch that makes typing easy.

2. *Use action verbs.* There are verbs of being and verbs of action, the latter divided into general action verbs and specific action verbs:

a. He *is* six feet tall and stoop-shouldered.	(Verbs of being)

b. There *are* some milling operators I was unable to telephone.
c. The slight delay *was* caused by a failure on our part to foresee the large response we received.

a. Joe *made* his application for a pension. (Verbs of general action)
b. I *contacted* by telephone most of the milling operators and *wrote* the others.

a. Joe *applied* for a pension. (Verbs of specific action)
b. I *telephoned* all but a few of the milling operators.
c. Because he *towered* above his contemporaries, he *developed* stooped shoulders.

Can you tell the difference? Action verbs are stronger than verbs of being, and specific action verbs have more force than general action verbs. They get their force from the specific image they call forth.

3. *Use the active voice in place of the passive voice.* The subject is acted upon in the passive voice, and does the acting in the active voice:

The Zintor Corporation *was forced* to raise its prices because the cost of raw materials *was increased.* (The passive voice)

The increased cost of raw materials *forced* the Zintor Corporation to raise its prices. (The active voice)

The second sentence has much more strength, because its force is expressed in direct action. Note the difference in the following:

The efficiency of the department of purchasing *can be maximized* by the installation of an IBM Executive electric typewriter in the purchasing office. (Weak)

The purchasing department *can maximize* efficiency by installing an IBM Executive electric typewriter in its office. (Strong)

The monthly statement for June *was mailed* to you Monday, July 10. (Weak)

We *mailed* you your June statement on July 10. (Strong)

Some reduction of mailing costs *was accomplished* by the office manager last month. (Weak)

Last month the office manager *reduced* mailing costs 10 percent. (Strong)

There is no doubt that verbs are more direct, more forceful, and stronger in the active voice than they are in the passive voice.

4. *Give direct answers.* Giving answers first and then explaining or supporting them strengthens your statement. The reader knows what to expect and look for, and you do not tax his patience while you labor to get to the point. You wouldn't want to have to read "Company policy provides leeway whereby we can . . ." when you can read "Your refund has been approved. You will receive. . . ."

■ You might stop and look back over the essentials of style, then test your mastery and skill in applying the principles and techniques to the following sentences. Point out the weakness or fault and the principle that applies, and rewrite for effectiveness.

1. As a reminder, to assure continuing warranty coverage you must have the following required maintenance services performed:
   a. Change engine oil every three months or 4,000 miles.
   b. You should have replaced the oil filter every second oil change.
   c. The carburetor air filter should be cleaned every six months and replaced every two years.
   d. Check operation of crankcase ventilator valve and have man clean oil filter cap every six months.
2. (From an ad) Solid oak posture chairs for secretaries with built-in padding.
3. Referring to the questionnaire you returned, you failed to answer two of the questions.
4. Our new system of record-keeping will result in a saving of time and convenience for the bookkeeper.
5. We wish to inform you we can offer you one-day laundry service on your shirts now.
6. Permit me to take this opportunity to thank you for your prompt action on my refund.
7. Your bank note has been endorsed as payment of the full amount of your loan plus interest and when we send it to you will be evidence that your loan and interest totaling $2,650 has been paid in its full amount.
8. The Acme (gas refrigerator) is quiet.
9. You can either include your check for $56.98 with your next remittance or we can return your check for $25.98 we received yesterday and you send us a corrected check for the full amount.
10. I am only responsible for making the entries on the records.
11. The plastic seat covers are so light and clear you hardly know they are on the car and because of the most unusual weave, air is being allowed to circulate and will keep them cool to the touch of your skin and very comfortable to sit upon.
12. The present conditions of the coal industry is poor and has been for over twenty years for they are being replaced with gas, oil, and electric heating systems.

13. You neglected to inform us the size and color of the shoes you ordered.
14. These blouses come in bright colors, plain and patterned.
15. These toy trains are very durable.
16. More value is represented in the savings offered by installation of storm windows.
17. Either our sales should be increased or our prices will have to be raised.
18. Your order came at a time in which we were very busy and therefore there had to be a slight delay, but the order should have been received by now. It was really shipped five days previously to the time we are writing you.
19. The new postal regulation and increase in postage was made effective several years previous to this date.
20. New power and smoothness have been given the ________ power lawn mowers by our very capable designers at the factory in New Jersey.
21. For news relating to the murder, a reward of $10,000 was made by contributors to a fund.
22. He was elected chairman by a majority of the committee.
23. Every secretary should have a dictionary on her desk and it should be consulted frequently.
24. In order to pay the arrears of premiums and policy loan interest it will require an 18-months' premium of $849 and the interest charge which would have been due May 10, 1968, of $107.42. This does not include any date interest since the check attached to the file is for $648.69, we would require a further remittance of $307.73.

■ Try your hand at transforming the following sentences[4] into a list of old sayings:

1. A warm-blooded vertebrate of the class *Aves*, grasped securely in the terminal prehensile portion of the upper limb of the human body, is equal in value to one plus one of the aforementioned vertebrates at liberty in the low foliage.
2. A mineral matter of various composition, when engaged in periodic revolutions, exhibits no tendency to accumulate any of the cryptogamic plants of the class *Musci*.
3. Bubbles of gas, rising from a liquid in a vessel, receptacle, or the like, to the surface of said liquid, is a phenomenon not witnessed by those who subject such liquid to constant, searching scrutiny.
4. Seeking a suitable place for the purpose of courting a state of dormant quiescence during the first part of the crepuscular period and forsaking said suitable place during the first part of the matutinal period results in myriad benefits to *homo sapiens*, among which benefits may be noted a substantial increase in body soundness, monies, and sagacity.

[4]Reprinted from *Effective Letters Bulletin*, by permission of the New York Life Insurance Company.

The next sentence was composed by an Eastern Michigan University student:

> The most insignificant modern currency, when withheld indefinitely, is therefore considered to have been sought after diligently and acquired thereof.

Why not try your hand at converting other old sayings into puzzling statements?

■ Evaluate the following letter. Discuss its faulty organization, its lack of essentials of style and tone for understanding, and its overall effect on the reader. Rewrite it the way you would say it.

Dear Madam:

Because you didn't include the size of the boy's jacket and the color of the girl's dress in your order I am taking this opportunity to write you. I realize you wanted the items ordered in your letter of November 10 to be shipped "Rush" to you. It is therefore necessary that I go ahead and send you the two coats, galoshes, and raincoats--for you did specify color and size for them. They are being shipped today and you should receive them in less than a week.

We are not having a rainy season now so you should have them in plenty of time.

We can not, however, send you the boy's jacket and girl's dress so you will not receive them with the other items you ordered. I am sure you will be happy with them when you do get them for the dress is very stylish.

Sincerely yours,

SECURING UNITY, COHERENCE, AND EMPHASIS

To achieve understanding, the communicator utilizes an effective style that should be direct, straightforward, interesting, persuasive, and readable. This requires careful application of the principles of unity, coherence, and emphasis, along with skillful use of language and application of the essentials of understanding.

Unity

The following paragraph is totally lacking in unity and coherence:

> Since I began work in the personnel department two years ago many changes have taken place. What is wrong is that the base-pay rate is too low. I feel that I'm not paid enough. Hourly wage employees receive $2.45 a hour or rather John Bonnett told me that was what he was receiving. Mr. Robert Dockett said he was offered $2.50 by Loughton Company. Employees have complained about their wages. We do pay overtime in some cases. I checked the base rate of five other companies doing similar work as ours, and found we are paying above average.

Unity denotes the state of being one. It demands that each simple sentence contain a clearly expressed single idea or meaning and that each complex or compound sentence make a single complete statement in each main clause. Related sentences form a unified paragraph. Each paragraph that presents unity of thought contributes to a unified section, until structurally the entire communication becomes a unified whole.

Including everything pertinent to one clearly defined purpose and eliminating irrelevant material, giving consideration to what the reader already knows and what he still needs or wants to know about the subject, enables him to concentrate on what is being said. An orderly arrangement of ideas flowing into other ideas and progressing to conclusions helps achieve unity and is also a major aid to coherence. (Lack of such an arrangement is the main weakness in the paragraph given earlier.) The relationship between a main idea and a subordinate idea in a sentence is indicated by placing the subordinate or lesser idea in the dependent clause and using a conjunction to point out the relationship. In paragraphs and larger thought units, the relationship is indicated by some transitional means. This provides an element of sequence and motion that moves the reader in a definite direction toward accomplishing the purpose of the communication.

Coherence[5]

To be coherent, a message must be understood and must hang together. These are the two aspects of coherence—relatedness and clearness. Like unity, coherence applies to sentences, paragraphs, sections, and the whole message. The relationship of all the elements in a sentence must be immediately apparent, and ideas must be clearly stated. By interlinking sentences so that thought flows smoothly from one to the next, a paragraph is given coherence. By arranging sentences in a clear, logical order and by relating them through the use of pronouns, transitional words or phrases, repetition of words or ideas, and parallel structure, a paragraph is given further coherence.

Likewise, by interlinking paragraphs so that thought flows smoothly from one to the next, coherence is given to a larger section or division of a message. This relationship can be accomplished by developing and arranging paragraphs in a clear, logical order, linking them by transitional phrases or sentences, relating them by repetition of ideas and progression of thought, and using topic sentences and topic paragraphs to control ideas and direct the flow of thought. Thus a message is tied together into a meaningful whole.

[5]See also the discussion of *clearness* on pp. 111–15.

Emphasis

The ideas, facts, and figures that make up a message are of varying degrees of importance. The degree of emphasis placed upon them indicates their relative values. Emphasis may be achieved by position, by proportion, or through mechanical methods.

Ideas of greatest value should be in the most prominent positions. The beginning and end of a paragraph, section, or division are emphatic positions. Placed at the beginning, main thoughts are given attention, for they are what the reader sees first. Placed at the end, important ideas leave the reader with his final impression. Sometimes a climactic effect is achieved by leading the reader through an analytical discussion that builds up to a conclusion at the end. In deciding which position to give an idea, consideration must be given to its relative importance to the reader and to the purpose of the communication.

Sentence structure also plays an important role. For example, putting the main idea of a complex sentence in an independent clause and the subordinate idea in a dependent clause, or stating two ideas of equal rank in main clauses of a compound sentence, can make the desired facts stand out. When a number of facts are given and long sentences are used, placing the most important fact in a short, simple sentence emphasizes it.

Material in a message takes up space commensurate with its importance. The more that details are used or illustrations given, and the fuller the development of a point, the more emphasis is given to what is being treated. This is achieving emphasis by proportion. Of course, undue weight should not be given to unimportant points and inessential details; superfluous words and hackneyed expressions should be avoided. Major ideas are emphasized by condensing minor ones. Negative ideas need not be developed at length; positive ideas should receive full treatment. Commonplace, conventional ideas should not receive the same attention as others. Lengthy introductions should be avoided. A very short sentence at the beginning or end will receive special attention. It is usually a summary, direct and to the point. For instance:

> A university is set up to seek truth. Its basic assumption is that knowledge is worthwhile and that knowledge will lead one to the truth. Its faculty and students must have freedom to find truth—freedom to investigate, learn, publish, and teach what they are convinced is the truth.

Repetition of an important idea or word also calls attention to it, as does the use of parallelism. A series or an itemized list calls for parallelism, as in the above illustration: ". . . freedom to investigate, learn, publish, and teach. . . ." If a verb phrase states one idea, a verb phrase should be used for stating all ideas.

A number of mechanical devices may be used to make an idea emphatic:

Leave a large amount of white space around
the idea or fact to be set off.

Use CAPITAL LETTERS; underscore; use *italics* or another style of print. Indent, set off a list of items, or use subject headings to highlight topics and make their relationships stand out.

Other methods of securing emphasis include the use of graphs, charts, tables, and pictorial forms for presenting figures, statistics, and other data. Such material may also be highlighted by spot tables. Careful selection and combination of words is also important. Precise, specific words will convey concrete ideas. Vivid words, appropriately used figures of speech, euphonic words, strong active verbs—all call attention to ideas and move a message forward.

WRITING ROUTINE LETTERS

Classified on the basis of the function they perform, there are eight major kinds of business letters:

routine	collection
claim	sales
adjustment	goodwill
credit	application

Although our approach to developing our ability to write effective letters has been to master and use the principles involved in all letter-writing and communicating situations (and not to learn how to write the various types of letters), it is well to recognize that there are different types of letters and that there are people who use highly developed skills in these particular functional areas.

Letters such as those written every day, many times a day, to handle recurring business transactions are routine in nature. Many are the secretaries who compose these letters and handle this type of correspondence by themselves, thus freeing their bosses to write and dictate the more individual letters called for in the more complicated situations of management, marketing, etc. Routine letters consist of orders and acknowledgments, letters of inquiry and answers to inquiries, letters of transmittal, and letters conveying miscellaneous information. It is highly important that the message be understood and have that extra measure of goodwill—then it cannot fail to accomplish its routine purpose. Thus, applying the essentials of style and tone will get results.

The primary purpose of a request or order is to obtain the items or services being requested. To achieve this it is essential to give some necessary information:

1. Identify the goods and state the quantity wanted.
2. Describe the goods clearly and completely.
3. Tabulate (when several items are wanted) for brevity and easy checking.
4. State clearly how the payment will be made.
5. Specify where, when, and how the shipment will be made.

Acknowledgments are made for promoting business and building goodwill. They should explain what is being done about the order or request. In accepting an order:

1. Quickly indicate appreciation (and welcome, if it is a new customer).
2. Restate or identify the order or terms.
3. Explain how the order is being handled—payment, transportation, shipping, and approximate arrival date.
4. Look forward to future business, especially in the case of a new customer, who should also receive resale material on present goods and a sales talk for other products.
5. Indicate an interest in serving the customer.

In refusing an order or a request, follow the organizational pattern of a *no* letter as presented earlier (see page 105).

Inquiries are direct requests for information or action. They should be short, concise, clear, and courteous. When asking a special favor, it is often wise to:

1. Give the reason for the request.
2. Identify oneself or otherwise manifest one's right to make the request.
3. State the request itself.
4. Include the advantage to the reader.
5. Offer to reciprocate or show some other form of appreciation.
6. Make it easy to reply.

Because there is an advantage in striking while the iron is hot, answers to inquiries should be made right away, often the same day they are received. All information called for should be given. If the inquiry has sales possibilities, answer it in terms of product or service advantages to the prospect and include descriptive material that is interestingly and convincingly presented. If samples are to be sent, have them carefully packed, wrapped, and tied. If a catalog or booklet is to be sent, send it with the letter—not under separate cover. In granting a request:

1. Express cheerfulness.

2. Give the information requested.
3. If necessary or possible, add relevant material.
4. Offer further assistance.

Letters of transmittal accompany reports,[6] catalogs, pamphlets, price lists, and other enclosures. They introduce and explain; they should clarify points and interest the reader. When the enclosures are advertising materials, the letter becomes a sales promotion letter, which the enclosures supplement.

Claim letters are written to secure an adjustment on goods or services that are at fault. In this respect they are similar to letters of request, order, or inquiry. Their purpose, however, is to have an error rectified by influencing someone to act in a definite way. Thus a claim letter is a problem in persuasion. Most business firms are glad to rectify their mistakes because they know the value of keeping the customer's goodwill. Therefore it is wise to cool off before writing the claim letter, to be reasonable and fair, and to assume that the business firm will make the adjustment, given the opportunity. In making a claim:

1. Explain what is wrong; provide specific details and evidence.
2. Describe the resulting inconvenience or trouble.
3. Request definite action.
4. Provide a motive for inducing the reader to act immediately.

Dear Sirs:

Until yesterday I was exceptionally well pleased with my Magic Pressure Cooker, which was given me as a gift on May 12.

Now it won't work. The gift package contained an instruction booklet, which I have very carefully followed. Yesterday, when I was preparing the evening meal, I detected a strange odor. When I located the source, I found that the rubber gasket had melted and run down into the food. I had over a two-pound beef roast ruined plus potatoes, carrots, and onions. The roast cost me $1.59. Of course, I had to cook another supper, and I had no meat.

As you should know, good meals are hard to cook and doubly so without a Magic Cooker. I know that you want to keep the high standards of your firm and will remedy the situation.

I would like a new Magic Pressure Cooker that will work or my money back so that I can buy another pressure cooker.

Very truly yours,

Mrs. Allan Smith

[6]See also the discussion and fuller treatment of letters of transmittal in Chapter 10, especially for their use with business reports.

The omission of sarcasm and a sharp tone goes a long way toward persuading the other person, for it indicates that the writer knows what he is talking about and doesn't have to resort to other means of arousing the reader.

MEASURING READABILITY

Readability is the quality of writing that results in clearness and interest for the reader. Much of the written communication between management and employees and between companies and the general public goes unread because the appropriate readability has not been maintained. Readability formulas have been developed for rating material by measuring its difficulty. The level of readability then is expressed in terms of the general educational level of the reader. Results determine whether or not the measured material will reach its intended reader.

The four most widely known readability formulas are those developed by Flesch, by Dale and Chall, by Farr, Jenkins, and Patterson, and by Gunning.[7] No one formula is definitely superior to the others. Although it is impossible to present enough information here about each formula for applying it, we will take time to present Gunning's method, which is one of the easiest to understand and apply. Gunning determined seven factors affecting readability: average sentence length in words, percentage of simple sentences, percentage of verbs expressing forceful action, proportion of familiar words, proportion of abstract words, percentage of personal references, and percentage of long words. He uses two elements in his formula, the number of words of three or more syllables in 100 words and the average sentence length in words.

Gunning's Fog Index[8]

To find the Fog Index of a passage, take these three simple steps:

1. *Determine the average sentence length.* Count the number of words in successive sentences. For long pieces of writing, take samples of 100 words. Divide the total number of words by the number of sentences. Do not count the articles *a, an,* and *the* as words.

[7]See Rudolf Flesch, *The Art of Readable Writing* (New York: Harper & Row, Publishers, 1949); Edgar Dale and Jeanne Chall, "A Formula for Predicting Readability," *Educational Research Bulletin,* Ohio State University (January 1948); James N. Farr, James J. Jenkins, and Donald G. Patterson, "Simplification of Flesch Reading Ease Formula," *Journal of Applied Psychology* (October 1951); and Robert Gunning, *The Technique of Clear Writing,* rev. ed. (New York: McGraw-Hill Book Company, 1968).

[8]From Gunning, *The Technique of Clear Writing,* pp. 38–41.

2. *Find the percentage of hard words.* Count the number of words of three syllables or more per 100 words. Don't count words that are capitalized, that are a combination of short, easy words (like *bookkeeper* and *butterfly*), or that are verb forms made into three syllables by adding *-ed* or *-es* (like *created* or *trespasses*).
3. *Figure the Fog Index.* Add the two factors (steps 1 and 2) and multiply by 0.4.

The following table is used to interpret the Fog Index or readability score:

Fog Index	*Reading Level by Grade*	*Reading Level by Magazine*
17	College graduate	
16	College senior	(No popular
15	College junior	magazine is
14	College sophomore	this difficult)
13	College freshman	
	DANGER LINE	
12	High school senior	*Atlantic Monthly* and *Harper's*
11	High school junior	*Time* and *Newsweek*
	EASY READING RANGE	
10	High school sophomore	*Reader's Digest*
9	High school freshman	*Saturday Evening Post*
8	Eighth grade	*Ladies' Home Journal*
7	Seventh grade	*True Confessions* and *Modern Romances*
6	Sixth grade	Comics

Effect of Readability Formulas

Readability formulas measure readability in a general way for the general reader and help the writer to see his material as the reader will or *to adapt his writing to the reader.* Carried to the extreme, however, a choppy, childish style may result from writing in too many short, simple sentences. The most familiar word may not always be the best choice, and even a short sentence may not be clear. Writing within a limited vocabulary range may become monotonous and deadening. The formulas should not be used as rules for writing, only for measuring the readability level. They do not consider either the reader's background and interest or many of the factors that go into effective writing. Nevertheless, they point to the necessity of clear sentences and understandable words to make writing readable. Thus the emphasis is on clearness in writing. The formulas have affected writing style to the extent of giving importance to the principles that follow.

For clear sentences:

1. Keep the majority of the sentences short and simple.
2. Make relationships clear in each sentence.
3. Vary sentence length and structure.
4. Use a small number of prepositional and infinitive phrases.
5. Use adequate conjunctions and transitional phrases for smooth reading.
6. Convey only one or two main thoughts in each sentence.
7. Let each sentence mean something in relation to the other sentences.

For understandable words:

1. Use familiar words.
2. Make words meaningful.
3. Avoid unnecessary words.
4. Use words with few syllables.
5. Select nontechnical terms.
6. Put action into the verbs.
7. Use a variety of words.
8. Select pictorial words within the reader's experience.
9. Use concrete rather than abstract words.
10. Apply concrete analogies, examples, and comparisons when abstract concepts must be given.

- Using Gunning's Fog Index, measure the readability of one of the letters you have written for this course. Discuss its score in relation to the intended reader's time, effort, and level of comprehension. How does it rate? Does it point up any changes you should make in your style?
- Look up one of the other readability formulas and apply it and Gunning's Fog Index to a given piece, such as:

  an annual report
  a magazine article
  a newspaper article
  an employee handbook
  an employee magazine
  a business letter

  Compare the results.

SUMMARY

Skill at getting ideas across is essential to everyone and can be developed by all who take the time to practice certain principles and techniques. The first of these is careful planning. Following a prescribed procedure for planning makes organization and comprehension possible, because the writer has full control over what he is doing and gives direction to his messages. Planning creates good organization, which results in understanding. Letters may be organized following a "yes" pattern, a "no" pattern, a psychological effect, or a relationship of the ideas expressed.

Routine letters, written every day to handle recurring situations, consist of orders and acknowledgments, letters of inquiry and answers to inquiries, letters of transmittal, and letters conveying miscellaneous information. Understanding results from application of the essentials of style and tone and from the inclusion of particular points to be covered according to the situation and the purpose to be accomplished.

Measuring the readability of a piece of writing and revising it to meet the level of your intended reader helps the reader to understand it. One of the best and easiest of the formulas to apply is the one developed by Robert Gunning—the Fog Index. It is based on sentence length and word length, recognizing that short sentences and short words result in ease of comprehension. An average sentence length of seventeen words meets the needs of most readers.

CHECKLIST FOR ESSENTIALS OF UNDERSTANDING

Application of the fundamental principles of clearness, completeness, conciseness, correctness, and strength is essential to understanding. The following checklist should prove useful to help you make sure that each of your letters possesses these desirable qualities.

For Clarity

Is there an easy-to-follow arrangement?
Do ideas flow smoothly from beginning to end?
Are thoughts linked together?
Do conjunctions show proper subordination and coordination of ideas?
Is the same point of view maintained in a given paragraph or section?
Are principles of parallelism applied?
Is concrete, simple language used?
Have technical and business terms been avoided?
Has the other person's language been used?
Is it conversational?
Has attention been given to layout and display possibilities for clearness?

For Completeness

Has the subject been treated fully?
Have specific, pertinent details been given?
Have nonessential details been eliminated?
Is there overuse of quotations?
Is there long, unnecessary description?
Has evidence been stated precisely?
Are the significance of facts and their relationships shown?
Does the reader find his questions answered?

For Conciseness

Are thoughts expressed in as few words as possible?
Are definite, precise words used?

Are unnecessary superlatives avoided?
Is there exaggeration?
Does the subject have a direct beginning?
Have adjectives been used judiciously?
Have irrelevant details been eliminated?
Have hackneyed expressions been avoided?
Are there any long, rambling sentences?
Has the reader's time and effort been conserved?

For Correctness

Is there freedom from error
- in grammar?
- in spelling?
- in punctuation?
- in typing?

Are facts accurate?
Have data been verified?
Has sound judgment been shown?
Is there conformity to good usage standards?

For Strength

Are specific, exact words used?
Are abstract, general words avoided or explained?
Have concrete examples been used?
Have words been selected for both their denotative and connotative meanings?
Do simple, short words predominate?
Is active construction used?
Is it direct and to the point?
Is it natural?

For Unity, Coherence, and Emphasis

Is there one central thought?
Do related sentences form a unified paragraph?
Is everything pertinent to one clearly defined purpose?
Is there an orderly arrangement of ideas?
Does it hang together?
Is a relationship clearly indicated?
Are sentence elements related?
Is the appropriate degree of emphasis given?
Do ideas of greatest value stand out?
Are important points placed first and last?
Is space commensurate with importance?
Do positive ideas receive full treatment?
Are negative ideas subordinated?
Does the message move forward?

FURTHER READING

FOR REFERENCE USE AND FOR IMPROVING YOUR MECHANICAL SKILL:

The American College Dictionary. New York: Harper & Row, Publishers, 1953.

Gavin, Ruth E., and E. Lilian Hutchinson, *Reference Manual for Stenographers and Typists,* 3rd ed. Chicago: Gregg Publishing Division, McGraw-Hill Book Company, 1961.

Gunning, Robert, *The Technique of Clear Writing*. New York: McGraw-Hill Book Company, 1952.

Hamburger, Edward, *A Business Dictionary*. Englewood Cliffs, N. J.: Prentice-Hall, Inc., 1967.

——, *A Business Vocabulary*. New York: P & H Sales Co., 1966.

Keithley, Erwin, and Margaret H. Thompson, *English for Modern Business*. Homewood, Ill.: Richard D. Irwin, Inc., 1966.

Lamb, Marion M., *Word Studies*. Cincinnati: South-Western Publishing Co., 1963.

Leslie, Louis A., *20,000 Words,* 5th ed. Chicago: Gregg Publishing Division, McGraw-Hill Book Company, 1965.

Morehead, Albert H., ed., *Roget's College Thesaurus in Dictionary Form*. New York: Signet Books, 1962.

Perrin, Porter G., *Writer's Guide and Index to English,* 4th ed. Glenwood, Ill.: Scott, Foresman & Company, 1965.

Random House Dictionary of the English Language, college ed. New York: Random House, Inc., 1968.

Silverthorn, J. E., and John W. Oberly, *College Vocabulary Building,* 4th ed. Cincinnati: South-Western Publishing Co., 1964.

Webster's New World Dictionary, college ed. Cleveland, Ohio: World Publishing Company, 1966.

FOR DEVELOPING YOUR ABILITY TO BE UNDERSTOOD:

Aurner, Robert R., and M. Philip Wolf, *Effective Communication in Business,* 5th ed. Cincinnati: South-Western Publishing Co., 1967, pp. 42–94, 116–24.

Damerst, William A., *Resourceful Business Communication*. New York: Harcourt, Brace & World, Inc., 1966, pp. 137–52, 347–63.

Dawe, Jessamon, and William J. Lord, Jr., *Functional Business Communication*. Englewood Cliffs, N. J.: Prentice-Hall, Inc., 1968, pp. 83–109, 240–62.

Devlin, Frank J., *Business Communication*. Homewood, Ill.: Richard D. Irwin, Inc., 1968, pp. 59–109, 161–88, 244–85.

Himstreet, William C., and Wayne M. Baty, *Business Communications,* 3rd ed. Belmont, Calif.: Wadsworth Publishing Company, Inc., 1969, pp. 77–101, 271–323.

Hunsinger, Marjorie, *Modern Business Correspondence,* 2nd ed. Chicago: Gregg Publishing Division, McGraw-Hill Book Company, 1967, pp. 39–52, 65–99. (A text-workbook for colleges.)

Janis, J. Harold, *Writing and Communicating in Business.* New York: The Macmillan Company, 1964, pp. 33–57, 78–109, 188–93.

Lamb, Marion M., and Eugene H. Hughes, *Business Letters, Memorandums, and Reports.* New York: Harper & Row, Publishers, 1967, pp. 2–19, 49–57, 89–115.

Reid, James M., and Robert Wendlinger, *Effective Letters: A Program for Self-Instruction.* New York: McGraw-Hill Book Company, 1964.

Stewart, Marie M., Frank W. Lanham, and Kenneth Zimmer, *College English and Communication.* Chicago: Gregg Publishing Division, McGraw-Hill Book Company, 1964, pp.12–46, 262–316.

Wells, Walter, *Communications in Business.* Belmont, Calif.: Wadsworth Publishing Company, Inc., 1968, pp. 48–128, 250–67.

QUESTIONS AND PROBLEMS

1. What is wrong with the way each of the following situations was handled?
   a. The bureau of business services at a midwestern university sponsored a special one-day seminar on "Lower Court Reorganization–Its Effect on the Business Community." Speakers were drawn from the state legislature, business and industry, the legal profession, and the school's faculty. The potential audience would likewise be composed of these various groups plus citizens interested in the problem. The wife of one of the faculty men received this announcement:

As a member of the League of Women Voters,

I know you will want to know that on March 4th a seminar on "Lower Court Reorganization — Its Effect on the Business Community" will be held at the Union Building.

We expect that the largest audience segments will be businessmen and attorneys, but the seminar will not be complete unless the League is represented by a goodly number of you.

We hope you will attend.

Cordially,

Director, Bureau of Business Services

   b. A dry cleaning establishment in a West Coast city where a large junior college is located sent the following letter to one of its customers who had just recently moved to Omaha, Nebraska.

      The facts are that Mr. Smithsonian stopped at the branch office just before moving and was refused his tuxedo because he had lost his claim check. He had to leave town without the tuxedo. He informed his roommate of the situation, asking him to check at the main office and to leave his new address.

> Dear Mr. Smithsonian:
>
> I'm very sorry you have been inconvenienced in not being able to get the tux you left with us for cleaning, removing spots, and pressing. Rules are rules, and we can't give out clothing without claim checks. This is a protection for you and us.
>
> The lady manager, however, at our campus branch office had been authorized to give you your suit and you may call for it at your convenience.
>
> Hoping we may continue to be of service to you and your family.
>
> Very truly yours,

c. A Tulane University fraternity received this letter:

> Greetings:
>
> The writer had the pleasure of speaking to Mr. Meyers of the Messers Mayers and Mann Hardware of 2410 Apple Street who furnished us your good name to contact regarding Carnival Throws.
>
> Our company has just been established in this type of business, which we will open and commence at the first of the new year, namely January 2, 197__.
>
> We would like to extend to you our fine service, and friendly cordian atmosphere which we take pleasure in inviting you to visit us. We believe you will profit by visiting our display of various Carnival Throws of which it will allow you to have a very nice Mardi Gradi in which you participate.
>
> At our place of business we would like to have the pleasure of your partronage and serve you in your needs for the Carnival Season.
>
> May we extend to you the finest of Season Greetings and look forwarded in seeing you at our display room which contains various Carnival Throw items.
>
> With best wishes,
>
> Yours very truly,
> CARNIVAL CENTER OF
> NEW ORLEANS
>
> J. C. Bachdan

2. The author of this text wrote a review of *Research Methodology in Business,* by J. F. Rummel and W. C. Ballaine (New York: Harper & Row, Publishers, 1963), for publication in one of the professional journals. The editor returned it with the request that it be reduced 50 to 75 percent in length. The reviewer decided to omit the second paragraph entirely, then to reduce the length by a careful editing job, eliminating unnecessary words, using active rather than passive construction, reducing several words to one word, etc. He came up with a concise, meaningful review of 180 words. It was published! See what you can do with the original review:

With its emphasis and presentation of material concentrated on quantitative research, *Research Methology in Business* makes a strong contribution to quantitative research methods, although it does not give the reader as comprehensive a guide to other research methods in business. The authors have intended the book for use in all graduate divisions and specifically colleges of business administration, as a guide to the scientific method underlying all good research. Basically, all research procedures are considered. General principles and techniques found successful in the field, office, and classroom are presented; and illustrative material is used from business administration and research projects and proposals.

Research is defined as a careful inquiry to discover new information or relationships and to expand and to verify existing knowledge. It is the manipulation of things, concepts, or symbols for generalizing, extending, correcting, or verifying knowledge that may aid in constructing a theory or in practicing an art. The book concentrates on research as a method of solving problems. The premise is that good research methodology reflects good thinking and that the steps in the thinking process as outlined by John Dewey might serve as procedural guides in the development and execution of research investigations. This philosophy is theoretically sound and practical.

The ten chapters in the text are arranged in the order in which the stages of a research project normally arise. Chapter I sketches the general nature of research; Chapters II and III present the principles for a selection of a research project and discuss overall planning and organizing. Chapters IV, V, VI, and VII treat methods of collecting data. These chapters deal with basic, elementary material that most graduate students should have already had. Nothing new is given although the details dealing with sampling are meaningful, and the suggestion for interviewing and observation pertinent. Chapter VIII, which introduces basic designs for experimental research, and Chapter IX, which presents techniques for using data processing for research projects, are the two best chapters in the book. Here the emphasis is on quantitative research; new ideas are presented; illustrations are very appropriately used. Chapter X, which is one of the weakest chapters, scantily treats writing the research report. It does, however, contain an excellent checklist at the end for judging effective research reports, and Appendix B, serving as a manual for the mechanics and form of research reports, helps to balance Chapter X. The criticism here is that much of the material is too elementary for the reader who is already familiar with research reports and is not sufficient for the reader who has not mastered the art of writing a report. Most readers would do better to consult one of the standard report-writing textbooks as a guide to presentation. Appendix A contains a good review of basic statistical concepts and computation.

The brevity of textual material makes it possible for the instructor to develop his own points of emphasis and to adapt to the specific needs of students and institutions. The emphasis on the quantitative approach seeks to know not only *what* but also *how much;* it considers measurement an important aspect of scientific research.

3. Do you agree that the next letter is too long to accomplish its purpose? Why? It was sent out by the gas company to homeowners and received a favorable response. See what you can do about rewriting it for conciseness.

Dear Customer:

We have now had a slight taste of Michigan summer. Needless to say, this is only the beginning and we will have many more hot, humid days, weeks, and even months before summer is over. The purpose of this letter, therefore, is to suggest that you consider the many advantages of installing central gas air conditioning in your home or business establishment. If you have a central gas warm air furnace, you already have half of a central gas air conditioning system. At present, more than 800,000 of our more than 940,000 customers enjoy the convenience, cleanliness, and most of all dependability and economy of natural gas heat. These and many more advantages can be yours with the addition of a central gas air conditioning unit to your gas furnace.

Why should you consider gas central air conditioning rather than electric? Here are a few of the many reasons. First, we can say without fear of being proven wrong that a gas air conditioning unit is the very best that can be had. It operates on the absorption refrigeration cycle rather than on the vapor compression refrigeration cycle as does the electric unit. The gas unit thus has fewer moving parts and consequently less chance of loss of efficiency and breakdown due to wear. One of its major features which differentiates it from an electric unit is that it <u>does not</u> have the electric motor-driven compressor that is prone to produce excessive noise. Second, a gas air conditioning unit is sold, serviced, and backed by your Gas Company. Service by trained Gas Company employees is available on call around the clock, seven days per week. Third, the cost of operation of a central gas air conditioning unit is substantially less than that of a comparably sized electric unit. Fourth, the installation of a gas air conditioning unit will entitle you to our special Gas Air Conditioning Rate for all gas you use for any purpose during the five-month air conditioning season. Under this rate you will not only get your air conditioning gas at a very low rate but will also save about 40% on the cost of gas used for all other purposes during the air conditioning season.

A central gas air conditioning unit will reduce the humidity in your home or business establishment, will filter out dust and pollen, and when added to your central warm air gas furnace will provide you with comfort control throughout the year. If you now have a central warm air gas furnace which adequately heats your home or business establishment, a gas air conditioning unit can be added. The ducts and furnace blower that deliver warm air to every part of your home or business establishment in the winter can deliver cool, dehumidified, and filtered air to the same area during the summer.

For those who install central gas air conditioning this summer, we also have available a time payment program which may be of interest to you. It provides that with a nominal down payment your unit can be installed and no further payments need be made until next November. At that time, the installed cost can be paid in full with no carrying charges being added, or you may choose to enter into a time payment program of up to five years with payments, including carrying charges, being added to your monthly gas bill.

If you are interested in central gas air conditioning and would like to learn more about our program, I invite you, without obligation on your part, to either call or fill out and return the enclosed card. One of our air conditioning representatives will survey your home, will determine the proper size unit for it, will advise you of the installed cost of the unit, and will furnish detailed information about gas air conditioning equipment, our rates, and the program. I look forward to hearing from you.

Sincerely,

Courtesy Michigan Consolidated Gas Company

4. To notify its customers about holiday delivery services, a dairy products company on the East Coast sent out the next two letters—one at Thanks-

giving and the other just prior to Christmas. Evaluate both letters, using the checklists on pages 131 and 132.

Dear Customer:

Thursday, November 22nd, is THANKSGIVING DAY. This is a day when friends and relatives gather together to worship and break bread. It is a day when we all give thanks to our Lord for our wonderful blessings.

In order that our route salesmen might enjoy this day off with their families, we will leave your Thursday order with your regular order Tuesday, November 20th. This, in most cases, will be equivalent to your regular weekend order. There will be no delivery THANKSGIVING DAY.

May I remind you also of our delicious Egg Nog now available for the remainder of the Holiday Season, as well as our other line of by-products such as eggs, butter, whipping cream, etc.

Kindly leave a note for your route salesman, or order in advance by calling 529-2224, for any additional products.

I would like to take this opportunity also to bring to your attention our new ALL-JERSEY MILK available for you. This is the milk that has the most for the children and adults. Look for details concerning such soon.

Please always remember that we value and appreciate your business and pledge to continue giving you the highest-quality milk and service available.

Yours truly,

Home Delivery Sales Manager

To Our Friends:

This is the time of year when friends greet friends. . . and the world is full of smiles. It's the time of year when we want to express to all our friends and customers the thoughts that are in our hearts.

These thoughts are about your patronage, your friendship, and how you have helped make our business success possible. We'd like for you to know how grateful we are to have the privilege of serving folks like you.

Since Christmas is unlike any other holiday, a time to worship and join together with our families and friends to help celebrate this glorious occasion, we feel that our "Home Delivery Salesman" should be home with his family and friends on Christmas and New Year's Day. We hope you agree with us likewise.

Therefore, in order to make this possible without having you short of milk, we will leave you a double order on Saturday, December 22, and Saturday, December 29th. This order will consist of your regular Saturday and Tuesday delivery. There will be no delivery Christmas or New Year's Day. As you know, we have done this for the past several years.

If you should need any additional items, or for a change in order, simply leave a note for your milkman specifying same or order in advance by calling 529-2224, "Home Delivery," and your milkman will be more than happy to serve you.

We extend to you many thanks for your past favors and pledge to give you faithful service throughout the coming year. Our entire organization joins with me in sending the very warmest Holiday Greetings with every good wish for the New Year.

Yours truly,

Retail Salesmanager

Is either letter any better than the other one? Rewrite them for clarity, conciseness, strength, etc.

5. A photography studio in California wanted to reach the parents of babies. A mailing list gleaned from vital statistics in the newspapers yielded a number of prospective customers, to whom the photographer sent the following form letter.

> To the Parents of the New Baby:
>
> I wish to congratulate you on the blessed event that has come into your lives and sincerely wish you great joy and pleasure with the new little stranger.
>
> At the same time I want you to know that I am one of the best Baby Photographers in the city. Just to prove my sincerity, enclosed herewith is a complimentary coupon to Smith-Hackett Studios.
>
> This will entitle you to one free photograph, size 9½ X 12, regular $8.95 value, beautiful black and white silver etching. You may have your baby's picture taken up to eight months old, and receive a special discount of 10% for any additional photographs, any number you might desire.
>
> There are no strings attached to this offer. I'll give you this photograph absolutely free of charge to prove I am outstanding in baby and child photography so that for many years to come I can treasure you as one of my valued customers.
>
> With very best wishes, I am
>
> Sincerely yours,
>
> James Richard Hackett
> Smith-Hackett Studios
>
> P.S. Don't lose your valuable complimentary coupon; bring it with you at time of sitting.

Much to his dismay he did not get the results he had anticipated. Do you wonder why? Rewrite the letter.

6. Your school library has just received three-year gift subscriptions to *Atlantic, Harper's, Credit World,* the *Journal of Psychology, Advanced Management,* and the *Wall Street Journal.* They were given by an alumnus who graduated fifty years ago and is now retiring from his own business; it will be taken over by his two sons, who are also alumni of your school. Write him a letter, expressing your appreciation.

7. As an instructor in business writing at your school, you would like to use the Champion Paper Company's film, *Production 5118,* to illustrate some of the points you've brought out in lectures. You want to show the film in two weeks to your 100 students. You have heard that some businesses loan films at no charge. And you must get this film without cost, since you have no budget for such things. By seeing the film, your students will learn more about business communication. Write your letter, addressed to the company's director of public relations.

8. Myers Sales and Service is a small family-owned and -operated business selling power lawn and garden equipment. They also service the mowers and other equipment they sell and operate a repair service for equipment sold by other firms. Recently they acquired a three-acre tract of land and enlarged their work and storage area to 5,000 square feet. During the spring, summer, and early fall months they have more service jobs than they can handle, partly because in their city of 25,000 people there are only two other small repair shops doing similar work. During the winter months, however, they have practically no business, and service jobs are few and far between.

   Mr. Myers has decided to actively seek customers who will have him pick up their mowers in the fall, store them for the winter, and deliver them in the spring ready for the new season. This will give him a chance to spread the work over the winter months and will help alleviate the rush and piled-up work during the spring. Accordingly he has set up the following price list for services:

Reel-type hand mowers	$ 5.00
Reel-type silent hand mowers	6.00
Rotary-type mowers	8.50
Riding mowers—3 to 5 hp.	15.00
Tractors with mower attachment–6 to 12 hp.	22.00
Power reels:	
18 to 22 inches	12.50
23 to 25 inches	15.00
26 to 30 inches	22.00

   He plans to steam-clean mowers, install new electrical contact points if needed, clean and adjust the carburetor and controls, change the oil, remove and clean the blower housing and cooling fins, and sharpen the blade or reel. Services are guaranteed. He has been in business for over twenty years.

   Write a letter that he can mail out to his customers to get them to take advantage of his "winter servicing and storage." To simplify the customer's action, you might also want to prepare a reply card.

9. As personnel research analyst in your company, you are presently developing a training program to help implement some newly developed policies for motivating employees. Your firm engaged a management consultant firm to conduct an employee attitude survey; conclusions indicated that contrary to management's expectations, pay and physical working conditions were not the prime motivations of employee performance. Pride in the company and the job, pride in self, and the opportunity for self-development appeared to be more important. You have just read "What Do You Mean I Can't Write?" by John Fielden (*Harvard Business Review*, May–June 1964, pp. 144–57). Write a memorandum to your manager suggesting that the thoughts contained in the article be made a part of your training program. Mention the key areas described in Mr. Fielden's approach and some details concerning each.

Why does he propose this system? What test does he recommend that you apply in appraising your persuasiveness?

10. As manager of the First Savings Bank, your city, you sit down at your desk this morning and begin to handle the day's correspondence. Here is the first letter you read:

Dear Mr. Transtappan:

Something is wrong at your bank. I was notified today by the State Federal Loan Association, who holds the mortgage on my new home, that the check I sent them last week for the monthly house payment of $252, including taxes and insurance, was no good at your bank--that you had turned it down.

My husband and I have kept money in your bank ever since we moved here five years ago, and we now have on deposit in our joint checking account $1,210.89.

You are giving us a bad reputation, and the mortgage company thinks I write rubber checks. If you don't do something about this, I'll withdraw our savings.

Sincerely yours,

Mrs. John R. Carsons

You check and find that Mr. and Mrs. John R. Carsons have a checking account balance of $1,210.89 and a savings account balance of $3,510.50. You check with a few of the tellers about Mrs. Carsons. They recognize the name and tell you that they remember the couple. In further conversation it comes out that Mrs. Carsons' card gives "Mrs. John R. Carsons" for her signature, but the check to State Federal had been signed "Sharon Lee Carsons."

You decide to write two letters, one to Mrs. Carsons and the other to State Federal Loan Association.

11. The Courtesy Chevrolet Center, Dayton, Ohio, apparently has a twofold problem—selling used cars and writing letters to get results. This is apparent from the following form letter:

Dear Mr. Hernandez:

We call to your attention a special value in which you may be interested.

Because our new cars are being so well accepted, we have been taking in a large number of good used cars in trade. I would like to suggest at this time that you take advantage of the convenience and flexibility enjoyed by so many Two Car Families and give your family a good second car or perhaps replace a second car which you already own.

Right now I have several fine values to offer you in a wide variety of makes and models. Some are exceptional and the early shopper will enjoy a wider selection.

Very truly yours,

How would you rewrite this?

PUNCTUATION REVIEW TEST

At this point it would be well to check up on your ability to use punctuation appropriately. The following exercise is given to be used at your instructor's direction—for review, diagnosis, or study. You can also test yourself, checking your answers by using Appendix C of this text as a guide. Put in correct punctuation marks, and change those that are incorrect. Good luck!

1. In typing a report use a good quality white bond paper that will take neat erasures and will stand handling
2. It was really simple John was not 15 would not be until late October consequently he could not take Driver's Education this summer.
3. You have maintained a monthly balance of 400 in your checking account this past year?
4. To indicate the possessive case of nouns plural nouns which do not end in *"s"* and indefinite pronouns add the apostrophe to the *"s."*
5. The apostrophe is used to indicate omissions in contracted words as in cant class of 67 and o clock
6. Its also used to form plurals of letters, figures and words as in three As he made 2s ifs etc
7. We will have to consider a half dozen advertising media before making a final decision perhaps direct mail or an announcement in the employee magazine or over the loud speaker or even a stuffing in the pay envelopes.
8. The production on the automobile parts however has been slowed down during the period of the threatened strike
9. To make the most of the situation the director of personnel called a meeting of all production foremen
10. Although it was difficult to maintain perfect order he did a creditable job under the circumstances
11. Did you notice particularly how he handled the obstinate foreman from the welding crew.
12. Delivery date for the carburetors spark plugs and writing connections has to be set back three weeks
13. We are happy Mrs Jones to send your refund check for $10.50
14. Johns letter which he wrote about the delay in shipment went off this morning.
15. The work plan he submitted however for his report wasnt done until 4 o clock this afternoon.
16. This is your problem Susan and only you can make the final decision.

17. For the party we will need to buy lets see what shall we need.
18. There are two uses for the colon after an introductory word phrase or statement calling attention to what follows and to separate two main clauses when the second explains or amplifies the first.
19. Mr. Henri Beauregard who is director of public relations at La Touriste Travel Bureau is a personal friend of mine. The tours he plans moreover are usually inexpensive yet inclusive?
20. Mr. Simon Kurachi who read his report very enthusiastically stirred up a lot of challenging ideas in the group!
21. Although the presiding chairman refrained from expressing an opposing point of view he did not agree with all that Mr. Kurachi said nor did he agree with the groups conclusion at the end of the meeting.
22. Are those up to the minute data.
23. To set off a quotation within a quotation use single quotation marks?
24. The price of the hosiery normally is 1.98 but they are on sale this week three pairs for 5.00.
25. Always avoid breaking ideas into short choppy sentences which will give a childish effect.
26. The governor elect hoped to be nominated as a favorite son in the next presidential election.
27. Bill bragged that he was a self educated man and had played football on the all American football team in 1968.
28. It was hard to believe but he had accomplished all this in a span of twelve years.
29. Keep related parts of a sentence together avoid dangling modifiers and use parallel sentence structure.
30. He read the advertisement for a job opening in the Detroit News June 10 but decided not to apply for the job because he was uninterested in traveling.
31. For the wedding she wore a light greenish blue dress and a white hat.
32. He was unable to get reservations for his secretary had not requested them in time.
33. The secretarys typing of the correspondence made a hit with her boss.
34. Bulletins since they generally follow a similar format are numbered in the same way as the memorandum report.
35. Mr. Smiths chances for making the meeting on time were nil for the traffic was far too heavy to make up lost time.

SPELLING RULES EXERCISE

You can't learn to spell by learning spelling rules, but often it helps. Review the standard rules presented here and fill in the blanks to help fix the words correctly in your mind.

1. Words ending in *l* do not drop the *l* before *ly*:
   especially

2. Words ending in a consonant and *y* change the *y* to *i* and add *es* to form the plural:
   city, cities

3. In combination of *i* and *e*, the *i* precedes the *e* except after *c*:
   believe
   deceive

   The exceptions are:
   either
   leisure

4. Verbs ending in *ie* change *ie* to *y* before adding *ing*:
   lie, lying

5. Words ending in *s, ch, sh, z,* or *x* generally form their plurals by adding *es*:
   couch, couches

6. Singular words ending in *o* preceded by a consonant generally form their plurals by adding *es*:
   echo, echoes

   The exceptions are:
   pianos

7. A few nouns ending in *f* or *fe* change the *f* to *v* and add *s* or *es* to form the plural:

   knife, knives

   self, selves

8. Compounds usually add the plural to the most important word:

   brothers-in-law

9. Words ending in a silent *e* usually drop the *e* before a suffix beginning with a vowel:

   arise, arising

   write, writing

10. A prefix or a suffix and a main word are generally written as one word:

    antedate

    postgraduate

11. Words ending in *y* preceded by a consonant change *y* to *i* before suffixes that do not begin with *i*:

    certify, certified

    reply, replied

12. A monosyllable or a word accented on the last syllable, when ending in a consonant preceded by a single vowel, doubles the consonant before a suffix beginning with a vowel:

    allot, allotted

    transfer, transferred

13. Some compound words vary their spelling according to their use in the sentence:

    Altogether unwilling to study, he wasted time.

    He gathered his office supplies *all together.*

Chapter Five

WRITING INTERESTINGLY AND THINKING CREATIVELY

By now you should have made great progress in developing your ability to think and write effectively, especially in sizing up a situation, planning and organizing, and expressing yourself well enough to be understood. Being understood, however, is not sufficient in the total communication process, for to accomplish its purpose of getting action, a message must interest and persuade. Thinking creatively plays its role here by enabling the writer not only to generate new and original ideas, but also to use his imagination in looking ahead, in considering the other person's interests and point of view, in evaluating alternatives to choose the best one, in arriving at decisions, and in finding newer and better means of expression. The purposes of this chapter and the next one are to help you understand the nature of creative thinking and to develop your ability to apply its principles to writing interestingly and persuasively.

THE NATURE OF CREATIVITY

Years ago, Thomas A. Edison made the statement, "There's a way to do it better—find it." With directness and clarity, Mr. Edison expressed the very essence of progress. Behind his inventions were years of intensive research and creative thinking. And in the spirit of the great inventor, today many thousands of companies around the world carry on a constant search for better products, for methods of product improvement, and for ways to convey their messages to the public.

Creative thinking implies the use of ingenuity to produce unusual solutions to the ordinary, everyday problems that confront us. It operates in research, decision making, problem solving, and communication. It is the ability not only to generate new ideas, but also to plan and look ahead. It is the power to visualize and understand. It is the constant search for a better way.

The pictures shown below are of several enterprising young men and their business endeavors. These boys put their minds to work and came up not only with new and original ideas, but also with unique and clever ways of expressing them. And they had the vision and foresight to follow through! Businesses are always looking for this kind of power, and people who have it are much in demand; American business has expanded as a result of the individual's ability to create ideas.

The young men's placards also result in interest and motivation for the reader. The boys put themselves in the other person's position and set aside their personal feelings and reactions by giving every consideration to the other person. This is often overlooked in discussions of cre-

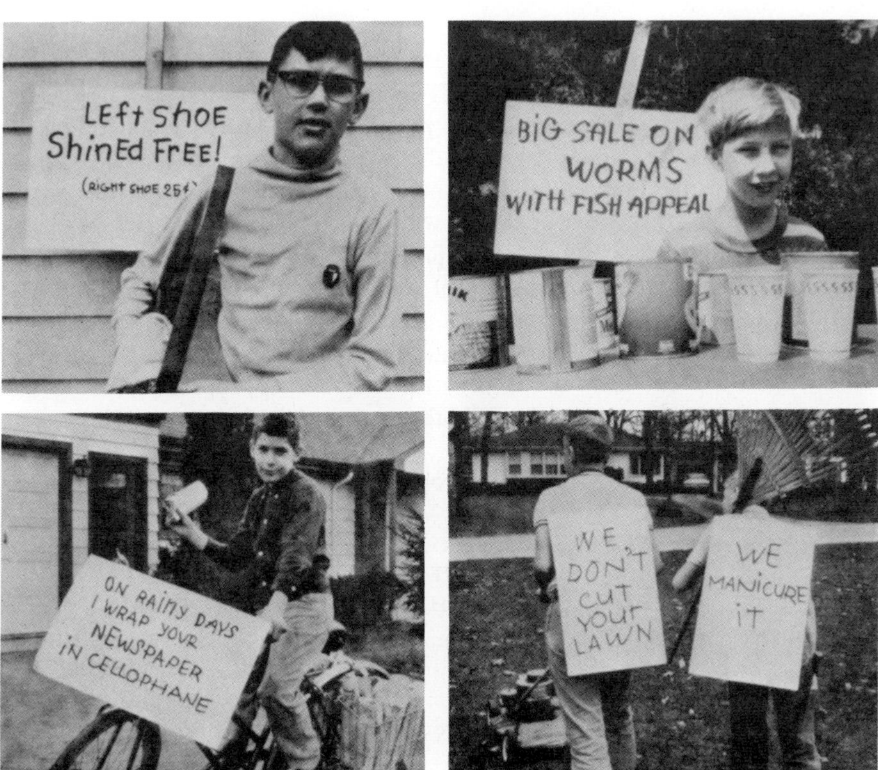

Courtesy Leo Burnett Co., Inc., Advertising, Chicago, Ill. From *Printers' Ink*, July 1965

ative thinking, but it is certainly vital and requires foresight, vision, and imagination.

CONSIDERING THE OTHER PERSON

Showing every consideration for the other person involves a four-point program, which is especially important in writing letters that will interest and persuade the reader:

1. Empathize—identify with the reader to understand him better and to write from his point of view.
2. Personalize—use the personal approach to direct the letter's message from one personality to another.
3. Adapt—satisfy a need, desire, or feeling of the reader.
4. Reflect—convey a personality and attitude that are pleasing to the reader.

Empathize

Empathy is the projection of one's personality into that of another in order to understand him better. By identifying with the other person you are able to see his point of view and understand his needs, desires, and feelings. You can apply your imagination to visualize how he will react to what you are saying and how you are saying it.

Simply using *you* before *I* in an opening sentence forces the writer to remember that he is dealing with someone other than himself. It does not, however, always do the job, and using *you* too many times results in insincerity, arousing doubt that the communicator has the best interests of his audience at heart. But showing a personal interest in *you,* indicating a benefit to *you,* recognizing the importance of *you,* taking the point of view of *you,* are ways of appropriately using empathy. Remember that it's the other person that counts and be concerned with what is good for him.

Note the following advertising copy that appeared in *Time* magazine:[1]

> A BETTER LIFE FOR YOU
> BEGINS WITH THE GUARANTEED BENEFITS
> YOU GET IN THIS "BETTERLIFE" POLICY
>
> The great thing about life insurance is its ability to take a load off your shoulders for years to come. Just how well your life insurance does this depends on the guarantees of your policy contract. Those benefits should be numerous enough and generous enough to cope with the many unpredictable situations in your future or your family's future.

[1] *Time,* September 21, 1959, pp. 42–43. Reprinted by permission of New England Mutual Life Insurance Company.

It is important, then, to know what you are getting when you buy life insurance. We raise these questions to give you an idea of what is involved.

How generous are the provisions if you want to change your policy from an "ordinary" life to a retirement plan, or vice versa?
Will you have . . .

Is the company currently paying a lot more than the guaranteed interest rate on funds left on deposit?
If you . . .

Will payment for coverage beyond the month of death be refunded?
Will the . . .

Here the New England Mutual Life Insurance Company is concerned with the reader's welfare. Because the company emphasizes the benefits to the reader and writes from his point of view, he becomes interested in the copy.

Examine the following letter. Does it show empathy with the reader? Does it interest you in a Chevrolet at this time? You will probably answer "no" to both questions. Why?

Dear Customer:

It's that time of year again! The last of the beautiful 19-- Chevrolets has been built, our final shipment has arrived, and our inventory has never been better.

Specifically, we have 221 new passenger cars and 50 new trucks in stock and ready for delivery right now. This total of 271 units assures you the widest possible selection of models and colors of the entire model year. Add to this our year-end rock-bottom prices and the result is the bonanza of bargains you have been waiting for.

You already know from newspaper and radio announcements that our close-out sale of this vast stock of new cars and trucks begins on Thursday, August 26. But on Wednesday, August 25, we're closing our doors to the general public early, and you, as one of our preferred customers, are cordially invited to visit our air-conditioned showroom between 7:00 and 10:00 P.M. for a special pre-sale offering of all these fine new cars and trucks while our stock is still at its peak. No gimmicks or give-aways -- just rock-bottom deals and refreshments!

So do plan to be with us on Wednesday evening, August 25, between 7:00 and 10:00. Bring the family. See you then.

Cordially,

Now examine the letter from *Today's Secretary* on pages 150–51. Your answer to the same two questions here should be "yes." It does have empathy with the reader, and it interests him in both a subscription and the free *20,000 Words.*

Involvement of the reader is the technique used in the letter from *Today's Secretary.* Empathy is developed. The reader participates in what is being said; she is caught up in it and moves happily along with it, for it contains action and ideas common to her experience

TODAY'S SECRETARY

THE MAGAZINE FOR SUCCESSFUL SECRETARIES

A Gregg-McGraw-Hill Publication • 330 West 42d Street, New York, N. Y. 10036

i before e
e before i
~~fullfil~~
fulfil

book-keep-ing

inacessible?
inacessable?

Dear Secretary:

Does this ever happen to you?

> It's 4:45 p.m., and all of a sudden the boss comes dashing out of his office and hands you a very RUSH! RUSH! letter.
>
> "Must be out by five tonight!"
>
> You start typing when suddenly a teaser word (we all have trouble spelling) like "bookkeeping," or "inaccessible," or "fulfill" bogs you down smack in the middle of a letter.
>
> What to do? Hunt for the dictionary (it's probably at the other end of the office) to look up the word, while precious minutes fly by, or take a chance on trying to spell an important word right--or wrong?

It happened to me--many times! That was before I heard about "20,000 WORDS." Now, no misspelling. No time lost. Letter and secretary out by five.

What's "20,000 WORDS"? A handy, good-to-have-by-your-typewriter, pocket-size dictionary that gives the correct spelling of the most commonly misspelled words--the tricky ones that give all of us trouble.

And, if you check and mail the enclosed postage-free reply card today, you will receive your copy of "20,000 WORDS" (as I did) as part of a marvelous, money-saving introductory subscription offer from TODAY'S SECRETARY. It brings you the next

> 10 issues plus "20,000 WORDS" for $5,
> a $6.46 value
>
> or,
>
> 20 issues plus "20,000 WORDS" for $7,
> a $9.96 value

* * *

TODAY'S SECRETARY is the one monthly magazine published specifically for you.

(over, please)

Every issue is a happy blend of features, facts and special articles geared to help you in your day-to-day work.

What does TODAY'S SECRETARY talk about?

It talks about <u>YOU</u>! Your attitude about your job--your boss--the company--the other girls--even yourself. It helps you to sharpen your skills: steno, typing, vocabulary, spelling. It discusses the human side of the job and gives you tips that will make your job much more enjoyable.

It talks about the <u>BOSS</u>! His attitude toward you--his likes and dislikes (how he takes his coffee)--work habits. It tells you how to judge his moods--how to judge office atmosphere.

It talks about the <u>JOB</u>! Your responsibility--interest--office routine--job security. It tells you how to prepare yourself for a particular situation (promotion, demotion, reassignment). Most important, it tells you what to do to keep your job secure.

It talks about <u>FASHION</u>! Yes, fashion! How you look is almost as important as how your letters look. Every issue has its own fashion section that gives you the very latest styles for office, cocktails, dinner, and dating.

In short, TODAY'S SECRETARY talks about everything and anything important enough to help you enjoy your job while climbing the secretarial ladder.

* * *

So take a tip from one secretary who knows. Don't let those trouble words keep you after five again. Subscribe to TODAY'S SECRETARY...today!

You'll receive your copy of "20,000 WORDS," which will be mailed to you immediately, plus...

<u>10 issues of TODAY'S SECRETARY for $5</u>

Or, if you prefer...20 issues for $7

Just check and mail the postage-free reply card today while this marvelous, money-saving offer is in effect. You'll be glad you did.

Cordially,

Sue Daniels

Sue Daniels,
Secretary to E. W. Edwards
Publisher, TODAY'S SECRETARY

SD
Enc.

P.S. If you decide to enclose payment with your order, we'll extend your subscription with one additional issue of TODAY'S SECRETARY, free.

(which she relives). The latter half of the letter also is written from the reader's point of view, stressing the benefits that apply to her.

Does the following opening of a sales promotion letter interest you men in Calumet Lodge? or in reading further into the letter?

> The wonderful smell
> of fish frying slowly
> over an open fire,
>
> the excitement of that "big one" on the end of your line, or just that fresh, cool air coming to you gently through the Northern pines are just a few of the reasons Calumet Lodge on Lake Linden in Upper Michigan is the vacation spot you've been looking for.

Does the following opening of another sales promotion letter interest you ladies in the Touch of Glamour?

> Dear Miss Danbury:
>
> "What is so rare as a day in June?" A day in July—the 24th, to be exact—on which Touch of Glamour, in the Vieux Carré, opens its doors to welcome you to a wonderful new world of inexpensive high fashion.

An advertisement for new prepared cake mixes also used the involvement approach:

> Put on your hat
> Grab your purse
> Rush to your nearest grocer
> Set before your family tonight . . .
> They will delight in . . .

The owner of a fishing lodge sent prospects a circular letter that said in part:

> You are sitting in the boat.
> There's a tug on your line, and you
> hasten to pull . . .

A businessman giving a speech opened with:

> Take a piece of paper and pencil.
> Jot down the first ten . . .

The reader and listener in these instances were put into the picture, and because they were involved, they became interested.

Personalize

Another way of showing consideration for the other person is through personalization. The informal, friendly salutation, such as *Dear Mr. Johnson, Dear Fred,* or *Dear Friend,* and the corresponding informal complimentary close such as *Sincerely, Cordially, Faithfully,* or others of the same tone, denote a form of personalization used in business letters. Omitting the salutation and incorporating the recipient's name in the first sentence, as well as repeating his name in the body of the letter, are personal gestures. Using his name in the address, instead of addressing the envelope and letter to the company or to the titled position the man holds, also helps achieve a personal effect. Even individual signing of the letters of a mass mailing adds a personal touch. Don't you, for instance, have a friendlier feeling for the person who signs his Christmas cards himself than for one who uses a printed signature? Adding a handwritten postscript to a typed letter also gives a personal touch. But these are somewhat mechanical, routine ways of achieving a personal effect.

True personalization entails taking a personal interest in the other fellow and having him feel it. Writing about things, people, and events of interest to the other person indicates the writer's interest in the same things. For example:

1. How about your game of golf?
2. I saw our mutual friend, Fred Smith, yesterday and he . . .
3. When you are in Chicago for your convention, get in touch with me . . .
4. Best wishes for a Merry Christmas.
5. I'm sure Grace also will like the Grecian vase . . .
6. How does your boy like first grade?

You will need to be careful in using the personal pronouns *we* and *I,* for it is very easy to fall into the trap of personalizing without using the "you" attitude to establish empathy with the reader. Note, for instance:

1. We do appreciate your interest in our company and wish we could assist you in compiling your report; however, as we do not have a company correspondence manual, we will not be able to comply with your request.
2. We are pleased to learn that you recently purchased a new Dodge vehicle. We are grateful that you selected one of our products for your transportation needs and are confident that it will provide you with maximum performance, comfort, and dependability.

Neither example shows real concern for the reader. The emphasis on

Newsweek- GREAT MUSEUMS OF THE WORLD

444 MADISON AVENUE, NEW YORK, N.Y. 10022

NOW - you can "visit" the world's great museums -- meet the Director of each one -- and take a guided tour of its treasures.

As your introduction to GREAT MUSEUMS OF THE WORLD -- you may examine Volume 1, LOUVRE-PARIS, for 10 days absolutely without cost or obligation ... and

CHOOSE AS A FREE GIFT a beautiful 21" x 27" masterpiece magnificently reproduced on canvas in full color.

Dear Reader:

Even if a trip to Paris isn't in your immediate plans ...

... you can still enjoy a personally conducted tour through the art-filled halls of The Louvre, the world's richest museum.

Now, The Louvre's great treasures are yours to enjoy for 10 days without cost or obligation when you examine the exquisite 9 3/8" x 11 5/8" full color volume titled, LOUVRE-PARIS.

Your tour starts with an 8 page introduction by M. Jean Chatelain, Director of the Museums of France, and M. René Huyghe of the Académie Française.

For the next 160 pages, you'll thrill to the primitive arts of Ancient Egypt ... the Statues by the great Greek and Roman sculptors ... the

Courtesy *Newsweek* magazine

we prevents the reader from becoming interested, and consequently keeps him from getting the message of helpfulness.

In contrast, examine the first part of a letter from *Newsweek* magazine. *You* personalizes the letter, and the message maintains empathy with the reader, largely because the reader is involved, something is given to him, and he is taken on a visual tour. Thus he can't help but become interested.

Agreeing with the other person in some way also puts the writer on a personal basis.

1. You have every right to expect good service.
2. Yes, Mr. Bronson, your shipment should have been sent immediately.
3. I agree that . . .

Personalization is really a kind of adaptation. It makes the other person feel that the message is for him and not for a group of people, and that he is important to the communicator, who is showing him every consideration.

Adapt

Talking *with* the other person instead of *to* him, writing the other person's language, speaking on his level, economizing his time and effort—all are ways of adjusting what one says to make it pleasing and interesting to the other person.

A letter should be adapted to the receiver. An individual is interested in anything that satisfies a need or desire for him. Psychologists agree that basically most people want health, wealth, power, reputation, love, family, friends, job success, security, food, shelter, and clothing. Buying a Cadillac makes a man feel important. A new Easter hat makes a woman feel young and gay. A new taste sensation from a different combination of foods is pleasing. A ride in a new sports car is thrilling. A deep freezer will save the homemaker money for other things in her food budget. A teenage girl is in love on her first date. Adapting what is said to the needs and desires of the recipient arouses his interest.

Panther Oil Company of Fort Worth, Texas, in its company magazine, tells its salesmen to sell the benefits of Panco lubricants.

> *Tell the customer:*
>
> Here's how Panco products protect your valuable machinery, Mr. Jones. See how easily it is handled? Proper lubrication relieves you of all your worries about maintenance.
>
> *Do not say:*
>
> Our lubricants are made from the finest ingredients known to science. They are the best on the market today.

"Sell the sizzle, not the steak" has long been star salesman Elmer Wheeler's good advice. In other words, sell the *benefits* of the product, not the product itself. A customer buys the benefits of long-lasting protection for his machinery. Selling benefits—adapting what is said to the needs of the other person—creates interest.

Being conversational, writing naturally, not only puts you at ease but also relaxes your reader. Write your own way. Talk about the things you and your reader have in common, people you know, and interests you can share, such as hobbies, sports, jobs, etc. This creates a friendly informality that is conducive to a give-and-take atmosphere. Knowledge of the other person will aid you in adapting your letter's message. The next letter, from an agent for Central Life Assurance Company, is adapted to its reader; it recognizes the situation—graduation from college—and seeks to help the reader.

A great deal of creativity in layout and form went into the letter on page 157, which adapts itself to the reader by talking conversationally about points of common interest.

Dear Mr. Szarek:

This is probably the umpteenth letter you've received from an insurance man and you're going to throw it away.

Before you do that, however, please consider two things.

1. Practically all of my clients have a degree such as you are about to receive and, just like you, many had never heard of me until I called them for the first time.

2. They would not be my friends and clients today if I were not able to give them an idea that was worth money to them.

With this in mind, I plan to get in touch with you in the near future. When I see you, please allow me not more than fifteen minutes to explain the type of work I do. If I can be of no service to you, which we will both know in much less than fifteen minutes, we may then go our own separate ways.

Sincerely,

Reflect

Suppose that, as manager of a retail furniture store, you receive the following letter from a new customer who has just opened a charge account:

Dear Sirs:

Unless you send out your appraiser and pick up the baby bed which was to have been traded in on the new bed and dresser I have purchased for my little girl's room you might as well get the furniture you delivered last week.

Your salesman has really fouled things up. The appraiser was to have come Tuesday of last week, the furniture was to be delivered Wednesday and the baby bed picked up at that time.

Your interior decorator was to have come out Thursday to suggest what I should do about replacing my old living room furniture.

Delivery was made Thursday when I was not home. The new bed was dumped (not set up) in the middle of my living room, the dresser placed in the dining room, and the baby bed stayed in my girl's room. My house is a mess now for the weekend.

Today they brought the linoleum for the family room floor. What about installing it? You were certainly in a hurry for the down payment.

I called the credit office and your service department. They don't answer. They are out for lunch. The linoleum was to have been installed on delivery.

I'm sorry I opened a charge account with you. My money is as good as anyone else's and I expect service. I'll not buy anything else from you.

Truly yours,

(Mrs.) J. R. Samuelson

What do you think of Mrs. J. R. Samuelson? What is your reaction to the letter she has written? She has expressed a very unfavorable attitude toward your store and services and she has not indicated a pleasing personality. The tone of your answer, however, must turn away her wrath, regain her confidence, and restore her as a customer.

Recognizing a person as a human being and showing him sympathy, warmth, and friendliness create harmonious relations. Agreeing with the person will help to turn away his wrath, while answering him in the same angry tone he used with you will only further his anger. Clear and

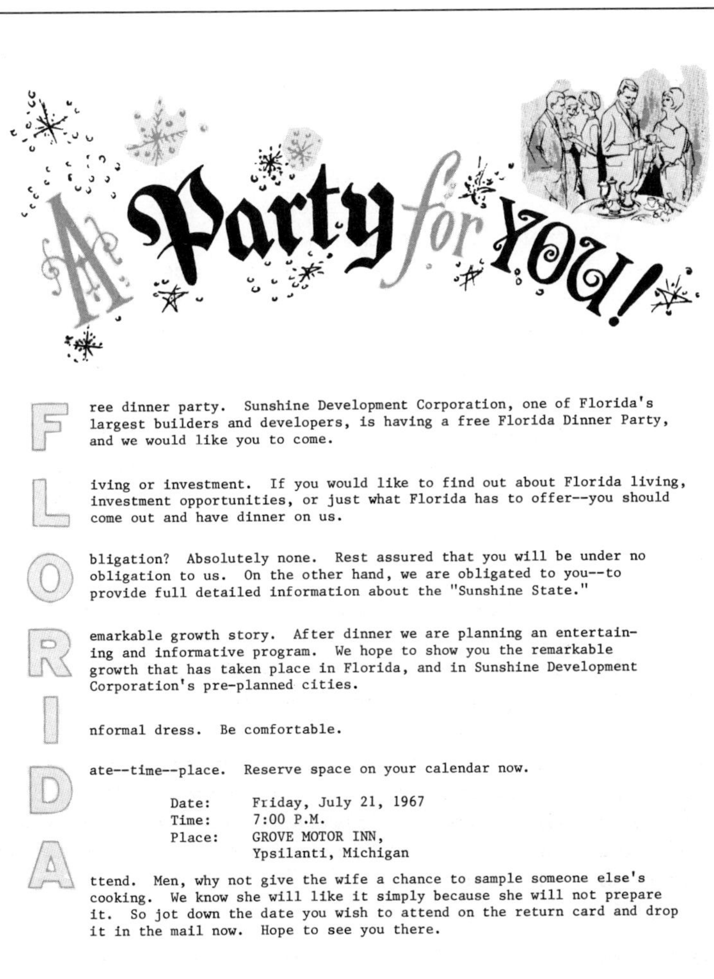

A Party for YOU!

F ree dinner party. Sunshine Development Corporation, one of Florida's largest builders and developers, is having a free Florida Dinner Party, and we would like you to come.

L iving or investment. If you would like to find out about Florida living, investment opportunities, or just what Florida has to offer--you should come out and have dinner on us.

O bligation? Absolutely none. Rest assured that you will be under no obligation to us. On the other hand, we are obligated to you--to provide full detailed information about the "Sunshine State."

R emarkable growth story. After dinner we are planning an entertaining and informative program. We hope to show you the remarkable growth that has taken place in Florida, and in Sunshine Development Corporation's pre-planned cities.

I nformal dress. Be comfortable.

D ate--time--place. Reserve space on your calendar now.

Date: Friday, July 21, 1967
Time: 7:00 P.M.
Place: GROVE MOTOR INN,
Ypsilanti, Michigan

A ttend. Men, why not give the wife a chance to sample someone else's cooking. We know she will like it simply because she will not prepare it. So jot down the date you wish to attend on the return card and drop it in the mail now. Hope to see you there.

Seating Limited
Adult Couples Only
Return Card Enclosed

reasonable explanations and constructive and positive action help him to understand the situation and pacify him.

Be cheerful, enthusiastic, and happy. "Smile and the world smiles with you" may be trite, but it works. Say:

> It is a pleasure to credit your account . . .
> *or*
> We are delighted to open your charge account.
> *or*
> We are happy to send our interior decorator to your house . . .

Let the person know that your attitude toward him is favorable, that you want to help him, that you think well of him and feel kindly toward him.

Sincerity cannot be faked. The communicator must be genuinely interested in the other person and his needs. It is a good idea to say, "I am sorry," if that is true, but not if it isn't meant or if there is nothing to be sorry about. Half-truths and insincere statements are recognized for what they are. The simple, natural unpretentiousness of effective language gives expression to what is felt in the heart and mind.

There are some "don'ts" to follow in transmitting a pleasing personality and a favorable attitude. Don't brag, patronize, or bully, for it will make the other person feel inferior and he will react by establishing his position or withdrawing entirely. Don't argue, question his word, or ridicule him, for he will be on the defensive and will retaliate with antagonism. Don't be gushy or coddle, for he will recognize the hollow ring in the strategy.

■ Which of the two direct mail letters opposite do you think pulled in the most subscriptions? You will probably agree that each one applies the four-point program of showing consideration to the reader: empathy, personalization, adaptation, and reflection. How?

The "analogy on the kangaroo" letter outpulled the "straightforward $2 saving" one by more than 2 to 1. Can you reason why? It all goes to prove that even showing every consideration to the reader can't be effective without the use of the writer's imagination. The kangaroo letter is much more creative that the "$2 saving" appeal by itself. And wasn't it written more interestingly?

Everyone has some natural capacity for creating ideas, a capacity that can be developed. The valuable things to know are how to train the mind in the methods by which ideas are produced and how to grasp the principles that are at the source of ideas.

HIS MOTHER DETERMINES

<u>HIS</u> VIEW OF THE WORLD—

WHAT DETERMINES YOURS?

Each of us must, perforce, rely largely on ready-made news and data in forming our own judgments.

None of us alone has the time or the specialized ability to select the vital facts from the never-ending stream of daily news and misleading half-truths, or to scan the trends that produce a complete picture of national and international events in politics, science, and the arts.

> But—unlike young Master Kangaroo—you <u>can</u> assure yourself of <u>all</u> the <u>significant</u> facts and new ideas for interpretation.

You <u>can</u> secure, in THE REPORTER, a new kind of journal-

an analogy on the kangaroo . . .

Courtesy *Printers' Ink*

Courtesy *Printers' Ink*

THE REPORTER

136 EAST 57th STREET
NEW YORK 22, N. Y.
Murray Hill 8-4033

PUT $2 BACK IN YOUR POCKET!

NOW — by accepting this special offer — you can give yourself two valuable presents: first, you get the next 18 issues — 9 full months — of THE REPORTER, America's most challenging magazine of news and comment on national affairs, world events, and the arts; and second, <u>you save</u> more than <u>41% under</u> the regular newsstand price!

Simply airmail the enclosed postfree card to me today, and you can be sure of not missing a single exciting issue in the next 9 crucial months — and you get TWO EXTRA FREE ISSUES for sending a check with the order, <u>so you put more than $2 savings back in your own pocket</u>!

> For less than 15¢ per issue — less than the cost of transit fare in most cities — you join such distinguished REPORTER readers as Senator Ralph Flanders and Adlai Stevenson, industrialists Paul G. Hoffman and James Zellerbach, artists and writers like Ethel Barrymore and André Malraux, and 110,000 others.

The enclosed reservation card assures you of some of the most provocative, entertaining, and authoritative material published today; exposures of vital facts hitherto kept carefully out of the limelight (such as THE REPORTER'S famous series on the China Lobby; or its

straightforward $2 saving?

AIDS TO CREATING IDEAS

Environment

Management can aid individual workers by providing an environment conducive to creating ideas. Creative people have to be free of conflict, management pressures, and anything else that gets in their way. They need to work in a friendly atmosphere and have the freedom to think and talk. For the stimulation of ideas they must be able to exchange ideas among men of a variety of experiences across all levels. There should be a free flow of communication that allows each one to contribute his best effort. Management can encourage cross-fertilization of ideas, new points of view, and creative approaches to problem solving.

Creative people are usually warm and sensitive and cannot work in a cold climate where there is no acknowledgment that they are doing well. They need recognition and the feeling of being accepted. Sometimes appreciation is more important than a raise. A we're-all-in-this-together climate that starts with management and goes through every part of the firm helps bring out creative effort in people. Being a part of the scene is also very important. To be involved in the issues and to know that people depend on his skills help the creative person to solve problems, and he is much happier for this involvement.

For example, given free rein and with no ideas barred, the packaging team of the Warren Featherbone Co., Atlanta, Georgia, came up with a very successful package loaded with sales appeal.[2] The company makes the Warren and Alexis lines of infant wear. Its best sellers are plastic pants and plastic-lined nylon pants for youngsters in diapers. Kleinert, Cutler, and Warren compete for top sales leadership in a market of more than $50,000,000 a year. A few years ago Warren's packaging was merely a container; it performed no selling function, which was hardly in line with the decline of personal selling and the increase in display and self-service found in the nation's retail outlets. Recognizing the need for new packaging, the company president and the general manager called in the packaging team and virtually said, "Give us what we need, not what you think we need." The team was free to tap its talents and came up with a functional package that was also lovely to look at and that had tremendous sales appeal.

The advertising director thought a box for infant wear should portray elements of tenderness, sweetness, and affection. Also on the team with her were a package designer and a free-lance artist. The three together outlined their objectives:

1. The package would be distinctive and bright for attracting attention. It would aim at impulse sales.

[2]"Creative Freedom Puts Sell in a Package," *Printers' Ink*, January 30, 1959, pp. 103–4.

2. It would appeal to the sentimental interests of people who buy baby products.
3. It would be appropriate to buy as a gift.
4. It would suggest freshness and cleanliness, two qualities of special importance to infant wear.

The box for Alexis plastic-lined Handi-Pantis illustrates how these objectives were achieved. The background is vivid yellow. A delicate illustration includes bluebirds and daisies, symbols of happiness and freshness. Peeking through an acetate window are line drawings of a boy in the package for boys' pants and a girl in the package for girls' pants. Size and price are printed on a pressure-sensitive label, easily removed for sale as a gift. A gift card is included with each package. The program proved a success—given the freedom to use its creative abilities to the fullest, the group produced a distinctive package to sell to retailers.

Management can do much to provide an atmosphere for creative people, but creative people are individuals and as such should exercise their individual creative talents. They also can do much toward providing an environment conducive to creating ideas. Objectives can be set, since having a goal or purpose gives some aim and direction for thinking. Time must be allotted for mulling over things, exploring in all directions, and even daydreaming. Training yourself to see different points of view, being exposed to a wide range of knowledge and to the experiences of others, keeping an open mind, being on the lookout for ideas, and listening to the other person all help to formulate a frame of mind conducive to creating ideas. An overt, outreaching personality, broad general knowledge, and varied experience all provide a storehouse from which to draw new combinations and ideas. Working in a creative climate brings a concomitant responsibility to create ideas and to take advantage of creative opportunities. Let yourself relax and daydream, exchange ideas, keep informed, and develop an awareness of what is going on about you. People who keep looking outside themselves keep on getting fresh ideas.

Association

In a creative climate, laws of association have free play; the individual with a frame of mind conducive to creating ideas is able to think creatively. A person's mind is a storehouse of all he has learned, felt, and experienced. The three laws of association—contiguity, similarity, and contrast—enable the imagination to move from one idea to another by providing points of relationship for new combinations and thus for new ideas. A man reads an article in a magazine on how to make a garden grow; he associates the facts with the wonderful garden he remembers his neighbor had last year, then with the wonderful garden he himself would like to have. What does he do? He buys equipment, seeds, etc., and starts making a garden. A teenage girl reads what to do to make a party tick. She associates these ideas with past experience and decides what she will do for her next party. These ideas lead to action. The ideas both these people have are the result of the law of contiguity at work in their minds. Contiguity means nearness. One idea follows another because it comes next to it. You might ask for the bread to be passed and then associate butter with it and ask that it too be passed. The two go together. Ideas also come as a result of their similarity to one another. You might be thinking of writing a letter to your mother and then think of writing your sister, for the two are alike or similar. If you also think of writing your father or brother, it is because the law of contrast (*father* contrasts with *mother*) produces the idea.

The use of questions stimulates association of ideas. Asking yourself questions like the following ones will help the laws of association work for you:

Contiguity:	*Similarity:*	*Contrast:*
What is this next to?	What is this like?	What is this smaller or larger than?
What does this go with?	What has this in common with that?	What is this different from?
What happens before or after this?	What is this the same as?	What is this unlike?
What is this a part of?	Are the parts similar?	What is its opposite?

Association also works through the senses—sound, smell, taste, touch, and sight. Therefore, asking how it looks and sounds will cause you to associate the "sense" of a thing and thus generate further ideas.

Analysis and Synthesis

Another aid to creating ideas is analysis, which is the breaking down of a whole into its parts. A division of thoughts results in separate ideas that may be studied individually or in relation to each other and to the whole. Interrelationships lead to new ideas. The analysis of each idea serves as a clue to another idea and thus increases the number of ideas. Parts are also studied for their possible cause-and-effect relationships. Analysis is used for clarifying thinking. The process of breaking something down helps to give a fuller understanding than would be possible otherwise. It pinpoints specific areas for further examination. Because it involves thinking from the general or whole to the specific or parts, it is a type of deductive reasoning.

In examining relationships it is often helpful to ask questions that begin with *how, why, when,* or *where.* Analysis also helps to establish a pattern, the common elements of a relationship, or a trend. In this respect it becomes helpful in formulating conclusions and involves the exercise of judgment.

Analysis works hand in hand with synthesis. Each function complements the other. Analysis breaks down; synthesis puts together. Analyzing several ideas for their relationships provides a basis for putting them together to form new combinations or a related whole. Synthesis thus helps to give a fuller understanding than would otherwise be forthcoming. It involves thinking from the specific to the general and in that respect is a type of inductive reasoning. Finding through analysis a common element, pattern, or trend from a number of specific instances or details provides the basis for synthesis. This is the inductive process for reaching a conclusion. Like analysis, synthesis involves the exercise of judgment. Analysis gives meaning to the parts and synthesis gives meaning to the whole.

Freewheeling

Sometimes synthesis does not immediately follow analysis. Instead, there must first be a period of freewheeling and concentration. Freewheeling is letting oneself go. It can be used at several stages in the creative process. One might freewheel before analyzing or after, before synthesizing or after. There are times when pausing to think, to mull over facts, to daydream, and so on, will produce ideas more quickly and easily than trying to concentrate on a few points in a limited time. In freewheeling for ideas, there are no set limits; the mind is kept open to explore in every direction.

Note the differences in the two following diagrams, each starting with "you" in the center:

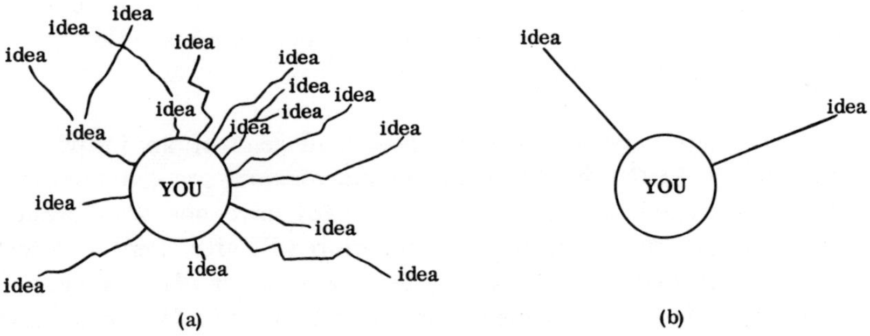

(a) (b)

In *a,* the mind explores all the possibilities it can. It goes in all directions. This is freewheeling. In *b,* the mind explores only two possibilities, and limits itself to fewer ideas as a result; the process is neater but also more barren. Freewheeling opens up new paths and numerous ideas that may lead you to a valid conclusion, a better solution to a problem, or an original thought and broader perspective than you might have reached otherwise.

After freewheeling you should stop and take stock of your ideas. Analysis may be helpful in providing relationships, and a synthesis of your ideas should follow. Between analysis and synthesis, however, concentration usually helps.

Concentration

Concentration is focusing on a particular fact, idea, or problem and solution. It calls for blocking out distractions and working intensely. Keeping one job clearly in mind and forgetting all others, finding a goal and doing everything to reach it, keeping certain ideas in mind and blocking out others, thinking about a selected number of pertinent facts and eliminating irrelevant, insignificant ones—these are ways of concentrating. Interest is a great aid to concentration, for finding relations between new materials and old interests focuses attention on the new materials. Keeping informed by reading widely makes material interesting and concentration easier. Sometimes taking notes or setting a deadline or quota of work to be done or ideas to be produced will help you to concentrate.

Incubation and Illumination

Concentration might be followed by freewheeling (further thinking in all directions to find more ideas) or by a period of *incubation.* When labor over a problem hasn't produced a satisfactory solution, there is a risk of frustration. The best thing to do is to get away from the problem, allowing the mind to let up. When concentration has produced a number of possible solutions, the subconscious mind should have a chance. Incubation is commonly referred to as "sleeping on the problem."

The conscious mind contains only a small part of an individual's mental powers. In the memory and the subconscious are countless multitudes of ideas and associations that perhaps have not been brought into use on a particular problem. Incubation will give them a chance.

In actual practice, incubation may be just a matter of breaking away from work, taking a coffee break, or going to lunch. The break gives the subconscious a chance to work on a problem on which you were previously concentrating. Doing routine tasks like washing and drying dishes or mowing the lawn gives the mind a chance to mull over ideas. Like freewheeling, incubation opens up new paths, new vision, a wide

perspective, and new ideas. Time, freedom, relaxation, a change of pace, a different task, some form of recreation or hobby—all play a part in incubation.

The hen's incubation period ends with the hatching of the eggs on which she has been sitting. For an individual a new idea, the answer to a question, or the solution to a problem might be hatched. The hatching-out process is commonly referred to as *illumination*. You see the light, you grasp the issue, you have the answer. It might be a new invention, the solution to a problem, or an advertising idea for promoting the sale of sugar. Although illumination naturally follows a period of incubation, it can occur anytime or anyplace. The lighting up might take place during concentration, analyzing, freewheeling, or the application of any of the other aids to creating ideas.

- ■ Think of ways in which the aids to creating ideas presented here can help you to be a creative letter writer.
- ■ Create opening paragraphs for direct mail promotional letters in each of the following situations. Consider your reader's interest, and be creative in what you say and how you express it.
  1. A new restaurant is opening on your campus and is seeking to do predominantly a lunch-hour business among students, faculty, and staff.
  2. You are the owner–manager of a men's (or ladies') clothing store in your campus business area and have been doing a successful volume of business among the students for over twenty-five years. You have decided to try a new approach this year by writing to graduating high school seniors in the spring or summer to attract them to your store in the fall.

DEVELOPING CREATIVE ABILITY

Understanding and using the aids to creating ideas whenever an opportunity arises will help to develop creative ability. *Increasing your sensitivity to problems and developing originality will also help to develop creative ability.* To recognize that a problem exists, to be able to see through obscure facts, misunderstandings, and misconceptions and recognize the real problem is to demonstrate a sensitivity to problems. Keeping in mind that there is nothing in existence that cannot be improved upon will help one to be sensitive to current problems and to find new ones. Every product on the market today, every business operation, every communication technique can be changed for the better. Being aware that problems exist and being willing to accept changes will increase creativity. A curiosity for discovery and learning will increase creative effort and output. Forming the habit of piling up a quantity of ideas and giving consideration to several solutions before making a decision can also be a challenge to creativity. A man is as big as his ability to think. A boy daydreams. His thoughts are far in the future. Thinking, dreaming, his mind sees more than his eyes do. Vision, looking beyond the commonplace, results in innovations. Then growth and development follow where the mind has marked the way. So it is in business today.

Originality can be used by the problem solver in varying degrees. In most day-to-day business problems great originality is not demanded or needed. Consideration must be given to the facts in the situation, and often an already accepted practice may be an adequate solution. Yet the difference between a good business executive and an ordinary one is often the ability to produce original ideas. Originality might be expressed in finding new ways to vary existing practices, devising new ways to adapt existing ideas to new conditions, or seeking to improve whatever is at hand.

One key to developing this type of originality is the systematic use of questions. Creative people are filled with curiosity. They constantly ask themselves and others such questions as, "Why is this made this way?" "Why do we follow this procedure?" and "How can this be improved?" They are constantly challenging what is and seeking to change it. The questioning approach is a habit that can be formed. However, it must be followed by a search for answers. Otherwise it might result only in faultfinding, and no positive, creative thinking will come out of it. Asking a creative question calls for finding a creative answer, whether the problem is to invent something or to design a product, package, or advertisement. The creative approach is to inquire and then to find the answer. The purpose of using questions is to stimulate the search for the answers.

Originality might consist of applying a principle, process, or practice that has never been applied before to a particular area. Looking for new applications of former practices or ideas, reading widely for new ideas, or drawing on all mental and emotional resources will open new doors.

Many changes and new ideas come about through new combinations.

Borrowing an idea and adapting it to a new use makes it different. Ideas change by adaptation and modification. Change the size, shape, or color of an object and it will be altered from what it was originally. Paint the walls of a white room dark green and the room takes on a new and different appearance. Rearranging a pattern—reversing certain elements, turning them around, trying an opposite pattern, producing a different effect, or combining like or unlike elements into a new composite—will also change an idea. Alex Osborn suggests using a checklist for stimulating creative thinking.[3] His list consists of questions that will invoke new ideas in their answers. Each person can make up a list to serve his own needs. Suggestive questions to include might be:

1. How can I change this?
2. How can I improve this?
3. What alternative do I have?
4. What can I add?
5. What can I combine?

These questions might be used in thinking of ideas to include in a report or letter, ideas for improving a product or existing condition, or better ways of doing things.

Anyone can increase his creative ability and put ideas to work for him. He can make use of the various aids available for creating ideas, such as environment, association, analysis and synthesis, freewheeling and concentration, incubation and illumination. He can increase his sensitivity problems and develop his originality. The vision, the foresight, and the creative imagination that result in newer methods, better products, and better living can be his.

■ To increase your ability to create ideas freely, quickly, and in quantity, you might try making a list of uses for various small items usually found about your home, office, or school. Followers of Alex Osborn maintain that when this is done for five to ten minutes each day for a week or more it develops one's creative power. You might check your own progress by counting the number of ideas you think of in a given time.

1. Suggest uses for empty frozen juice cans.
2. Suggest uses for empty milk cartons.
3. Suggest uses for wire coat hangers.
4. Suggest uses for paper clips.
5. Suggest uses for empty typewriter ribbon spools.
6. Suggest uses for 3- by 5-inch file cards.

The more you let yourself go, the more uses you will think up. Also, you will find that the more specific and detailed the uses are, the more you'll think of. A general classification, such as "use as a container," when pursued specifically might disclose as many as fifty uses.

[3]Alex F. Osborn, *Applied Imagination* (New York: Charles Scribner's Sons, 1963).

- Exercising your imagination each day keeps it active and thus increases your ability to think creatively. Making assumptions and foreseeing their results is one way of accomplishing this.
  1. Assume that you have produced a fruit from crossing a blackberry and a cherry. Write a description of the resulting fruit, which would combine the characteristics of the blackberry and cherry. Use your five senses to create ideas through association. How does it feel? taste? smell? sound? look? How can it be used? What reaction would consumers have?
  2. Assume almost any fruit or vegetable combination, such as cucumber and squash, orange and cantaloupe, banana and honeydew melon, lemon and orange, apple and peach, and green beans and peas. What would you call the resulting product? Describe it, and think up uses for it. You might even consider combinations such as apple and onion. "Pomme de tears"?[4]
  3. Assume that starting this instant every infant born in the United States is born with two thumbs on each hand, with the second thumb next to the little finger. What changes would this physical characteristic bring about in the United States or even in the world?
- To increase your ability to see the other person's viewpoint:
  1. Bring to class three cartoons from magazines or newspapers. Write new captions for each. Share them with the class. You'll be surprised at how good the rewritten captions are!
  2. Assume some change in one of your school policies or one of the employee policies where you work. Predict the reactions of the students or employees. Foresee the effect of the change on the group.

BEING IMAGINATIVE IN WRITING LETTERS

Applying creative thinking to messages so that the reader is stimulated to see and feel what is depicted usually sustains his interest in what is being said. The imaginative, creative letter writer is clever, uses techniques for variety and vividness, and exercises foresight by seeing things for himself and determining their effects on people.

Cleverness

The dictionary defines *clever* as possessing quickness of intellect, or being talented or good-natured. Cleverness might be a deft way of handling a situation or problem. It involves speed and originality: acting quickly, tactfully, directly, and subtly, as Abraham Lincoln did in the Lincoln–Douglas debates; acting forcefully and effectively as Doug-

[4]There have been many jokes based on this exercise. On his Cypress Gardens television special in September 1968, Johnny Carson asked what the results would be crossing a banana and an orange. The answer: a great corsage if you're taking a monkey to a prom. In Spring 1968, "Rowan and Martin's Laugh-In" crossed an orange and a cactus. The result: spiked orange juice.

las MacArthur did when he made his resignation speech before Congress and said, "Old soldiers never die, they just fade away"; saying the unusual at the appropriate time; saying the same thing in a new and different way; using touches of humor and figurative language. These are ways of showing cleverness, and originality is the key to its success.

The concluding portion of an article on dieting in *Time* magazine shows originality of expression:

> Where will it all end? Optimists claim that all the dieting is producing a new, slim American who will look as grand as the fashion ads. But there are mutterings that if it keeps up long enough, the Communists will overpower the U.S. without firing a shot. Americans will all get so skinny that the Reds will take over the country merely by sucking up the citizenry with vacuum cleaners.[5]

Trying an original format and layout for advertising copy, creating an original opening to a sales letter, devising a different headline for a news item, using action captions as subject headings in a report, beginning a speech with a humorous incident, and sparking a conversation with clever statements represent opportunities for originality and cleverness.

On the spur of the moment, a customer of Northern Luncheon Napkins decided to count them to satisfy his curiosity that he had received eighty as printed on the box. He found that there were only seventy-eight. Two napkins hardly justified a complaint, but he did take advantage of the occasion to drop the sales manager a short note on his discovery. This is what he wrote:

> I thought you would like
> To know about this right away
> Perhaps the two lost napkins
> Will return to old Green Bay!

To his surprise, he received quite a humorous answer from Dr. F. S. Charlton, the patent agent for Northern Paper Mills, American Can Company, Neenah, Wisconsin:

> We're sorry you got 78
> It seldom happens really
> To make it up please try this pack
> We're sending you quite freely.[6]

Dr. Charlton was clever in answering a packaging complaint with a reply that would amuse the customer instead of one that would further strain the relationship.

[5]*Time*, November 21, 1960, p. 23.

[6]"Letters to the Editor," *Printers' Ink*, April 23, 1965, p. 71.

Variety

Imagination helps inject the element of variety into what is being said and how it is being said. Vary the length of words and sentences. When using predominantly words of three or fewer syllables, vary the text by using some longer words that are within the experience of the audience. When using an average of seventeen words per sentence, vary the sentence length by using some longer and some shorter sentences. The principle of variety in length can also be applied to paragraphs, sections, or other parts of longer works to avoid monotony.

All kinds of sentences should be used for variety—declarative, interrogative, exclamatory, and imperative; simple, compound, and complex. Different arrangements of sentence elements help. Instead of starting with the subject, begin with the verb, a prepositional phrase, an adverb, or some other part. Use a subordinate clause before the independent clause.

Don't begin every letter in the same way. Consider the reader, the circumstances of the situation, and the nature of the message when looking for ways to create different beginnings. Instead of a conventional introduction, use a humorous incident, narrate briefly the situation that gave rise to the problem, use an attention-getting caption to arouse curiosity, show need or use to the reader, appeal to a psychological need, or emphasize a point of special personal interest. Often there is too little imagery and ingenuity, too much talking and too little saying anything. Clever cartoons and creative copy keep prospects chuckling and remembering.

Cole Steel Office Machines, Inc., personifies its Cole Dictator as a stenographer and then runs a simulated "Situations Wanted—Female" ad about "her." This is imaginative copy that is different. The copy reads:

> Available: The world's fastest stenographer. Seeks permanent position. Understands and speaks every language. Will work in large or small office. Perfect for details, guaranteed 100% accuracy.
>
> Will work 24 hours a day—Seven days a week—Never late—Never home ill—Needs no instructions—Never forgets anything—No personal telephone calls—Will travel anywhere without notice.
>
> Ideal business personality. Very attractive appearance, will never marry, lives only for work . . . days, nights, weekends. Excellent references!
>
> An electronic marvel that dictates and transcribes—the new hi-fidelity Cole Dictator.[7]

The theme runs into the coupon, which asks, "Won't you please give me an interview?" Because this copy is interesting and imaginative, it entertains readers and stimulates action.

[7] *Printers' Ink*, October 9, 1959, p. 56.

Checking over the mail from newspaper ads for Stern's Nurseries of Geneva, New York, Mr. Samm Sinclair Baker, advertising consultant, came to an ad headlined "Giant Strawberries." Mr. Stern commented, "The ad is just about breaking even. Yet these are most superior strawberries, huge, delicious, exceptionally satisfying to every gardener who plants them. Reorders prove it. The ad ought to pull a lot better."

The two studied the ad; then Mr. Baker said, "The word *giant* is rather vague."

"But that's what they are, giant strawberries."

Baker asked, "How big are they?"

"Gigantic. Much larger than most strawberries."

"An inch big? Two inches?"

"Yes, many measure up to two inches long and even more."

"As big as plums?" Baker persisted.

"Oh yes," Mr. Stern agreed, "many are as big as plums."

Mr. Baker crossed out "Giant Strawberries" in the headline and crayoned in "Plum-Size Strawberries."[8]

The ad ran with that change in the Sunday newspapers. Mail orders tripled again and again. The ad ran and produced profitably for over fifteen years. This proves that a crucial amount of dollar pulling power can be packed into just two four-letter words, when they have been arrived at creatively and used imaginatively, and when they convey truth and arouse emotion.

Vividness[9]

Vivid descriptions arouse interest and stimulate action. Specific details, descriptive words, and action words are vivid. Note the differences in the following descriptions.

General:	*Specific:*
Our candies are made of the best and purest ingredients, selected with utmost care and combined with superlative skill.	Our candy is a lemon fondant made from real fruit, freshly grated, and vanilla caramel produced from pure country butter and cream. These are rolled together and then covered with melt-in-your-mouth chocolate.
Food budgets go farther.	Save a half to two-thirds on your food budget.
The building materials are well over government specifications.	The building materials are 52.7 percent above government specifications.

[8]*Printers' Ink*, January 8, 1965, p. 22.

[9]See also Chapter 4, under *strength*, pp. 118–20.

Telephone: Midway 2-2246
Cable Address: DANCO

DANUSER *Machine Company*

ESTABLISHED 1910

Manufacturers of Earthmoving Equipment and Farm Tools 500 EAST THIRD STREET • FULTON, MISSOURI

HERE IT COMES, MR. PROCTOR.

Reference is made here to your recent request for Danuser Digger information.

You will be anxious to study the enclosed literature describing this heavy duty, trouble free Digger. There you will see it illustrated and find the specifications with some of its features described. The message that is most difficult to convey to you on paper is what you actually will experience when you see and operate one of these units.

IT'S FAST. Two holes in the time it takes to read this letter.

IT'S RUGGED. The very best of new materials are used.

IT'S EASY TO OPERATE. Simple controls easily reached from the tractor seat.

IT'S ECONOMICAL. Engineered and manufactured to last for years.

IT'S TROUBLE FREE. Ask a Danuser owner.

IT'S COMPLETE. 4 inch to 24 inch diameter augers available.

To help you further to get some first hand "local" information, we are asking our distributor, the John Reiner Company of 726 Hiawatha Boulevard, in Syracuse, to contact you. The Danuser Digger is sold in New York through this distributor and local implement dealers.

Mr. Proctor, your interest is very much appreciated. You will start receiving dividends from this interest just as soon as you put a Danuser Digger to work for you.

Yours very truly,

M. W. Finkenbinder

Courtesy Danuser Machine Company

An unusual twist often creates imaginative vividness, such as that existing in these headlines:

Downyflake 1-Minute Waffles
No more waiting for waffles;
No Batter, no Bother.

Wesson Oil
Rates kisses for the Mrs.

Chase and Sanborn Coffee (with diagrams)
Fresher here, because of
pressure here.

Quick Elastic Starch
Now you can make starch hot or cold!
Just get the box that's red and gold.

Arrow Shirts
Plaids, lads! . . . and some
checks you'll gladly endorse.
or
The colorful white shirt.

Snickers Candy Bar
It's a Milky Way
gone nutty!

The direct mail sales letter on the opposite page interests and persuades because of its specific details, which not only are vivid but also give convincing evidence.

Appeals

It takes imagination to determine what appeal to use to interest the reader and to work out how best to present the appeal to the individual or group concerned. The letter from Father Flanagan's Boys Town (page 174) is designed to hit the "composite man" on a list. It offers the pleasure of helping boys get a better deal. It utilizes numerous appeals both to reason and to emotion, so that if one does not hit home to a particular reader, another one will.

Emotionally the letter from Boys Town gets the reader's sympathy, shows him appreciation, appeals to his love for his fellowman and country, emphasizes the joy of giving, and ends on a religious note. On the side of reason, facts and figures are given to show the need for help and the past results that have been achieved, and a citizen's card and seals that serve a practical purpose are given as a tangible inducement to help. These appeals were powerful, and the mailing proved successful.

FOR HOMELESS ABANDONED BOYS REGARDLESS OF RACE OR CREED

"He ain't heavy, Father . . . he's m' brother"

THE ORIGINAL BOYS TOWN
ESTABLISHED 1917
FATHER FLANAGAN'S BOYS' HOME
FATHER NICHOLAS H. WEGNER, DIRECTOR
BOYS TOWN, NEBRASKA

My dear Mr. :

I wish you could see only once, as I do daily, the hungry, thinly clad and forlorn homeless boys who come to Boys Town. They are the victims of family tragedies -- death, divorce, and in some instances, crime. They come to us alone, unknown and unwanted. Denied the joys of normal boyhood, they know too well the bitter taste of privation and neglect.

You have been helping me give them a good home, sympathetic care, wholesome food, and teach them a high-school education and a practical trade. In their spare time they are kept busy in athletics, in Boy Scouting, in our choir and band, hobbies, and in our system of self-government. They are doing useful things, and learning to work and play shoulder to shoulder with their companions. The more than 7,000 who have been here during the past thirty-five years, of all races and religious creeds, and from every State, are now useful citizens throughout the country, a credit to themselves, to Boys Town and to the Nation.

I am enclosing your 1971 Honorary Citizens Card. Please sign it in the space indicated. I am also sending you a sheet of seals picturing our work here at Boys Town. With almost 1,000 boys here now, and more coming to us continually, our success depends upon the continued generosity of friends like you. If you will keep and use these seals, and send me a contribution of whatever amount you care to give, you will help me provide a brighter future for more helpless, homeless boys.

For us it is so little, but for them it is everything. You will not see their smiles, but if you could accompany your gift to Boys Town, you would realize how much genuine happiness and gratitude it will bring. Thank you--and God bless you.

Sincerely,

Father Wegner

Courtesy Father Flanagan's Boys' Home

The following checklist will help in adapting your appeal to the reader. Ask yourself:

1. Will my idea appeal to his reason or business sense?
2. Will it strike his imagination?
3. Will it appeal to his convenience or personal drive?

4. Does he have any hobbies or special interests to appeal to?
5. Why will it be to his advantage to do what I ask?
6. What idea will be sure to grip his interest?
7. What strong point will bring favorable action?
8. Have I handled his needs profitably for both of us?

The *Atlantic Monthly* uses snobbery of a very special brand, as shown in two letters, here and on the next page, that have met with great success. A quality magazine reaches readers who feel they are people of "quality." Although some recipients were amused, they still bought subscriptions. There is no doubt about it: creativity in using appeals imaginatively pays off by interesting the readers.

Why we're offering you the ATLANTIC MONTHLY for half the regular subscription rate

Dear Reader:

"Profile matching" is a method of matching characteristics of one group with those of another. We used it to locate your name as one whose interests would most likely coincide with those of our readers. (Indeed, you may already be one of them.)

If we are correct, The ATLANTIC is a magazine you, more than most, will appreciate and value each month.

What do you have in common with ATLANTIC subscribers? You are, for instance, more likely to: own an imported car than the average person—own a piano or tape recorder—have purchased over three times as many books and more than twice as many records last month than the average person—have taken a trip to a foreign country in the last five years, and are much, much more likely to be active in civic affairs.

Oh, yes. . .if you drink, your favorite whiskey is probably bourbon (although I confess to being a scotch and martini man myself).

Of course, there's a margin for error in "profile matching." Therefore, we offer you this opportunity to judge for yourself:

The enclosed card will bring you the next eight issues for just $2.84—half the regular rate—and the lowest you'll ever be offered.

Included in the eight issues of The ATLANTIC you'll receive will be at least two special, expanded issues which will probe controversial areas in American life. Recent projects have covered mental health, the campus, cars, children, divorce, and hospitals.

Also in this and every issue:

The ATLANTIC Reports—on Washington and key spots around the world, will take you to the "inner realms" for the stories behind the issues of the day. . .presented in a lively fashion, they bring the key points into sharp, clear focus.

Accent on Living. . .In a lighter vein these

Reprinted by permission of *Atlantic Monthly*

You are one of a
very special group
to receive this
half-price offer

Dear Reader:

Ask the people next door. . .

. . . confirm the fact that their name is not in the group selected to receive this letter.

Yours is. Why?

Because we believe you are one of the special individuals for whom The ATLANTIC is edited.

You are not a casual choice. . .this letter was mailed to you after matching the known backgrounds and interests of our subscribers against lists of book clubs, organizations, and professional societies. We then selected the people like yourself whose interests we felt matched those of current ATLANTIC readers. Of course, we could be wrong. . .

. . .so, to enable you to judge for yourself how "right" The ATLANTIC is for you, at minimum cost. . .

> . . .we'll send you the next twelve issues
> for only $4.25--one-half the regular rate.

Included in the twelve issues of The ATLANTIC you'll receive will be at least two special, expanded issues which will probe controversial areas in American life. (Your first issue will contain an intimate examination of Divorce in America.) Recent projects have covered mental health, the campus, cars, children, and hospitals.

Also, in this and every issue:

> The ATLANTIC Reports--on Washington and key spots around the world, will take you to the "inner realms" for the stories behind the issues of the day. . .presented in a lively fashion, they bring the key points into sharp, clear focus.
>
> Accent on Living. . .In a lighter vein these

Reprinted by permission of *Atlantic Monthly*

SUMMARY

The purposes of this chapter have been to help you understand the nature of creative thinking and to develop your ability to create ideas and apply the principles of creative thinking to writing interestingly. Creative thinking is the ability to generate new ideas, to plan, and to look ahead. It is the power to visualize and understand. It is the constant search for a better way and implies using ingenuity to produce unusual solutions to the ordinary, everyday problems that confront us.

Putting yourself in the other person's position and setting aside personal feelings and reactions to give every consideration to the other person are often overlooked as being an integral part of creative thinking. But they are certainly vital and require foresight, vision, and imagination. This can be done with a four-point program, which is especially important in writing letters that will interest and persuade the reader:

showing empathy, personalizing, adapting to the reader, and reflecting a pleasing personality and attitude. Empathy is identifying with the other person, being able to see his point of view, and understanding his needs, desires, and feelings. True personalization entails taking a personal interest in the other fellow and having him feel it. Talking *with* the other person instead of *to* him, writing his language, speaking on his level, economizing his time and effort—all are ways of adapting the message to make it interesting. Writing naturally and conversationally reflects one's personality and attitudes.

Everyone has some natural capacity for creating ideas, a capacity that can be developed. Management can aid workers by providing an environment conducive to the creation of ideas. It is the individual's responsibility to take advantage of this environment and to generate ideas. In a creative climate, laws of association—contiguity, similarity, and contrast—have free play to allow points of relationship, new combinations, and new ideas to come forth.

Analysis and synthesis are other aids to creating ideas. Breaking down a whole into its parts is analysis; putting the parts together to formulate a whole is synthesis. The two work together. Similarly, freewheeling and concentration complement each other. Freewheeling is letting oneself go in all directions to open up new paths and ideas. Concentration focuses attention on a particular fact or idea.

Concentration might follow or precede freewheeling. It might also be followed by incubation, commonly referred to as "sleeping on it." This means letting up on active thinking and allowing the subconscious mind to work on the problem. The new idea, answer, or solution appears in illumination, or the hatching-out process.

Using the aids to creating ideas whenever an opportunity presents itself will help the individual to increase his ability to create ideas. Increasing originality and sensitivity to problems will also help to develop creative ability.

Imagination is necessary for creating interesting letters. Being clever, using a variety of techniques, being vivid, using special psychological appeals—all play an important role in expressing creativity.

The following checklist of questions will prove helpful in evaluating material to make sure that it has been presented in an interesting and imaginative manner:

1. Have I shown the reader every consideration? Have I written from his point of view? Have I made him feel important? Have I shown consideration for his concern and well-being? Have I shown an interest in things that interest him? Is my material personalized? Have I used his name? Have I adapted my message, tone, and style to his needs? Have I used his language? Have I been conversational?

2. Have I reflected a pleasing personality and attitude? Have I been courteous and sincere? Have I treated him as I would want to be treated? Have I been cheerful and agreeable?
3. Have I used creative imagination in presenting my material? Have I used a variety of sentence lengths? paragraph lengths? Have I devised a clever opening? Have I been original in format and layout? Have I used vivid language appropriately? Have I included specific details?
4. Are my appeals appropriate to the reader's needs and desires? Has he been made a part of the message?

FURTHER READING

Alexander, Tom, "Synectics: Inventing by the Madness Method," *Fortune*, Vol. LXXII (August 1965), 165–68, 190, 193, 194.

Crawford, Robert P., *The Techniques of Creative Thinking*. New York: Hawthorn Books, Inc., 1954.

Drucker, P. F., "Big Power of Little Ideas," *Harvard Business Review*, Vol. XLII (May 1964), 6–8, 10, 12, 16, 19, 180.

England, A. O., "Creativity; an Unwelcome Talent?" *Personnel Journal*, Vol. XLIII (September 1964), 458–61.

Foster, Florence P., "The Human Relationships of Creative Individuals," *The Journal of Creative Behavior*, Vol. II (Spring 1968), 111–18.

Ghiseln, Brewster, ed., *The Creative Process*. New York: The New American Library, Inc., 1955.

Gisser, P., "Industrial Creativity; It's Different," *Printers' Ink*, Vol. CCXC (April 9, 1965), 49ff.

"How To Develop Ideas," *Nation's Business*, Vol. 43 (January 1955), 76–81.

"How To Put Ideas To Work," *Supervisory Management*, Vol. IX (July 1964), 4–8; (August 1964), 20–23; (September 1964), 18–21.

"Ideas: Ten Ways To Sell Them," *Nation's Business*, Vol. LIII (June 1965), 84–90.

Klare, G. R., and Byron Buck, *Know Your Reader*. New York: Hermitage House,1954.

McCollum, L. F., "Challenging Horizons for Creative Managers," *Advanced Management Journal*, Vol. XXXII (July 1967), 3–8.

Mason, Joseph H., "How To Develop Ideas," *Advertising Age*, Vol. XXVIII (March 3, 1958), 43–46.

Mooney, Ross L., and T. A. Razik, eds., *Explorations in Creativity*. New York: Harper & Row, Publishers, 1967.

"New Techniques in Evaluating TV Commercial Strength, Weaknesses," *Advertising Age*, November 20, 1967, pp. 73–74.

Osborn, Alex, *Applied Imagination*, rev. ed. New York: Charles Scribner's Sons, 1963.

——, *How To Become More Creative.* New York: Charles Scribner's Sons, 1964.

Parnes, Sidney J., "Can Creativity Be Increased?" *Personnel Administration,* Vol. XXV (November 1962), 2–9.

Prince, George M., "The Operational Mechanism of Synectics," *The Journal of Creative Behavior,* Vol. II (Spring 1968), 1–13.

Roman, Michael D., "Empathy: Key to Salesmanship," *Advanced Management Journal,* Vol. XXXIII (April 1968), 27–30.

Smith, Paul, ed., *Creativity: An Examination of the Creative Process.* New York: Hastings House, Inc., 1959.

Steinmetz, Cloyd S., "Creativity Training: A Testing Program That Became a Sales Training Program," *The Journal of Creative Behavior,* Vol. II (Summer 1968), 179–86.

"Think in Terms of Your Audience, Not Yourself," *Advertising Age,* Vol. XXXVIII (November 20, 1967), 8, 92.

"Tips on Getting Better Ideas," *Supervisory Management,* Vol. X (December 1965), 38, 39.

Torrance, E. P., "Examples and Rationales of Test Tasks for Assessing Creative Abilities," *The Journal of Creative Behavior,* Vol. II (Summer 1968), 165–78.

Wallace, W. H., "Some Dimensions of Creativity," *Personnel Journal,* Vol. XLVI (June 1967), 363–70; (July/August 1967), 438–43, 458.

Walter, Otis M., "Creativity and the Rules of Rhetoric," *The Journal of Creative Behavior,* Vol. I (Fall 1967), 383–90.

Young, James Webb, *A Technique for Producing Ideas.* Chicago: Advertising Publications, Inc., 1956.

QUESTIONS AND PROBLEMS

Exercises for Ideation

1. Start with a can of tomato soup, add seasonings and other ingredients, take away substances, change its form. Do anything you want, but in the end come up with something other than tomato soup to eat or drink. Campbell Soup Company has used this sort of ideation in their advertising, showing soup as a basis for a lunch or a meal and adding other foods, and by showing numerous casserole dishes and other concoctions in which soup has played a part.
2. Listing ways of improving something is a form of ideation for developing increased creative power:
   a. List ways of improving either the basic materials or methods of manufacturing of a particular product.

b. Suggest ways of increasing attendance or membership in some organization to which you belong.
c. Suggest ways of making your communication classroom a more pleasant and efficient place.
d. List ways in which television sets might be improved.
e. List the "of-the-month clubs" with which you are familiar. Think up others that might succeed.
f. Suggest special features that might be added to *Reader's Digest* or some other specific magazine with which you are familiar.
g. List ways to improve the letters you write.

3. Create a list of ideas on the following problems:
   a. How to reduce absenteeism in your classes
   b. How to be entertaining on a date
   c. How to celebrate birthdays (or some other holiday)
   d. How to raise funds for some specific cause
   e. How to write imaginative openings to business letters
   f. How to motivate people to do what you want them to do
4. Improve the following sentences by rewriting them for empathy, personalization, adaptation, cleverness, variety, vividness, and appeal:
   a. I am indeed happy to inform you that we are expanding our services in order to be able to sserve you better than we have in the past twenty years we have been in the sheet metal business.
   b. You are the most important person in the world to me. That is why I have written your name in gold and am writing you now. The Golden Boy ball-point pen will prove just as valuable to you as your name is to me.
   c. The plastic slipcovers you ordered, sir, for your office furniture are just as durable for use in family rooms and living rooms where they get a lot of general rough wear.
   d. Made from tree-ripened fruit, sugared and boiled, these candied grapefruit are truly delectable.
   e. Each year thousands of people return from their vacations disappointed. Why?
   f. A slouchily dressed man is of little interest to a lovely girl, but a man who selects his wardrobe from our store will always be popular with the ladies.
5. Rewrite for vividness:
   a. The work sox are very durable.
   b. Gas heat is easier and cheaper to use than electricity.
   c. The shirts come in various colors and stripes.
   d. The ________ refrigerator operates silently.
   e. It's easy to use an electric clothes dryer.
   f. He shot a long string of small game.

Puzzles Requiring Creative Thinking

A few years ago the American Can Company launched a corporate advertising program in a number of the nation's leading magazines to accomplish three purposes:

a. To interest and involve the reader through a "puzzle" theme
b. Once the reader has been interested and involved, to deliver meaningful information concerning the company
c. As a result of the information, to create a definitive understanding of the company by the employees, stockholders, community, and customers

The advertising program has proved very successful. The ads were creative; they interested and involved the reader and related the informational copy to each specific puzzle concept. Three of the ads are reproduced on pages 182–84. Try your skill at finding solutions. Discuss how the concept in the puzzle relates to the copy and thus creates an effective, creative and interesting ad. What would the company gain from these three ads?

Additional puzzles from the series are reproduced on pages 185–86 to allow you to try your creative skill at reaching solutions. Puzzles like these help you to look at things and people from different points of view, and to devise different approaches to problem situations.

Special Projects

The following projects are thought-provoking and will require time, effort, and imagination to accomplish their objectives. Thus they should be started now, spanning your study of Chapters 5 and 6 and perhaps taking from a week to ten days for completion. They may also be assigned in part should your instructor so choose:

1. Your company prepares and sells a full line of canned and frozen fruits such as peaches, grapefruit, pineapple, pears, and cherries. Always on the lookout for product diversification and for an increased consumer market, management has come up with a new product—Gourmet Fruit Salad. They haven't decided yet whether the packaging should be canned or frozen, or what the label should look like. The salad is to be made up of sliced mandarin oranges, pineapple chunks, and fruit cocktail (in large sections and pieces). A serving suggestion that could be placed on the label might be:

add:		add:
marshmallows		dates, nuts, and
and sour cream	*or*	mayonnaise
and serve chilled		

Several decisions must be made: the size of the can or package, the weight of the contents, and the price per can to the retailer and consumer.

You have been asked to create five promotional advertising pieces to be used:

a. A label design for the can or package. This will include a picture, message or copy, format (layout), etc.
b. Newspaper and magazine advertisements, including illustrations and appealing copy and layout to attract attention, interest, conviction, and action.

(Project 1 continued on page 187.)

CAN YOU CONNECT THE DOTS WITH FOUR STRAIGHT LINES WITHIN THE GREY AREA WITHOUT LIFTING YOUR PENCIL?

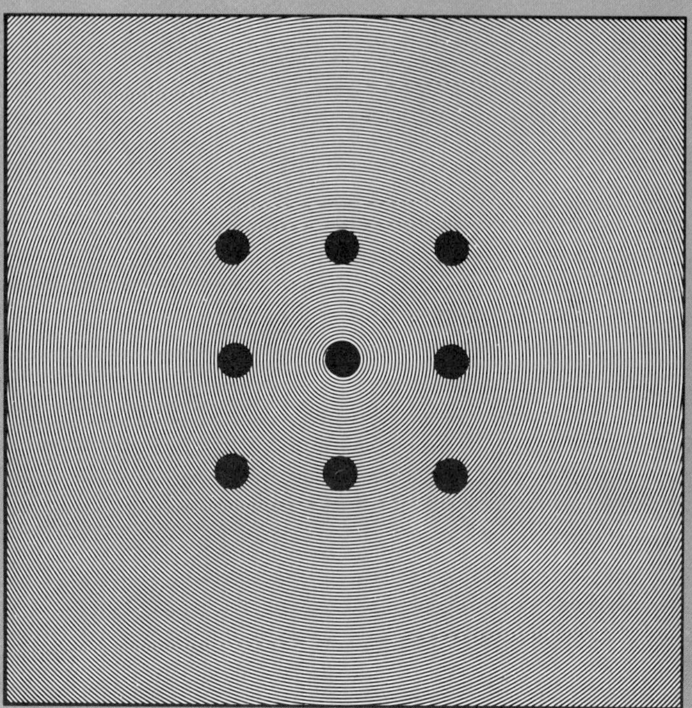

Most people are so boxed in by their thinking it doesn't occur to them to extend the lines above and beyond the dots. Once they do, they're on the way to solving the problem.

Unleashed thinking is what we strive for at the American Can Company. Our research people are encouraged to go above and beyond, to "blue sky" it. Imagine glueing steel? They did! And now American Can does!

Instead of soldering a seam, we overlap the sides and bond them together. We end up with something called the MiraSeam can.

Its innovational seam is stronger. (If you try to split it, you'll split the steel first.) Better. Cheaper. Plus it works with both aluminum and tin-free steel. Since tin is scarce, and expensive, our MiraSeam can is considered the most revolutionary development in containers in 20 years.

It happened because we spend 20 million dollars a year on research. Not only in cans, of course, but in all the areas into which we have diversified: container and packaging products, consumer products, service products, chemical products.

You never know what important development we'll come up with next. You only know we will come up with it!

American Can Company.
Creative products
that shape your future.
100 Park Avenue,
New York, N.Y. 10017.

Reprinted by permission of the American Can Company

WHICH ONE OF THE 4 INTERLINKED RINGS MUST BE CUT SO ALL THE RINGS WILL BE FREE?

Choose the correct one and watch them spread out.

To us, the American Can Company, spreading out is second nature. Back in 1901 when we started, we only made tin cans. Over the years we've diversified so much that anyone who knew us then, would hardly recognize us now.

Just last January, for instance, we set out in two brand new directions. We acquired The Butterick Company, Inc. (a home sewing pattern business) and the Printing Corporation of America (among other things they print textbooks and high quality art books).

This is a far cry from the humble tin can, but it's a good example of our desire to grow in the areas of leisure and education.

It means that today, at the ripe young age of 67, we're now diversified into five major areas: container and packaging products, consumer products, service products, chemical products and printing services.

Altogether we produce well over 1700 different products! While all you have to produce is the right answer to this 4-ring problem.

American Can Company
Creative products that shape your future.
100 Park Avenue
New York, N.Y. 10017

Reprinted by permission of the American Can Company

DRAWING THREE STRAIGHT LINES
CAN YOU ENCLOSE EACH ITEM IN ITS OWN AREA?

Where do you draw the lines?

We try not to draw them when it comes to solving problems.

Like the problem we had recently. We figured there ought to be a quicker way to cut and crease our cartons. So first we created a whole new type of die. The first breakthrough in 50 years! The old ones were made by hand, these are chemically milled. Then we linked them to a rotary press (a kind never used before in carton cutting and creasing!) Result: Impact Graphics' dies now do the job twice as fast. For less money.

This is something that will mean as much to the paperboard business, as another innovation of ours did to the can and glass businesses. An innovation called bulk palletizing. A long name for a simple way to ship things. We used to pack cans and bottles in individual cases. Now we layer them on wooden racks. It's a whole lot faster. Cheaper. And easier. For you and for us.

If there's a better way, we find it. In all the areas into which we've diversified: container and packaging products, consumer and industrial paper products, chemical products.

This is progress. This is growth. This is the American Can Company today.

We'd be the last ones to suggest drawing a line anywhere—but how about under the top three items. Just to speed things up!

American Can Company problem solvers in packaging, paper, chemistry 100 Park Avenue New York, New York 10017

Reprinted by permission of the American Can Company

CAN YOU MAKE THE TOP GROUP OF CIRCLES THE SAME SHAPE AS THE BOTTOM GROUP BY MOVING ONLY 3 CIRCLES?

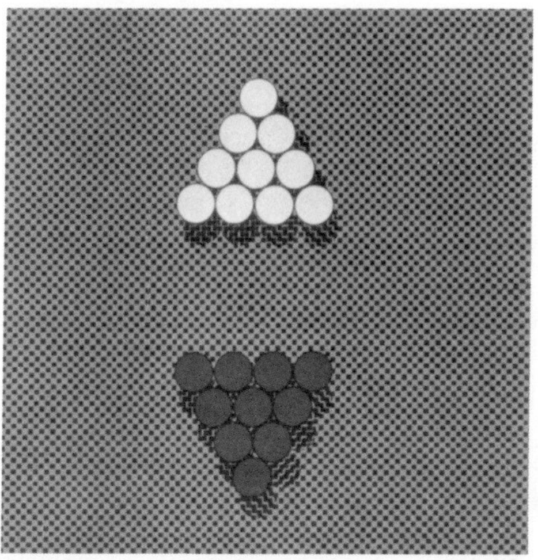

Reprinted by permission of the American Can Company

HOW MANY TRIANGLES OF ANY SIZE ARE IN THIS STAR?

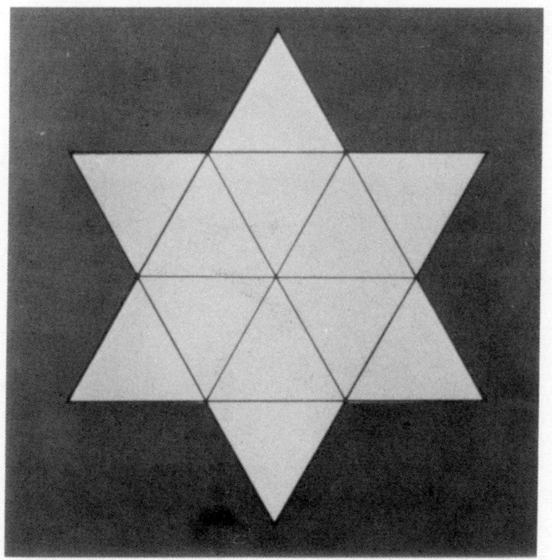

Reprinted by permission of the American Can Company

CAN YOU ARRANGE THESE 8 PENCILS TO MAKE 3 SQUARES OF EQUAL SIZE?
(No part of any pencil may extend beyond the edge of any square)

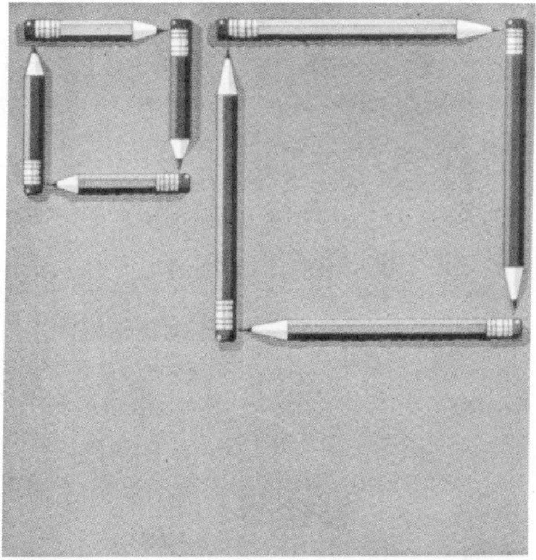

Reprinted by permission of the American Can Company

CAN YOU RENUMBER THE REST OF THE SQUARES SO THAT EACH ROW, COLUMN, AND DIAGONAL OF THREE SQUARES TOTALS 15? (NO NUMBER MAY BE REPEATED)

Reprinted by permission of the American Can Company

HOW MANY SQUARES CAN YOU COUNT?

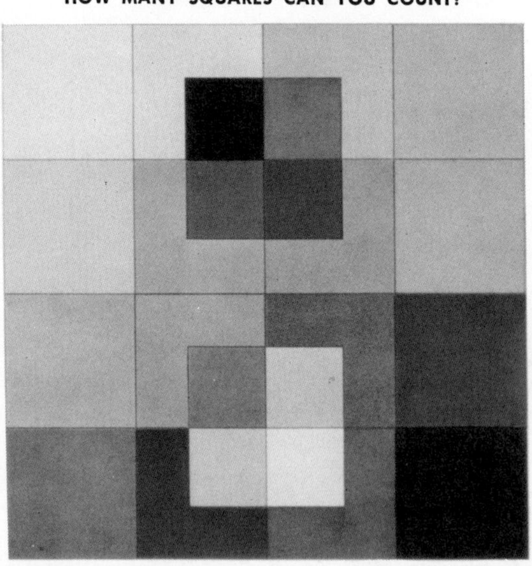

Reprinted by permission of the American Can Company

c. A news release or feature story that may appear on a newspaper's feature or financial page.

d. A radio or television commercial to introduce the new product. The television commercial would include a "frame" presentation:

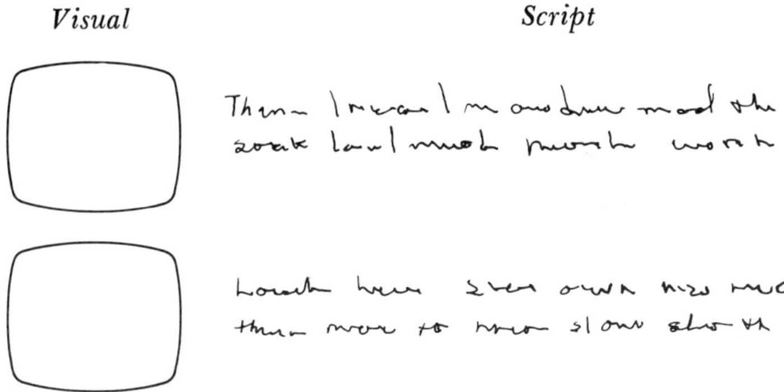

Be sure to specify the length of the commercial; common practice is to use either sixty or twenty seconds, or else a series of "quickies." Both radio and television commercials have to be timed to the second, but can depend upon sound for part of their effect on the listener.

e. A letter to the retailer to sell him on stocking the new Gourmet Fruit Salad. You could create another name for it and a "brand" name for your fruit products, of which it is only one.

Include all these promotional pieces as part of a total advertising program. Submit them with an accompanying memorandum directed to top management to get acceptance of your ideas and plans. You will have to present some rationale for each element in order to persuade management that it will be effective.

2. Invent a household gadget. It may combine features of several now existing or may change one into some other useful item. The homemaker is interested in gadgets that will save time, effort, and money. Draw a diagram of your invention and write an explanation or description of it. Include kinds of materials, dimensions of the parts, colors, uses, etc. Write a letter to a manufacturer selling him on the idea of producing your invention. You may include your diagram and description as an enclosure with the letter. This project could be developed further by adding any or all of the promotional pieces in problem 1 above.

3. A variation of problem 2 is to invent a toy. Here you will have to think of an age group and a use: "to entertain the three-year-old" or "to teach the five-year-old how to ________." Children like toys that imitate the actions of others (people and animals), make noises, are colorful, and move.

Growers Vow to Let Cherries Rot in Revolt on Crop Price

By ROBERT L. PISOR
Of The Detroit News Staff

TRAVERSE CITY, July 10.—Angry cherry growers have sounded the first murmurs of a threatened full-scale revolt, vowing to let their fruit rot rather than sell at the going price of 4.8 cents a pound.

More than 60 farmers have pledged to leave over 5,000 tons of cherries on the trees, and many promised to get their friends and neighbors to sign the holdout oath and join an organization known as the Cherry Growers Honor Group.

SEEK MORE HELP

The rebels also appointed envoys to go south into the Grand Rapids-Benton Harbor cherry region to convince other growers to join the revolt against a price level considered totally inadequate. The western Michigan area produces most of the world's red tart cherry crop.

The dissident farmers in this cherry-growing area may even have trouble selling their cherries at the 4.8 cents they are protesting: processors rejected the price when it was offered by the Great Lakes Cherry Producers Marketing Cooperative Inc., an organization of 2,200 growers.

Ironically, the blow came as this cherry capital was celebrating its annual National Cherry Festival.

The cooperative now is bargaining with individual processors on the 4.8-cent rate, a price growers regard as below their break-even point.

THREAT OF VIOLENCE

Violence to back up their demands for a higher price also was threatened when 250 growers and their wives met last night to air their grievances at a meeting at Glen Lake, 20 miles west of here.

"Let's picket the plants," "Let's tip over the trucks that are going to sell at 4.8 cents a pound," and "Let's show them we're going to stand together to get a decent price, just like the milk producers and labor unions do," were some of the shouts from the crowd.

The meeting was called by Paul T. Johnson, an Empire cherry grower who drew up a pledge to sell at a minimum of seven cents a pound or let the cherries rot.

"We have enough tonnage right here to rock the packers," Johnson told his applauding audience. "We'll make the packers so nervous they'll give us seven cents a pound out of fear we'll ask for nine cents.

SOME ARE CAUTIOUS

About half of the farmers present pledged all or part of their 1965 crop to the holdout plan, but others, including some of the largest growers, adopted a wait-and-see attitude.

But all cheered men like John T. Miller, of Arcadia, who shouted that he had 400 tons to pledge to the holdout campaign.

"Let 'em hang in the trees. I would just as soon go fishing for three weeks. I'm tired of working for nothing," Miller shouted.

A former member of UAW Local 600 at a Detroit Ford plant, Miller said a tight, militant organization of growers was absolutely necessary, adding:

"If we hadn't had unions, we would all still be peasants. It's about time the growers got organized to protect our investments and hard work."

Miller said the holdout scheme could come to picketing, stopping trucks and even iolence if enough growers joined in the holdout movement.

PICKING TIME NEAR

The call for revolt comes just a week before migrant workers are scheduled to start picking in a second straight year of a bumper crop of cherries.

The U.S. Department of Agriculture estimates that Michigan will produce 120,000 tons of red tart cherries this year, compared with 190,000 tons last year. Both figures represent more than 60 percent of all cherry production in the United States.

But while the level is down 35 percent from 1964, it is still far above the five-year Michigan average of 82,000 tons of cherries a year.

Last year's crop brought five cents a pound from packers, and a 38,000-ton carryover of unsold canned and frozen cherries has forced the price down even further this year.

Even packers admit that 4.8 cents a pound is an unreasonable price for cherries.

CAN'T BREAK EVEN'

Clete W. Bowers, sales manager for Cherry Growers Inc., a grower-owned processing plant in Traverse City and second largest processor in Michigan, said:

'The growers can't even break even on five cents a pound. They must pay three cents a pound to migrant workers to get the cherries picked and they must also pay for fertilizing, spraying, pruning, buying equipment and paying help."

But, he continued, the 4.8-cent price had been set and other processors had to go along to remain competitive.

The marketing cooperative claims to represent 51 percent of the total tonnage of cherries grown and its decisions are almost always adopted by processors throughout the country.

The Grand Traverse area, which grows more than half of Michigan's red tart cherries, is the hardest hit by the low price.

Most of the growers place the blame on family distribution. claiming there are many parts of the United States which don't receive cherries at all or receive only poor quality cherries, killing off hopes of resales.

Robert P. Morrison, a Williamsburg grower who also acts as a middleman between growers and processors handling millions of pounds of cherries each year, said:

"There are stores right in Traverse City, the capital of the cherry world and the site of the National Cherry Festival, that never have had cherries on their shelves.

"What we need is better distribution, more advertising and more research on new products."

NOTE OF DISSENT

Only one dissenting voice was sounded at the meeting at Glen Lake. Peter Lutz, a former director on the board of the Great Lakes Marketing Cooperative who quit in protest of the 4.8-cent price, said growers would have to accept a federal marketing order or develop a "terrifically strong" growers' organization to win fair prices.

He called the meeting "small potatoes" and said any revolt would have to include farmers across the nation in "one giant marketing cooperative" to be successful.

"We would have to collect large dues, large enough to build a fund to actually pay growers to keep their cherries on trees and force the prices up, the same way a union supports its members when they go on strike for higher wages," Lutz said.

But most of the farmers said they had nothing to lose by starting the revolt immediately.

One who drew applause from the crowd summed up the feelings of many of the growers when he said:

"If I don't sell my cherries this year or have to sell them at 4.8 cents a pound, I wont sell them next year or I won't be here. I'll bulldoze the trees out."

Courtesy *The Detroit News*, July 11, 1965

4. The news story from the *Detroit News* reproduced above points up several problems: the price controversy, the role of the union for the cherry growers, and the need for national promotion of cherries all year to prevent the lack of sale to consumers that occurred the previous year and to increase consumer demand for cherries. How do you view the problems?

Attacking the problem from the same point of view as Mr. Robert P. Morrison, who said in the article, "What we need is better distribution, more advertising, and more research on new products," what ideas can you generate as solutions? After you have created as many promotional ideas as possible, evaluate them and decide on several that would appeal to the consumer and interest him in buying and eating more cherries throughout the year. Write a letter to the National Cherry Growers' Association persuading them to adopt your ideas and put them into effect. You will need to present not only your ideas but also the reasons why they would be effective. Wouldn't it be good strategy also to submit some sample promotional pieces that could be used?

5. A situation like the one in problem 4 could exist in Georgia for peach growers, Florida for orange growers, California for grape growers, or your own state for whatever farm product it raises abundantly. Create ideas, plan promotional pieces, and write the association an interesting and stimulating letter.

Problems for Class Discussion and Letter Writing

1. Any communication must be receiver-oriented: it must be thought out in terms of the receiver's frame of reference and desires. Therefore, the communicator must know his receiver. Divide the class into groups of two students each. Designate one as *A*, and the other *B*. For ten minutes (or some specified short time period) let each pair interview or converse with each other. During the conversation each student must find out enough about the other to identify an action or belief that he has a reasonable chance of convincing him to take, or change, or at least give consideration to.

   After the conversations allow each student five minutes to plan his communication. Then have one of the pairs come to the front and have *A* convince *B* in three minutes. Have the class criticize this, then let *B* have three minutes to convince *A*.[10]

2. The following short case study lends itself to creative problem solving and class discussion:

   The home office of the American Insurance Company employs 200 people. They are hired on the basis of interviews and tests and are then given on-the-job training for three months under the direction of their department heads. Every six months each one is considered for a pay increase, but he may be passed over if the department head does not recommend him.

   In the accounting department there are four women who have been with the company for seven to ten years. Three men in this department have also been with the company for seven to ten years. The position of senior cost accountant, the department supervisor, has been filled by three different people in the past three years, in each instance by a younger man hired from the outside. Management recognized the worth of the older staff members, but felt that they were not eligible for promotion.

   The women employees have been displeased, and their work shows it.

[10]Adapted from Edward J. Holder, "Communication Curriculum for Basic Sales Training," *Training in Business and Industry*, Vol. V (August 1968), 40.

An excessive amount of talking and visiting goes on. The topic of conversation is known to the rest of the office force. General morale is low.

Discuss what you would do in this situation.

a. What is the problem and what are its causes?
b. What alternate courses of action could be taken?
c. What would you recommend be done?
d. What effect would your solutions have on the employees involved?

3. Assume that your instructor has a small manufacturing company south of your town. He has been manufacturing walking canes like mad, but he hasn't been selling many. He hates to lay off workers, so the canes have piled up. Will you help him out? List as many ideas as you can for advertising and promoting the sale of walking canes among male college students. If you can create a fad, he will have no trouble selling them. Or perhaps you might have ideas for changing or converting them to something else in order to create a new product and demand. Write him a memorandum or letter giving him the benefit of your ideas and the reasoning behind them.

4. Think up at least three appropriate premiums to be given with the purchase of

   a. Men's shoes
   b. An outboard motor
   c. A washing machine
   d. A refrigerator
   e. A hair dryer
   f. A living room sofa

   A premium should have a low cost to the store using it, be related in some way to the product with which it is given, be of interest (satisfy a need or desire) for the receiver, and be lasting enough to remind the user of the store. Write a letter to a retail store owner, giving him your suggestions in order of importance, and interesting him in using them.

5. You are the owner–manager of a vacation resort and want to attract businessmen for weekends or for short stays of a few days. You will have to visualize a particular type of facility and supply details such as the advantages, location, and services. You will also need to use special psychological appeals to interest the businessman. Make your decisions, such as:

   1. Should it be a lodge, cabins, or a hotel?
   2. Should it be an out-of-the-way place or in a hub of activities?
   3. Should it have fishing, boating, and golfing?
   4. Should it have a conference room and meeting rooms?

   Analyze the reader and his interests, visualize what you have to offer, then plan and write your letter.

6. In an editorial in the local press, the editor welcomed the college students for a new year in the community and expressed his concern about bridging the gap between "gown and town," stating that there was too much separation and that the two factions did not work together cooperatively. Write a letter to the editor with ideas and suggestions for greater cooperation between the two factions. How can business serve the students? In what university activities can they participate jointly?

How would you bridge the gap? Is it merely a communication gap or something else? Can the students improve or serve the community? A community often considers students to be beer-drinking, protesting, long-haired weirdos who stay up all night carousing. Can you change the image?

TEST YOUR CREATIVE ABILITY

1. Dr. Sarnoff A. Mednick, of the University of Michigan, has developed the Remote Associative Test (RAT). Test items consist of sets of three words: for example, rat, blue, cottage. The person taking the test finds a fourth word that will serve as a connecting link. The answer in this example is *cheese*: rat cheese, blue cheese, and cottage cheese.

Creativity Test[11]

Fill in the blank to the right of each set of words with a fourth word that is an associative connecting link with the others:

1.	rain	pay	mate	________
2.	off	side	ball	________
3.	egg	seed	food	________
4.	ball	nut	market	________
5.	ski	high	rope	________
6.	back	weight	scratch	________
7.	acid	pin	egg	________
8.	motion	tennis	card	________
9.	moth	pin	chain	________
10.	frame	moving	window	________
11.	stick	hare	upper	________
12.	dog	boat	cat	________
13.	hole	master	board	________
14.	hop	cow	boy	________
15.	life	house	river	________
16.	maid	graph	candy	________
17.	knife	milk	fingers	________
18.	pie	crab	tree	________
19.	case	mark	bank	________
20.	spread	river	time	________
21.	cleaner	walker	main	________
22.	house	ship	tennis	________

If you score twelve or more correct answers you are as creative as the average Harvard student and the average University of Michigan honor or graduate student. If you answer eight or fewer, you are doing poorly.

2. Business is stepping up its search for creative people. Corporate concern is practical and urgent. Dow Chemical, the IBM Corp., General Electric, Lever Brothers, and the AC Spark Plug Division of General Motors are among firms currently using creativity tests in their selection and promotion of employees. Psychologist Eugene Raudsepp, co-founder of Prince-

[11]*The Detroit News Magazine*, August 18, 1968, p. 27.

ton Creative Research, assembled some sample tests for *Nation's Business,* two of which are reprinted here so you may test your ability.[12]

Which Traits Describe You?

Object: Check the adjectives that you believe really describe you. Your selections can be clues to your creativity.

determined	life of party	stern
responsible	dynamic	sociable
tolerant	polite	sensitive
independent	informal	restless
inventive	impulsive	reflective
enthusiastic	excitable	rational
clear-thinking	popular	preoccupied
understanding	cheerful	practical
individualistic	obedient	peaceable
industrious	self-demanding	organized
dependable	unassuming	moody
absent-minded	worrying	masculine
logical	polished	loyal
versatile	fashionable	good-natured

Your Choice Shows Creativity

Object: Check the responses that you feel apply to you.

1. Would you rather be considered:
   a _____ a practical person?
   b _____ an ingenious person?
2. If you were a teacher, would you rather teach:
   a _____ fact courses?
   b _____ courses involving theory?
3. Does following a schedule:
   a _____ appeal to you?
   b _____ cramp you?
4. When there is a special job to be done, do you like to:
   a _____ organize it carefully before you start?
   b _____ find out what is necessary as you go along?
5. Do you often get behind in your work?
   a _____ yes
   b _____ no
6. Do you prefer specific instructions to those that leave many details optional?
   a _____ yes
   b _____ no

[12]From "Test Your Creativity," *Nation's Business,* Vol. 53 (June 1965), 80–83. © *Nation's Business*–the Chamber of Commerce of the United States. Reprinted by permission.

7. Do hunches come to you just before going to sleep?
   a ______ yes
   b ______ no
8. Do you often fret about daily chores?
   a ______ yes
   b ______ no
9. Do you like to introduce the speaker at a meeting?
   a ______ yes
   b ______ no
10. Do you get your best ideas when you are relaxed?
    a ______ yes
    b ______ no
11. Do you sometimes feel anxious about the success of your efforts?
    a ______ yes
    b ______ no
12. Do you like work in which you must influence others?
    a ______ yes
    b ______ no
13. Are you fundamentally contented?
    a ______ yes
    b ______ no
14. Do you like work that has regular hours?
    a ______ yes
    b ______ no
15. Do you spend many evenings with friends?
    a ______ yes
    b ______ no
16. As a child, were you inclined to take life seriously?
    a ______ yes
    b ______ no
17. Do you frequently daydream?
    a ______ yes
    b ______ no
18. Do you remember the names of people you meet?
    a ______ yes
    b ______ no
19. Do you like to keep regular hours and run your life according to established routine?
    a ______ yes
    b ______ no
20. Is it hard for you to sympathize with a person who is always doubtful and unsure about things?
    a ______ yes
    b ______ no

Chapter Six

WRITING PERSUASIVELY

All communication is persuasive. The element of persuasion is present in some degree in every communication situation. To persuade is to get someone to accept a belief or idea or to take action. It is using word power to invoke emotion and to stimulate action. You get people to do things by making them *want* to do them. People want to be well thought of; they want to get ahead in business; they want to make money; they want to do more work in less time with less effort. Thus they can be persuaded to do the things that will satisfy these wants and needs.

Following the suggestions in Chapters 4 and 5 will help you to develop your persuasive power, for being understood is the first step in influencing and motivating people; interesting the reader or listener follows. Having developed your skills in these areas to some extent, you are now ready to apply them further and to add the ability to persuade, for persuasion is a necessary element in every communicating situation. Thus the purposes of this chapter are to help you understand the art of persuasion and to develop your ability to apply its principles effectively in your writing, especially in writing sales letters and promotional materials.

THE ART OF PERSUASION

A colleague of mine, who decided that he wanted to have aluminum siding put on his house, telephoned a company that sells and installs it. He told the secretary who answered the phone that he would like to have a representative call and give him an estimate, that although he did not think he could have the work done this fall, he wanted some idea of its cost so that he could plan to have it put on in the early spring. Arrangements were made for the representative to be at my colleague's house at 4:00 P.M. the following Wednesday. Both men drove into the driveway at the same time. The representative was indeed prompt, and my friend noted this in his favor.

They lost no time in getting started. My friend (let's call him Chuck) immediately told the representative, Mr. Johnson, what he had said on the telephone, adding that he was rushed for time but was especially interested in an estimate so that he could plan ahead. Mr. Johnson immediately began asking all sorts of questions: what kind of siding he wanted, what color, what width, how far up on the house. Chuck kept interrupting him with, "These are decisions I'll make later. All I want now is some idea of cost, so I can plan for it."

Mr. Johnson seemed surprised to learn that it was not to be put on now and said to call him in the spring; he would give the estimate then. When pressed, he commented that labor and material costs would increase.

"How much?"

"I can't say."

"Fifty percent?"

"No."

"One-third?"

"No."

So the conversation went, ending with Mr. Johnson's refusing to give an estimate then and there. He said that it was too much work and time when the sale wouldn't be made until spring, and insisted that Chuck should telephone when he was ready.

The sale was lost; the prospect was no longer a prospect. What went awry? No persuasion took place; yet the truth is that that salesman could have "sold" my friend. Three persuasive elements were never recognized or practiced. The sales representative did not read his prospect correctly; his credibility rating with the prospect was low and he did nothing to raise it; and his message contained nothing of a persuasive nature. Incidents such as this happen daily. There are factors inherent in every communicator, message, and receiver that must be considered and brought into interplay in order for the message to be persuasive.

The Credibility of the Writer

The writer must be credible as a person and in what he says. Everything the receiver knows and perceives about what the sender does and

DICK WEBER

P.O. Box 300, Florissant, Missouri 63030

March 26, 19__

Dear Fellow Bowler:

I know of your active interest in bowling--a sport that has been very kind to me--so I'd like to be first to tell you about a remarkable new bowling ball. It's called the Dick Weber All-Pro Ball, and its specifications are the most exacting for any ball on the market. The maker is AMF.

If you have ever missed a spare by one wobbling pin that failed to fall (and what bowler hasn't?), you will particularly appreciate the fact that this new ball is actually bigger. While staying within the ABC's maximum specs, the new Dick Weber All-Pro Ball is guaranteed to exceed the ABC's minimum circumference specs by fully 1/4".

This extra 1/4" may not seem like very much, but it can be just enough to mean an extra spare. And how many more games could you have won, if only you had made just one more spare!

This guaranteed bigger size is only one of the many premium features and advantages that results from the industry's toughest specifications and rigid quality controls. I have personally inspected every step of manufacturing and testing at the factory to be certain of this. The enclosed folder tells the complete story and why we say this new ball is "built to outscore them all."

After you read it, I'd like to invite you to see the ball at your favorite bowling center or pro shop. To induce you to stop in soon, I am enclosing a coupon good for a free $1.50 Buffing Bag if you buy one of the balls before May 31st.

Don't forget to tell the man that Dick Weber sent you!

Cordially,

Dick Weber

Dick Weber

P.S. If he does not have the new ball in stock yet, please ask him to call his man from AMF.

The Reporter of Direct Mail Advertising, June 1968, p. 27. Reproduced by permission.

says tells something about him that affects his credibility. A person who is competent and dependable and who gets things done has a high credibility rating. These characteristics become apparent through knowing the person and his past performance, and through the establishment of friendly relations. The writer who reflects a pleasing personality, shows concern for the other person, is sincere, is confident and believes in what he says, and is enthusiastic, is *credible*. The reader perceives most of this from what the writer says and how he says it, but he also recognizes some of it from the writer's social standing, reputation as an authority, or status in the company, even though he may not know him personally.

The letter on page 196 rates high in credibility. Dick Weber is a name well known in bowling circles. His reputation makes him an authority. The reader quickly associates the larger-sized ball as being within the ABC's specifications and realizes its advantages. The guarantee furthers credibility, since the reader has nothing to lose. The coupon for a buffing bag adds an incentive—and so it all adds up to persuasion, with the biggest element being credibility.

Message Credibility

You can't always separate the credibility of the writer from that of the message. For instance, at a meeting of his employees, a supervisor said, "Whenever I enter the shop, I want to see every man performing his job cheerfully. I will appreciate any idea you have as to how this can be brought about." The next day there was a note in the suggestion box: "Take off your rubber heels."[1]

A message is credible when the recipient accepts it and is motivated to action. Each one of us has physical and psychological needs, desires, and wishes. Whenever we hear or read of something that will fulfill them, we become interested and are motivated to act. We tend to ask, "What's in it for me?" Thus, letters that emphasize the benefits, advantages, and uses of a product are likely to be persuasive. Note the two letters on page 198. The second one is a rewrite of the first and is much better. It persuades by emphasizing benefits.

Tell the reader what he wants to know. Should you write about the product (or main idea)? Yes! But do it in terms of the reader and his concerns. The two letters on page 199 well illustrate persuasiveness by relating the facts in terms of the reader and what they will do for him. Thomas Publishing Company sent them to industrial purchasing agents to sell the *Thomas Register*. The second letter is far more persuasive than the first.

To write persuasively, you must know what you have to say, analyze your reader so that you can predict his reaction, write from his point of view, and thus motivate him to act favorably so that you can accomplish your purpose.

Knowing Your Reader

You must know your reader in order to meet his wants and needs. Analyze him by considering his storehouse of knowledge and experience, and try to find out what is in his mind. He has feelings as an individual personality, is seeking recognition, and wants to be recognized. You can't know everyone personally; however, you can know some of

[1] *Personnel Administration*, Vol. XXV (November–December 1962), 30.

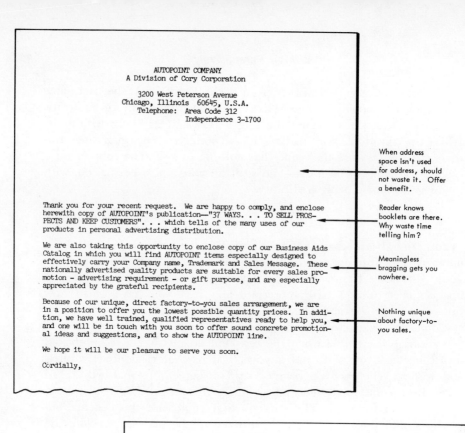

AUTOPOINT COMPANY
A Division of Cory Corporation

3200 West Peterson Avenue
Chicago, Illinois 60645, U.S.A.
Telephone: Area Code 312
Independence 3-1700

When address space isn't used for address, should not waste it. Offer a benefit.

Thank you for your recent request. We are happy to comply, and enclose herewith copy of AUTOPOINT's publication—"37 WAYS. . . TO SELL PROSPECTS AND KEEP CUSTOMERS". . . which tells of the many uses of our products in personal advertising distribution.

Reader knows booklets are there. Why waste time telling him?

We are also taking this opportunity to enclose copy of our Business Aids Catalog in which you will find AUTOPOINT items especially designed to effectively carry your Company name, Trademark and Sales Message. These nationally advertised quality products are suitable for every sales promotion - advertising requirement - or gift purpose, and are especially appreciated by the grateful recipients.

Meaningless bragging gets you nowhere.

Because of our unique, direct factory-to-you sales arrangement, we are in a position to offer you the lowest possible quantity prices. In addition, we have well trained, qualified representatives ready to help you, and one will be in touch with you soon to offer sound concrete promotional ideas and suggestions, and to show the AUTOPOINT line.

Nothing unique about factory-to-you sales.

We hope it will be our pleasure to serve you soon.

Cordially,

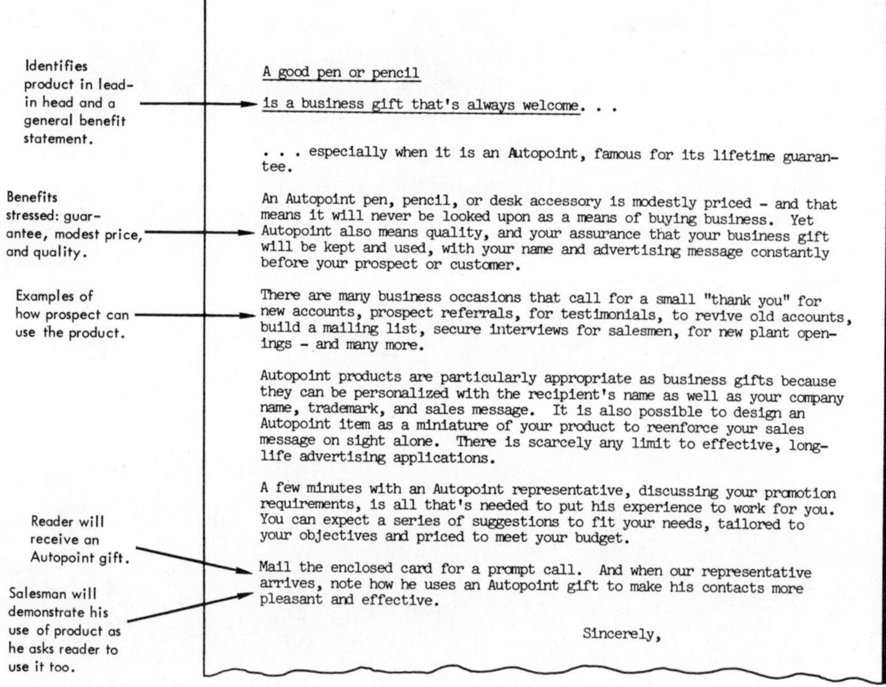

A good pen or pencil
is a business gift that's always welcome. . .

. . . especially when it is an Autopoint, famous for its lifetime guarantee.

An Autopoint pen, pencil, or desk accessory is modestly priced - and that means it will never be looked upon as a means of buying business. Yet Autopoint also means quality, and your assurance that your business gift will be kept and used, with your name and advertising message constantly before your prospect or customer.

There are many business occasions that call for a small "thank you" for new accounts, prospect referrals, for testimonials, to revive old accounts, build a mailing list, secure interviews for salesmen, for new plant openings - and many more.

Autopoint products are particularly appropriate as business gifts because they can be personalized with the recipient's name as well as your company name, trademark, and sales message. It is also possible to design an Autopoint item as a miniature of your product to reenforce your sales message on sight alone. There is scarcely any limit to effective, long-life advertising applications.

A few minutes with an Autopoint representative, discussing your promotion requirements, is all that's needed to put his experience to work for you. You can expect a series of suggestions to fit your needs, tailored to your objectives and priced to meet your budget.

Mail the enclosed card for a prompt call. And when our representative arrives, note how he uses an Autopoint gift to make his contacts more pleasant and effective.

Sincerely,

Identifies product in lead-in head and a general benefit statement.
Benefits stressed: guarantee, modest price, and quality.
Examples of how prospect can use the product.
Reader will receive an Autopoint gift.
Salesman will demonstrate his use of product as he asks reader to use it too.

The Reporter of Direct Mail Advertising, June 1968, p. 43. Reproduced by permission.

ATTENTION: PURCHASING AGENT

Here at Thomas Register—

We made nearly 200 changes an hour, eight hours a day, every day of last year just to keep up with the growth and change of industry!

THAT ADDS UP TO MORE THAN A MILLION CHANGES IN 19__!

Changes in names. . .addresses. . .new products. . .new phone numbers. . . new titles. . .tradenames. . .it's a never-ending job for our more than 100 editors and reporters. But it has to be done if we are to maintain the Register's reputation as America's most complete, comprehensive and authoritative source of "who makes what and where to find him."

THIS YEAR'S EDITION, LARGEST YET, OBSOLETES ALL EARLIER ONES

Don't "make do" with an older set of the Register--the more than a million changes render even last year's edition dangerously obsolete.

This latest edition consists of seven volumes plus an index. The individual volumes are light and easy to handle. We continue to improve the quality of printing, and you will, we feel, be impressed with the strides we made this year.

ALWAYS "SOLD OUT," WE'RE SELLING OUT EARLY THIS YEAR

At this writing the remaining inventory is dwindling rapidly and we cannot guarantee delivery for much longer. So if you want to be sure that you have an up-to-date set of Thomas Register at your side in the months ahead, order now. The price, including shipping, is only $30.00.

Cordially,

Florence K. Brett
Circulation Manager

P.S. At $30.00 for the complete seven volume set plus sturdy wire rack stand, the cost figures out about fifty cents a pound. In these days of soaring prices, isn't that a rare bargain? Send in your order today.

Talks about what is happening at Thomas Register. Tells about product in terms of what goes on at the Register office. (The reader couldn't care less.) We, our, and us are mentioned eight times.

Can you afford

another day - or week - or month's delay?

How often when you write for information about a new product or service do you wait days longer because the address wasn't right? How often does the wrong phone number make another call necessary?

Serious delay in reaching that important supplier happens much too often when you use an out-of-date directory. And with today's business pace, even last year's directory is woefully behind the times.

That's why Thomas Directory keeps more than 100 editors and reporters busy keeping up with business changes. New names and addresses, new products, phone numbers, titles, trade names--with current data your inquiries hit the mark faster, bring facts to you faster.

More than 1500 changes a day--that's the speed with which your old directory is traveling toward uselessness, and costing you delay and extra expense along the way. It's a cost you can eliminate when you order the current edition of Thomas Register.

For just $30, delivered, you get seven volumes of the right information about American business. Just one false start or unnecessary delay eliminated and the current Thomas Directory is paid for. Locate one new source for an important product and you may well pay for new directories far into the future.

We estimate directories on hand will be sold out within 30 days. Try to "make do" with what you have and your old directory can only get older, while your cost of using it keeps mounting.

Your order received within the next ten days brings a bonus, a handy wire storage rack, along with your copy of the most complete, and accurate, and easy-to-use reference to American business available anywhere. Immediate shipment.

Sincerely,

Emphasis is on what the reader will get out of it. He will buy better, faster, and easier. Talks about the reader first, last, and throughout the letter.

The Reporter of Direct Mail Advertising, August 1968, p. 32. Reproduced by permission.

the characteristics of the group of which he is a part. On the basis of what is known, you can assume some additional facts and characteristics. The more you know about him, the more you will be able to adapt your message, increase its credibility, and persuade him to act.

Much has been said and predicted about the youth market, the population explosion, and the information explosion. At the beginning of the 1970s, half the population of the United States is under the age of twenty-five. The protests and the rebellion of youth during the late 1960s told us a few things about the youth market of today. Just as youth rejects traditional goals, it rejects traditional advertising. It is persuaded by honesty. Its slogan is "Tell it like it is"—directly and truthfully. Young people demand the "soft sell" rather than the "hard sell." They have no patience with sham values and are much more interested in today's fun or benefits than in later success. They are more openly emotional, and they respond to humor. Knowing these factors and characteristics should help you to be persuasive with them.

The letter on page 201 makes some sensible, logical statements about management skills with which the reader cannot argue. But the facts invite a "So what?" response. The statements are impersonal; they do not involve the reader. They do not answer his question, "What does it mean to me?" The last sentence does motivate; but what reader will get that far?

The rewrite of that letter, on page 202, begins with a strong statement that grabs the reader's attention. It talks about management training in terms of involvement and directs its statements to the reader. The emphasis is on immediate benefits, and the message is geared to the reader's needs and use. He is bound to be persuaded to act. Involving the reader in something of interest and use to him becomes a persuasive act in itself, for who can resist something that is closely related to him?

■ How persuasive are you? Every day you are faced with at least one situation in which you must persuade someone to do what you want. Here are ten typical situations.[2] What would you do in each instance?

1. You're trying to persuade your landlord to paint the apartment.
   a. "After three years we deserve some attention."
   b. "It wouldn't cost much, compared to what we paid in rent."
   c. "Maybe I could do some of the painting myself."
   d. "My boss is coming to dinner next week. He's bringing lots of new people into town—potential tenants."
   e. "I'd paint it if I were you—this isn't the only apartment in town."

[2]Reprinted with permission from the December 1966 *Reader's Digest*. Copyright 1966 by the Reader's Digest Association, Inc. Condensed from *Contemporary*. The test was devised by John H. Wolfe, President, John Wolfe Institute, Houston, Texas, for use in management and sales training.

LOUIS A. ALLEN
Associates, Inc.

Management Educators
615 University Avenue
Palo Alto, California 94361
415/322-6421

February 1, 19__

Mr. Everett M. Pippin, Advertising Manager
David C. Cook Publishing Company
850 North Grove Avenue
Elgin, Illinois 60120

Dear Mr. Pippin:

Some call it a gift. Some say it's acquired. Others refer to it simply as the ability to lead and motivate people. Call it what you will--most executives agree it's the one asset that determines a manager's success more than anything else.

Curious thing, how the effects of this intangible something send morale up or down. Mostly it happens in little ways--in momentary contacts between manager and the managed. A word that shows understanding. Phrasing of instructions that stimulates accomplishment. The cutting remark that collapses a man's ego. Advice that takes the ball away from the runner. An expression of interest in a man's personal objectives. (All symbols that show how a manager feels about his subordinates.)

A bit ironic, isn't it, that the destinies of such big companies--such big investments in plant, production and people--are shaped by such intangible things as how its managers manage.

Yet most managers are good men with good intentions, convinced at the moment they're handling things in the right way. Trouble is, too few have the gift of natural leadership. Too many haven't taken time to think if there's a better way. Most are trying to get along with some basic abilities that could be remarkably improved with short, but intensive training in techniques used by successful managers.

If improving leadership skills is both a desire and a problem in your company, give us your managers for two days in this Leading and Motivating People program.

The men we return still won't be gifted leaders. But with improved leadership skills--gifted or 'got'--they'll know how to get results through other people.

Sincerely,

The Reporter of Direct Mail Advertising, April 1968, p. 43. Reproduced by permission.

2. You're trying to quiet a noisy drunk at a party.
   a. "Think what you'll feel like tomorrow!"
   b. "There's a very interesting girl over there. Sober up a little and I'll introduce you."
   c. "Can't you see, everybody is getting worried about you?"
   d. "You're too loud. Shut up."
   e. "I just heard you won the golf tournament. Tell me about it."
3. You're trying to talk the teacher into passing your teenage son—though she knows his homework papers were mostly done by you.
   a. "But Tommy tries so hard. Can't you give him credit for effort?"
   b. "The principal happens to be an old friend of mine!"
   c. "I'm the one who goofed and I was wrong. Why not flunk *me* and give Tommy a chance to make it up?"

Dear Mr. Jones:

Send us your managers for two days. They will be better managers when they come back.

On-the-job management training is not fast enough today to keep up with expanding business. Better management now, not next month or next year, is important to maintaining growing sales and profits.

You can get better management now, more effective leadership, greater skill in motivating employees, by sending your managers to the next Allen Management Seminar.

In two days of intensive study, discussion, and role playing in leadership situations, your managers learn how to get maximum cooperation from co-workers, how to improve working relationships and communications, and how to counsel others effectively.

Allen Seminars give your managers the practical, theoretical, emotional, and intellectual foundation for greater skill in getting results from and with other people. They quickly learn how to understand and motivate their co-workers, a skill that is seldom developed in formal business education.

No one is born with management skill. It is learned. Hundreds of aggressive and skillfully managed firms have sent their managers to Allen Seminars, some many times. They recognize the effectiveness of intensive training—that packs more management improvement into two days than can normally be gained from a year or more of short weekly meetings.

Select your men now to send to the next Allen Seminar. Each group is limited to 25 executives, so it is important to make reservations early. Once you see the results of intensive Allen training in people management, you will want to send all of your executives.

Sincerely,

The Reporter of Direct Mail Advertising, April 1968, p. 32.
Reproduced by permission.

d. "My brother, the actor, is visiting and we'd like you to meet him."

e. "If Tommy only passes this course he'll get into a good college."

4. You're soliciting a charity donation from a thrifty prospect.
   a. "Give me $10 and I'll fix the receipt so you can deduct $25 from your income tax."
   b. "Don't you agree it's better to take care of our needs locally, so the government won't have to step in and raise taxes?"
   c. "It's your civic duty, you know."
   d. "If *you* give, my collection record will be perfect."
   e. "This is a very worthy cause!"
5. A hoodlum sticks a gun in your back, and you're trying to save your money.
   a. "You're out of luck. I left my wallet in my other suit."
   b. "Watch out, buddy, I just graduated from karate school."
   c. "Gee, I worked all week for that money!"
   d. "Please! I can't face my wife if I come home broke."
   e. "My wallet is in my hip pocket."
6. You've been promoted over an older employee and you want his cooperation.
   a. "I'm going to need your help to get this job done."

   b. "My new boss will be retiring soon, and when I get his job I'll put you in this one."
   c. "Sorry I was promoted over you. You really deserved the job."
   d. "Now I'm boss and you'll just have to do things my way."
   e. "Look at it as a fresh opportunity to show how good you are."
7. You're trying to get your boy to practice the piano when he wants to watch TV.
   a. "You'll make me so proud if you learn to play well."
   b. "Be a good kid. We all have to do things we dislike."
   c. "Let's make a deal. If I let you watch this show, will you practice when it's over, without complaining?"
   d. "If you learn to play well, think how popular you'll be."
   e. "All that money for lessons will be wasted if you don't practice."
8. You need your secretary to work overtime, but she has a date.
   a. "Cancel the date, and I'll buy you the best steak in town when you finish this report."
   b. "The chief told me I just have to get this report out today."
   c. "I know it's an imposition—but *please*."
   d. "It's either stay and finish this, or back to the stenographers' pool."
   e. "You're the only one I'd trust to do this right."
9. You're trying to sell your husband on a second honeymoon.
   a. "I saw Dr. Mason today, and he said you've *got* to get some rest."
   b. "You take a lot of business trips. Now I want a trip."
   c. "Doesn't ten days on a Caribbean island sound tempting?"
   d. "Gee, honey, I'd really love a vacation."
   e. "Wouldn't it be great—just the two of us alone together?"
10. You're trying to talk a policeman out of giving you a ticket.
   a. "Give me a break—this once."
   b. "Listen, would this five-dollar bill square things?"
   c. "Believe it or not, I've never had a ticket before."
   d. "I guess I was going pretty fast, and just didn't realize it."
   e. "I'm on my way to an important appointment and I just can't be late."

■ As an experiment in oral persuasion, prepare a three-minute presentation to influence the thinking of the class. Allow a free choice of subjects. The presentation might include a lecture, a discussion, questions and answers, visual aids, or supporting materials and evidence. Before each presentation each speaker should tell the class what he is attempting to do to them; whether it is convincing them that personnel management is the most challenging job in business, persuading them to join a little-theater group, convincing them that mutual funds are the best way for a young executive to save money, persuading them to donate a pint of blood to the community blood bank, or convincing them that the voting age should be eighteen.

After each speaker announces his objective, but before he speaks, the class members should grade themselves on a minus-five to plus-five scale in terms of how they feel about the proposition. After each speech, the class members grade themselves again; thus the degree of persuasion can be measured. Each presentation can be analyzed. A good practice would be to ask why a student was or was not persuaded. The experiment should drive home the point that persuasive communication is getting people to arrive at *your* conclusion through *their* thought processes.

TECHNIQUES FOR PERSUASIVE WRITING

You persuade people to do things by making them want to. What do people want? They want to be well thought of, to get ahead in business, to do more work in less time and effort, or to make more money. Approval motivates people. Be genuinely interested in other people: show your appreciation, make them feel important, and show concern for them. These things will give a high credibility rating not only to you but also to your messages. Other techniques for persuasiveness include emphasizing the positive aspect, presenting evidence and supporting material, and using sales psychology to create confidence and invoke action.

Be Positive

Emphasizing the positive aspect and either eliminating or subordinating the negative goes a long way toward convincing people that what is being said is worthwhile. Negativism suggests the opposite, often antagonizes, and invokes an unfavorable response. Consider the effect of the following sentences:

Negative:	*Positive:*
This toy is made of plastic that will not break.	This toy train is made of durable polyethylene plastic to withstand a boy's hard play.
Our store opens at 9:30 and closes at 5:30.	For the convenience of our cusomers, our store is open from 9:30 to 5:30.
In view of what you say, we shall have to make good the supposed damage.	We shall be delighted to send you a new shipment.
Since you failed to stipulate the size and color, we cannot send you your merchandise.	Let us know the size and color you wish and your merchandise will be on its way.
We are sorry that the book cannot be sent you until next month.	*The Hidden Persuaders* will be sent you as soon as the reprint is available next month.
Unfortunately, I have had no practical business experience.	In college my courses in management dealt with practical solutions to business problems.

The half-dozen following sentences illustrate some important do's and don'ts in emphasizing the positive aspect:

Do:	*Don't:*
Tell what a product will do.	Tell what a product will not do.
Mention specific details of construction or use.	Use general terms that say nothing and leave the reader to guesses.
Take action pleasantly.	Do something grudgingly.
Give the other person a chance to save face.	Blame the other fellow or tell him he is wrong.
Tell what you can do.	Tell what you cannot do.
Mention strong points.	Play up weaknesses.

Suppose that in the mail order business, a customer who ordered five items was informed that shipment of two of the items would be made in two weeks (as they were not then in stock), but that the others were being shipped at once. The letter would first give news of the shipment being made immediately, then explain why the other two were not being shipped and inform the customer that they would be sent in two weeks.

A letter declining an invitation to speak, because of a previous commitment, would not begin by saying "no." It would begin by being appreciative of the invitation or by showing an interest in the inviting group. Both of these instances involve the psychology of saying "no." In such cases, the positive approach is to put good or favorable items first, to offer explanations, and to emphasize whatever is helpful and constructive.

The positive approach can add up to a sale:

> A salesman was trying to sell an adding machine to a small town druggist. He finished his sales talk but had no customer reaction; he repeated major points—no response. Finally he closed with "and every progressive merchant I know has an adding machine."
>
> "Certainly," the druggist replied, "I've had one for years."
>
> That was the opening the salesman wanted; he asked to see it, to evaluate trade-in value. The druggist took him into the back of the store. The salesman took a look and let out a derogatory "ugh." Starting to comment further on its age, the salesman was asked to leave and protested. . . .
>
> The next day he reported the incident to his boss and they decided to return to the druggist. The boss wanted the facts and the sale. The salesman waited in the car for over 15 minutes. When the boss came out he had the old adding machine and had made the sale. His comment was, "Get driving fast; the druggist is still angry with you and I don't want him to face you today."
>
> The boss further explained that the druggist felt he had been insulted. "I might have accepted his offer of a trade-in for my old machine, but he acted disgusted with it and I ordered him out."

The boss had countered, "May I have a look at the machine? Why, it's a good machine. It's in good working condition, too. You must take a great deal of pride in how it has worked for you all these years. Now let me show you how our new machine will save you even more money and time."

Moral: Look at things from the customer's point of view.[3]

Offer Evidence and Proof

Because it offered concrete evidence in the finished photograph shown to the audience, one of the most convincing commercials on television some years ago was the one-minute "live" Polaroid demonstration on the Jack Paar show. The Polaroid Land Camera produced a finished snapshot exactly sixty seconds after a picture had been taken. Although there was an element of risk every time the commercial was presented, the corporation was so sure of its product that in 1959 it spent $2,500,000 in its ad budget, with 75 percent going to television. Polaroid was selling the idea that photography can be fun, and the suspense created by wondering how the picture was going to turn out increased audience interest and lent unlimited credibility to the camera. The demonstration was one convincing type of evidence used to persuade.

Closely allied to demonstrations used in advertising and selling persuasively are the free trial offer, the guarantee, the sample, shipment on approval, the refund, and the offer of free aid or services. This type of evidence creates confidence in a product and firm. It reflects the company's own confidence in its products and indicates its willingness to make good any shortcomings. The confidence of the company inspires confidence in the customer. The prospect takes no risk; he pays only if satisfied, and he is disarmed immediately because he is guaranteed satisfaction and service or his money back.

Another type of evidence useful in selling and advertising is the test. There are three kinds, ranked in order of their persuasive power: tests by the prospect (the ninety-day home trial), tests by an independent research agency, and tests by the company itself. We are prone to look upon company tests as biased and on those made by an independent agency with the attitude, "Well, they were paid to say that was the result," or, "They aren't telling the whole story." Testimonials given by the man in the street, for the same reason, generally carry more convincing weight than those given by a famous person. To say "Mr. Jonathan Wedding, who lives on the next street over, installed storm windows last fall and reports that his fuel bill was reduced 15 percent" is much more believable and persuasive than to say "Mr. Cary Grant installed storm windows last fall and reports that his fuel bill was reduced 15 percent." There is a persuasive element, however, in an ad-

[3]"The Sale I Never Forgot," *Printers' Ink*, August 1, 1958, p. 49.

vertisement claiming that a particular brand of lipstick is used by Raquel Welch or Jane Fonda, for women wish to look beautiful, and to some of them a certain type of beauty is exemplified in the movie celebrity. Unconsciously and unadmittedly they hope to look like the actress by using the lipstick.

One of the most powerful types of persuasive evidence is simply the use of facts and figures as supporting statements to ideas or conclusions. Specific details are useful in backing up conclusions. When they are tactfully and tastefully presented, their implications become highly believable. In using supporting statements of facts and figures it is well always to make apparent the authority or source and to follow a logical presentation. Both the writer and reader might well ask:

1. Are the facts and figures pertinent and essential?
2. Are they representative?
3. Are they accurate and reliable?
4. Does the statement seem probable?
5. Is the information the result of observation or hearsay?
6. Are the data up-to-date?
7. What effect will the data have?
8. Are there sufficient data to justify a conclusion?
9. Are the cases typical?

Facts and figures must also be evaluated for their consistency with other evidence, their interest to the reader, and their general usefulness in accomplishing the writer's purpose.

Apply Sales Psychology

Presenting the message in a positive, constructive manner and following the four steps of sales psychology can persuade and move the reader or listener to action. A successful sales formula has always been *attention, interest, conviction,* and *action.* These are the stages the customer goes through mentally and psychologically before he buys any product. Beginning in a friendly way, starting at the reader's point of interest, finding a common ground, arousing curiosity—all are aimed at getting attention, whether you are selling an idea, a product, or a service. Once the reader's attention is focused, his interest develops. Being sympathetic, showing respect for the prospect's advice and ideas, talking about benefits, using appeals—all further his interest in the subject or product. Talking in terms of the reader's self-interest, being specific, using evidence to prove a point, showing him how he will profit—all these are convincing. Telling a person what to do, making it easy for him to act, supplying an impulse for immediate action—all lead the person to action. The psychological steps of selling are extremely useful in organizing your sales messages to be persuasive.

The Dy-Dee Service letter opposite persuades the reader to mail back its reservation form. Its headline caption gets the reader's attention because of the awareness it expresses of the coming event. The reader immediately becomes involved; her interest is furthered by the specific advantages described—protection, convenience, and economical, safe, and efficient service. These advantages convince her that the Dy-Dee Service is for her. The free gifts are offered as incentives, and action is made easy. The final impulse in the last sentence moves her to act immediately.

Many advantages are stated, so that if one or two should not appeal to any given reader, others will. The letter, which is organized according to the psychological sales steps, moves fluently from one benefit to another, contributing to a total persuasive effect.

WRITING SALES LETTERS THAT SELL

Selling is presenting facts and qualities about a product or service in such a way as to persuade the other person (the customer) to buy the product or to take some action toward buying. Writing a sales letter can be just as creative and dynamic as any other method of salesmanship. Linking the needs, wants, and interests of a prospect with your product is a fascinating game.

Although selling has not been reduced to a formula, to succeed in its purpose a sales letter must create attention, arouse interest, convince or create a desire, and evoke action. These are the sales steps or psychological stages of selling, and thus could be thought of as a formula for organizing a sales message. However, there are also other requirements that a successful sales letter must meet.

A sales letter should show sincerity, integrity, goodwill, and a genuine interest in serving the reader. It also must prove logically, clearly, and fairly that the product offered will satisfy the prospect and must persuade him to want to possess it and use it. This means that it must meet the basic requirements of any effective letter by using all the principles and techniques at the writer's command to assure that it will be understood, will be considered interesting and persuasive, and will motivate the prospect to action. You have been developing the skills to accomplish these objectives, especially in Chapters 4, 5, and 6; now it behooves you to apply all you have learned to the task of writing sales letters that sell. The planning of a sales letter begins with an analysis of the prospect and the product.

1895-1965 Cyril B. Lewis/Founder

Hope F. Lewis/President • Horatio B. Lewis II/Vice President • Beatrice Clark, R.N., Stanford C. Stoddard/Directors • Donald J. Miller/Sec. • Peggy W. Lewis/Treas.

12626 GREENLAWN
DETROIT, MICHIGAN 48238
PHONE (313) 933-0390

A Baby Due Soon . . . and
What About The Diapers?

Can it be that you have decided against the protection our exclusive Diaseptic Process diapers give? Remember, our diapers . . . the finest Johnson-Johnson make . . . are checked every month by a national laboratory to be sure they contain clinical properties that act to prevent diaper rash. No other diapers can guarantee your baby this protection.

Aside from protection, think of the convenience. All of the Diaseptic Process diapers your baby needs, delivered ready to use in sanitary plastic bags each week. There is no worry about running out of diapers . . . no worry about washing and folding diapers when you are ~~dead~~ tired.

In addition to protection and convenience, DY-DEE Service is economical, too. Are you aware that automatic washers were never constructed for diaper washing? They do not get the water hot enough to sterilize and they do not rinse thoroughly enough to get out every bit of soap . . . two of the main factors in diaper rash. In addition, they still save you at the most only 54 cents a week over diaper service.

So think it over. In addition to reserving DY-DEE Service the enclosed card entitles you to a copy of Dr. Spock's "Baby and Child Care" as well as a subscription to Baby Talk Magazine and a stainless steel baby feeding spoon. It will take you just a minute to fill in the reservation form and mail it back to us. It's already addressed and needs no postage. Why not do it now and then rest assured that your baby will have all the cleanest, whitest, softest, safest diapers he'll need . . . when he needs them.

Cordially,

Peggy W. Lewis

Mrs. Peggy W. Lewis
Communications Director

jb
enclosures
file: A42-3

P.S. Now all suburbs can call us without charge on our new toll-free number: 800-552-4513.

Serving Michigan Hospitals and Homes Since 1933 • *Symbol of Diaper Service Quality and Safety*

Courtesy The DY-DEE Service, Detroit, Mich.

Know Your Product and Prospect

There is no doubt about it. The more you know about what you are selling, the better able you will be to present a persuasive sales message. Your prospect cannot be convinced unless you yourself are convinced. The more you speak and write about the qualities and uses of the product, the more confidence your prospect will have in you and in the particular item you are selling. This means learning all you can about design, construction, materials, and processes. The sales writer must uncover facts that will answer these questions:

1. How is the product used?
2. Where is it used?
3. When is it used?
4. Why is it used?
5. Why isn't it used more?
6. Has it any new uses?

These answers should not come just from reading advertisements or fly sheets, from scanning catalogs or sales literature. They should come from a first-hand acquaintance with the product, which can be obtained by personally trying it out, by going into the factory to observe it and inquire about it, or by talking with its users. This can reveal simple facts that make good talking points, and that might otherwise be overlooked.

Knowledge about a product should also include facts and ideas about competing products, services, and companies. This will give you a basis for comparing quality, performance, uses, and cost. Although you should not knock the other fellow or his product to your prospect, this knowledge may provide you with good talking points that will place your own product in a favorable light.

You must make your message vital to the customer. To do this, you have to understand him as an individual or as a member of a group of people.[4] Otherwise, how can you connect your product with his specific wants, needs, or other interests? An analysis of the customer's wants, likes, dislikes, and interests will help you to show that you care about him as a person and will enable you to tailor your sales message to his interests. A key question to ask is, "Why should he do what I am asking him to do?"

Your prospect will like facts about your product that will enable him to do a better job or to live more happily. This means that you need to know him: his job, his duties there, his attitudes, and how he feels; for human desires and satisfactions form the basis for selling. In this way you can describe persuasively how the products and services you of-

[4]See also pp. 11, 12, 85–89, and 148–58.

fer will satisfy him. The customer is always asking, "What's in it for me?"

Just as selling is based on knowledge of the product, so it is also based on knowledge of what makes people tick. This requires the sales writer to have first-hand knowledge of human nature, an understanding of human instincts and emotions, and the ability to make his product appeal to the customer.

Create Attention-Getting Openings[5]

An attention-getting opening will cause the reader to say to himself, "This is for me; it's worth reading," and he will read on. Any attention-getting opening will recognize its reader and relate the product or service to him. This is possible because from his analysis, the writer has knowledge of what the reader likes, wants, and can use.

The attention-getting opening may take the form of a question, a statement, or a command. It may be positioned on three lines to take the place of an inside address, placed as a headline across the top of the page, or divided to lead the reader by short, successive stages to the point of the letter.

1. *When using a question,* avoid one with a straight "yes" or "no" answer. Induce the reader to answer as you wish. Lead him on to seek the answer or solution to a problem, as:

   Are you wasting your secretary's time?

2. *When using a statement,* be agreeable. Say something of importance or significance to the reader. Relate the idea in the statement to your product as a benefit or advantage to him:

   Carpets come clean, easily and quickly, with the Knox Deep Cleaner.

3. *When using a command,* involve the reader immediately, for you have made a decision for him and are asking that he follow it. Make certain that it is something he will want to do and will do without hesitation:

   Set before your family tonight a mouth-melting orange chiffon pie . . . watch the looks of sheer delight as . . .

The following opening of a letter inviting membership in the American Torch Club demonstrates the use of several lines in place of the inside address. After emphasizing a benefit, it leads directly into the heart of the letter and motivates with its snob appeal:

A personal invitation to you from the Board of Directors of the American
Oil Company to enjoy the special privileges of Charter Membership
in the AMERICAN TORCH CLUB—a full year's membership at
HALF PRICE—A SAVING OF $6.00

[5]See also pp. 90–92.

> The American Oil Company is pleased to announce that you are among those of our credit card customers who are eligible for Charter Membership in the exclusive, new and most unique credit card club in the world—the American Torch Club.
>
> Membership is limited. Only credit card holders like yourself, with the necessary qualifications and exemplary record, can qualify.

Sometimes the message begins on the envelope and continues inside. The reader recognizes this as a sales promotion technique and therefore knows that he will be subjected to a sales talk; nevertheless, when the technique is used effectively, the reader's curiosity is aroused and he opens the envelope and reads on. On page 213 is an example of such a message that a weekly science magazine used in soliciting subscriptions.

The form and layout of the opening of a sales letter will do a great deal to make a favorable impression and attract attention. True attention, however, must also create interest, for the two merge with only a shade of difference between them. For this reason effectiveness is dependent upon the relationship of the attention ideas to the product and reader: the ideas must direct the reader into some major point connecting him with the product. Appeals, advantages, benefits, and reader involvement are always strong beginning ideas. Keep in mind that:

1. The profit motive attracts customers.
2. Curiosity arouses the interest to read further.
3. The sympathy appeal, appropriately used, opens hearts.
4. Civic pride motivates action.
5. Special interests influence prospects.
6. Appeals to basic human wants, such as comfort, security, health, and convenience, attract attention.
7. Appeals to emotions, such as love, patriotism, pride, and ambition, involve the reader and create interest.
8. "Selling the sizzle, not the steak," or appeals to the five senses—sight, sound, taste, smell, and touch—generally are impressive.
9. The use of humor on a sophisticated level can be effective.
10. "Telling it straight" impresses the reader with the writer's credibility.

Note the following sample openings and the reasons why they are effective:

Yes, there is a special hospitalization plan that is available *only* to those who don't drink—and for good, sound business reasons.	(Benefit appeal to special group)

________ MAGAZINE

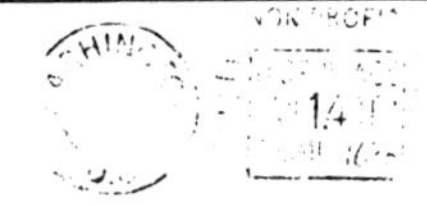

You will soon hold in your hand
a new paper
that disintegrates, disappears
when dropped into water.
Your sample is enclosed.

MRS LELAND BROWN Z
1929 WITMIRE ST
YPSILANTI MICH 48197

__________ MAGAZINE

Here is a square of the new disintegrating, disappearing paper . . .

Tear off a part of it and drop it into water. See what happens in less than a minute. This new achievement of ingenious scientists can be made into bags or packets to enclose industrial, agricultural and household materials for measured use when dropped into water. It is non-toxic, has no odor.

And note its security possibilities for diplomatic or military agencies, for research laboratories where if it is necessary, records, letters, formulae and maps can be disposed of quickly and completely without tell-tale evidence.

This new paper has been described in ________, the magazine that brings each week to its readers all that is recent in science. From no other single source can you get so many advanced ideas, so much stimulating science information . . . in so short a time at each reading.

You can know about wonderful new developments in science, practically as soon as the scientists working upon them, by reading ______ ____.

You can read by the F-5 Portalite a mile or more away! That, better than anything I can think of, demonstrates the intensity and power of the F-5 used as a searchlight.	(Reader involved in using product)
You can fill a better job and command a better salary, and here's a free lesson that shows you how.	(Appeals to security and money)

Readers may not read every word and sentence in a letter, but they will glance at the opening; they will read further if they see something that will help them make more money, lead a happier life, raise their status, or satisfy some personal want, need, or desire. So pack as many benefits as possible in the first sentence. Then the reader will read on through the remainder of the letter.

Develop a Central Selling Point

Once the prospect's attention has been obtained, lead him into the central selling point. Give him the details, facts, figures, descriptions, and advantages that will cause him to visualize the product not only as it is but also in operation.

When you analyze your product and prospect, numerous ideas will come to you about points that you can use in talking about your product to a particular customer. The central selling point is decided upon by asking:

> "Of all the talking points I can use, which one will be most persuasive for this prospect?"
>
> "To which one central idea can I relate all the selling points so that I can make a united effort for total persuasion?"

Selecting the best idea and making it the backbone of your letter will allow you to arrange your supporting ideas around it. The central idea may be stated at the beginning, at the end, or somewhere in the middle. At the beginning, it lets the reader know what to expect. At the end, it provides a summary or final point. In the middle of the letter, it is the focus, with ideas pointing toward it and away from it.

There are a number of ways to develop the central idea: by descriptive or analytical details, by comparison and contrast, by cause and effect, by illustration or example, and by narration. Description enables the reader to visualize the product as it is and in use. Details provide concrete evidence and add interest and emphasis. They may consist of descriptive words, figures, specific points—all to help the reader understand. Comparison and contrast may be used separately or may be intermingled. They indicate relationships between points and are also useful in analysis and description. Illustrations serve as an application of the general idea and help the prospect to see himself involved in similar situations. Narrative creates the illusion of reality.

Look at the following description of old-fashioned Louisiana Strawberry Shortcake as described on a Toffenetti menu:

> The Louisiana sun, the earth enriched by a thousand years of erosion, the blissful warm rain plus the tender care of lovely maidens of the South, bring forth to you the most luscious, delicious strawberries you ever tasted. Fresh, sweet, ripe, and gorgeously red as the lips you love to kiss.

This may cause you to picture the strawberry shortcake and may persuade you to order one. It does not, however, necessarily appeal to your sense of taste, as is usually done in selling food items.

The following excerpt is from a direct mail letter to sell campers Chuck Wagon Foods.[6]

> . . . Complete and tasty meals packaged for one to six people are ready in a jiffy. All the time-consuming work is done at the Chuck Wagon plant. You add water, heat, and a meal is created.
>
> Chuck Wagon Foods are made to take the load off your back. Why tote fresh or canned foods that are mostly water? There is far less weight with Chuck Wagon and no refrigeration needed—guaranteed to keep for a year. Chuck Wagon food per man-day weighs just 1½ lbs.
>
> Note the interesting and appetizing menus listed in the catalog. Each meal is balanced, nourishing, and adequate for the huskiest camper. . . .

Facts about the food are given in terms of reader benefits. The reader is assured that Chuck Wagon Foods are good to eat, easy to prepare, and easy to carry, and that they require no storage care. Thus the sales points are related to the central point of *convenience;* they develop or reinforce it and at the same time create interest and persuade.

"Be specific and vivid" is always good advice when you are describing something. Note the following excerpt from a letter written to interest a prospective out-of-town buyer in looking at a house:

> I know your family would fit into our house, for it has three bedrooms and a fourth room that can be used as a study or bedroom. There are two and one-half baths, with one of them attached to the master bedroom. We think the architect must have known that large families were going to live here because all the rooms are big. The kitchen and dinette are large enough for everyone to get into at the same time. The living room with its fireplace is big enough for two davenports with room to spare. If your family is as active as ours, you will appreciate the recreation room in the basement and the big fenced-in back yard.

The central selling point appears in the first part of the first sentence. The facts presented all support the idea of "large house for your family." The reader can visualize his family living comfortably in the house.

Sizing up their alumni as prospects for fund-giving, Miami University views them as reaching a gift-giving peak twenty-five years or longer after graduation. They have found that fairly informal, personal letters work best, that an element of nostalgia that recalls pleasant memories produces friends and increases contributions. One of their letters, reproduced on page 216, shows the development of a theme with the central selling point permeating the entire letter.

[6] *The Reporter of Direct Mail Advertising,* March 1968, p. 46. Reprinted by permission.

To Be Read With A Smile

REMEMBER THE FANTASTIC
PITCHING OF SATCHEL PAIGE?

Ted Williams, one of history's greatest hitters, with a lifetime batting average of .344, got one hit in forty-one tries off Old Satch.

That's an average of .024!

Joe DiMaggio, the pride of the Yankees, outfielder magnificent, clutch hitter extraordinary, did a bit better.

Two for sixty-five ... a sparkling .030!

Satch did let some of the weaker batters hit once in a while, and when Bill Veeck asked him why, Ol' Rockin' Chair replied: "I just like to help keep those po' boys in the league."

I have something in common with Terrible Ted and Joltin' Joe. All year long, I've been swinging away ... trying to make a hit with you on behalf of the Miami University Fund. Unlike Ted Williams and Joe DiMaggio, I'd be happy with a single. But, says our official scorer ...

My 1967 batting average is .000!

By bunching single gifts into meaningful clusters for scholarships, the Alumni Center, faculty research, and many development projects, the Miami University Fund has helped alumni and friends do great things for Miami year after year. Now we're in the last of the ninth for 1967, and it's now or never in this ball game.

Even though you've had good reason for pitching a no-hitter so far, I hope you're now in the mood to relax, relent, remit, and ...

Keep this po' boy in the league.

Gratefully,

John E. Dolibois

The Reporter of Direct Mail Advertising, April 1968, p. 39. Reproduced by permission.

Use Action Endings[7]

Assuming that the listener or reader has been interested and persuaded, he is ready for action. Most business letters state the action the reader is to take, explain and make action easy, and provide an extra impulse or inducement to act. The following ending is typical of a direct mail sales letter selling a magazine subscription:

> Use the handy order form and postage-free envelope enclosed today to send us your instructions. That way, we'll have sufficient time to give your Christmas order all the careful attention it deserves.
>
> Remember, ________ is one gift you can give with confidence to everyone on your list whose time—like your own—is limited but whose interests are not.

Often a special inducement such as a booklet, sample, free trial, premium, or introductory price is offered to the reader. A time limit might be placed on the offer so that the reader may be persuaded to act now. A limited supply also tends to have the same result—immediate action. Stressing what the reader will gain, restating the central selling point, and utilizing a special appeal are good motivating techniques.

In addition, an action ending should include a reason for action, and should be clear and specific, expressed in a natural personal tone, aided by appropriate enclosures, and stated positively.

The action ending is always in line with the purpose of the letter:

Will you please indicate on the enclosed card when it will be convenient for you to see our representative?	(Having a representative call)
Drop the enclosed card in the mail today. We'll then send the slacks to you for a week's inspection *free*.	(Making a sale by direct mail)
Let us help you save on your next season's fuel bill. Telephone 482-6841.	(Obtaining an order by telephone)

A homey style was used in a service station sales campaign, consisting of a letter and two picture postcards with messages, which won one of the annual awards of the Direct Mail Association. (See pages 218–20.) The copy was created by Paul J. Bringe, sales manager of the Milwaukee Dustless Brush Company, for his son Richard, owner of Dick's Center Service in Milwaukee, Wisconsin. The cards introduce a new service station operator, and the copy is based on selling the individual and service rather than products. The letter is an appeal to the reader to

[7]See also pp. 92, 93, and 96.

help the little fellow, something everyone likes to do—especially when it doesn't cost any more money. With the letter, Dick enclosed a picture of his son, Stevie, looking out the window for his father.

Card #1

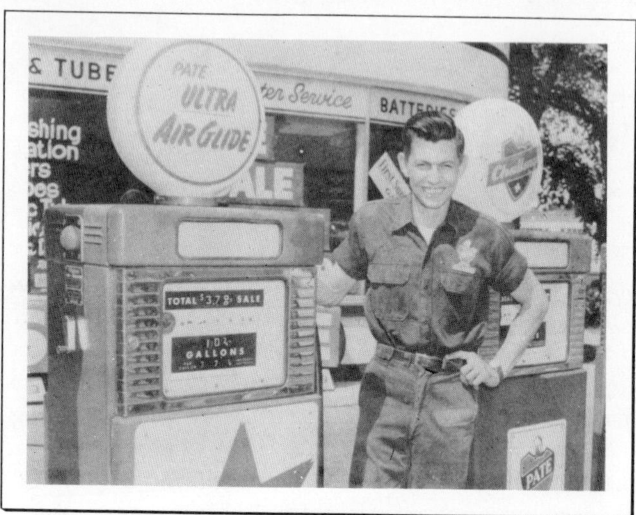

Hello Neighbor:

I am Dick Bringe, operating the Pate Service Station at Center & Pierce. I'd like the chance to take care of your car as I do my own--with gas & oil, but perhaps more important, with repair work you may need to keep your car in first class shape.

I've got the latest equipment for good repair work--tune-ups, muffler and tail pipes, brake adjustment and reline, and voltage regulators and generators. There's a good tow truck here too, ready to help you out anytime.

When your car doesn't sound right or act right, let me have a look at it. Nine times out of ten I can tell you what's wrong, and where to get it fixed reasonably, if I can't do it myself.

Dick Bringe - Dick's Center Service
632 E. Center St. Co 4-3260

BULK RATE
U. S. POSTAGE
PAID
MILWAUKEE, WIS.
PERMIT NO. 4666

The Reporter of Direct Mail Advertising, November 1958, p. 28. Reproduced by permission.

Card #2

Hello Neighbor:

Your Pate Station at Center and Pierce is pretty busy these days but not too busy to give your car the attention it should have. The time to avoid car trouble is before it happens - that's my specialty. Nothing I like better than putting your car in first class shape -- and at a reasonable price.

Snow tires are getting popular, and with good reason. I've got a special on them. It isn't as expensive as you might think to be ready for any kind of storm. Ask me about snow tires next time you come in.

When you have a repair job, big or small, check with me first on the cost. My overhead is small so I don't have to charge as much as the big shops -- and I guarantee everything I do.

Dick Bringe - Dick's Center Serv.
632 E. Center St. CO 4-3260

BULK RATE
U. S. POSTAGE
PAID
MILWAUKEE, WIS.
PERMIT NO. 4666

The Reporter of Direct Mail Advertising, November 1958, p. 28. Reproduced by permission.

DICK'S CENTER SERVICE

632 E. Center Street CO 4–3260

Hello Neighbor:

This is a picture of Stevie.

It's not a very good picture, I'll admit, because you can't see his face. He thinks he's heard his Dad's car come up the drive so he is investigating.

Stevie is pretty small but, in a way, he is partly responsible for the service and careful attention your car gets at this Pate Station. When the hours stretch out and a quick change in the weather brings service calls one after another, I think of Stevie peeking out that window.

Then suddenly everything is fun to do and every job goes faster.

Of course, Stevie can't really fix your car, not yet at least. It's up to me to do that. Sometimes, when I'm late getting home and he has made three or four trips to the window, I like to think he understands why I am late--and thinks it's all worthwhile.

When a young man has a wife, and Stevie, and Pamela, he's got to do a mighty good job of taking care of your car. That's just what I want to do.

Will you give me the opportunity?

Sincerely,

Dick Bringe

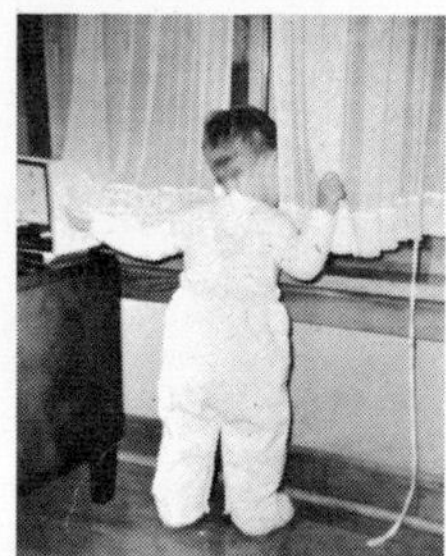

Tune Up
Lubrication
Brake Reline
Mufflers and Tail Pipes
Washing
Pickup and Delivery

The Reporter of Direct Mail Advertising, November 1958, p. 29. Reproduced by permission.

The cards and letter in the service station series have elements common to most sales letters.

1. *An effective opening to catch the reader's eye:*

   "I am Dick Bringe, operating the Pate Service Station at Center and Pierce. I'd like the chance to take care of your car as I do my own. . . ."

   "Your Pate Station at Center and Pierce is pretty busy these days, but not too busy to give your car the attention it should have."

2. *A smooth transition into the sales talk:*

   "Stevie is pretty small but, in a way, he is partly responsible for the service and careful attention your car gets at this Pate Station. . . ."

3. *A central selling point:*

   Use of the personality behind the efficient "service with a smile."

4. *Specific details to attract and develop interest:*

   ". . . latest equipment for good repair work—tune-ups, muffler and tail pipes. . . ."

   "Nine times out of ten I can tell what's wrong."

   ". . . putting your car in first-class shape—at a reasonable price."

   "I guarantee everything."

   "My overhead is small."

5. *Effective endings, stimulating action:*

   "If you prefer, you can simply give me a telephone call at. . . ."

   At the bottom of the service station cards—"Dick Bringe—Dick's Center Service, 632 E. Center Street, CO4-3260."

   At the close of the letter— ". . . mighty good job taking care of your car. That's just what I want to do. Will you give me the opportunity?"

This series also makes full use of principles and techniques that are common to all letters; these principles and techniques contributed to the success of the series:

1. The mailings are adapted to the purpose and the reader.
2. They give full consideration to the reader, stressing benefits and making him feel important as an individual.
3. They contain a positive, courteous attitude, shown sincerely and simply, which creates goodwill.
4. Originality and ingenuity make them something other than run-of-the-mill letters.

■ Collect sample sales letters and analyze them for their persuasiveness. Why are their openings attention-getting or not? What is the central selling point in each and how is it developed? What motivates the action?

■ Collect sample advertisements and analyze them for their attention-getting effectiveness, interesting appeals, and ability to stimulate action. Is there any similarity in the techniques and principles of sales letters and advertisements?

■ After analyzing advertisements and letters, draw some conclusions about persuasive techniques that are applicable and effective. You might compile your results in a memorandum report on:

  1. Creating attention-getting openings
  2. Developing the sales story

3. Using imagination in writing sales messages
4. Using humor to sell and promote products
5. Applying the right degree of showmanship in selling

OPPORTUNITIES FOR PERSUASIVE WRITING

Sales letters form the most commonly used type of persuasive writing in business today. They require the writer to apply the principles of persuasion in specific situations, and a person who can do this effectively in selling can also do it when other persuasive opportunities present themselves. In any sales letter the customer or prospect is persuaded to take a specific action step, which in reality accomplishes the purpose of the letter. Sales letters are written to:

1. Sell direct through the mail
2. Induce a customer to come into a store
3. Advertise a product
4. Create inquiries about a product
5. Answer sales inquiries
6. Introduce or pave the way for a representative to call
7. Regain inactive customers
8. Raise funds or obtain contributions
9. Cultivate a customer
10. Induce one department's customer to become the customer of another department

Sales letters may be used with enclosures that do part of the selling. For instance, with a letter that concentrates on getting attention and interest, a brochure containing facts and figures will help to convince the reader, and the two together will lead him to buy. Sometimes a series of letters is used as part of a campaign; in a four-letter series, sent over a period of time, each letter may do one phase of the selling.

Although sales letters comprise the most commonly used type of persuasive letter-writing in business today, some claim letters, requests, and refusals are highly persuasive, and opportunities in other situations often present themselves. Collection letters collect past-due accounts and keep accounts current. Intra-office memorandums used vertically and horizontally across organization lines stimulate action through persuasive messages.

Collecting Past-Due Accounts

Difficulties increase in writing collection letters, for the letter must be courteous, sincere, and simple, and must present disagreeable material in agreeable terms, treat an unpleasant subject in pleasant words, and impel the receiver to pay the amount due. It must do this without arousing resentment and must maintain goodwill to keep the customer and firm on friendly business terms. Because of the increased difficulties, the whole area of collection and credit has become highly specialized, and a large body of knowledge has evolved. Those of you who obtain work in credit and collections can prepare yourselves by further study and experience on the job. For this reason it is sufficient here to recognize that the concepts, principles, and techniques of persuasive writing are applicable to collection situations—the reader must be persuaded to act (to pay up).

Collection letters generally state what the customer received for his promise to pay, review the case (including the amount due and the terms), give a reason or motive for payment, appeal to the reader, and request payment. The opening paragraph may use an attention-getting device, state the business at hand, create a favorable attitude, or say something that pleases. The body of the letter should make a mental and emotional appeal for payment. The ending should explain what is to be done, state how and when action should be taken, and provide an inducement for action.

The letter below was successful in collecting membership dues for the New Orleans Chamber of Commerce Association.

Form letters are often used in collecting money. The secret of their success lies in the fact that they are not always recognizable as form let-

Dear Mr. Smith:

Your Help is Wanted!

Asking a member for membership dues is never a pleasant task, but nevertheless, it is a task that must be performed if your Chamber is to cope successfully with the multitude of complexities arising from our tremendous industrial growth and increasing population.

We are calling this matter of your unpaid dues to your attention with the thought that our previous bills have been overlooked or misdirected--your check may be on its way. If not, we feel that you will take care of this at once.

The growth of your business depends upon the industrial expansion of New Orleans.

Help them both now!

Sincerely yours,

President

ters. A collection series follows the steps of collection through three major assumptions.

1. The assumption that the customer will pay:
   a. Notification—the usual statement
   b. A reminder—a statement plus a sticker or note, or a short letter
2. The assumption that something is wrong:
   a. An inquiry—a discussion, a request for money or an explanation, an offer of help and cooperation
   b. Appeals—element of urgency
3. The assumption that the customer is not going to pay, and that strong persuasion is necessary:
   a. A demand—a strong request for money, appeals to self-interest or fear
   b. An ultimatum—must be carried out
   c. Action—a credit bureau, a legal suit, or a collection agency

Some do's and don'ts in writing collection letters are:

1. Set the tone and topic early.
2. Be friendly, helpful, and considerate.
3. Don't seem annoyed or mistreated.
4. Don't antagonize by implying dishonesty or poverty.
5. State the amount due and request payment.
6. Develop points convincingly—by explanation, analogy, anecdote, or dramatization.
7. Use the "you" attitude whenever possible.
8. Sell the reader on paying and retain his goodwill.
9. Give the customer a chance to save face.
10. Don't continue to assume that it is an oversight.
11. Don't threaten or issue an ultimatum until you are ready to carry it out.
12. Use appeals appropriate for each stage of collection:

Stage:	*Appeal:*
Notification and reminder	Humor, oversight, and cooperation
Inquiry and discussion	Cooperation, fair play, and pride
Demand and urgency	Self-interest and fear
Action	Fear and loss of credit

Most people pay long before the account goes into the later stages of collection. At that point the company is dealing with only a very small percentage of customers, and perhaps it would be just as well not to continue them as customers.

Motivating Action Through Intra-Office Memorandums

Often memorandum reports are used to speed up the flow of information within the company and little persuasion is needed. The reader recognizes that he needs the information to make an analysis or decision and readily acts upon it. There are times, however, when a solution to a problem or a course of action is recommended and persuasion is necessary to motivate the reader to act.

Motivating the reader to act requires logic in handling evidence, proof, and supporting statements. A clearly written memorandum indicates sound reasoning and reliable data, for the writer had to reason through his material to organize and present it logically. The report writer avoids hasty generalizations in his own thinking by making sure that he has enough data to draw valid conclusions. He studies an adequate number of specific cases as evidence and picks out the general trend or conclusion to which they point. When working from an assumption, he discovers adequate supporting facts and instances to prove it to be a workable one.

Many fallacies of reasoning can occur; the way to avoid them is to think logically and critically. Pass judgment, draw an inference, and reach conclusions only after thinking through the facts. Weigh the pros and cons, study the advantages and disadvantages, make comparisons, and test your conclusions. Consider *all* the evidence; see the *total* picture. Prevent generalities and ambiguities by taking these precautions:

1. State your ideas definitely.
2. Be exact.
3. Use explicit words.
4. Qualify general statements.
5. Use illustrations and examples.

Argumentative exposition is a type of logical reasoning that presents factual and reasoned proof to prove a point, conclusion, or recommendation. The four steps taken in the process might be used as a basis for organizing a report:

1. Discuss the problem.
2. Explain the main issues.
3. Submit proof and evidence.
4. Draw conclusions and make recommendations.

The discussion of the problem should point to a need for a change or improvement, or should state a recommendation or proposition. The main issues are determined by their importance and use. Proof may be factual or reasoned. When opinions are cited, they should be those of authorities. Statistics, tables of figures, and the like show concrete evidence. Along with factual and reasoned proof, use persuasion to influence action. Every consideration should be given to winning the reader over. Anticipated objections should be presented and refuted. The entire presentation should marshal its data to convince the reader.

A common situation that requires persuasion is the purchase of new equipment. Operational efficiency might be developed as a major point; then all the facts and data would be used to prove that the new equipment is necessary to either maintain or increase efficiency. In another situation a decision may be made to purchase the *X* brand of typewriters instead of brands *Y* or *Z*, and the manager must be persuaded that *X* is the best choice. Comparisons of all three brands would be made according to factors such as cost, special features, advantages, size and weight, discounts, and availability of service and repairs. This would prove the advisability of brand *X* and thus persuade the reader to purchase it.

Numerous opportunities exist for persuasive writing. In fact, there are those who would say that all communication is persuasive, and they are right in that each communicating situation may have an element of persuasiveness in it.

SUMMARY

To persuade is to get someone to accept a belief or idea or to take action. In some degree the element of persuasion is present in every communicating situation. There are factors inherent in the communicator, the message, and the receiver that must be considered and brought into interplay to achieve persuasion.

The writer must be credible as a person and in what he says. His credibility is based upon his dependability, trust, and sincere enthusiasm. The reader perceives this from what the writer says and how he says it; in addition, credibility is recognized from the writer's social standing, reputation as an authority, status in the company, and personality traits, when they are known. A message is credible when the recipient accepts it and is motivated to action. The reader has physical and psychological needs, desires, and wishes that should be fulfilled. Letters that emphasize benefits and advantages to the reader are credible and thus invoke favorable reader reaction. To stimulate action, you need to know your reader and to analyze and consider his knowledge, experiences, feelings, and personality. The more you know about him, the better able you will be to increase the credibility of your message.

Reader involvement becomes a persuasive act in itself. What person can resist something of which he is a part? You persuade people *to do* by making them *want to do*. Several techniques are helpful:

1. Be positive.
2. Offer evidence and proof.
3. Apply sales psychology.

Selling is presenting facts and qualities about a product or service in such a way that the other person (the customer) is persuaded to buy the product or to take some step toward buying it. Writing sales letters is a very creative and dynamic task. Linking the needs, wants, and interests of a prospect with your product can be a fascinating game. To succeed in its purpose, a sales letter must:

1. Create attention
2. Arouse interest
3. Convince
4. Create desire
5. Evoke action

It must show sincerity, integrity, goodwill, and a genuine interest in serving the prospective customer. It proves logically, clearly, and fairly that the product is for him.

The planning of a sales letter begins with an analysis of the prospect and the product, for the more one knows about them the better able he is to be persuasive and thus to make a sale. The sales presentation begins by creating attention. The trend today is not to do this with a device, but to make a direct sales point about some advantage or benefit that will appeal to the reader. After the opening, the sales presentation leads the customer by developing the central selling point; the writer uses all his ideas in a sales talk that explains and supports the central point in an effort for total persuasion. This involves description, facts, figures, evidence, and proof. It convinces the reader and creates a desire for the product. The sales letter ends with a suggestion for a single, easy, and motivated action.

Although sales letters comprise the most commonly used type of persuasive writing in business today, opportunities often present themselves in other situations. The job of collecting past-due accounts and of keeping accounts current is a persuasive one. And a great deal of persuasiveness is necessary to motivate action with intra-office memorandums.

Collection letters generally state what the customer received for his promise to pay, review the case (including the amount due and the terms), give the reasons or motive for payment, appeal to the reader, and request payment. Form letters are often used, and seven steps are taken in the total collection process: notification, reminder, inquiry, appeals, demand, ultimatum, and action.

Motivating the reader to action through intra-office memorandums requires logic in handling evidence, proof, and supporting statements. One type of reasoning that is useful is argumentative exposition. The four steps in this process can be followed as a basis for organization:

1. Discuss the problem.
2. Explain the issues.
3. Submit proof.
4. Draw a conclusion and invoke action.

Numerous opportunities exist for persuasive writing in business. In fact, every situation has its element of persuasion.

FURTHER READING

Aurner, Robert R., and M. Philip Wolf, *Effective Communication in Business,* 5th ed. Cincinnati: South-Western Publishing Co., 1967, pp. 326–487.

Baker, Richard M., and Gregg Phifer, *Salesmanship: Communication, Persuasion, Perception.* Boston: Allyn & Bacon, Inc., 1966.

Bettinghaus, E. P., *Persuasive Communication.* New York: Holt, Rinehart & Winston, Inc., 1968.

Campbell, James H., and Hal W. Hepler, eds., *Dimensions in Communication.* Belmont, Calif.: Wadsworth Publishing Company, Inc., 1970.

Dawe, Jessamon, and William J. Lord, Jr., *Functional Business Communication.* Englewood Cliffs, N. J.: Prentice-Hall, Inc., 1968, pp. 137–58.

Devlin, Frank J., *Business Communication.* Homewood, Ill.: Richard D. Irwin, Inc., 1968, pp. 291–368, 432–60.

Hodgson, R. S., *Direct Mail and Mail Order Handbook.* Chicago: Dartnell Corporation, 1964.

Howland, Carl I., Irving L. Janis, and Harold H. Kelley, *Communication and Persuasion.* New Haven, Conn.: Yale University Press, 1953.

Menning, J. H., and C. W. Wilkinson, *Communicating Through Letters and Reports,* 4th ed. Homewood, Ill.: Richard D. Irwin, Inc., 1967, pp. 61–76, 307–407.

Thayer, Lee, *Communication and Communication Systems.* Homewood, Ill.: Richard D. Irwin, Inc., 1968, pp. 220–39.

Wells, Walter, *Communications in Business.* Belmont, Calif.: Wadsworth Publishing Company, Inc., 1968, pp. 273–302.

Yeck, John D., and John T. Maguire, *Planning and Creating Better Direct Mail.* New York: McGraw-Hill Book Company, 1961.

QUESTIONS AND PROBLEMS

1. Bring to class examples of communication and discuss their application of persuasive principles. Include not only letters and memorandums, but also excerpts from newspaper items, magazine articles, and speeches over the radio or on television.
2. Invite a famous person such as S. I. Hayakawa, Rudolf Flesch, or Robert Gunning, or another author of a communications textbook, to talk with members of your class in business communication. You will need to be persuasive, for there are numerous demands on such a person's time and energy.
3. Arrange for a speaker from industry to come and speak before a meeting of the student body in your school.
   a. Write the letter persuading him to come.
   b. Prepare a school newspaper writeup that will promote student and faculty interest.
   c. Design the layout and copy for either a bulletin board announcement or a poster promoting attendance at the meeting.

   This project should be carried out to completion.
4. The two letters on page 230 represent the version before Paul Bringe (consultant and writer) rewrote it, and his revision. Analyze the first letter for its weaknesses, thinking of how it can be improved, and the second one for the ways in which it is more effective than the first. Can it be improved further? Why is the second letter more effective than the first?
5. Paul Bringe also rewrote the first letter on page 231, which resulted in the second letter. Why is the second letter more persuasive? Can you improve its effectiveness?
6. Use a local school situation as a basis for writing a persuasive letter. Select one of the following problems and write a letter that can be sent to all the students or used as an open letter to the student body and published in your school newspaper:
   a. There should or should not be Saturday classes at your college.
   b. The "No Smoking" signs in the classrooms should be enforced.
   c. Students should attend pep rallies.
   d. The faculty should support athletic programs.
   e. Parking regulations should be changed.
7. Use a community situation as a basis for writing a persuasive letter. Select one of the following problems and write a letter that can be sent individually or published as an open letter in your city's newspaper:
   a. Request the creation or improvement of city parks.
   b. Make an appeal for contributions to the Red Cross, Cancer Drive, Heart Fund, Community Chest, or United Fund.
   c. Request a change of a traffic sign or signal light from one location to another.
   d. Request that a particular street be made one-way in order to facilitate the flow of traffic around your campus.

DEAR SIR:
THE POSITION YOU HOLD WITH YOUR FIRM AND IN YOUR COMMUNITY HAS MOTIVATED OUR NECESSITY TO CONTACT YOU.

WE ARE DELIGHTED WITH THE PLEASURE OF BEING ALLOWED THIS OPPORTUNITY TO TELL YOU OF THE FACILITIES OF ONE OF DETROIT'S LEADING DINING ROOMS AND COCKTAIL LOUNGES. WITH FIVE BEAUTIFUL PRIVATE ROOMS — KEYED TO SERVE — BUSINESS MEN'S LUNCHEONS, AFTERNOON COCKTAILS, EVENING DINNERS, PRIVATE PARTIES, WEDDINGS, SHOWERS, ETC. WE ARE OFFERING YOU THE FINEST IN FOODS, SUPERB SERVICE AND DISTINCTIVE ATMOSPHERE. THE ADVANTAGES OF EDDIE PAWL'S PRIVATE BANQUET ROOMS, WE BELIEVE SHOULD BE BROUGHT IN DETAIL TO YOUR ATTENTION.

THE CONTEMPORARY MAIN DINING ROOM ---CAPACITY FROM ONE HUNDRED TO THREE HUNDRED, IS AVAILABLE FOR EVENING AFFAIRS, DINNERS, COCKTAILS AND DANCING. ALSO AVAILABLE IS OUR P.A. SYSTEM AND SPEAKER'S STAND.

THE NEW KING ARTHUR FASHIONED INN SIGN ROOM WITH A COZY FIRE PLACE, CIRCULAR TABLES AND LEATHER CAPTAINS CHAIRS, IS THE PERFECT SETTING FOR THAT SPECIAL PARTY OF THIRTY TO SIXTY GUESTS.

THE AUSTERE, YET WARM WALNUT ROOM WITH PRIVATE BAR SEATING UP TO EIGHTY PEOPLE, THE STAG PARTY SIZED CUB ROOM WITH A CAPACITY OF TWENTY-FIVE PEOPLE COMPLETES THE INDIVIDUALITY THAT EDDIE PAWL HAS DISPLAYED SO ELOQUENTLY IN HIS ANTICIPATION OF YOUR EVERY NEED.

STOP IN FOR AFTERNOON COCKTAILS AND ALLOW US THE PLEASURE OF SHOWING YOU OUR FACILITIES. WE WILL BE MORE THAN HAPPY TO OFFER YOU SPECIAL PRICE CONSIDERATIONS.

WITH YEARS OF EXPERIENCE IN PARTY PLANNING AND WEDDING ARRANGEMENTS TO OUR CREDIT, WE FEEL THAT WE ARE MORE THAN EQUIPPED TO EASE YOUR BURDEN.

THE FALL OF THE YEAR BRINGS TO MIND RETIREMENT PARTIES AND HOLIDAY AFFAIRS, SO PICK UP THE PHONE AND DIAL ---TU. 4-7300 AND ASK FOR THE CATERING DEPT.

THANKING YOU FOR TAKING THE TIME FROM YOUR BUSY DAY TO READ OUR LETTER, WE REMAIN,

RESPECTFULLY
EDDIE PAWL'S

EDDIE PAWL

How to enjoy the finest service...

delectable food ...

delightful drinks...

dancing if you like...

...all in surroundings so pleasant you will want to come back often.

Have you considered Eddie Pawl's as the very best place for your business meeting or social affairs? Here you can be a gracious host with never a moment of concern about the details that make your important occasions successful.

Here you will find outstanding accommodations for groups of up to 300 people. The main dining room, for example, handles 300 for evening affairs. The Walnut Room accommodates 80, the King Arthur Room up to 60, and the Cub Room 25.

Though I might try to describe these delightful rooms for festive occasions, that won't do. You must see them yourself to appreciate the congenial surroundings and picture how successfully your entertaining can be done here.

Will you be my guest for cocktails some afternoon soon so that I might personally show you our facilities? It will be my great pleasure and of course there is no obligation whatever.

Phone me now at TU 4-7300 to set a date and tell me your preference in cocktails. The welcome mat is out. Will you come soon?

Cordially,

EDDIE PAWL

The Reporter of Direct Mail Advertising, January 1964, p. 34.
Reproduced by permission.

Dear Friend,

We are happy to announce that in the first quarter of 1967, we established a record all time high in sales volume, in the history of this company.

We are extremely grateful to our friends, all our customers and employees for making this possible. Your confidence justifies our 67 years of management under the original president. We are proud that 3 generations of Miller's are active in the management of this leading Delmarva furniture firm and will continue our high, fair standards of business that have made us the leader in the industry.

In appreciation to everyone for making Miller's the outstanding furniture chain it is, we would like to declare a 20% dividend of all purchases made from any of our four stores during Wednesday, April 26th through Monday, May 1st, 5 days of shopping with a fabulous 20% discount on anything you wish to purchase. You'll have an unrestricted choice of furniture, bedding, carpeting and decorating merchandise.

Of course, our policy of NO CHARGE FOR CREDIT will apply. We do all our own financing, therefore, we never charge a single penny for interest, service charges or delivery charges. You'll save as much as 18% per year on budget terms alone.

Park your car in any parking lot wherever our stores are located and we will gladly pay your fee while you're shopping. In Wilmington, there is a 1,000 car parking lot right across the street from our store.

Don't miss the dividend, enjoy a big 20% discount from Wednesday, April 26th to Monday, May 1st. We will be looking forward to seeing you.

Sincerely yours,

You are invited

to a most unusual

birthday party

You are invited to help us celebrate a glorious five-day birthday party, from Wednesday, April 26th, through Monday, May 1st.

Please don't bring a present.

This is a reverse birthday party. You get the present - a whopping 20% discount on anything and everything you buy in any of Miller's five stores during these five shopping days. Nothing is excluded - your choice of furniture, bedding, carpeting, and other home accessories. Your savings can be as large as you want them to be because you save on everything.

Miller's has grown and prospered during the last 67 years. This growth and progress we owe to you and to thousands of other good customers. The 20% discount birthday present is a small token of our appreciation for your confidence and goodwill.

Parking is no problem. Park on any lot close to our stores and we will pay your fee when you come in.

Credit is no problem. You may charge any or all purchases and never pay a penny in interest or service charges.

Delivery is no problem. Delivery is free to your home on everything you buy.

Three generations of Millers invite you to their five-day birthday party. Come and get your share of the dollar-saving 20% discount while the party lasts. There is no easier way to get the finest in furniture at exceptionally attractive prices.

Sincerely,

***The Reporter of Direct Mail Advertising*, July 1967, p. 37. Reproduced by permission.**

e. Appeal to the public to support a school bond issue or some other issue.

8. Write to either the U. S. senator or the state senator from your district to persuade him to vote for or against a particular bill being presented to the legislature at this time. Would individual personal letters tend to be more persuasive than letters from groups or organizations? Would letters signed by numerous people be more effective than those with single signatures?

9. Forest Lake is a private lake, about 135 miles north of Detroit, right off Highway I-75. It is surrounded by 1,400 acres of beautiful woodlands. It is now under development by the Forest Lake Development Company, Troy, Michigan. Every year thousands of dollars are invested in lake properties for leisure, retirement, and income purposes. Plans are under way for a water ski run that will please even the experts. Fish abound. The water is 45 feet deep. A nice sandy beach surrounds most of the lake, which is 2½ miles in diameter. Michigan is known as a sporting and recreation state.

   Write a letter to prospective buyers interesting them in finding out more about the lake. This should open the door for your sales representative so that he can persuade or sell them a piece of land or a building. You can make any assumptions consistent with the facts given. This includes adding specific details and appeals that your imagination might provide.

10. You are the automobile dealer in your city for ________. (This can be any make of car in which you are interested.) You have just recently been able to offer a leasing plan to firms operating a fleet of cars for their management people to use on business trips. There has been a tremendous increase in the number of firms leasing rather than owning automobiles. Advantages are the lower overall costs and modest rental rates. Gasoline is the only expense to the lessee; the cost of insurance, licensing, and maintenance is borne by the leasing company. The rental fee is tax-deductible as a business expense and there are no mileage restrictions. The firm is relieved of records for owning and maintaining the cars. Write a letter to be sent to business firms that will persuade them to investigate your leasing plan.

11. Several days ago, Mr. James Dupont, a professor at one of your state's universities, came in and looked over your new cars. He told you that he was interested in checking Dodge, Ford, and Chevrolet before buying. You made him a trade-in offer for his four-year-old Plymouth Valiant and invited him to bring his family in to see your new models. Ten days later, he hasn't come in. You could telephone him or drive over to his house, but you decide to write him. Write a letter that will persuade him to come in and test-drive your new model.

12. What do companies teach their employees regarding effective written communication? What principles do they stress, and how important do they feel it is to write well? These are a few questions students in com-

munication classes ask. To get a first-hand view, write three companies for answers. Ask for a correspondence or communication manual. Perhaps you can also obtain an interview. The manuals could be placed in the reference section of your library for further use. Your instructor may have you use this information to make a comparative analysis of three company manuals as a report project to be submitted at a later date.

13. As part of one of your management courses, you have been asked to visit a large business firm to interview someone familiar with its formal organizational structure. This will provide data for a short report on formal organizational structure that will also include material from a selected bibliography on the subject. The assignment is due in two weeks. Request the interview. Your instructor may choose to have you make the interview and either write up your findings or combine them into a report later.

14. You represent the First National Bank of your home town. This morning's mail brought the following letter:

    Four years ago, I moved from one location to another in this city. I had to request three times that my address be changed in your records. This is absurd inefficiency on your part. I moved again in January of this year [it is now August 6]. I am about to submit for the sixth time notice of change of address. I have sent one post office notice, three times filled out your forms for change of address, sent one notice by mail after your requesting my new address, and twice told you orally. Three times I've received notices from you that you have made the change. Yet last month, and now, I've received bank statements bearing 201 Fox instead of 1201 Fox. Now—why should I bother to have you make the correction?

    Disgustedly yours,
    Samuel Martin

    What can you say? Answer Mr. Martin's letter.

15. The following letter promoting this textbook for college and university teachers to use in their classes is certainly not very persuasive.

Dear Professor:

Your copy of COMMUNICATING FACTS AND IDEAS, Second Edition, by Leland Brown is being mailed to you with our compliments. Outstanding features and highlights of the book are given in the brief that accompanies your examination copy.

COMMUNICATING FACTS AND IDEAS provides a scholarly blending of principles and procedures of communication with psychological and sociological principles. The subject matter emphasizes the philosophy and policy considerations that are basic in sound communication training.

COMMUNICATING FACTS AND IDEAS, Second Edition, sells for $9.95 list. Compare your copy with the book you are presently using in your classes. You will find that this book can help you in presenting the dynamics of communication. A comprehensive instructor's manual will be furnished to those instructors who adopt this book for class use.

Sincerely yours,

By being too general, the letter gives little or no information about the purpose, contents, or use of the book; no reference is made to tone or style, or to the main features of the book. Having read and studied half of the book, you should have a fairly good concept of its strong (and weak) points. Write the letter that you would send.

16. For the past year you have been sending a complimentary subscription of *Training in Business and Industry* to a number of people in personnel and training in companies and to a select group of educators in management and communications. It is no longer economical to continue on a complimentary basis. The fact is that you sent the copies in order to get these people interested and to sell them on the magazine so that you could increase your subscription list. Higher advertising rates are possible when longer lists of readers are reached.

    Write the letter to persuade them to renew. The rates are: 1 year, $10; 2 years, $15; and 3 years, $20. You will reduce rates to companies for two or more subscriptions: 1 year, $8 per subscription; 2 years, $12.75; and 3 years, $17.

    You might want to check a copy of the magazine in your library to see what it is like. It contains a special-events calendar of professional meetings, book reviews, and free training aids, among other things. Articles deal practically with personnel and training problems, new ideas, concepts, programs, and methods.

17. The advertisement for a folding food and cake cover on page 235 appeared in *Printers' Ink* on October 8, 1965. It lends itself very readily to use as a promotion-premium item. It also appeals to women as an inexpensive gift item. You are planning to sell it through direct mail but are wondering which of these two target markets to reach. To help you make a final decision, you plan to test it out both ways with small samples. Prepare the letter you would send to companies, and the one you would use for the homemaker.

18. The three advertisements on page 236 appeared in the *Wall Street Journal* on November 1, 1968. Assume that you are employed in the advertising department of Merrin's, and want to use direct mail advertising to sell these jewelry items. They would make wonderful gifts for a wife or girl friend. One good target market would be executives in the upper ranks of management in large corporations. Select one of the three pieces and write a letter selling it to executives for gift-giving. Attach to the letter a memorandum to your boss persuading him to use direct mail, the top-management target market, and your letter.

19. Assume that you are the collection manager of Brown's Modern Appliance Shop, 4015 Washington Avenue, Indianapolis, Indiana. Most of the credit you extend to customers is on the installment plan. You require 5 percent as a down payment, with the remainder divided into monthly payments. The credit thus extended is for twelve-, eighteen-, and twenty-four-month periods, depending upon the price of the article sold and the wishes of the customer. One of your customers is Mrs. Elizabeth Ann Jones. The account is in both her name and her husband's. You have the following information about them: They are in

A Perfect Self-Liquidating Premium Item

FOLDING FOOD & CAKE COVER

Ideal for 1,001 Product Promotion Tie-ins

Unique . . . Attractive . . .
Foolproof . . . Sturdy

Specs: Open—12¼″ x 6⅛″
Closed—12¼″ x ⅜″

Convenient: Simply snap open, fold closed

Strong wire frame covered with clear plastic on sides and either clear or colored top. Quilted top (as shown) available at additional cost.

Designed and priced to meet the requirements of a one dollar self-liquidating premium.

Prototype sample available to qualified companies
(I.E. Potential volume purchasers)

ALLIED PRODUCTS CO. **101 First St., Benicia, Calif.**

their forties. He makes $12,500 annually working for Kaiser Aluminum Company. She takes in sewing and makes around $100 a month. They have one child, a son, Ralph, age twelve. He has a paper route, and he makes about $4 per week, which he uses as spending money. They have a good credit rating and usually pay promptly. Three years ago they bought a $36,500 house on which they pay $255.00 per month. They have a 1969 Chevrolet, which is paid for. They belong to the Christmas savings club at the Hibernia Bank, where they have a checking account that they usually exhaust each month.

Assume that one year ago, you sold them a Zenith combination radio, TV, and phonograph for $750.00. On May 10, during a sales campaign on window fans that you conducted, you sold them a Reed window fan costing $259.50 and extended credit over an eighteen-month period. They have made all twelve payments to date on the Zenith, but the payments were extended over twenty-four months, so they have one more year to go.

"Enchanted Love" NECKLACE

in Treasured JADE

Double her pleasure with genuine deep-green Jade—clasped with a 14K gold Chinese symbol that says "Enchanted Love." Each bead is hand-knotted and beautifully matched for color and size. An exceptional value at **$135.00**

Elegantly Gift Boxed • Satisfaction Guaranteed
If Diners' Club, American Express or Carte Blanche account, give number & signature.
Mail orders postpaid. **Write Dept.**

merrin
530 MADISON AVE. (CORNER 54th) NEW YORK 22, N. Y. PLaza 3-8688

Courtesy Sherman Sackheim & Co., Inc., Advertising

Now assume that it is July, and you have not received any payments on the Zenith since the purchase of the Reed fan, although the payments on the fan have come in.

a. Write the reminder that you would have sent on June 1.
b. Write the letter that you would send them on July 1.

What is the difference in these two stages of collection?

20. Assume that you still have received no answer from the Joneses (problem 19). Write to them again. What accounts for your different appeal and tone in this letter?

21. Assume that Mrs. Jones comes in with her payments for May, June, and July. She still owes for August (delinquent) and her September payment is due in nine days. Would you write to her or wait? Why?

22. You have been employed in the credit-collection department of the Record Department Store for the past two years—since you were graduated from high school. You are currently assisting the new credit man-

ager to develop a modern collection system for the store. He has suggested that you read up on the subject to review some of the principles and practices of writing collection letters. You have gone to the library and discovered a few books but have not yet read them. He drops by your desk and says, "The general manager is pressing me for a proposed collection program and to give him some idea of what we are thinking and planning. Can you prepare a memorandum to him for my signature? Include the concepts and the essentials. We can fill him in later." Write the memorandum.

23. Your company is planning to purchase an accounting machine, a postage meter, an opaque projector, a tape recorder, and some other business machines. One of them will be used in connection with the work for which you are responsible. Investigate several brands and prepare a persuasive memorandum recommending the best one.

24. You have been made chairman of arrangements for a one-day conference for middle management in your company. About 350 men will be brought together for a general meeting at the beginning of the day and again at night. The group will also be divided for smaller meetings according to interest and problems. Included will be luncheon at 1:00, dinner at 8:00, and midmorning and midafternoon coffee breaks. You have been asked to check three possible motels and conference centers and to recommend the one that best fits the needs of the conference. You will have to consider the facilities available, menu possibilities, comparative costs, and services. After you have gathered the information, prepare a memorandum for your boss. Recommend your choice and persuade him to approve your decision.

Chapter Seven

CREATIVE PROBLEM SOLVING

Much of the emphasis in this book thus far has been on understanding and applying sound principles of communication through business letters and memorandums and in developing the power to think and express yourself in any given communicating situation. In Chapters 7–10, we will be stressing the role and importance of business report writing, and will try to develop your ability to gather, organize, and evaluate facts and ideas; to reach conclusions and solve problems; and to handle problem situations through reports. The purpose of this chapter will be to help you discover and recognize the relationship of creative problem solving to report investigation and presentation.

All preparation of reports begins with a problem to be solved, a need to be fulfilled, or a purpose to be accomplished. A problem is a situation that calls for taking a definite decision or course of action to reach a desired outcome. All your life you have had to make decisions and solve problems. When your alarm went off this morning, you decided to turn it off. Once this decision was made, you were faced with another one. Businessmen are constantly faced with problems to solve and decisions to make, because they are dependent upon wise decisions and practical solutions for the survival, operation, and growth of their companies. Some problems are important ones; others are minor. Some decisions are made unconsciously, following a pattern established through other similar decisions. At other times, however, one has to gather and analyze factual information and reach conclusions that will serve as a basis for further decision making. Problem solving thus involves clear thinking and sound judgment.

Although thinking begins when a problem, large or small, is examined and defined, in the early stages of problem solving, it involves a search for a set of facts or principles that will help to explain the problem situation. Thinking through to the problem's solution involves three major stages of progression:

1. Understanding and defining the problem
2. Finding the solution (including alternatives)
3. Putting the solution into action

A creative person becomes sensitive to problems as they arise and develops skill in methods of attack and solution. He maintains an open mind and is always on the lookout for a better way to do things.

The careful thinker will work step by step through several stages before he decides upon the best solution and takes action to put it into effect. First, he will seek a full understanding of the problem and of the situation in which it has occurred. Then he will plan an investigation of its causes and results; he will determine what is already known and what he will need to find out, and he will decide how to obtain the necessary data. His third step will be to gather all data, both facts and ideas, by appropriate research methods. Some of the material he obtains will lead him to other material, and he will create ideas of his own. His fourth step will be to organize and interpret his material; here he will create further ideas and reach conclusions. Fifth, he will propose and consider all possible solutions. Sixth, he will decide which solution is best, and as the seventh and final step, he will determine action for putting his solution into effect.

Much creative and logical thinking enters into each step in problem solving. Both kinds of thinking involve evaluative judgment and result in decision making. At this point, note that the steps in the creative process follow rather closely the basic steps of problem solving and that they may be appropriately applied during any *one* step of problem solving.

Alex Osborn lists the steps in the creative process:

1. Orientation—pointing up the problem
2. Preparation—gathering pertinent data
3. Analysis—breaking down relevant material
4. Hypothesis—piling up alternatives by way of ideas
5. Incubation—letting up, to invite illumination
6. Synthesis—putting the pieces together
7. Verification—judging the resultant ideas[1]

[1]Alex F. Osborn, *Applied Imagination*, rev. ed. (New York: Charles Scribner's Sons, 1957), p. 115.

UNDERSTANDING AND DEFINING THE PROBLEM

At first there is no particular problem, merely a situation. When the situation is examined and a source of difficulty found, the problem can be defined. Thus, a first concern of problem solving is learning how to recognize problem situations.

1. *Set goals.* Once a goal is established, you can look for barriers that stand in its way. You can work toward achieving the goal and eliminating any action that is detrimental to its accomplishment.
2. *Imagine an ideal situation.* By setting up a criterion of what conditions *should* be like, you can compare and evaluate the circumstances that prevail and recognize signs of trouble or underlying causes.
3. *Observe what is taking place.* By observing operations, you can discover areas in which problems might arise.
4. *Listen to others.* You may pick up complaints or grievances that will indicate something is wrong, or you may hear suggestions for improvement.
5. *Ask questions.* Asking questions about all phases of an operation may yield clues. It will also give other people a chance to communicate with you.
6. *Read.* You can profit from the recorded experience of others and gain knowledge it would take you years to amass through your own experience. Guidance in professional reading for gathering facts and ideas used in solving problems is provided in Chapter 8.

Setting goals, imagining an ideal situation, observing, listening, asking questions, and reading are all desirable methods for developing the ability to recognize that something is at fault or needs improving—in other words, that a problem exists.

After a problem situation is recognized, it can be analyzed to determine its difficulty. It is best to begin by examining all the known facts of the situation. Then the unknown facts can be discovered; they can be included or explored for further data if they are found to be relevant. The problem solver also searches for details that will explain why something has happened. To discover the relation between an effect and its cause is to find symptoms of trouble. Such details will provide clues and ideas that should be set down on paper or recorded mentally for further analysis.

In some problems, issues stand out clearly, whereas in others they may be complex and obscure. Reviewing all the factors involved helps to point out the basic problem, as does isolating the parts of a problem and analyzing each separately, to find their relationships to each other and to the central problem. Sometimes a series of questions can be asked about the people and the action concerned in the situation. The problem may involve a clash or conflict of personalities or interests, or the lack of or misapplication of a sound principle.

When the problem solver has sufficient knowledge of the problem, he can break it down into several elements, outlining wherever possible to provide a framework for his further investigation. He can also try phrasing the problem in one sentence. This can be stated as a question to be answered, as the statement of a need to be fulfilled, or as a purpose to be accomplished. For example:

> The United Supply Company, a coffee packer in Miami, Florida, at present owns a fleet of trucks that it uses for distributing its products. Costs have been increasing in the last few years, and several of the trucks now need to be replaced. Some of the coffee companies in other parts of the country are renting trucks to reduce costs.

In this situation the facts point to the problem, but the problem must be stated separately from the facts. As a question, it could be phrased:

> Should the United Supply Company rent trucks?

As a statement of purpose, it might be expressed as follows:

> To decide whether or not the United Supply Company should rent or own trucks, an examination of comparative costs must be made.

The final step in understanding a problem is to devise principles or hypotheses that might help in arriving at workable solutions. The solution to a problem has to meet certain requirements. The principles help to determine the direction in which effort will be made. They do not tell *how* a problem is to be solved, but they do indicate the objectives that the solution must accomplish if it is to be put into action. The problem solver at this point must visualize a new situation in which these criteria exist; he can apply them in thinking up alternative solutions.

FINDING SOLUTIONS

Data collected to solve a problem help the mind to turn out solutions. Searching and analyzing create new insights from relationships of facts and ideas and may yield several possible solutions to a problem. The problem solver will rethink the problem after he has collected all his data and will direct his thoughts to devising solutions. It is here that he will utilize all his thinking faculties. He will find out what others have done under similar circumstances; he will scrutinize all angles; he will speculate on what might happen; and above all, he will give himself free rein to think and explore all possibilities. Then—after he has several solutions—he will evaluate them and decide which one is best.

Gathering Data

A full understanding of the problem will give the problem solver knowledge of what is known and what needs to be known. He can then plan his investigation and collect the necessary data. Data are obtained through various research methods:

1. *Bibliographical research*—the use of printed sources, records, and materials from company files and reports
2. *Questionnaire studies*—surveys of opinions, attitudes, beliefs, etc., that may indicate a trend, an average, or a quantitative measure for reaching conclusions
3. *Interviews*—the determination of objective facts such as events, conditions, practices, policies, and techniques, and of subjective data such as attitudes, preferences, opinions, and emotional reactions
4. *Observation*—often combined with the interview, in which actions and reactions are noted; useful in watching procedures and practices to determine what is being done and how

Gathering data is such an important aspect of report investigation that we will give it additional study in Chapter 8.

Brainstorming for Ideas

As a group method for piling up a quantity of ideas and possible solutions, brainstorming has proved itself very valuable. Some twenty years ago, Alex F. Osborn, of the Batten, Barton, Durstine and Osborn advertising agency, originated brainstorming as a method by which groups of people could use their brains to attack a problem from all sides to find the best possible solution. Since then, numerous case histories show use of the method in government and public affairs, the armed services, business, and industry. Brainstorming sessions have been held to find ways to reduce employee absenteeism, to improve purchasing methods, and to promote suntan lotion in the summer months.

Such idea-producing conferences are relatively fruitful when certain rules of the game are understood and followed by the participants.

Here are Osborn's four basic guides:

1. *Criticism is ruled out.* Adverse judgment of ideas must be withheld until later.
2. *Freewheeling is welcomed.* The wilder the idea, the better; it is easier to tame down later than to think up in the first place.
3. *Quantity is wanted.* The greater the number of ideas, the more likelihood of winners.
4. *Combination and improvement are sought.* In addition to contributing ideas of their own, participants should suggest how ideas of others can be turned into better ideas or how two or more ideas can be joined into still another idea.[2]

Ideas produced at brainstorming sessions must be recorded and later evaluated. Someone should be appointed to write down the ideas suggested. The list should be reportorial, however, rather than stenographic. Group members should receive a copy, and the committee or persons assigned the responsibility of evaluation and selection will need copies. The suggestions can be evaluated through testing and experimentation in several ways:

1. By setting up criteria for judging them
2. By projecting them into the future, assuming that they are put into action, and examining the effects
3. By checking them for their practical value as solutions
4. By verifying their validity through past experience, statistics, or originality

At a brainstorming session, there must be a leader who is responsible for presenting the problem and maintaining the spirit of the session. Encouragement may be needed by some in the group. The members should feel that they are playing a game with friendly rivalry and that each is free to say whatever comes to mind. Suggestions should flow easily. When necessary the leader may prime the group by suggesting a few ideas, thus maintaining a ready flow and a spirited give-and-take.

Brainstorming can be effectively used in problem solving, especially for piling up ideas and devising principles or hypotheses that might offer solutions.

Role Playing for Perspective

Equally effective as a technique useful in problem solving is role playing. It is especially helpful in defining problems and in evaluating possible courses of action or proposed solutions. Role playing is a de-

[2]Osborn, *Applied Imagination,* p. 84.

vice for putting oneself in another person's place and determining what to do in his situation. The very nature of role playing forces one to deal with human relations, as it provides the opportunity for individuals to see their mistakes and correct them. It also allows them to see the problems and points of view of other people. As an informal method of getting to the root of a problem, role playing is very helpful. Characters are assigned roles to play in a real-life drama and actually act out the parts of characters involved in a given situation. No script is needed and informality is desirable. Actors portray not what they think the characters *should* do but what they think they *would* do under a particular set of circumstances. A group of observers then analyzes the actions and from the results determines the best possible solution.

Role playing has recently attained wide recognition as a method used in industrial training programs for salesmen, agents, supervisors, and other types of employees, although it has actually been used for a number of years. Originally it was the outgrowth of Dr. J. L. Moreno's work with the mentally disturbed. The purposes of role playing include obtaining a better comprehension of the problem or situation at hand. Acting out and then discussing the situation results in understanding the factors involved. Alternative solutions might then be acted out and a decision reached as to the best possible solution. Or by acting out the situation that gave rise to the problem, the solution itself might become readily apparent.

Many advantages are inherent in role playing:

1. It requires the person to carry out a thought or decision he may have reached. For example, a conferee may conclude from a case study that Mr. *A* should apologize to Mr. *B*. In role playing, *A* would go to *B* and apologize. Role-playing experience soon demonstrates the gap between *thinking* and *doing* and makes clear the fact that good human relations require skill.

2. It effectively accomplishes changes in attitude by placing people in specified roles. This makes it apparent that a person's behavior is a reflection not only of his personality, but also of the situation in which he finds himself.

3. It trains a person to be aware of and sensitive to the feelings of others and increases his understanding of the effect his own behavior has on other people. For example, the person who enjoys making wisecracks may discover how they often hurt others.

4. It develops a fuller appreciation of the important part played by feelings in determining behavior in social situations.

5. It permits training in the control of feelings and emotions. For example, if a person is repeatedly placed in the role of supervisor,

he can learn not to become irritated by complaints and to express fewer complaints of his own.[3]

There are two types of role playing. In *multiple role playing,* the entire audience participates. Because all members become involved in the problem, this type gives wide opportunities for people to try out new attitudes and behavior patterns. The leader divides large groups into subgroups and presents the problem each group is to solve by role playing. He then issues a set of written instructions to one person in each group, who is designated as chairman. The chairman in turn passes out instructions to members of his group. After twenty minutes or so of role playing in each group, the acting is halted and the results are discussed. Multiple role playing thus provides a wide sample of group behavior for comparisons in working out solutions.

In *single role playing,* one group performs while others watch. In this way, all see the same performance and are able to discuss the details that led to a certain effect. Role players benefit from the discussion of their behavior, as they are often unaware of the effect it has on other people. Single role playing may consist of as few as two people. One person, for instance, could be an employee and the other a supervisor. The leader would explain the problem situation and the role players would then act it out. Their behavior might lead to a possible solution; in any event, it would point up some causes and effects of the problem.

Brainstorming and role playing are both worthwhile group techniques for creating ideas with which to make decisions and solve problems. Each gives an insight into a problem and works toward a solution. Each involves thinking through the problem situation, devising alternative solutions, and arriving at the best solution—fundamental parts in the problem-solving and decision-making processes.

Arriving at the Best Solution

Using the special group techniques of brainstorming and role playing helps to provide ideas and solutions in problem solving. However, individual creative thinking is also necessary. First, it helps you to visualize the problem in relation to other problems and to understand its nature in relation to causes and effects. Then, by looking ahead, you can foresee what will be needed in the way of facts and materials for finding an appropriate solution. By following clues, piling up ideas, and exploring as many solutions as possible, you will be able to arrive at the best solution. Putting yourself in the place of the person involved in the problem encourages fresh ideas and reactions and helps you to predict

[3]N. R. F. Maier, A. R. Solem, and A. A. Maier, *Supervisory and Executive Development* (New York: John Wiley & Sons, Inc., 1957), pp. 2, 3.

what might happen under certain conditions. Reflecting on questions such as "What would I do?" "Would I be interested?" or "Would I be convinced?" will provide you with ideas that might not otherwise occur to you.

Creative thinking alone cannot solve all problems, but it works hand in hand with logical thinking. Each complements the functioning of the other.

Logic is structured thinking. When you argue a proposition, bringing out the relationships among ideas, you are relying on logical reasoning to make the line of argument a valid one. When you draw conclusions from premises, extract universal truths from individual cases, and infer particulars from general laws, using statistics, surveys, relevant facts, or valid reports, you are reasoning and using logic. By using data, you supply *proof*; you search for *evidence,* consider *facts,* and formulate a *conclusion* that follows.

After you have thought of several possible solutions, you will need to evaluate them and decide which is best. Here the criteria arrived at in defining the problem can be applied to determine which solution meets them. Considering the advantages and disadvantages of each alternative helps point up which one is best. The standard procedure for evaluating solutions is to test them for effectiveness, practicality, and pertinence:

1. *For effectiveness, ask:*
    a. Will it solve the problem?
    b. Does it meet the established criteria?
    c. To what extent will it contribute to a solution?
2. *For practicality, ask:*
    a. Can it be put into practice easily?
    b. Are necessary personnel and material available?
    c. Is there enough time?
    d. Does it create new problems?
3. *For pertinence, ask:*
    a. Has every factor been considered?
    b. Is the solution an answer to the specific situation?

PUTTING THE SOLUTION INTO ACTION

The problem solver has to decide what is to be done, by whom, at what time, and where, when he considers putting his solution into action. These decisions are dependent upon the lines of responsibility and authority of the people affected by the solution and responsible for it and upon the relationship of the problem solver to the person for whom he has found a solution. Further insights into what to do come from visualizing the effect of the solution. Predicting the outcome may help in overcoming barriers to putting it into effect.

There are times when the solution may be put to work for a test run. This enables the problem solver to avoid mistakes and smooth out the "kinks," should there be any. In a number of instances the problem solver will need to persuade others to approve the solution and his plans for putting it into action. This may be done through *conferences, discussions,* or *reports.* Holding conferences with everyone concerned to brief them on what is to be done involves them actively; psychologically, whenever a person is made to feel a part of some course of action, he is more easily persuaded to carry it out. Group discussions also provide the means of persuading others and of developing ideas about further adjustments to be made. Often the solution and its discussion are presented to others in a written report.

The Need for Reports

The need for reports is great today, not only to present solutions to problems and recommend action to be taken, but also to keep people informed and give them the data needed for making decisions. Without reports as a means of communication, it would be difficult indeed to operate a business, for operational efficiency depends on the quantity and quality of the information that flows through all the personnel. Different kinds of information must be disseminated; with division of labor and delegation of authority, reports are helpful as a unifying force to build cooperation and knit together the activities of the various departments. Reports are used to exchange data, to run accurate checks on events, and to record day-by-day operations. An executive receives information from which he weighs results, makes decisions, and initiates appropriate action. Reports are also used to measure costs and performance, to facilitate long-term and current planning, to present solutions to problems, and to recommend courses of action.

The Definition and Nature of Business Reports

A business report is a factual presentation of data or information directed to a particular reader or audience for a specific business purpose. It is a highly specialized type of communication, presenting a collection of facts to be transmitted to someone who will make use of them. It is flexible in subject content, organization, form, and use.

A business report may record past transactions or accomplishments, release new information or ideas, give an account of conditions past and present, analyze conditions for determining future policies, or recommend a course of action to be followed. Data may consist of notes, quoted material, statistics, tables, charts, figures, and so on—all the result of some method of investigation and research—or the report writer may have first-hand information that he presents from his own experience and knowledge.

Before a report is written, facts are classified, arranged, examined, evaluated, interpreted, and recorded. The emphasis in writing is on presenting the facts to accomplish a specific purpose. They must therefore be clearly stated. Visual aids help, as does the division of material into sections and the use of subject headings. Because the report is directed to the reader and his use, it must be adapted to his needs. Thus every report is different, varying according to the reader, the nature of the material, its purpose, and the writer.

THE FUNCTIONING OF REPORTS

There are, broadly, two kinds of business reports: the informative report and the investigative report. The informative report keeps an executive up to date with events, developments, and projects. It lets him know what is going on and serves as a basis for his decision making. Informative reports are also used with employees to develop an understanding of the aims, objectives, organization, policies, regulations, procedures, problems, and future outlook of the company. The development of positive attitudes, loyalties, respect, and teamwork is essential to an integrated management employee team that has a sense of responsibility, trust in the company, and the ability to work toward common interests.

The investigative report presents the results of an investigation of data or of a problem. It carries the presentation a step farther than the strictly informational report, for the data are interpreted, analyzed, and used for drawing conclusions or determining a course of action. Often a problem is presented and recommendations for the best solution are given. The emphasis is on an analysis of the results of research or the proposed solution to the problem.

Reports function in the four general areas of communication that are carried on by a business enterprise:

1. *Employee reports:* booklets, pamphlets, memorandums, and newsletters—reports to inform, to build favorable attitudes and loyalties, and to create good employee relations.
2. *Operational and technical reports:* manuals, procedural statements, orders, records, and facts for decision making—reports to give and receive information vital to carrying on the business of the firm.

3. *Management reports:* solutions to problems, decisions made, and policies formulated—reports to aid management in its functions of planning, decision and policy making, and problem solving.
4. *Customer and public reports:* sales promotional materials, pamphlets, annual reports, and news reports—reports to advertise and sell the company name and products, to create goodwill, and to build good relations.

Within a company, reports pass between those who supervise and those who carry on the work, between those who are the policy makers and those who carry out the policies—between employees and employers, subordinates and superiors, management and labor. Outside a company they are sent to stockholders, customers, the general public, and interested individuals. Moving vertically through the organizational channels, horizontally between departments and individuals on the same level, and radially inside and outside the company, reports inform, analyze, and recommend.

In the downward flow of communication, reports are largely informational: they increase their readers' general knowledge of the work and organization; they give opinions, information about employee benefits, or notices about such things as Red Cross and Community Chest drives. They also transmit policies, procedures, and orders. In the upward flow of communication, reports contain financial statements or statistics that show the present condition of the business and that become part of its record. In the horizontal interchange of reports, the aim is to coordinate the work of the various departments or divisions. Radially, reports reach everyone. The annual report, for instance, goes to employees, stockholders, the general public, and other groups.

Effective communication through reports is necessary for the life of any company. The informed worker feels like part of company operations and works smoothly and happily for the company. Facts and their analysis are necessary for all decisions. Problems must be investigated and an effective solution found.

One test for the effectiveness of a business report is to check how well it accomplishes its purpose. The following checklist of factors that make a business report effective is a good guide to use, especially as an aid for revising the contents of a report before it is finally prepared for distribution:

1. An effective business report meets the needs of the situation, the purpose, and the reader.
2. It is well planned and organized.
3. It adapts its format and presentation to its purpose, message, and reader.

4. It reflects good, clear thinking.
5. It presents material for easy and quick comprehension.
6. It interests the reader.
7. It makes effective use of visual aids as they are needed.
8. It motivates action.
9. It solves the problem in the best possible way.

Good report writing is the result of good, clear thinking. Confronted with the problem of preparing a report, the careful thinker will work step by step through several stages before he decides upon the best solution and presentation. He will apply his ability to think creatively, logically, and critically, for the steps in the thinking processes are, as discussed earlier, very much like those in problem solving and report preparation. The steps in report investigation and presentation are as follows:

1. Seek a full understanding of the problem and the situation.
2. Plan an investigation.
3. Gather all facts and data; create ideas.
4. Organize and interpret the material, create further ideas, and reach conclusions.
5. Propose and consider all possible solutions.
6. Conclude which solution is best.
7. Determine action for putting the solution into effect.
8. Outline the material for presentation.
9. Write up the report.
10. Revise, proofread, type, and edit the report.

PLANNING REPORTS

Successful reports are well planned. Planning consists of setting up definite procedures for conducting an investigation, for handling its results, and for writing the report. It enables the writer to establish policies pertaining to the objectives, scope, cost, time limit, and outline of the report. It clarifies his thinking and work by providing him with a guide for conducting his research and presenting his findings in report form. The basis for any report planning is an analysis of the situation, the problem, and the reader.

The working plan charts the investigation and clarifies the researcher's thinking. Usually it takes the form of an informal outline; sometimes, in being submitted for approval, it is written as a letter; and in some companies it consists of blanks to be filled in on a printed form provided for this purpose.

The plan will include as many of the following elements as are applicable to a given report problem situation:

1. A statement of the problem
2. The need and use for the report
3. Its purpose and objectives
4. Its scope and limitations
5. Divisions of the subject matter
6. Methods and procedures for gathering data
7. A tentative bibliography
8. Methods of organizing the data
9. A tentative general outline of the report
10. A statement of expected results or a tentative conclusion
11. A statement of the cost and time required
12. Definition of terms (technical and other specialized terms)
13. A work-progress schedule

The purpose is the long-range goal the report seeks to accomplish when it is completed. Objectives are short range and are attained as steps toward accomplishing the report's purpose. They are specific in nature and deal with the immediate aspects of a larger problem. For instance, the purpose of a report might be to determine whether or not to open a branch store in a suburban shopping center. Before a decision can be made, several questions must be answered, such as: Do we have the extra finances? How much will it cost? Is there a suitable building? Is there a potential market? These questions indicate the objectives that must be achieved in accomplishing the purpose.

The scope sets boundaries. It indicates the extent of the material to be covered or the quantity and nature of the data. Within those boundaries, limitations of subject matter, time, cost, and procedure apply. Major methods for gathering data for a report are bibliographical research, questionnaires, interviews, observation, experimentation, and letters. Determining sources of data and how they will be used is an important decision. Once the writer has done this, he can look ahead to determine how he can organize his data, for while in the process of collecting material, he can be organizing and saving time by doing two things at once. (This is one reward for careful planning and foresight.) As soon as he has analyzed the problem, the writer can set up a tentative general outline, which may consist of major topics arranged in an orderly sequence, or of main topics with as many subdivisions as possible, to clarify and simplify the task of outlining the final presentation later.

A tentative conclusion should be merely something toward which the writer directs his work. All factors and data should be examined; in the end he may reach an opposite conclusion. The work-progress schedule is used as a means of budgeting time proportionately so that a project can be completed in the time allotted to it. Because the same elements are included, the working plan can be used as a basis for outlining and writing the report's introduction. The working plan is a statement of what is proposed, and the introduction a statement of what was done.

SUMMARY

A problem is a situation that calls for a definite decision or action to be taken to reach a desired outcome. Problem solving involves clear thinking and sound judgment. It consists of three major steps: defining the problem, finding solutions, and putting the best solution into action. The creative problem solver will become sensitive to problems as they arise and skilled in methods of attack and solution.

To learn how to recognize problem situations, you should set goals, imagine an ideal situation, observe, listen, ask questions, and read. After a problem is recognized, it can be analyzed for further definition. Find the difficulty, work from the known to the unknown, discover cause-and-effect relationships, sense the problem in a general way and break it down into its parts, isolate the problem from the situation, and devise principles or criteria that may help in finding solutions.

When a full understanding of the problem has been reached, the researcher will know what he still needs to find out. He can then plan and collect the data necessary for the problem's solution by using bibliographical research, questionnaires, interviews, observation, or experimentation. He might also use group methods: brainstorming for more ideas or role playing for a better perspective. All this will provide data and ideas that will help in arriving at possible solutions.

It is necessary next to evaluate and come up with the best solution to solve the problem, using both logic and creative thinking. Afterwards, the solution must be put into action, which involves making decisions such as what, by whom, when, where, and how. This decision making requires conferences, discussions, and reports.

A business report is a factual presentation of data or information directed to a particular reader or audience for a specific business purpose. Broadly, there are two kinds of reports: informative and investigative. The beginning of the investigation and presentation of any report is the problem situation; the general steps of creative problem solving also apply to the investigation and preparation of reports:

1. Planning the investigation
2. Gathering facts, data, and ideas

3. Organizing, interpreting, and reaching conclusions
4. Proposing possible solutions
5. Determining the best alternative
6. Putting the solution into action
7. Outlining the material for presentation
8. Writing up the report
9. Revising and editing

Successful reports are well planned. Planning consists of setting up definite procedures for conducting an investigation, handling its results, and writing the report. The working plan charts the investigation and clarifies the researcher's thinking.

FURTHER READING

Anderson, C. R., F. W. Weeks, and A. G. Saunders, *Business Reports,* 3rd ed. New York: McGraw-Hill Book Company, 1957.

Brown, Leland, *Effective Business Report Writing,* 2nd ed. Englewood Cliffs, N. J.: Prentice-Hall, Inc., 1963.

Dawe, Jessamon, and William J. Lord, Jr., *Functional Business Communication.* Englewood Cliffs, N.J.: Prentice-Hall, Inc., 1968.

Kogan, Zuce, *Essentials in Problem Solving.* New York: Arco Publishing Company, Inc., 1957.

Lesikar, Raymond V., *Report Writing for Business,* rev. ed. Homewood, Ill.: Richard D. Irwin, Inc., 1965.

Robinson, David M., *Writing Reports for Management Decisions.* Columbus, Ohio: Charles E. Merrill Publishing Co., 1969.

Sigband, Norman B., *Communication for Management.* Glenwood, Ill.: Scott, Foresman & Company, 1969, pp. 75–87, 122–30.

CASE STUDIES

The case study method of teaching and learning is a well-established approach to problem solving. The student learns by doing. After he has studied a number of cases, he will have established a pattern or approach to solving problems. This approach includes the three fundamental stages of problem solving. Although no one solution may be the correct one, the student goes through the thinking process of problem solving and thus develops a sensitivity to problems, evolves a method of attack, and gains experience in arriving at solutions.

The following case studies are presented for use as a basis for class discussion and for presentation as reports. After reading each one, define the problem or problems, find alternate solutions, and decide on courses of action appropriate in each situation.

1. NYLIC's Mr. Trumbull

The case study shown in the illustrations on pages 255–57, which appeared in *Effective Letters Bulletin,*[4] is presented here for class discussion purposes. It presents not only the problem confronting NYLIC, but also what NYLIC did to solve it. Can you improve further on the solution?

a. What was the problem?
b. Suggest how the solution can be improved.
c. Answer Mr. Trumbull's letter.

2. The Office Manager's Problem

The general office of the Richland Manufacturing Company employs 150 people. They are hired on the basis of interviews and tests. Successful applicants are placed on a three-month probation period. Every year employees are considered for a pay increase.

In the secretarial pool there are five women who have been with the company for five to ten years. There are two men in the department—the office manager (you) and a supervisor. There are twenty-five girls, the majority of whom have been with the company less than two years—five of them less than six months.

General morale has been good. There are good facilities, good equipment, and good working conditions. The company gives fifteen minutes for a coffee break in the middle of the morning and again in the middle of the afternoon. There is an unwritten policy, however, that only one-third of the girls can be out at any one time.

Recently, one of the vice-presidents came through the office at midmorning and found only a half-dozen of the girls at work. That same morning the sales manager telephoned one of the girls for some mimeographed work he needed for a sales conference and was told that Miss Harris was out for coffee. He called back in half an hour and was given the same message. The vice-president stopped and told you (the office manager) that he didn't like this situation one bit. The sales manager called the vice-president in charge of marketing and told him what had happened. That afternoon you got a call from the vice-president in charge of personnel who said that he had been asked to look into the situation and wanted your help and suggestions.

Your first impulse was to protect your girls, but you knew that the coffee-break problem existed and had become worse in the past three weeks. Miss Harris, one of the worst offenders, is also one of your best workers, has been with the company two years, and shows promise of leadership among the girls. You also realize that something needs to be done. The girls are not producing work as fast as they did two months ago, and the incidents that have been noticed by the other people are typical of what is going on. As office manager, you have to do something.

[4]NYLIC's *Effective Letters Bulletin,* September–October 1958. Reproduced by permission.

Afterthoughts and notes of interest to business correspondents, published bi-monthly as part of New York Life's continuing Effective Letters Program.

Effective Letters

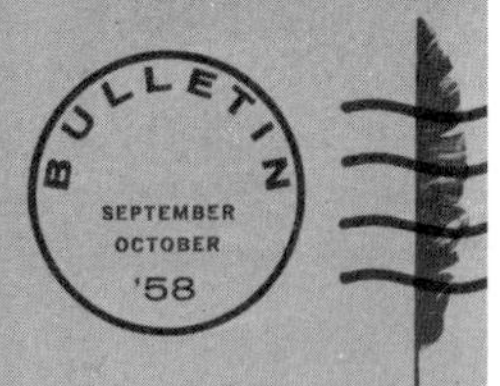

Dear Mr. Trumbull:

When an endowment policy matures, the owner receives a check along with a letter telling him how the amount was figured. Quite a while back, we sent such a letter to a man we'll call John Trumbull. The check was the right amount, and he wrote back to thank us for it. In the last paragraph of his letter, almost as an afterthought, he mentioned that acceptable as the check was, our letter was not acceptable—in fact, it was not a letter at all, and he enclosed it so that we could see what he meant.

August 18, 1949

Dear Mr. Trumbull: Re: Pol. No. 52)3 566

We are herewith enclosing our check in the amount of $1,013.93 for the proceeds on the maturity of Policy No. 52 063 566 on August 6, 1949.

You are no doubt gratified that Policy 52 063 566 has now matured. It may be a matter of interest to you to know how the figure of $1,013.93 was determined and accordingly, we are herewith enclosing a statement advising you of the manner in which this figure was arrived at by us.

Please do not hesitate to contact us if we may be of future service to you, Mr. Trumbull.

Sincerely yours,

Albert A. Alberts

Albert A. Alberts
Office Manager

In a report to the personnel director, write your analysis of the problem and your suggestions for changes.

3. Communication Problems

The other day Joe Chambers, salesman, and Bob Allen, interior designer —both at J. D. LeBlanc, Inc., sellers of office furniture, systems, and stationery—were holding a conference with the president, vice-president, and purchasing agent of the Argus Oil Company. Argus was a promising sales

We saw what he meant.

Reading that letter was rather like listening to a record of your own voice being played back and thinking, "Why, that doesn't sound like me!" The letter didn't sound like us, look like us. Not only that, as we read it, one fact became embarrassingly clear: it was not a "real" letter, but a pretend letter — that is, a form pretending to be a letter.

Like any other business, we are concerned with public relations. How many of our policy owners, like John Trumbull, were constantly being irked by such inept, unattractive communications? It was not a comforting thought. But what could we do?

The only thing to do, we finally decided, was to make it perfectly clear that we were sending out a form. Why should it have to look like a letter when it wasn't? Why not have regular printed forms with the message on the right-hand side of the page and on the left, fill-ins pertinent to the message? We tried it right then with the now-famous Trumbull Form and it came out like this:

Policy	Enclosed please find our check for the amount indicated at left. This check represents the indicated face value of the policy numbered at left which matured on the date shown. The check also includes accredited dividends, as indicated.
Maturity Date	
Face Amount $1,000	
1958 Dividend $6.43	
Termination Dividend $7.50	Please do not hesitate to contact us if we may be of future service to you.
Amount of Check $1,013.93	
	Hometown General Office

Good as far as format was concerned, but — back to the voice recording again — it just didn't sound like us, or more correctly, perhaps — the way we wanted to sound. So as long as we were involved in changing format, this was as good a time as any to overhaul language, too.

prospect, for it was furnishing a new suite of offices in a new building. Prior to the conference, Joe Chambers had held several conversations with the oil company men. He had measured the office floor space; he had suggested furniture that would be appropriate for the needs of the men; and he had reported the details to Bob Allen. Bob had drawn up suggested floor plans and office layouts; he had selected suitable draperies, carpets, and other accessories to fit in with the decor the company wished to use. At this conference Bob hoped to get approval of his plans for decorating, and Joe hoped to clinch the total sale.

But during the conference the vice-president asked, "What material is

POLICY
52 063 566
MATURITY DATE
8/6/59
FACE AMOUNT OF POLICY
$1,000
CURRENT DIVIDEND
$6.43
TERMINATION DIVIDEND
$7.50
DIVIDEND DEPOSITS
none
AMOUNT OF CHECK
$1,013.93

We are pleased to enclose our check for the amount indicated at left. Your policy matured on the date shown and the check represents the face value of the policy plus accredited dividends.

If you have any questions about this, let us know, won't you? It will be a pleasure to be of service to you.

HOMETOWN GENERAL OFFICE

POLICY
1958 DIVIDEND

This was the finished product — and the first Nylicom.* We have now revised over 500 forms, turned them into Nylicoms and they are being sent out daily by the hundreds.

A Nylicom has no salutation, no closing; it does not pretend to be a letter. It is, admittedly, a "middle-of-the-roader," an honest-to-goodness printed form, with fill-ins obviously typed in, with language as courteous, clear and untechnical as we could make it.

The results? Well, for one thing, they are more efficient. The typist has to set only one margin, fill in the blank spaces on the left-hand side and send it off. We've had no compliments to speak of, but then, we've had no complaints. And the other day, we heard that a company which ran across one of our Nylicoms is considering adopting them for their business.

P.S. — Mr. Trumbull — if you read this — thank you.

**A word made up of the initial letters of New York Life Insurance, and the first three letters of the word "communication."*

the sample carpeting made of?" Bob answered that he did not know. Neither did Joe. The purchasing agent noted that the plans called for wall-to-wall carpeting for one of the offices to measure 17 by 24 feet, and he remembered this particular office as being 15 by 20 feet. He called this error to the attention of Joe Chambers, who remeasured the room and found it to be 15 by 20 feet. The sale was lost.

THE COMPANY

J. D. LeBlanc, Inc., has been in business for twenty-five years, and in its present location ten years. It occupies a four-story building with samples and showrooms on each floor, and a warehouse five blocks away. Office furniture is the main business; LeBlanc carries the Leopold line of wood furniture and the Steel Age line of steel furniture, and sells around $50,000 worth of each line a year. The company also handles office supplies and office systems and can completely furnish and equip an office. About three years ago, because of competition, LeBlanc began an interior designing service for its customers. The service is free and helps the salesmen sell a complete line of furnishings as well as furniture and supplies. Selling is direct to the consumer; to professional men such as doctors, lawyers, and dentists; and to all sizes and kinds of companies: banks, city and state offices, oil companies, and insurance brokers. The furniture is received directly from the manufacturers. The same two lines have been handled for twenty-five years.

PERSONNEL

J. D. LeBlanc, the owner and manager of the firm, is fifty-seven years old; he also functions as sales manager. He was graduated from Soulé Business School and began work as a bookkeeper and accountant. He also worked as a salesman for an office equipment firm before going into business for himself. There are four salesmen who concentrate on selling outside the store and two salesmen who sell to customers coming into the store. The latter two are also assigned additional duties and responsibilities. Tom Franklin, 37, has been with the firm fourteen years. He began as an inside salesman and was promoted to being an outside man. Joe Chambers, 28, has been with the company for three years. He was hired as an outside salesman because Mr. LeBlanc thought he had an excellent sales personality. Herman Blazes, 48, has been with the company only six months. Formerly he was in business for thirty years selling stationery and office supplies. At present there is an opening for the fourth outside salesman. Dan Fisherman resigned last month after being with the company for less than one year.

The two inside salesmen are Henry Mannering and Lee Manbow. Henry also does the billing and some of the correspondence work. Lee is responsible for inventory and bookkeeping. There are also three delivery men. One works inside the office, telephoning and making delivery arrangements; one is the driver of a small truck; and one is a cabinet worker, to touch up and service furniture that is sold. For large pieces of furniture, an independent drayage is used.

The interior designer, Bob Allen, 23, has been with the company only three months. This is his second job. He formerly worked for nine months with the interior decorating service at Sears. Prior to that, he was a student in the School of Architecture at Auburn, Alabama, where he majored in interior decorating.

There has always been a turnover in salesmen for Mr. LeBlanc, and he has found it difficult to get and keep experienced men. He states that an inexperienced man, trained first inside and then outside, usually leaves because of his inability to make sales. Salesmen have a weekly drawing account for expenses. It is applied as a loan and charged against sales commissions. Salesmen are paid on a commission basis, varying from 5 percent to 18 percent and, on some special jobs, up to 33⅓ percent, depending upon the items sold.

COMPANY COMMUNICATION WITH THE FACTORY

Very little paperwork is done. About 75 percent of the products sold come directly from the factories and about 25 percent from local distributors. One of the responsibilities assigned to one of the inside salesmen is to expedite orders and shipments. He is in charge of the inventory and has to see that a shipment is ordered and installed properly and completely.

A *production schedule* is a monthly list of merchandise the factory is going to produce during a specified period; it covers a period of about one to eight weeks. The factory forwards this schedule to the dealer ahead of production so that the dealer can order the merchandise he needs. Lee Manbow plans the purchase order from the production schedule and purchases items needed to maintain the inventory in balance as well as to fill current orders. Normally this procedure works well; sometimes, however, incorrect items are ordered and received, causing an oversupply or undersupply. Needs are estimated, and these estimates are not always accurate. LeBlanc and the factories have been dealing with each other for over twenty-five years and have established good rapport.

A *detailed order form* is forwarded to the factory with a transmittal letter for ordering specific merchandise. A sample form is shown on page 260. To keep track of the status of orders, it is necessary to write letters reminding the factory to ship certain orders on a promised date. Everything is left up to the memory of the person handling these orders.

The *thirty-one-day-folder system,* which has individual folders for each letter of the alphabet, is used. Each folder has numbers from 1 to 31 printed across its top. Orders are filed under the name of the company to which an order was sent. The follow-up comes by tagging the correct date on which the order should be checked.

COMMUNICATION WITH TRANSPORTATION CARRIERS

Communication with transportation carriers involves tracing merchandise and insuring speedy and proper delivery. Deliveries may be made to the main store, the warehouse, the customer's office, or any other place the customer designates. Sometimes the LeBlanc company cannot answer customer inquiries concerning delivery dates and places. The salesmen do not know the status of orders enroute, nor are they responsible for knowing.

COMMUNICATION WITH CUSTOMERS

Communication with the customer consists of sales solicitation, drafting of bids or proposals, and clear and concise billing and collection. In the office furniture business, a large part of the soliciting is done by personal contact; sales leads are dependent upon the ingenuity of the salesmen, who must be observant and alert to new office buildings going up and to the expansion plans of companies that are likely prospects. LeBlanc, Inc., subscribes to the *Daily Journal of Commerce,* which gives local business news of this nature, and to the *Dodge Reports,* dealing with local building and business. Sometimes a good prospect is found simply by talking to the elevator boy in an office building.

PURCHASE ORDER

J. D. LeBLANC INC. No 7799

618 GRAVIER ST.

NEW ORLEANS, 19

OFFICE FURNITURE, SYSTEMS AND STATIONERY

SHIP TO VIA

QUANTITY	CATALOG NO.	DESCRIPTION

*FIT ALL WOOD DRAWERS LOOSELY FOR USE IN SOUTHERN HUMID CLIMATE.

**ALL INVOICES DATED AFTER 24TH OF ANY MONTH WILL BE CONSIDERED AS PART OF THE FOLLOWING MONTH'S BUSINESS.

J. D. LeBLANC, INC.

BY____________________

NOTE: PLEASE ACKNOWLEDGE AT ONCE AND ADVISE WHEN YOU WILL SHIP

Courtesy J. D. Le Blanc, Inc., New Orleans, La.

Circular letters and sales promotion letters prepared by the manufacturers are available and are used by the salesmen at random. A salesman will occasionally write a letter to accompany the promotion piece. The following is a sample letter, sent to doctors who were finishing their residency or internship at Charity Hospital. A similar letter was mailed to students being graduated from Tulane and Loyola law schools.

Dear Doctor:

We enclose leaflets showing our new contemporary design of office furniture by Leopold. This Document Group was awarded the highest honor in furniture design. It is very beautiful, functional, and efficient.

The entire group, as well as the complete line of Leopold desks, Precision chairs, steel desks, and aluminum chairs, is now on display in our showrooms at 618 Gravier Street - not far from Charity Hospital - and we shall be delighted to demonstrate it to you. However, if you prefer, we can have one of our Office Furniture Counselors call on you and make a floor plan of your new office without obligation.

We would take pleasure in opening an account for you and easy terms can be arranged to your satisfaction.

Yours very truly,

Courtesy J. D. Le Blanc, Inc., New Orleans, La.

Procuring any sizable order demands the preparation of some written material describing the furniture and quoting its price and general attributes. Bids are used by a great number of concerns to purchase their merchandise. Individual salesmen prepare these reports and bids. The interior designer works on the order with the salesman whenever a complete office is being

J. D. LEBLANC, PRESIDENT

J. D. LEBLANC

A. W. LEBLANC, SECTY.-TREAS.

OFFICE FLOOR PLAN LAYOUT WITHOUT OBLIGATION

Leopold

OFFICE FURNITURE, SYSTEMS AND STATIONERY

618 GRAVIER STREET NEW ORLEANS 12, LA. MAGNOLIA 7764

FILING CABINETS AND INDEXING SERVICE

Steel Age

SOLD TO

DELIVER TO

INVOICE No.

DATE

SALESMAN

YOUR ORDER No.

TERMS: NET CASH

QUANTITY	STOCK No.	DESCRIPTION	PRICE	AMOUNT

INVOICE

Courtesy J. D. Le Blanc, Inc., New Orleans, La.

planned. He prepares layouts of floor plans and selects accessory items such as draperies, carpets, and pictures, of which he submits samples.

The company at present uses a multicopy invoice billing system that provides copies to the bookkeeper, delivery man, salesman, and customer. The form being used is shown on page 261. A copy of the invoice is sent for collection purposes in billing the customer. Monthly statements are also mailed.

SUMMARY

The rapid growth of J. D. LeBlanc, Inc., from its inception twenty-five years ago has caused deficiencies and weaknesses in company operations and communications, internally and externally. Mr. LeBlanc wants to know what changes and improvements he should make to increase sales and to continue company growth.

4. A Problem in Decision Making

In July 1970, Mr. John Miller, of the policy loan department of the Policy Settlement and Service Division, Universal Life Insurance Company, was asked to review the file on Policy XY93892 for determining what action should be taken on unpaid interest on a $1,500 loan. About the time the loan was made, records for policy owners in metropolitan New York were being transferred from the premium remittance department of the home office to metropolitan branch offices. In the file were the following two letters:

Ward and May, Inc. **Insurance**

16 John Street
New York, New York 10038
November 7, 1969

Universal Life Insurance Company re: John Doe - #XY93892
150 Jefferson Avenue
New York, New York 10020

Gentlemen:

Will you please furnish the assured in the Captioned policy with a history of any policy loans made or in force in 1966 or 1967 as well as statement of interest payments made during those years.

Sincerely yours,

WARD AND MAY, INC.

F. Ward

Courtesy New York Life Insurance Company

UNIVERSAL LIFE INSURANCE COMPANY
150 Jefferson Avenue New York, N.Y. 10020

December 5, 1969

Mr. John Doe
16 John Street
New York, New York 10038

Dear Mr. Doe: Re: Policy #XY93892

We have been requested by Mr. Fred Ward to furnish you with a history of any policy loans made or in force in 1966 or 1967 as well as statement of interest payments made during those years.

After reviewing our records, we find that a loan of $1,500 was made June 29, 1965 and subsequently cancelled on April 28, 1968. However, we have been unable to locate the proportionate interest charge of $74.46 which was due on May 27, 1966. In 1967 the annual interest due of $90.00 was remitted.

We are very sorry, Mr. Doe, that the May 1966 interest payment was overlooked, and that we now have to call on you to remit the interest due of $74.46. However, if by any chance you can furnish us with some evidence of payment, we would appreciate having it so we can credit your account.

Will you kindly send our 49th Street Branch, located at 200 East 49th Street Branch, located at 200 East 49th Street, New York, N.Y. 10017, your remittance for $74.46, and we will be pleased to send you our acknowledgement.

Sincerely yours,

Robert Johnson
Manager, Premium Accounting

Courtesy New York Life Insurance Company

It was within the realm of Mr. Miller's responsibility to decide and take necessary action whenever routine circumstances existed, but if there might be a question raised about cost to the company, or if there were several equally satisfactory courses of action, he usually referred the case to someone in the Policy Settlement and Service Division for a "higher-up" decision. In this instance, he sent the memorandum report shown on page 264.

Mr. William Withers received the memorandum along with other reports and letters calling for his decisions. Because of his experience in the company and his knowledge of the insurance business, he is in the habit of making quick, sound decisions. However, he does consider the facts of each case and judge alternative courses of action on the basis of their effect on the company and on the policy owner.

Answer the memorandum.

OFFICE MEMORANDUM Date July 9, 1970

To Executive Assistant Withers Subject: Policy XY93892

From John Miller Doe

Please note the correspondence on the attached file, which was referred to me for review.

When we completed the loan for $1500 on June 29, 1965, we established an interest charge of $74.46 due on April 27, 1966. This action took place at the time the records in the Premium Remittance Division were being transferred to the Metropolitan Branches. You will notice this transfer took place on or about August 3, 1965. Apparently the loan was not indicated on the transfer record. Incidentally, I have seen several cases where this happened. I have verified that the Comptroller's Department did not bill for the interest because the history shows that only the premium was paid. Because of these two compensating errors the omission was not detected. The insured does not reply to letters sent him.

To complicate the matter, on March 9, 1968 the insured assigned this policy to the Midlands Trust Company, and on April 28, 1968 they repaid the loan. It is quite likely that the Actuarial Department "Bank Letter" advised the bank that the policy was charged with a loan of $1500 and that interest was due from April 28, 1967. Unfortunately, both the Actuarial File and the cancelled loan file have been destroyed.

There appear to be three courses of action available.

1. Waive the interest in view of the Company error.

2. Advise the insured that the shortage is a lien to be adjusted from any future settlement.

3. Establish a loan on the record as of a current date for the unpaid interest.

Either of these latter two courses brings us face to face with the assignee who may object on the basis of previous correspondence. May I have your opinion?

Courtesy New York Life Insurance Company

Chapter Eight

GATHERING FACTS FOR DECISIONS AND REPORTS

To make good, sound decisions, to find solutions to problems, and to write effective business reports, facts are necessary. Without such knowledge, you must resort to guesswork, and in today's competitive business world, too many wrong guesses can put a firm out of business. The presence or absence of essential facts at the moment of decision may mean the difference between a sound decision and a faulty one; it may mean the difference between a workable solution and one that creates further problems, or between an effective report that results in action and one that is rejected.

It is important, therefore, always to be informed and to know the sources of information and business data that are available for use when needed. Your purposes in studying the material in this chapter are to become familiar with ways of keeping informed and with the sources of business data, and to increase your skill in bibliographical research.

You should read through this chapter rather rapidly, for parts of the material included will be a review for you. You should then spend time applying the techniques and suggestions to report-writing situations. In this way you will increase your ability to use bibliographical material effectively. The chapter may well serve for later reference use.

WAYS OF KEEPING INFORMED

It is up to everyone to keep himself well informed. There are several methods you may use to keep abreast of current information and activity.

By subscribing to business periodicals and reading them regularly, you can keep up to date on both theoretical and technical advances. By being a member of trade or professional 'associations, you can participate in their activities, obtain information from their publications, meet people with interests similar to your own, and discuss subjects of importance at conferences, conventions, and other meetings. By using the sources of business information in libraries or having a basic business library of your own, you can look up information as it is needed and, in general, can keep abreast of what is going on in fields other than your own.

Periodicals

The following periodicals deal with business subjects in general. Reading several of them regularly will help you to develop a breadth and understanding of events, problems, and subjects that are of interest and importance to most people, even those outside the business world.

GENERAL BUSINESS MAGAZINES

Atlantic (Monthly)	Timely articles in the fields of politics, economics, and social affairs. Serious literature with literary tone and style.
Business Week (Weekly)	National and international business news. Statistical data reflect current trends.
Changing Times (Monthly)	Covers diversified subjects with wide general appeal.
Dun's Review and Modern Industry (Monthly)	Covers finance, credit, production, labor, sales, and distribution. Presents advanced thinking on problems of technique.
Fortune (Monthly)	Thoughtful articles on current business problems. Presents business titans. Emphasis on big business.
Harper's (Monthly)	Emphasizes contemporary history, politics, science, literature, and the arts. Includes fiction. Seeks to chronicle the pattern of ideas, social attitudes, and trends in the United States. Written in popular but stimulating style.
Harvard Business Review (Bimonthly)	One of the best journals for any field of business. Articles based on university research. Material presented on a broad scale.
Journal of Business (Quarterly)	Emphasizes scientific and professional interests. Includes reviews.

The Nation (Weekly)	Concentrates on political, social, economic, and industrial affairs. Frank presentation of critical public issues.
Nation's Business (Monthly)	Interpretative articles on Washington developments, management, labor, and economic trends. Topics of political and general interest.
Newsweek (Weekly)	Emphasis on material written by specialists. Contains signed articles. News columns unsigned. Impartial review of science, events in government, and business activities in the United States and abroad.
Survey of Current Business (Monthly)	Includes indexes for income payments, industrial production, commodity prices, statistics on construction and real estate, domestic trade, employment, wages, finance, foreign trade, transportation, communication, etc. Some reports on business and industry.
Time (Weekly)	Popular news magazine. Offers significant news that is editorially evaluated and interpreted. Appealing style.
U. S. News & World Report (Weekly)	Comprehensive coverage of news in depth. Objectively reported.

Numerous business periodicals present a wealth of information and material of interest and use to the businessman. Some are highly specialized and deal with technical subjects. Others present material from a layman's point of view. Trade journals are helpful to special groups of business people who deal with particular industries, theories, or practical problems. Professional journals are written for members of a given profession; they keep the reader up to date on what is taking place in his field. Reading periodicals will help to overcome provincial reactions to ideas and events by recording contemporary thought and by supplying a knowledge of new techniques, procedures, and concepts in your field. They present current situations, problems, and solutions. Being acquainted with periodicals outside a special field will also help in providing business information, whether it is needed to make a decision, solve a problem, or merely converse intelligently with other business people. The following list of business periodicals is arranged alphabetically by special functional areas. You should read regularly those dealing with your work and should familiarize yourself with the others, reading some occasionally and others as you need to in order to keep informed or to gather particular data.

ACCOUNTING

MAGAZINE	PUBLICATION FACTS	COMMENTS
The Accountant's Digest	L. L. Briggs, Burlington, Vt. (Quarterly)	Digests of articles currently appearing in the accounting periodicals.
The Accounting Review	American Accounting Association, Menasha, Wis. (Quarterly)	Articles cover the education of accountants, practice and theory of accounting, and importance of the profession. Includes detailed book reviews.
Business Budgeting	Budget Executives Institute, Oxford, Ohio (Bimonthly)	Articles on budgeting, decision making, and forecasting.
The Financial Executive	Financial Executive Institute of America, New York, N.Y. (Monthly)	Accounting and related topics presented on the executive level. News on laws and events of interest to members of the Institute.
The Journal of Accountancy	American Institute Publishing Company, Inc., Concord, N.H. (Monthly)	Articles by practicing accountants cover theory, practice, and problems of accounting. Annotated books and articles a regular feature. Official organ of the American Institute of Accounting.
The N. A. A. Bulletins	National Association of Accountants, New York, N.Y. (Monthly)	Research publication of the Association. Covers general aspects of accounting and applications to problems of specific companies.

ADVERTISING

MAGAZINE	PUBLICATION FACTS	COMMENTS
The Advertiser	The Advertising Publishing Company, New York, N.Y. (Monthly)	Articles and reports on agencies, media, promotions, and general advertising news.
Advertising Age	Advertising Publications, Inc., Chicago, Ill. (Weekly)	Newspaper of advertising. Covers current developments. Provides wide coverage of current information.
Editor and Publisher	Editor and Publisher, New York, N.Y. (Weekly)	Current proceedings and events briefly related. Good news magazine for advertising men.

MAGAZINE	PUBLICATION FACTS	COMMENTS
Marketing Communications	Decker Communications Incorporated, New York, N.Y. (Monthly)	Covers advertising, selling, and marketing fields. Emphasizes latest techniques and developments. Formerly *Printers' Ink.*
The Reporter of Direct Mail Advertising	The Reporter of Direct Mail Advertising, Garden City, N.Y. (Monthly)	Covers all aspects of direct mail. Emphasizes techniques, news, and campaigns. Includes case histories.
	BANKING AND FINANCE	
Banking	American Bankers Association, New York, N.Y. (Monthly)	Articles cover the field of banking. Special sections on banking news, legal notes, methods, and ideas.
Barron's	Barron's Publishing Co., Inc., New York, N.Y. (Weekly)	Current data on government, business, and specific companies. Statistics on bond quotations, over-the-counter markets, stock quotations, indexes, economic and financial indicators, and Dow Jones averages.
The Commercial and Financial Chronicle	William B. Dana Co., New York, N.Y. (Semiweekly)	Contains general corporation and financial news, investments, bank clearings, bond offerings, dividends, exchange rates, and quotations.
Federal Reserve Bulletins	Board of Governors, Federal Reserve System, Washington, D.C. (Monthly)	Articles on national and international trade and finance. Board announcements and tables of financial, industrial, and commercial statistics.
Financial World	Guenther Publishing Corp., New York, N.Y. (Weekly)	Covers a range of financial information from the investment market to development in specific securities.
Journal of Finance	American Finance Association, Chicago, Ill. (Quarterly)	Authoritative articles and scholarly reviews dealing with business, consumer and public finance, governments, money, and banking.
The Magazine of Wall Street	Ticker Publishing Company, New York, N.Y. (Biweekly)	Articles on business activities and trends, and government activities. Statistical data on firms. Analyses of investment opportunities.

MAGAZINE	PUBLICATION FACTS	COMMENTS
The Wall Street Journal	The Wall Street Journal, New York, N.Y. (Daily except Saturday and Sunday)	Current happenings in financial circles. Carries stock market quotations, Dow Jones averages, and corporation reports as regular features. Also reports national and world affairs and discusses their relation to business conditions.

ECONOMICS

MAGAZINE	PUBLICATION FACTS	COMMENTS
The American Economic Review	George Banta Co., Inc., Menasha, Wis. (Quarterly)	Scholarly discussions of current economic problems. Detailed and authoritative.
Economic Indicators	Council of Economic Advisors Report, Washington, D.C. (Monthly)	Charts show data at a glance, ranging from expenditures for new plants to corporate profits for various years.
The Economic Journal	The Economic Journal, St. Martin's Press, New York, N.Y. (Quarterly)	The journal of the Royal Economic Society. Features articles on economic topics of interest to many countries.
Journal of Political Economy	The University of Chicago Press, Chicago, Ill. (Bimonthly)	Articles are scholarly but timely, relating to current economic problems and issues in government and in the political economy of the United States. Book reviews included.
The Quarterly Journal of Economics	Harvard University, Cambridge, Mass. (Quarterly)	Articles on theory and practice in present-day economics. Largely theoretical information.
The Southern Economic Journal	Southern Economic Association, Chapel Hill, N.C. (Quarterly)	Covers many phases of economics. Articles largely by members of the Southern Economic Association.

LABOR AND INDUSTRIAL RELATIONS

MAGAZINE	PUBLICATION FACTS	COMMENTS
The American Federationist	AFL–CIO, Washington, D.C. (Monthly)	News of conventions, industry, and government pertaining to labor. Official publication of AFL–CIO.
Industrial and Labor Relations Review	New York State School of Industrial and Labor Relations, Cornell University, Ithaca, N.Y. (Quarterly)	Articles, reports, conferences, and news items dealing with labor and management problems and related topics.

MAGAZINE	PUBLICATION FACTS	COMMENTS
Industrial Relations Magazine	Dartnell Corporation, Chicago, Ill. (Monthly)	Covers all aspects of industrial relations and employer–employee relations.
International Labour Review	International Labour Office, Geneva, Switzerland (Monthly)	Topics related to labor internationally. Treats world labor problems and specific problems of various nations.
Labor	Labor, Washington, D.C. (Monthly)	National newspaper owned by railroad labor organizations. Contains news of developments, laws, and conventions.
Monthly Labor Review	U.S. Department of Labor, Washington, D.C. (Monthly)	Reports on trends in employment and payrolls, hourly and weekly earnings, hours, agreements, accidents, disputes, etc.
	MANAGEMENT	
Administrative Management	Geyer-McAllister Publications, New York, N.Y. (Monthly)	Covers methods, personnel, and equipment for offices and administrators.
Administrative Science Quarterly	Cornell University, Ithaca, N.Y. (Quarterly)	Articles written to advance understanding of administration through empirical investigation and theoretical analysis. Book reviews and abstracts.
Advanced Management Journal	Society for the Advancement of Management, New York, N.Y. (Monthly)	Articles on specialized phases of management and problems. Book reviews. Official publication of SAM.
Journal of Data Management	Data Processing Management Association, Chicago, Ill. (Monthly)	Articles covering data processing and computer science. Association news and book reviews.
Management Review	American Management Association, New York, N.Y. (Monthly)	Covers industrial relations, office management, production, marketing, and finance. Book reviews.
Management Science	The Institute of Management Sciences, Providence, R.I. (Quarterly)	Research articles from top management's viewpoint. Scholarly and theoretical.
Operations Research	Operations Research Society of America, Baltimore, Md. (Bimonthly)	Highly technical articles dealing with the science of management and coordinated research efforts in industry, government, and military science.

MARKETING

MAGAZINE	PUBLICATION FACTS	COMMENTS
Credit and Financial Management	National Association of Credit Men, Philadelphia, Pa. (Monthly)	Data on laws, court decisions, etc. Articles on problems. News and conventions of interest to credit men.
The Credit World	The Credit World, St. Louis, Mo. (Monthly)	Features articles on problems in retail credit.
Industrial Marketing	Crain Communications, Inc., Chicago, Ill. (Monthly)	Devoted to problems of advertising and selling industrial products. Presents sales promotion ideas, marketing facts, case histories, trends, etc.
Insights	Advertising Publications, Inc., Chicago, Ill. (Weekly)	Covers current news, happenings, and problems in advertising, sales, and promotion. Full of timely ideas on markets, products, and campaigns.
Journal of Marketing	American Marketing Association, Chicago, Ill. (Quarterly)	Articles by teachers of marketing and research experts. Presented from scientific point of view. Book reviews. Research in marketing summarized.
Journal of Retailing	School of Retailing, New York University, New York, N.Y. (Quarterly)	Analyses of retailing problems. Includes special surveys and concise book reviews.
Purchasing	Conover-Mast Publications, New York, N.Y. (Monthly)	A variety of topics treated for purchasing agents. Emphasis on new products.
Sales Management	Sales Management, Inc., New York, N.Y. (Semimonthly)	Articles on sales methods, programs, and media. Department on trends, tools of selling, etc.

PERSONNEL

MAGAZINE	PUBLICATION FACTS	COMMENTS
Personnel	American Management Association, New York, N.Y. (Bimonthly)	Covers all aspects of personnel management, hiring, training, paying, etc.
Personnel Administration	Society for Personnel Administration, Washington, D.C. (Bimonthly)	Covers personnel practices in government agencies.

MAGAZINE	PUBLICATION FACTS	COMMENTS
Personnel Journal	The Personnel Journal, Inc., Swarthmore, Pa. (Monthly)	Reports on conferences and research. Book reviews. Articles on labor relations and personnel practices.
Supervision	Supervision Publishing Company, New York, N.Y. (Monthly)	Articles on industrial and operating management. Helpful to personnel directors and supervisors. Case studies.
	PRODUCTION	
Factory	McGraw-Hill, Inc., New York, N.Y. (Monthly)	Articles on production, industrial relations, and maintenance. Current items on new equipment and developments.
Mill and Factory	Conover-Mast Publications, New York, N.Y. (Monthly)	Covers management, production, and maintenance. Has a calendar of events and a directory.
Modern Management	Society for the Advancement of Management, New York, N.Y. (Monthly)	Articles on factory operations and labor relations.

Although the list of periodicals presented here is not a complete one, it is representative of the magazines available and is fairly comprehensive. There are also several other magazines worth knowing about. The *Columbia Law Review, Harvard Law Review,* and *Yale Law Review* are published by their respective law schools. Several professional associations put out publications in addition to those included in the above list:

The American Statistician, American Statistical Association, Washington, D.C.

Appraisal Journal, American Institute of Real Estate Appraisers, Chicago, Ill.

The Journal of Business Communication, American Business Communication Association, University of Illinois, Urbana, Ill.

The Journal of Communication, International Communication Association, General Motors Institute, Flint, Mich.

Public Relations Journal, Public Relations Society of America, New York, N. Y.

Research, Professional, and Trade Associations

A number of organizations and associations publish material in pamphlets, books, reports, and newsletters. They carry on research and make their results known to members and interested persons. Membership in the association in one's field, and knowledge of other organizations and their services and publications, is very useful professionally. Participating in meetings, conferences, and other activities of organizations provides opportunities for meeting and knowing people, exchanging ideas and problems, stimulating thinking, and keeping well informed in other ways.

There are five major business research organizations, national in scope, that carry on a tremendous amount of research each year and make available in printed form a wealth of material, which businessmen need to keep informed, to make decisions, and to solve problems.

1. *The National Industrial Conference Board, 247 Park Avenue, New York, N. Y.* The NICB, an impartial and nonprofit institution for research and education in economics, business, and management techniques, is supported by subscribers, including business firms, schools, trade associations, libraries, and labor unions. Its chief purpose is to promote the development of private productive enterprise. It assembles, analyzes, interprets, and disseminates information regarding economic conditions and policies in the United States and in other countries. It holds conferences and serves as a public information bureau.
2. *The American Management Association, 1515 Broadway, New York, N. Y.* Founded in 1913, the AMA works closely with business, reprints articles, publishes pamphlets, disseminates materials, publishes several monthly magazines for members, conducts research, and puts on special training conferences. The purpose of the association is the advancement of an understanding of management, commerce, and industry. All phases of management are covered. There are local chapters of the AMA in most of the large cities where there are industrial and educational facilities and opportunities.
3. *The Chamber of Commerce of the United States, Washington, D.C.* The Chamber is a federation of over 3,100 local chambers of commerce and trade associations throughout the United States. Founded in 1912, its prime purpose is to obtain the mature judgment of businessmen upon national questions and to present and interpret these views to the public and to government agencies. Bulletins, reports, surveys, and so on present the results of research and study and are made available to members and to the general public. The International Chamber of Commerce is the international counterpart of the Chamber of Commerce of the United States; it promotes friendly relations among nations, facilitates trade, and stimulates commerce. The State Chamber of Commerce is the state counterpart, and the urban Chamber of Commerce is

the local counterpart—acting as a clearing house for industrial problems and constantly working to improve the community for its people and for business.

4. *National Association of Manufacturers, 2 East 48 Street, New York, N. Y.* The purpose of the NAM is to plan programs for studying economic trends and for assembling views of industry to make the American competitive enterprise system work more efficiently. Organized in 1895, the NAM provides industrial information and strives to protect domestic industrial interests, to improve foreign commerce, and to support legislation for furthering association aims.
5. *National Bureau of Economic Research, 261 Madison Avenue, New York, N. Y.* The bureau conducts impartial studies. It provides detailed knowledge of quantitative measures of activity and objectively derived data for policy makers to use in making sound decisions. Research deals with questions of national significance such as national income, capital formation, business cycles, prices, and wages. Staff members and associates carry out the research of this nonprofit organization. Conferences are held, issues discussed, and an exchange of ideas made. The results of research are published as part of either a general or a special series, a pamphlet, or a report.

There are three other economic research organizations—The Brookings Institution, 722 Jackson Place, Washington, D. C.; The Twentieth Century Fund, 330 West 42 Street, New York, N. Y.; and the Committee for Economic Development, 444 Madison Avenue, New York, N. Y.

Representative of the wide number of professional associations available for membership according to areas of professional interest and development are the American Business Communication Association, American Marketing Association, American Economic Association, American Statistical Association, National Association of Purchasing Agents, and Society for the Advancement of Management.

The ABCA (American Business Communication Association) is a professional society for the advancement and promotion of business writing—in business, government, and education. It publishes the *Journal of Business Communication* during the school year and holds an annual convention and spring regional program meetings for exchanging ideas and solving common problems.

The American Marketing Association is a professional society for men and women engaged in marketing activities in both business and education. It holds semiannual conventions, in which businessmen and educators exchange views. It publishes quarterly the *Journal of Marketing*.

The American Economic Association encourages economic research, particularly the historical and statistical study of industrial activity. It publishes quarterly *The American Economic Review.*

The American Statistical Association seeks to promote the use of statistical data and techniques and to encourage the use of statistics in research and practical affairs. It publishes quarterly the *Journal of the American Statistical Association.*

The National Association of Purchasing Agents collects information on market trends for various commodities, engages in research studies on problems of interest to its members, and gathers information on the reliability of vendors. It also seeks to improve government purchasing methods, to stimulate university course work in purchasing, and to promote the profession with industry, government, and the general public.

The SAM (Society for the Advancement of Management), through its publications and meetings, promotes the study and application of the science of management, makes special investigations, and analyzes and appraises the results of managerial research, experiments, and experience. The *Advanced Management Journal,* which comes out monthly, is its official publication.

For reference purposes and for convenience in writing for available information when it is needed, the following list of trade and professional associations may prove helpful. The names of the organizations indicate their major concern and the group their membership includes.

Administrative Management Association, Willow Grove, Pa.
Air Transport Association of America, 1107 16th Street, N.W., Washington, D.C.
Aircraft Industries Association, 610 Shoreham Building, Washington, D.C.
American Accounting Association, 6525 Sheridan Road, Chicago, Ill.
American Arbitration Association, 9 Rockefeller Plaza, New York, N.Y.
American Association of Advertising Agencies, 420 Lexington Avenue, New York, N.Y.
American Finance Association, 90 Trinity Place, New York, N.Y.
American Institute of Accountants, 13 East 41st Street, New York, N.Y.
American Institute of Certified Public Accountants, 270 Madison Avenue, New York, N.Y.
American Institute of Management, 120 East 38th Street, New York, N.Y.
American Railway Engineering Association, 59 East Van Buren Street, Chicago, Ill.
Association of American Railroads, Transportation Building, Washington, D.C.
Association of Export Advertising Agencies, 60 East 42nd Street, New York, N.Y.
Association of National Advertisers, 330 West 42nd Street, New York, N.Y.
Bankers Association for Foreign Trade, San Francisco, Calif.

Direct Mail Advertising Association, 17 East 42nd Street, New York, N.Y.
Industrial Relations Counsellors, Inc., RKO Building, Rockefeller Center, New York, N.Y.
Institute of Internal Auditors, 120 Wall Street, New York, N.Y.
Institute of Labor Studies, 54 Prospect Street, Northampton, Mass.
International Communication Association, Executive Secretary, General Motors Institute, Flint, Mich.
International Council of Industrial Editors, 2108 Braewick Circle, Akron, Ohio
National Association of Accountants, 505 Park Avenue, New York, N.Y.
National Association of Building Owners and Managers, 134 South LaSalle Street, Chicago, Ill.
National Association of Purchasing Agents, 9 Park Place, New York, N.Y.
National Association of Real Estate Boards, 22 West Monroe Street, Chicago, Ill.
National Federation of Sales Executives, 630 Fifth Avenue, New York, N.Y.
National Planning Association, 1606 New Hampshire Avenue, N.W., Washington, D.C.
National Retail Dry Goods Association, 101 West 31st Street, New York, N.Y.
Outdoor Advertising Association of America, 165 Wacker Drive, Chicago, Ill.
Public Relations Society of America, 2 West 46th Street, New York, N.Y.

Library Sources of Business Data

In a business library, there are a number of books that can provide information and data helpful in keeping abreast of what is what in related areas, as well as in providing specific facts needed for decisions and solutions. Current trends and developments, statistical compilations, guides to markets, changing methods, administrative practices—all are part of the factual data businessmen need and use. Much of this type of information is contained in directories, handbooks, yearbooks, almanacs, encyclopedias, and the publications of various subscription services. Some of these are general references; others are specialized according to the fields they cover. Handbooks and yearbooks give a general survey of the subject matter covered. They are highly factual, provide a quick refresher or renew familiarity with a particular business field, and often serve as the source for a principle. A few handbooks are revised annually, thus keeping their information up to date. The following list of handbooks shows the varied nature of the material they cover:

Accountants' Handbook
Corporate Secretaries' Manual and Guide
Cost Accountants' Handbook
Current Abbreviations
Financial Handbook

Handbook of Business Administration
Handbook of Insurance
Handbook of Labor Unions
Management's Handbook
Marketing Handbook
Production Handbook
The Real Estate Handbook
Sales Manager's Handbook
The United States Government Organization Manual
United States Postal Guide

Yearbooks appear annually and give a summary of the year's specific facts and data:

Commerce Yearbook	Information on commerce, trade, and industry.
Shipping World Yearbook	Shipping data for the year.
Statistical Abstract of the United States	Summary statistics in industrial, social, political, and economic fields in the United States. Statistics on population, education, employment, military affairs, social security, vital statistics, manufacturing, and commerce.

The *American Labor Yearbook, The Spectator Insurance Yearbook,* and *Social Science Abstracts* all give business information.

Directories present facts such as names, addresses, products, and sources of supply. Their data are listed alphabetically or are classified according to convenient categories. They give assistance to individuals seeking specific facts for current use and enable them to get quick results in locating a person or firm. Corporation directories give financial data that may be used in judging the worth of a firm or in determining investment possibilities. Some major directories are:

Ayer's Directory of Newspapers and Periodicals	Covers Canada, Newfoundland, Bermuda, and Cuba as well as the United States. Lists publications, publishers, editors, and circulations.
The Congressional Directory	Alphabetical lists and short sketches of U.S. senators, representatives, and congressional committees, and outlines of special agencies, commissions, and main departments of government.
Directory of House Organs	Lists internal and external publications, and sales magazines. Gives publications, editors, and companies.

MacRae's Blue Book	A buying guide. Arranged under product headings.
Marquis' *Who's Who in America; Who's Who in the East; Who's Who in the Midwest;* etc.	Directories of recognized individuals distinguished for their attainments and positions.
Moody's Manual of Industrials	Separate volumes deal with public utilities, railroads, government and municipalities, banks and insurance, real estate, and investment trusts. Data pertain to the finances, history, organization, and operation of the companies.
Poor's Register of Directors and Executives	About 90,000 names of executives and directors of manufacturing and mining concerns, utilities, railroads, banks, insurance companies, law firms, etc.
Standard's Corporation Manual	Same data as in Moody's, but for corporations only.
Thomas' Register of American Manufacturers	A complete and informative guide for purchases. Locates products, manufacturers, trade names, trade organizations, and papers.

Almanacs and encyclopedias give ready factual information of both a general and specialized nature. Specialized services screen, digest, clarify, forecast, tabulate, evaluate, and analyze data covering a wide range of topics. The three leading general encyclopedias on the market today are:

Encyclopædia Britannica
Encyclopedia Americana
New International Encyclopædia

Illustrative of specialized encyclopedias and almanacs are:

The Economic Almanac	Useful for executives and labor officials.
Encyclopædia of Social Sciences	Covers area of social science, including business subjects.
Encyclopedia of Banking and Finance	Helpful to investors and banking investment institutions.
Exporters' Encyclopædia	Gives complete export shipping data about each country in the world.
The Management Almanac	Helpful for labor and management.
World Almanac and Book of Facts	Brief information on all phases of human endeavor. Includes statistics.

Dictionaries supply not only definitions of terms, but also brief statements of fact and biographical information. Following is a list of several dictionaries that are of special interest to businessmen and students:

Dictionary of Business and Finance, Thomas Y. Crowell Company
The Dictionary of Occupational Titles, U.S. Government Printing Office
Encyclopedia Dictionary of Business, Prentice-Hall, Inc.
Henius' *The Dictionary of Foreign Trade,* Prentice-Hall, Inc.
Who's Who in America, Marquis–Who's Who, Incorporated, Chicago, Ill.
Who's Who in Commerce and Industry, Marquis–Who's Who, Incorporated, Chicago, Ill.

Several other sources of business information are worthy of inclusion here. They may be found in most libraries, and a number of business firms subscribe to the special services:

Commerce Clearing House Services
Dun and Bradstreet Credit Service
Prentice-Hall Tax Services
Publications of state governments
Publications of the Bureau of the Census
Publications of U.S. Department of Labor
Rand McNally Services
Standard Rate and Data Service

Familiarity with the types of information these library sources contain will enable you to locate factual material quickly whenever it is needed for decisions, solutions, or reports, or just for keeping abreast of developments in related areas.

SOLVING PROBLEMS INVOLVING RESEARCH

A firm, considering the question of whether or not to expand its facilities, engaged in an investigation of the possibilities for expansion. Facts about the financial condition of the firm, its policies, the physical plant and equipment, marketing methods, and labor conditions had to be obtained from company records and from conferences with concerned people within the company. It was also necessary to estimate the competitive position of the company within the industry and to determine national and regional trends and the outlook for the future. Bibliographical research helped supply the necessary information for solving the problem.

Bibliographical Research

Bibliographical research is the process of using printed materials as sources of information. It is invaluable in each of the following uses:

1. To provide essential data for the solution of a problem or to give information on a particular subject
2. To indicate what others have done and how an investigation fits into the general pattern of knowledge
3. To show the findings and opinions of authorities in the field
4. To reveal whether or not a similar study has already been accomplished, and if so to indicate any possible need for further investigation
5. To provide an understanding of the background of the subject

Solving a problem involving bibliographical information calls for six major steps to be taken:

1. Compiling a working bibliography
2. Evaluating, eliminating, expanding, and organizing the working bibliography
3. Reading and taking notes
4. Analyzing, interpreting, and organizing material from these notes
5. Integrating material from the notes with other facts and ideas for reaching conclusions
6. Preparing a final bibliography

The first three steps are discussed here. Steps 4 and 5 are included in Chapter 9, and step 6 is dealt with in the bibliography section of Appendix C. The objective in compiling a working bibliography is to obtain a complete list of available material on the subject being considered. This list, which includes such facts as the author, title, and publication details for each item, serves as a guide in the investigator's research and is helpful in directing his reading of essential and significant printed material. Later it may be used in preparing the final bibliography as a part of a finished report. Then it becomes a list of sources the investigator used, serving as a guide for the reader if he desires further information on the subject.

Prepared bibliographies and general and special indexes are helpful aids in compiling a working bibliography. Numerous lists (typewritten, mimeographed, or printed) have been prepared on a large variety of subjects. A number of prepared bibliographies may be obtained by writing to the Library of Congress, Washington, D. C. Many libraries subscribe to services such as the Public Affairs Information Service, which provides a weekly *Bulletin,* cumulated five times a year and annually. It lists books, pamphlets, government publications, reports of public and private agencies, and periodical articles related to economic and social conditions, public administration, and international relations.

The PAIS *Bulletin* is published by the H. W. Wilson Company. Another publication of the H. W. Wilson Company is *The Bibliographic Index*. This is a cumulative bibliography of bibliographies and is sold on a subscription service basis. Various associations, college schools of business, and libraries publish lists of printed materials, and most professional magazines print bibliographies in their fields from time to time.

General and special indexes to periodicals should always be checked for current articles as well as for older ones. Most libraries of any size will contain several indexes to periodicals. The *Industrial Arts Index,* first published in 1913, was issued monthly and cumulated quarterly and annually until 1958. It lists articles pertaining to business, industry, and commerce; over two hundred specialized technical and business magazines are indexed, including publications of a number of technical societies and associations in Great Britain, Canada, France, Germany, and the United States, as well as publications of the U. S. Bureau of Foreign and Domestic Commerce. All fields are covered; arrangement is by author, title, and subject. Since 1958, the H. W. Wilson Company has divided the *Industrial Arts Index* into two indexes: The *Applied Science and Technology Index* and the *Business Periodical Index*. These now provide wider coverage of subject matter and the indexing of more magazines than were formerly included in the *Industrial Arts Index*. Both of the newer indexes are issued monthly and cumulated quarterly and annually. The *Applied Arts Index* is also issued monthly, and has been cumulated annually since 1957. It indexes articles on architecture, engineering, and the applied sciences.

In contrast to the indexes listing articles pertaining to industry, the *Reader's Guide to Periodical Literature* indexes articles of a popular and general nature. Over one hundred magazines are indexed. Monthly supplements are issued, which are cumulated semiannually and annually. Entries are alphabetical by title, subject, and author. For articles published prior to 1900, *Poole's Index to Periodical Literature* should be consulted. It was published annually from 1802 to 1916. The arrangement is by subject only. Special indexes list articles in particular fields:

The Accountants' Index
Agriculture Index
Art Index
Education Index
Engineering Index
Index to Legal Periodicals
The Management Index
A World List of Scientific Periodicals

The only index to newspaper items is *The New York Times Index;* although it indexes only those items appearing in the *Times,* the coverage is correspondingly complete, since the *Times* regularly provides one of the most comprehensive news coverages in the world. It is published semimonthly and is cumulated annually.

To locate any book in a particular library, the investigator simply checks the library's card catalog, which lists all the books in the library by author, title, and subject. There are times, however, when the researcher will want to check books available elsewhere than in his own library. The H. W. Wilson Company's *Cumulative Book Index* indexes all books published in the United States. It is issued monthly and cumulated semiannually and annually. The *United States Catalog* lists all books published prior to 1928. *Publishers' Weekly* is a book trade journal, listing and describing the books published each week. It is published by the R. R. Bowker Company, 62 West 45 Street, New York, N. Y.

After a complete listing of all sources of data has been made, the next step in bibliographical research is to evaluate, eliminate, expand, and organize the working bibliography. This is accomplished by considering the authors, the material they have written, and the use of the material for your purposes. Several of the *Who's Who* publications and the *Book Review Digest* for the year the book appeared are sources of information of this sort. Other published reviews of books also contain information about the author. A quick perusal of the text itself, noting the information given on the title page and examining the preface and table of contents, will help to indicate the extent of coverage of the subject, whether or not the material is biased, the basis for the facts presented, the method of presentation, and so on. Information of this sort may be checked as the bibliography is compiled or after it has been com-

Bibliographical Research

Barzun, Jacques, and H. F. Graff
The Modern Researcher
Harcourt, Brace
New York
1957

Chapters 2, 4, 14,
and 15
especially good

Bibliography card for a book

Communication Policy

Exton, W., Jr.
"Improving Communication Policy"
Advanced Management
November, 1959
pp. 19-22

Bibliography card for a magazine article

pleted. Comments as to the worth, authoritativeness, and type of information may be written on the bibliographical card for later reference. A convenient method is to record bibliographical information on 3- by 5-inch cards to facilitate their arrangement for reading purposes and for ease in typing the final bibliography.

For convenience in reading and taking notes, it is wise to arrange together all references pertaining to each aspect of the subject so that you can read them in succession rather than having to move from one aspect of the subject matter to another. In this way, the proper relationships, any duplication, and later possible uses of the material should be made readily apparent. The reader may also compare what he reads and evaluate his material for its completeness and pertinence to his purpose.

The following suggestions are helpful for understanding and retaining what is read:

First:

1. Scan for the particular information you want. Reject what you can. Select what is needed and usable.
2. Have something definite to look for. Find the main thought. Look for topic sentences. Read for main points or for specific details.
3. Get a single, first impression of the whole piece you are reading, whether it is a chapter of a book, an article in a magazine, a report, or some other reference.

As you read:

1. Break down what you are reading into parts. Look for the meaning of each part and its relationship to other parts and to the whole.
2. Examine what you read for its relationship to aspects of your problem and to your purpose.
3. Examine factual statements and figures for their accuracy and logic.
4. Distinguish between vague and definite statements, between hasty generalizations and careful judgments, between opinion and accuracy.
5. Compare information from different sources.
6. Distinguish between facts or events and principles or ideas.
7. Look for a common thread or principle running through the material. Use this as a basis for classification of the subject matter.

Then:

1. Understand how the material you are reading is applicable to other situations and circumstances, and to your own problem.
2. Develop a critical attitude toward what you read. Look for evidence; look for original ideas. Ask yourself whether or not the material is trustworthy, genuine, and sincere.

3. Form a variety of associations among the points you wish to remember. Think about what you are reading. Find an interest in the material. Associate it with experiences in your past and present.
4. Focus your attention on obvious, foreseeable uses to which you are going to put your material, but don't overlook other possibilities. Read with an open mind.

During reading, notes should be taken for later analysis and use in drawing conclusions, reaching decisions, and presenting information or courses of action to someone else. Cards are preferred to notebooks for recording notes because they can be more easily rearranged later. An advantage of looseleaf notebooks, however, is that they have more space available for recording details. Although note cards can be of any convenient size the usual sizes are 3 by 5, 4 by 6, and 5 by 8 inches. Each card should contain only one fact, classified under a heading indicated at the top corner of the card. If you always include the author, title, and page number on the card, you can avoid spending endless hours later tracking down facts needed for footnotes.

```
Listening                    Wiksell
                             Do They Understand You?
                             page 86

     "Listening is more than just the process
of hearing. It involves a receptive attitude.
One must concentrate actively to understand
and interpret what is being said. Finally, one
must remember and apply what one has heard."
```

Example note card for a quotation

It is better to assimilate new knowledge along with your own ideas than to take a great many literal notes. Putting down your own thoughts helps. Whole paragraphs or sections can be summed up in a few sentences stated in your own words, keeping the original purpose in mind. What is recorded will vary, but in general it will include:

1. The main points
2. Important facts
3. Authoritative statements or opinions
4. Evidence or proof
5. Statistics
6. Figures
7. Amounts
8. Original ideas
9. Little-known facts or details of significance
10. An unusual or apt way of saying something
11. Conclusions

It is usually best to record information in the form of brief summaries or as a single fact or bit of data. A summary indicates the main idea or point of view of the author and is stated in the words of the note taker. There are several other methods of taking notes: direct quotation, paraphrase, précis, and outline. Record a direct quotation word for word with photographic accuracy, so as not to misinterpret or change the author's meaning. Frequent use of quotations, especially long ones, should be avoided. In quoting, omissions of words are indicated by ellipses (. . .). The whole quotation is enclosed in quotation marks.

The précis is an exact, sharply defined statement. Specific phrasing of expressions and style used by the original author should not be copied.

To paraphrase is to express, interpret, or give meaning, using one's own words rather than those of the author.

An outline records the main points, but shows the relationship of several ideas in its subdivisions.

After the material has been read and recorded from bibliographical sources, the next steps are to analyze, interpret, and organize the notes, then to integrate the note material with other facts and ideas, and to use it to reach conclusions. These two steps call for thinking creatively, logically, and critically and for organizing and outlining facts and ideas. They are discussed in Chapter 9. The handling of bibliographical material frequently calls for the use of quotations and footnotes, and for the arrangement of a final bibliography. Rules pertaining to the mechanics for these usages may be checked in the bibliography and footnote sections of Appendix C.

Other Business Research Methods

The use of questionnaires, interviews, observations, company and departmental reports, and individual inquiry provides other sources for gathering facts to make sound decisions and to find solutions to problems. Although it is outside the scope of this book to discuss the techniques and procedures of each of these research methods, it is important that we be cognizant of the fact that there are methods other than bibliographical research.

Questionnaires are used to secure information on behavioral characteristics, to gather opinions or attitudes, or to obtain facts. Finding out what a person or group of people thinks or feels, and why, is a basis for making relevant decisions. Knowing what a person does and why, how he reacts as part of a group, is important in understanding him and his group, as well as any problem connected with them. The use of questionnaires calls for preparation, planning of the sample to be surveyed, and tabulation of the results.

Interviews help determine objective facts such as events, conditions, practices, policies, and techniques. They also help in gathering subjective data such as attitudes, preferences, opinions, and emotional reactions. Such information is especially helpful in dealing with problems in marketing, personnel work, and industrial relations. Interviews should be planned, notes taken, and the results evaluated later.

One of the chief sources for gathering first-hand information is observation. Often it is combined with an interview in which the investigator gains information from conversing with the other person; from seeing his reactions, he forms a mental impression of what the other person perceives and observes. Observing the production line in a factory and noting the procedures being followed, in order to find out the steps used in the production process, is *uncontrolled observation,* viewing things as they are. If the conditions under which the observing is being done are set and prearranged, or the observer decides to try a new procedure and sets it up for observation, this is *controlled observation,* which is a type of experimental research. Observation calls for planning and for evaluating results.

A communication system set up within a company will provide for company and departmental reports, considering them essential for disseminating operational and technical information necessary for running the business. Management at all levels should make use of these reports to keep informed on what is going on in the firm and to secure information whenever it is needed. Data-processing machines and computers make available a vast amount of factual information that otherwise might not be obtainable—certainly not without tremendous effort and time being expended. The alert businessman will take advantage of the data made available in this way, and he will make further inquiry as needed.

SUMMARY

If one is to make good sound decisions and to find solutions to problems, facts are needed. The presence or absence of facts at the moment of decision may make the difference between a sound decision and a faulty one. It is necessary to be well informed at all times. Subscribing to business periodicals and reading them regularly, being a member of trade or professional associations and participating in their activities, and using sources of business information in libraries or having a basic business library are ways of keeping abreast of what is going on in general and of getting information as it is needed. The various lists provided in this chapter are valuable references to be used when seeking facts from periodicals, associations, or sources of business information.

Bibliographical research is one of the chief methods a student uses for gathering data to solve problems. A business firm, however, also makes use of questionnaires, interviews, observation, company records and reports, and individual inquiry for securing data to make sound decisions and solve problems.

Solving a problem or writing a report involving bibliographical research calls for compiling a working bibliography; evaluating, eliminating, expanding, and organizing the working bibliography; reading and taking notes; integrating material from the notes with other facts and ideas to reach conclusions; and preparing a final bibliography. The thorough researcher will carefully work through the steps of bibliographical research.

FURTHER READING

Barzun, Jacques, and H. F. Graff, *The Modern Researcher*. New York: Harcourt, Brace & World, Inc., 1957.

Brown, Leland, *Effective Business Report Writing*, 2nd ed. Englewood Cliffs, N. J.: Prentice-Hall, Inc., 1963.

Coman, E. T., Jr., *Sources of Business Information*, rev. ed. Englewood Cliffs, N.J.: Prentice-Hall, Inc., 1964.

Dawe, Jessamon, and William J. Lord, Jr., *Functional Business Communication*. Englewood Cliffs, N. J.: Prentice-Hall, Inc., 1968, pp. 344–69.

Johnson, H. W., *How To Use the Business Library*, 3rd ed. Cincinnati: South-Western Publishing Co., 1964.

Keithley, Erwin M., *A Manual of Style for Writing Reports*. Cincinnati: South-Western Publishing Co., 1959.

Lesikar, Raymond V., *Report Writing for Business*, rev. ed. Homewood, Ill.: Richard D. Irwin, Inc., 1965.

Manual of Style. Washington, D. C.: U. S. Government Printing Office, 1966.

Tarabian, Kate L., *A Manual for Writers of Term Papers, Theses, and Dissertations*, 3rd. ed. rev. Chicago: The University of Chicago Press, 1967.

QUESTIONS AND PROBLEMS

1. Find five books, five articles, and three references of another kind on one of the following topics and arrange them all in correct bibliographical form:

Business letter writing	Employee publications
Business report writing	Information theory
Communication theory	Logic
Conferences in industry	Management communication
Creative thinking	Office management
Direct mail advertising	Public relations

2. Locate and read three articles on the same subject in three different magazines. Summarize them and review them critically for a member of management in a business firm. Your instructor may ask you to write an analysis of the subject, integrating material from each article. This could be done as a memorandum.
3. Compile and arrange an annotated bibliography of recent books and articles written in your field of major interest.
4. The following list of problems could be used for a bibliographical research report. Select one, do the research, and write the report:[1]
   a. How much economic competition is desirable?
   b. Is creeping inflation dangerous to the national economy?
   c. Should we have public development of our power resources?
   d. Should the U.S. government take over the ownership and operation of the railroads?
   e. Does the consumer need more protection?
5. *Career report project*: Explore the possibility of a career in your chosen field of interest.
   a. Start by thinking about your area of major interest (accounting, marketing, management, teaching, etc.). Then narrow your thinking to some one aspect until you arrive at a particular position or job—this may be copywriter in an advertising agency, cost accountant in a CPA firm, etc.
   b. Next, list a dozen or so topics or questions that would give you information about this career; for example:

Educational requirements	Number of jobs available
Beginning salary	Number employed
Average salary	Present work trends
Promotion opportunities	Skills and duties

   c. Gather and organize information on these topics; use bibliographical sources, interview professors, interview people in the position in a company, write letters to the government and professional associations for material, etc.
   d. Determine a purpose or use for a report of this sort:
      Decision making?
      Advising?

   Present your information and analyze it to reach conclusions and recommendations that relate to your purpose. It will be up to you to decide what parts of a report to include as preliminary or supplementary material and to what degree your style of writing will be formal or informal. Be sure to read and use Chapters 9 and 10 in organizing and presenting your material as a business report.
6. The following editorial is just as relevant today as when it was written. After reading articles and books relating to the problem, present the

[1]This problem or any of the following ones should be assigned now, but one to three weeks should be allowed for its completion so that Chapters 9 and 10 can be read, studied, and applied to the situation.

issues and come to a conclusion, which you support. What stand should management take? What is the trend today among the business firms you know?

Management outlook BW

November 2, 1968

Is profit an outdated objective?

There's a new impetus to the search for a more general managerial objective than that of making as much money as possible.

Doubts about profit maximization as the ultimate business objective are increasingly being voiced by friends of the free enterprise system. Social involvement—once the preserve of the radicals who first raised the question—is claiming more and more corporate managers to its causes.

Indeed, the idea is a plank in the platform of GOP candidate Richard M. Nixon. And as business takes a bigger role in the attack on social ills, its actions cast more doubt on profit, measured in money, as its basic goal.

The view broadens

Uncertainty about the soundness of profit as the touchstone of business management stems from a revision in the classic notion of management's responsibility.

Classically, management serves as trustee for the owners. The modern idea is that the professional manager serves as trustee for all parties connected with the enterprise: owners, employees, customers, suppliers, creditors, government, and the public.

The statement of the late Harlow H. Curtice—that he placed his responsibility to the general public ahead of his responsibility to the shareholders of General Motors—no longer surprises as it did 15 years ago.

Support from the top

This expansion of the trusteeship of the professional manager has brought with it the view—by no means universal—that business has a social responsibility.

Here, too, the profit conception comes into question. William C. Stolk, former chairman and currently a director of American Can Co., recently suggested that if business is to deal successfully with social problems corporate managers will have to re-examine the profit concept.

Henry Ford II has said "to subordinate profit to broad social goals would be totally irresponsible. On the other hand, socially responsible behavior is essential to the long-term growth and profitability of the corporation."

Professor Ezra Solomon of Stanford is on the side of Stolk and Ford. He has suggested that—at least in making financial decisions—management should be guided by "net present worth maximization." Net present worth, or wealth, "reflects the most efficient use of a society's economic resources, and thus leads to a maximization of society's economic wealth," he avers.

Subversive doctrine?

Not everyone agrees with this view. Conservative economist Milton Friedman, in a 1963 book called Capitalism and Freedom, wrote: "Few trends could so thoroughly undermine the very foundations of our free society as the acceptance by corporate officials of a social responsibility other than to make as much money for the shareholders as possible."

He calls the concept of a social responsibility of business "a fundamentally subversive doctrine." He added that "if businessmen are civil servants rather than employees of their stockholders then in a democracy they will, sooner or later, be chosen by the public techniques of election and appointment."

Still, doubts about money as the best measure of profit are growing, and will continue to do so in proportion to business attacks on social ills.

Business Week November 2, 1968 **Management 71**

Business Week, November 2, 1968. Reproduced by permission.

7. Choose a controversial topic such as one of the following for study and analysis:
   a. Changes in the Electoral College in electing a president of the United States
   b. Federal aid to education
   c. Guaranteed annual income for all
   d. Fluoridation for dental health
   e. Government in private business
   f. Lowering the voting age
   g. Changes in abortion laws
   h. Reforms in automobile insurance practices

   Read widely on the issue or problem you choose, to get a full understanding of both sides of the issues involved. Then, with your own ideas and the material you have read, formulate a conclusion or a position that you hold. Present your conclusion with supporting ideas, facts, and data in such a way that you will convince others to agree with you.

8. Turn in a written report of an interview you conduct with a business executive. Preferably, this individual should be a member of top management (above the department manager level). Use your own initiative in arranging for an interview (you might try the personnel department of a local concern, or work through a relative or friend).

   As a basis for your report, you may ask these questions or others:
   a. How important is it to be able to write an effective report?
   b. What do you look for in a good report?
   c. What format do you favor?
   d. Do you train your subordinates in any way to be better communicators?
   e. How can college better prepare its students to write acceptable reports?

   Read the chapters on report writing, plus whatever other references you feel may be helpful, *before* the interview. Remember—to write well you must have something to say, then be able to say it to the satisfaction of the person to whom you are writing. You are free to determine your own title, format, and contents.

9. The following situation calls for two reports: an immediate one in less than a week to help Mr. Reiner by giving him specific information and your plans for investigating further, and a later one to give him your decision, supporting data, and implementation of your recommendation. Write either or both as your instructor directs.

   You are the personnel manager of the Channing Engineering Company. You have been working there for one year, having been first employed as assistant personnel manager when you were graduated from college, and then promoted when the personnel manager resigned. It was a sudden advancement, and you know that to hold this position, you must prove your ability.

At 9 o'clock on Monday morning, your phone rings. It is Mr. G. R. Reiner, the president of the company. He says, "Will you come in to see me when you have a moment this morning?" You stop work on the new organization chart you are making and go to Mr. Reiner's office.

"Sit down," he says, motioning to a chair near his desk.

You notice that he looks tired—not physically, but tense and drawn. He picks up a letter on his desk. "I just received this letter this morning, and I'd like you to read it."

You recognize the letterhead. It's from a trucking concern in Pittsburgh that handles most of the firm's business. The president, Mr. M. A. Highby, is a good friend of Mr. Reiner's. The gist of the letter is that Mr. Highby attended a conference in Buffalo last summer called "The Creative Problem-Solving Institute." For several days business executives discussed the need for creativity in business and the techniques that have been designed to develop this creativity. It is an enthusiastic letter, and Mr. Highby ends it:

> . . . I know, Gordon, that you have been losing some of your business to the Burton Industries, and as a close friend I offer this suggestion. Please don't take offense, but the reports are that your company is simply not keeping up, that you aren't in line pricewise and that you aren't up to date on all your designs. I hesitate to say this, but do you think something like this creative business might help? Maybe it could, maybe that's not it at all, but at least you can think about it. Give my best to Mary, and I'll see you next week in Chicago.

Mr. Reiner tosses you a pamphlet enclosed with the letter. The title is *Report of Proceedings of The Creative Problem-Solving Institute.* "He sent this along. Keep it. Incidentally, what you read in that letter and what we say here this morning are strictly between us."

"Of course, sir."

"To put it bluntly, he's right. We're losing money. We lost the Harbor Industries account yesterday, and we're taking the Ajax account at a loss. You know our problems in quality control and employee turnover rate."

"But . . ."

"I know," he says with a quick wave of his hand, "you are working on it. But there is something more basic than that. It may be me, I don't know." He gets up and walks to the window, staring out at the parking lot. "Maybe it's production, pricing, promotion—or maybe all of them. We seem to . . . well . . . to have run down." He pauses, and then, as if coming back from a reverie, turns toward you. His face is set now.

"I want you to look into this. Seems crazy, but I know Highby, and he doesn't jump off the deep end for nothing. Find out what this creative business is, what you're supposed to do and how, and what others are doing. I want to know everything you can find out about it—good and bad—and I want your recommendation as to whether or not we should do anything on it."

As you leave the office, Mr. Reiner says, "Do a good job for me. I know you don't have much time to work on it, but do the best you can." You walk out of his office and get busy.

What are the procedures you would use if this problem were given to you under these circumstances? Prepare the report or reports you would present to Mr. Reiner.

TEST YOUR FAMILIARITY WITH BUSINESS SOURCES AND BIBLIOGRAPHICAL RESEARCH

Since the purposes of this chapter have been to increase your familiarity with ways of keeping informed and with the sources of business data, and to increase your skill in bibliographical research, it will be to your advantage to stop and test your increased knowledge, and then apply it to the problems and cases that follow.

1. It is highly important to be informed and to know where to get facts when they are needed. There are three ways of accomplishing this and thus of keeping abreast of current information and activity:
   a.
   b.
   c.
2. Fill in the blanks in the columns:

Periodicals	*Comments*
a. ____________________	Articles on current business problems. Emphasis on big business and top management.
b. *Harvard Business Review*	____________________ ____________________ ____________________ ____________________
c. *Business Budgeting*	____________________ ____________________ ____________________ ____________________
d. ____________________	Timely articles on political, economic, and social affairs. Serious literature.

e. *The Journal of Accountancy* ______________________

f. ______________________ Covers advertising, selling, and marketing fields. Emphasis on developments. Formerly *Printers' Ink*.

g. ______________________ National and international trade and finance. Tables of financial, industrial, and commercial statistics. (Monthly)

h. ______________________ Charts showing data at a glance, ranging from expenditures for new plants to corporate profits.

i. *Administrative Science Quarterly* ______________________

j. *Monthly Labor Review* ______________________

k. *Insights* ______________________

l. *Journal of Marketing* ______________________

m. ______________________ Articles on factory operations and labor relations.

n. ______________________ Production, industrial relations, maintenance, new equipment, and development.

o. ______________________ Covers all aspects of personnel management, hiring, training, paying, etc.

3. List the five major research organizations and the kinds of information and help they have available:
   a.
   b.
   c.
   d.
   e.
4. What are the professional organizations that you as a businessman may wish to join? Why?
   a.
   b.
   c.
   d.
   e.
   f.
5. The kinds of material available in handbooks consist of:

   ____

   ____

   ____

   Some handbooks are:

   ____

   ____

   ____

6. The benefits of yearbooks to the businessman are: ______________

   ____

   ____

7. The *Statistical Abstract of the United States* contains:

   ____

   ____

8. Identify the following sources by telling what they contain and how they can be used:
   a. *MacRae's Blue Book*
   b. *Thomas' Register of American Manufacturers*
   c. *Moody's Manual of Industrials*
   d. *The Congressional Directory*
   e. *Encyclopedia of Banking and Finance*
   f. Dun and Bradstreet Credit Service
   g. *World Almanac and Book of Facts*
   h. Publications of the Bureau of the Census
   i. Prentice-Hall Tax Services
   j. *Publications of U.S. Department of Labor*
9. Six major steps in bibliographical research are:
   a.
   b.

c.
d.
e.
f.

10. Four uses of bibliographical research are:
a.
b.
c.
d.

11. One can bring a printed bibliography up to date by:

___

12. To locate a book in the library:

___

13. For information about a book not in the library, consult:

___

14. Three indexes to periodicals that a student in business administration will find most useful are:
a.
b.
c.

15. Important suggestions for reading and taking notes for a report are:
a.
b.
c.
d.
e.

16. The purposes of footnoting are:
a.
b.
c.
d.

17. Three ways of arranging a final bibliography are:
a.
b.
c.

18. In footnoting, *Ibid.* is used to ___; *op. cit.* to ___; and *loc. cit.* to ___

19. Research methods other than bibliographical ones that are often used in business reports are:
a.
b.
c.
d.
Why?

Chapter Nine

INTERPRETING AND OUTLINING MATERIAL FOR REPORTS

While you are gathering facts and creating ideas to solve a problem, you must organize, interpret, and think through these facts. As you do this, you evaluate the data; at this point you are concerned with making them meaningful and useful. When you have accomplished this, the next step is organizing the data for presentation in a report; this results in an outline. This chapter will concern itself with helping you to arrange facts, ideas, data, and material so that you can interpret and reason with them, and will show you how to organize them in a well-planned outline to be used as a guide in writing reports.

Many fallacies of reasoning occur from lack of sufficient data, an inadequate definition of the question, failure to understand the terms, dependence upon testimony that is of little value, unconnected results, or the belief that something is a cause when in reality it is an effect of another cause. Such fallacies may often be prevented by avoiding generalities, ambiguity, and hastily drawn conclusions. Generalities often confuse or antagonize the reader. Ambiguity is relative to the context: a word or statement is ambiguous when the reader is not sure which of its possible meanings is intended. Being specific will always help to prevent both generalities and ambiguity. The writer should think through his ideas and data; be exacting rather than vague; and consider the explicit distinctions of the words he uses.

Hasty generalization results from drawing conclusions from too few data. It is a more judicious use of evidence to set up a generalization after studying adequate specific cases. Generalize only after you have sufficient accurate, reliable data, and after you have considered the relationships, the consistencies, or a common pattern or characteristic.

REASONING LOGICALLY

Logic is the study of the structure of reasoning. When you draw conclusions from premises, extract universal truths from individual cases, and infer particulars from general laws, using statistics and facts, you are reasoning and using logic. Logic uses known factors to arrive at unknowns. It uses information to obtain *proof*. With logic one searches for *evidence* and considers *facts* with knowledge and experience to formulate a *conclusion*.

Link Belt News, Link-Belt Divisions, FMC Corporation

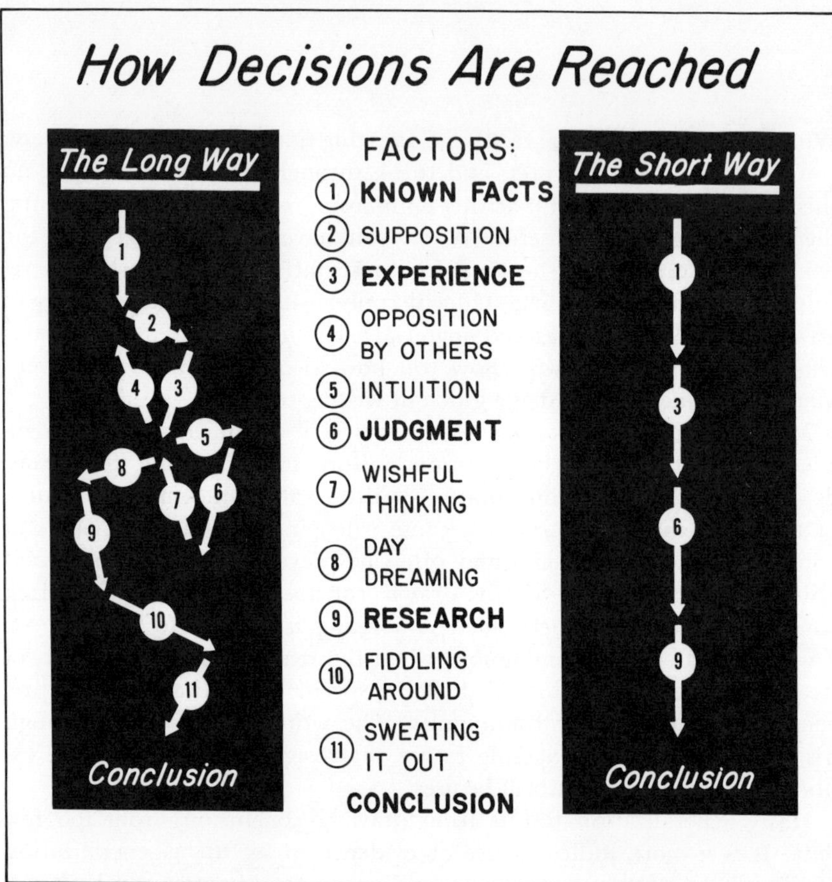

Reasoning is used to interpret, to see relationships, to evaluate, and to verify. It is by nature analytical and critical. Thus it enables you to:

1. Evaluate and select ideas suited to your purpose
2. Achieve order, harmony, and balance in ideas and thoughts
3. Adhere to the subject or problem at hand
4. Sift significant points from irrelevant ones
5. Insure the logical rightness of the parts and the whole
6. Compare and choose for optimum results

Logical thinking operates in all research, decision making, problem solving, and report investigation and presentation. Several patterns of reasoning are considered here that will help you to see relationships and meaning in data and to sharpen your reasoning powers.

Inductive Reasoning

Inductive reasoning is a logical thinking process in which we reason from an awareness of particulars to an understanding of their essence or nature. It shows us that something is so. We examine specific facts, isolated cases, or particular experiences to achieve a generalization, conclusion, inference, hypothesis, or principle; this affirms the truth or validity of the facts or situation examined. Conclusions are reached by:

1. Considering testimonial evidence
2. Examining a sufficient number of details
3. Reasoning from a hypothesis or generalization through the proof or evidence that supports it
4. Examining cause-and-effect relationships
5. Using statistical data to measure central tendencies or probability relationships

A friend of mine who recently purchased a new Ford station wagon told a neighbor the other day that he had plenty of room for hauling groceries, camping equipment, baggage, or anything else he needed. Furthermore, he said that a professor friend of his went on a trip last summer and also drove a new Ford station wagon. The professor maintained that he had plenty of room for his wife and five children, with all their baggage and supplies. Another man who has a Ford wagon uses it for fishing trips, taking as many as six men and their equipment, and also has sufficient room. Find further testimonial evidence about the roominess of the Ford wagon. After examining the evidence, you may decide that the statements all have a common element—the Ford wagon is a roomy car. This conclusion, reached from testimonial evidence, is not based on complete facts, but it might increase your interest

Here are 8 important reasons why the Bell & Howell overhead projector is the most advanced and efficient in the world.

Maybe No. 8 should be No. 1.

8 It's from Bell & Howell. You benefit from the superior design, reliability and performance that you expect and receive from Bell & Howell. For full details, mail the coupon.

Bell & Howell Co., 7100 McCormick Road
Chicago, Illinois 60645 Dept. OP2

Gentlemen: please send me full information on the versatile new Bell & Howell Overhead Projector.

Name________________

Title________________

Company________________

Address________________

City________ State________ Zip________

AUDIO-VISUAL PRODUCTS DIVISION

Inductive reasoning in advertising

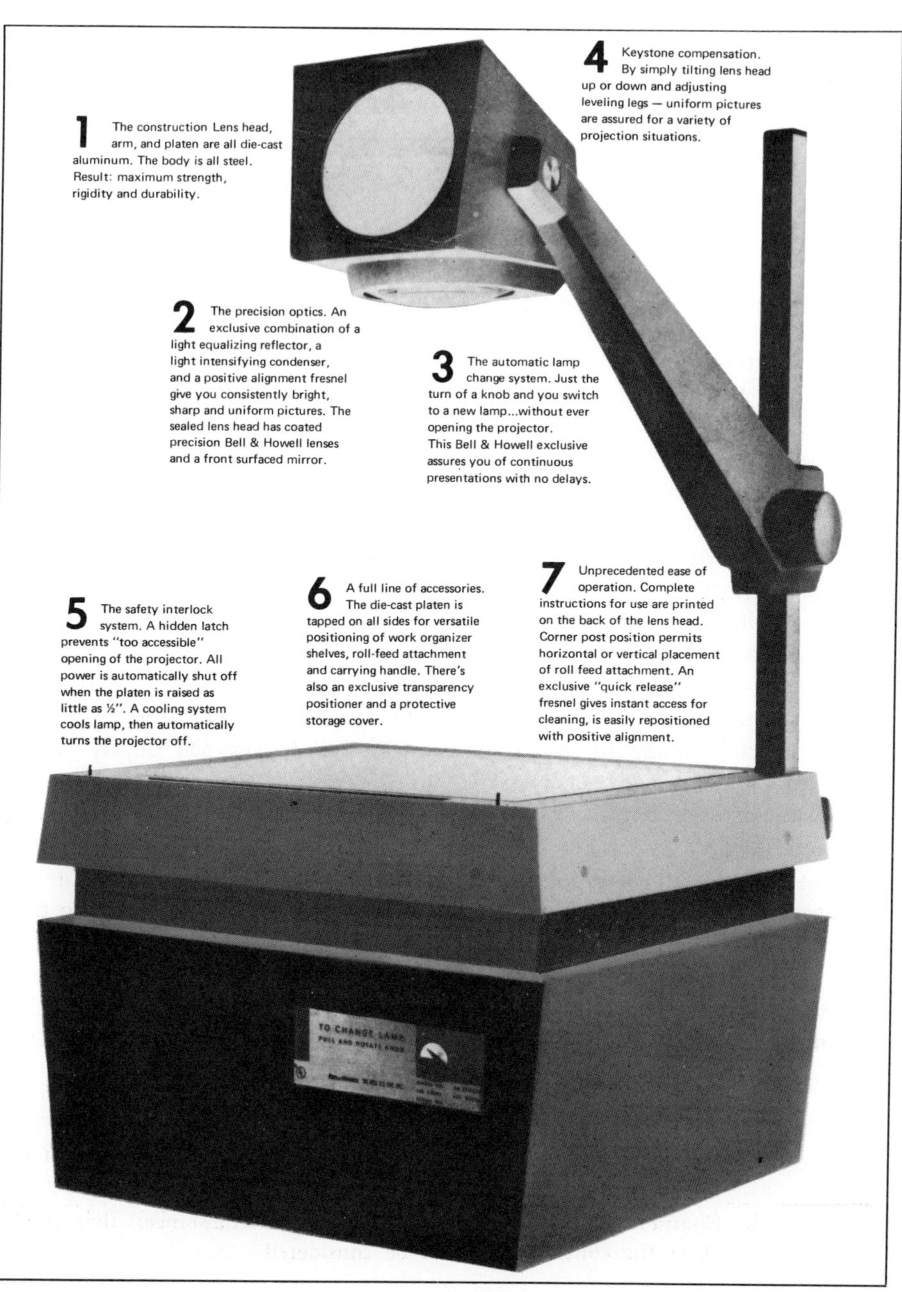

1 The construction Lens head, arm, and platen are all die-cast aluminum. The body is all steel. Result: maximum strength, rigidity and durability.
2 The precision optics. An exclusive combination of a light equalizing reflector, a light intensifying condenser, and a positive alignment fresnel give you consistently bright, sharp and uniform pictures. The sealed lens head has coated precision Bell & Howell lenses and a front surfaced mirror.
3 The automatic lamp change system. Just the turn of a knob and you switch to a new lamp...without ever opening the projector. This Bell & Howell exclusive assures you of continuous presentations with no delays.
4 Keystone compensation. By simply tilting lens head up or down and adjusting leveling legs — uniform pictures are assured for a variety of projection situations.
5 The safety interlock system. A hidden latch prevents "too accessible" opening of the projector. All power is automatically shut off when the platen is raised as little as ½". A cooling system cools lamp, then automatically turns the projector off.
6 A full line of accessories. The die-cast platen is tapped on all sides for versatile positioning of work organizer shelves, roll-feed attachment and carrying handle. There's also an exclusive transparency positioner and a protective storage cover.
7 Unprecedented ease of operation. Complete instructions for use are printed on the back of the lens head. Corner post position permits horizontal or vertical placement of roll feed attachment. An exclusive "quick release" fresnel gives instant access for cleaning, is easily repositioned with positive alignment.
TO CHANGE LAMP

Courtesy Bell & Howell Company

in the Ford wagon if you are looking for a roomy car. Although you may go to look at one, you probably won't buy it without comparing it with other cars. You might also evaluate the limitations of this testimony and seek further factual details on what each family's baggage amounted to and what each man considered a roomy car.

The other day, teenaged Johnny Jones dressed for school but looked outside before leaving to decide whether or not to take his raincoat. He saw the sun shining and trees and shrubbery blowing slightly in the breeze, and heard birds singing. He also noticed several children waiting on the corner for their school bus; they were hatless and coatless, with no umbrellas or boots. Johnny decided that it was not going to rain and did not take his raincoat. His decision was based on a conclusion formulated from examining a number of details and finding that they all pointed to one thing—no rain.

Last week a county school board met to decide on a possible site for building a new elementary school. The site under consideration was in a subdivision that had been developed in the past three years. Among the arguments presented to show the need and desirability of the proposed site were the following: at present, school children in that area and surrounding areas are being taken five miles by school bus to an overcrowded school. It has been expanded and added to during the past five years, but now there is no more room for further building. A survey recently made in the subdivision disclosed over 300 pupils of elementary school age and over 200 pupils of junior high school age. Consideration was also given to the expected future growth of the area, to the size of the areas available for the building and playground, and to cost. The arguments presented showed that an elementary school was necessary and desirable at the proposed site, and the board voted to purchase it.

Inductive reasoning is valuable in supporting conceived ideas and in testing their adequacy. Three general rules should be followed in using inductive logic:

1. Details, facts, or cases must be of a sufficient number to make the argument valid.
2. Specific instances or cases must be typical and representative of the class of which they are a part.
3. Contradictory evidence or extenuating circumstances that might affect the conclusion should be considered.

Causal Relationships

Cause-and-effect relationships also call for inductive reasoning. Causal argument is based on the fact that nothing happens without cause and that every event is a cause or potential cause of some other event.

Any observed activity, process, or event may be examined for its probable causes or consequences. One effect may result from many causes; and one cause may have many effects:

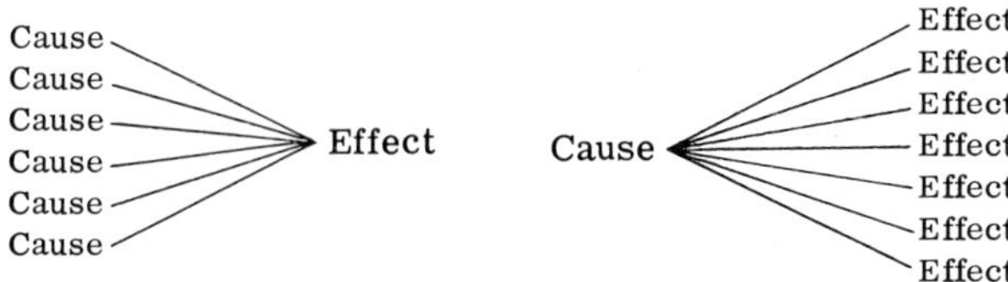

Results can be foreseen from a study of cause-and-effect relationships and then avoided, if they are undesirable, or obtained, if they are desirable.

Causal reasoning can be tested by asking the following questions:

1. Is the cause adequate to produce the effect?
2. Could other causes have produced the effect?
3. Is there anything that can prevent the cause from bringing about the predicted effect?
4. Has the cause been mistaken for the result?
5. Does any causal connection exist at all?
6. Are the conclusions based on causal relationships supported by other known facts and types of reasoning?

Much of the reasoning used in determining and analyzing problems in business is causal. In addition, much of the reasoning used in considering alternative solutions to a problem or plans to be put into action is also causal, for one must consider the effect of the solutions on people, on the company, and on factors such as cost, production, and equipment.

Deductive Reasoning

Deductive reasoning begins with a statement or accepted general principle, moves to its application in a specific instance, and reaches a conclusion in respect to it. Deductive reasoning is the reverse of inductive reasoning, which moves from numerous specific instances to establish a general principle or conclusion.

Induction and deduction are mutually supplementary. Induction helps us to draw conclusions from facts; deduction helps us to find new facts to be derived from the general principle. Again, induction tells us what ideas are implied by certain data; deduction tells us what data may be implied by the ideas. Often induction supplies the premise for a deduction. To deduce is to infer something about a particular case from a general principle by logical reasoning. In deductive logic we reason from the general to the specific, from the universal to the individual case, from the major premise to the conclusion. Deduction is thus analytical, for it reasons from the whole to a part or from all cases to a specific case. Induction synthesizes; it reasons from specific cases to the general, and it puts the parts together to form a whole.

A classic example of deductive reasoning is the following:

All men are mortal.
I am a man.
Therefore, I am mortal.

This example, known as a *syllogism,* illustrates three elements of deductive reasoning: the *major premise, minor premise,* and *conclusion.* In deductive reasoning we reach an inference from the relationship of the two premises. A common term or element is contained in both premises; this provides continuity, so that we may infer the conclusion. For example,

Major premise: All students who do not study will fail this course.
Minor premise: William Wright, who is a student in this course, is not studying.
Conclusion: William Wright will fail this course.

Here the relationship, often called the *middle term,* is "not studying."

Major premise: Banks in New York City are closed on the Fourth of July.
Minor premise: Chase Manhattan Bank is in New York City.
Conclusion: Chase Manhattan Bank will be closed on the Fourth of July.

A successful advertisement for a television program a few years ago ran:[1]

Women Are Wonderful.

Ann Colone's a Woman.

Ann Colone's Wonderful.

If there's a misogynist in the house, our authority for the major premise, Women Are Wonderful, is *TV Radio Mirror,* which made the comment

[1]Reprinted by permission, *Printers' Ink,* May 26, 1961, p. 42.

> while giving WANE-TV's Ann Colone its gold medal award for "Best TV Women's Interest Show—Midwest States."
>
> The minor premise (minor only in formal logic terms) is axiomatic. Ann's a most attractive, vivacious, witty and entertaining lady.
>
> The conclusion, shared by viewers, visitors and vendors alike, is inescapable. She's wonderful in providing everything from exercise gymnastics to festive cooking hints, from parakeet keepers to parachute jumpers, from the Dukes of Dixieland (in person) to the Chief of the Congolese Lunda tribe (in person). And there's always time to discuss and help community activities. . . .

These examples are all *categorical syllogisms.* The first statement (major premise) is an unqualified one, describing a classification with no exceptions. Two other types of syllogism are also recognized and used often: *hypothetical* and *disjunctive syllogisms.* The hypothetical syllogism contains a condition in its major premise; for example,

Major premise:	If the sun shines today, we will go on a picnic.
Minor premise:	The sun is shining now.
Conclusion:	We will go on a picnic.

Here the major premise's "if" clause is termed the *antecedent,* and its other clause is the *consequent.*

In using the hypothetical syllogism, remember that the minor premise must either affirm the antecedent or deny the consequent for the syllogism to be correct. If it affirms the consequent or denies the antecedent, no conclusion can be drawn.

The disjunctive syllogism presents alternate possibilities, indicated by "either . . . or . . ."; for example,

Major premise:	Either this man forged the check or he is innocent.
Minor premise:	He forged the check.
Conclusion:	He is not innocent.

In using the disjunctive syllogism, remember that the possibilities enumerated in the major premise must be all-inclusive and that the two terms must be mutually exclusive.

Sometimes either the major or minor premise may be implied, rather than expressed. This is technically called an *enthymeme:*

Premise:	Public schools begin the school year the first Tuesday after Labor Day.
Conclusion:	The E. J. Whitney School will begin the school year the first Tuesday after Labor Day.

If one of the premises, or even the conclusion, is omitted, the reader can fill in the missing part himself. Syllogisms are not often found in practical conversation or reports *per se,* but are abundant in the form of enthymemes; for example:

1. Is Jim an honor student? He's a member of the debating team.
2. Hal must live at home, since we know he doesn't stay in the dormitory.
3. Bill would like to be president of his professional fraternity, but he's not very popular.

The major use of syllogisms is to test the accuracy of our thinking. In our thinking, we do not always proceed from a major to a minor premise, and then to a conclusion. By setting down our judgments in syllogistic form, we can often determine the grounds upon which they are based.

The major premise states the universal or broad fact, and the minor premise is the particular or limiting statement. The predicate of the major premise should be the same as that of the conclusion. The two premises indicate necessarily and sufficiently the ground upon which the conclusion rests. Introducing the conclusion with *therefore, because, hence, then,* or *thus* indicates that it follows and is based on the two premises. Every syllogism, to be valid, must satisfy these basic qualifications:

1. The major premise must be an all-inclusive statement.
2. The middle term must be used again at least once.
3. A term applied in the conclusion must also be contained in the premises.
4. When one premise is negative, the conclusion must be negative.
5. Only one premise can be negative.

Whenever a syllogism violates any one of these rules, it is not valid.

Definition and classification are two other forms of deductive reasoning. A definition gives the essence of the word being defined and differentiates it from others in its own class. The definition consists of the *term* to be defined; its *genus,* or the class or concept to which it belongs; and the *differentiae,* or the characteristics that distinguish it from other members of its class. For example: a college social fraternity is a student organization formed chiefly to promote friendship and welfare among its members, and usually having secret rites and a name consisting of Greek letters. Education is a science dealing with the principles and practice of teaching and learning.

Some pertinent principles helpful in using definitions are:

1. Use clear and direct language. (Words simpler and more familiar than the term being defined should be used.)
2. Do not use the term to be defined in the definition.

3. Be sure the genus is large enough to include all members of the term. (This makes the definition exact and clear.)
4. Make sure the differentiae completely differentiate. (Essential and secondary characteristics may be given.)
5. Avoid terms such as "is when" and "is where."

The purpose of a definition is to establish a concept, idea, or process; it may be accomplished in a single statement, or it may be expanded into a paragraph by enumerating a number of differentiae, by explaining the differentiae, or by discussing the meaning or use of the term. For instance, the following definition of Delta Sigma Pi establishes an idea but requires further development of the differentiae to make it meaningful:

> Delta Sigma Pi is a professional fraternity for students.

Details are needed to clarify *professional* and *students*. After these terms are explained, the reader will have not only a basic definition but also a development of it so that he can distinguish Delta Sigma Pi from other professional fraternities.

The differentiation of characteristics in definitions is a type of classification. When we are concerned largely with sorting a given group of things into classes, we are dividing and classifying. Satisfactory classification will have these features:

1. A controlling purpose that must be constant at each stage
2. A clear basis for the classification
3. Mutually exclusive species that will not overlap at each division
4. An exhaustive subdivision at each stage

Classification is an integral part of the outlining principle of division; it will be discussed more fully later in the chapter.

Analogy

Analogical reasoning is based on the assumption that if two things are alike in several important and known respects, they will also be alike in other (unknown) respects. Many people, noting the similarities between the League of Nations and the United Nations, concluded that the United Nations would fail, since the League failed. Other people noted the differences between the two world organizations and concluded that the United Nations would succeed, because they felt that the differences were more significant. Analogy is useful in comparing and contrasting, because one item illustrates others. Analogy also adds vividness, clarity, and interest for the reader.

Certain distinctions may be made between analogy and deductive or inductive reasoning. In deduction, you reason from the general rule to a specific case. In induction, you consider specific cases and move to a general rule. And in analogy you reason from one specific case to another specific case. There are two kinds of analogy: literal and figurative. Because literal analogy compares two phenomena in the same class, it is often used in presenting proof or evidence. Figurative analogy, on the other hand, is more effectively used in illustration because it compares phenomena in different classes. It makes a point clear and vivid, pictorially or dramatically, as do the parables of Jesus in the New Testament.

You may test the soundness of the analogies you use and read by asking:

1. Are the similarities more important than the known differences? The presence of many similarities does not mean that things are basically similar.
2. Can the differences in the cases be accounted for? Differences become important only when they apply to the point being considered.
3. Are the asserted facts of the analogy true?
4. Are the conclusions drawn from the analogy supported by other known facts and types of reasoning? Analogy is one of the weakest types of argument and thus needs support.

THINKING WITH STATISTICS

Much of the data presented in reports consist of figures and statistics, which are used to draw conclusions and inferences and thus to support and prove the points they make. For this reason we are concerned here with organizing figures and statistics in order to find the relationships among them. Simply converting two figures to percentages shows their relationship to each other and to the total. Suppose, for instance, that you are exploring the students' desire for a university student directory. Out of 789 students sampled, 624 responded "yes" and 165 "no." The relationship is better shown in percentages: 79 percent responded favorably and 21 percent negatively. The percentages show the proportion, which is more significant than the number.

Another common method is to plot the frequency distribution of a series of numbers to determine their pattern or trend. Assume that you are investigating the high turnover rate of the checkout girls in the grocery store you manage. You are examining their educational backgrounds, ages, and other factors that might have a bearing on your future selection of girls for the job. Classifying the girls according to their ages would give you data for consideration. Assuming that you have 14 girls, the age distribution would be something like this:

Ages	*Number of Girls*
16–17	5
18–19	3
20–21	1
22–23	1
23–24	0
over 25, under 35	1
over 35, under 45	3
Total	14

This would show you that over half the girls are teenagers.

Averages

Often numerical data are arranged in tables to help in selecting averages and indicating trends. Three major statistical averages commonly used are the *mean,* the *median,* and the *mode.* To obtain the mean, sum the figures and divide by the number of cases. This results in the arithmetic average. To obtain the median, arrange the figures in rank order and find the point that has an equal number of cases above and below it. The mode is the figure that appears the most often. The three averages refer to three different ideas. Although the mean is the true average, there may be no specific case that falls in that position; the mean may fall instead between two cases in the list. The median does exist, and there are as many cases above it as below it. The mode is the case with the highest number of instances.

Any consideration of averages must also consider the range and the extremes of the figures and to what extent they affect the central figures selected. Knowing the range makes the average more meaningful. Statisticians use formulas and measurements to show the degree of the spread of data and in checking or proving the validity of a sample survey.[2]

Sampling

Questionnaires are used to secure information on behavioral characteristics, to gather opinions or attitudes, and to obtain certain facts. Information thus obtained helps management to make decisions and establish policies. In marketing, questionnaires provide a wealth of product and consumer data. Public polls and employee surveys measure attitudes

[2]See any textbook on statistics for details and reference in using such formulas as *standard error of deviation.*

and determine reactions to specific problems. They are based on sampling, which in turn depends on probability theory, one of the most common forms of induction. The conclusions are not inevitable; they are drawn from proof found in the instances examined. The process of complete enumeration, which establishes proof by perfect induction, is called *total sampling*. This can be done only with small groups. Generally, imperfect induction, based on part of a total group, is used and the conclusions are applied to the total group. This is *partial sampling*. Three problems are involved in sampling: selecting the kind of sample, determining its size, and testing its validity. Sampling is a big subject in itself and we are more concerned here with interpreting the results of its data than with studying the sampling process or its techniques and uses. There are several excellent books on the subject for those who are interested in pursuing it further.

By thinking with statistics and reasoning logically, you will be able to make data and ideas meaningful, for you will understand their relationships and will be able to reason through to conclusions. This is an important step in organizing and thinking. Then you will be ready to outline your material for presentation in a report.

OUTLINING

An outline serves two functions: as a guide to organizing the material and as a guide to writing the report. It forces the writer to think through his message, understand the relationships between its various aspects, and clarify his thinking. It helps tremendously in writing, by making clear to the writer what comes next and how it fits in.

Using Reasoning Patterns

Since reasoning inductively calls for marshaling specific instances or details to point up a conclusion, it involves going from the specific to the general. It treats parts, then the whole. By organizing facts and ideas, it is especially useful for the researcher, as well as for the reader or listener who needs to be led step by step along the way. Although it makes comprehension easier, it demands that the writer or speaker see the relationship of the instances or details in proper perspective when he draws his generalizations and validates his conclusions.

The following outlines illustrate an arrangement of major divisions according to an inductive reasoning pattern:

Who killed Joe?

1. Mary was last seen with Joe.
    a.
    b.

2. She could not explain her whereabouts at the time of the slaying.
    a.
    b.
3. Blood found on Mary's clothing matched that found on Joe's.
    a.
    b.
4. Mary's fingerprints were identical with those found on the weapon.
    a.
    b.
5. Mary must have killed Joe.

Let's contribute to the American Cancer Fund

1. The American Cancer Society performs research that fights against cancer.
    a.
    b.
2. It educates the public by giving facts about cancer.
    a.
    b.
    c.
3. It offers services that aid and comfort the stricken.
    a.
    b.
4. It gives you a chance to protect yourself and your family.
    a.
    b.
5. The American Cancer Society needs your dollars.
    a.
    b.
6. You should contribute to the American Cancer Fund now.

Deductive reasoning calls for clear statements of premises, recognition of common points of relationship, and an understanding of definition and classification. It goes from the general to the specific, treating first the whole, and then the parts. It is especially useful in argumentation and in proving a point. It demands that the writer or speaker have full command of the situation, and it presupposes the audience has knowledge of and interest in the subject at hand.

The major divisions of the next two outlines follow a deductive reasoning pattern:

Drinking and driving do not mix

1. Drivers must be alert to avoid accidents.
    a.
    b.
    c.
2. Drinking slows reflexes.
    a.
    b.

3. Drinking and driving cause accidents.
    a.
    b.

Government spending

1. The Democratic Party does not want to increase government spending.
    a.
    b.
2. The President is a Democrat.
    a.
    b.
3. The President does not want to increase government spending.

Applying Principles of Outlining

There are three guiding principles that should be understood and applied in outlining: *consistency, division,* and *parallelism.* Being consistent is maintaining uniformity by conforming to a predetermined pattern. The outliner must use a uniform style in the type of outline he composes. An outline may be either sentence or topic, general or specific. It is possible and sometimes practical to mix the general and specific types by couching main points in general terms with details stated specifically, or vice versa, and to mix the sentence and topic types by presenting major divisions in topical form and all subdivisions and details in sentence form, or vice versa. The guiding principle is to be consistent from the beginning to the end of any one given outline. When the first main topic, for instance, is in sentence form, all main topics must be in sentence form. When the main topic is expressed in general terms, all main topics must be expressed in general terms.

A general outline indicates the main topical divisions and subdivisions, but it does not present the details necessary for developing them. Many reports can follow the same general outline pattern, since only major divisions are indicated; thus these outlines are useful for gathering and organizing material. Here are some general patterns that can be followed.

Logically a report might be organized as:

I	*or*	II	*or*	III
Introduction		Statement of problem		Problem
Main issue		Analysis of problem		Causes
Subdivision		Need for changes		Results
Subdivision		Proposed solutions		Possible solution
Main issue		Discussion of solutions		Discussion
Conclusion		Conclusion		Conclusion
Recommendations		Recommendations		Recommendations

Psychologically a report might be organized as:

I	*or*	II	*or*	III
Recommendation		Attention		Conclusion
Conclusion		Interest		Evidence
Supporting facts		Conviction		Alternatives
Discussion		Action		Discussion
Summary				Summary

Variations of the basic patterns might be used, as:

I	*or*	II	*or*	III
Summary		Present situation		Summary—What has been done
Nature of problem		Weaknesses		Work to be completed
Findings		Proposed corrections		Future plans
Conclusion		Discussion		
Recommendations		Pros and cons		
		Conclusion and recommendations		

A specific outline gives the detailed facts not included in the general outline, and it serves as a guide for further development of the topics in writing a message. Unlike the general outline, it pertains only to one report, speech, or communication type. The following outline, for example, is specific; it is also a sentence outline:

AN OUTLINE
OF A SPEECH ON FOREIGN AID

I. U.S. foreign aid should be reduced.
   A. Foreign aid is the financial assistance of the underdeveloped countries by the developed countries—principally the United States.
      1. U.S. foreign aid began April 4, 1917.
      2. The amount spent on foreign aid to date is over $120 billion.
   B. There are three types of foreign aid.
      1.
      2.
      3.
II. Military aid to the NATO countries has not been satisfactory.
III. Economic assistance is no longer needed from the United States.
   A. Europe now has a $14 billion favorable balance of trade.
   B. The Arab countries earn over $84 million a month from the petroleum industry alone.
   C.

IV. There is anti-American feeling in almost every country the United States has helped.

  A.
    1.
    2.
  B.
  C.

V.
  A.
  B.

VI.

Consistency

Consistency in form includes uniformity of typing details, such as margins, indention, capitalization, punctuation, and other mechanics of writing. It also means following either the numeral–letter or decimal system of outlining. In the numeral–letter system, the principle of alternation is applied by alternately using numbers and letters. Roman numerals, for instance, may be used to indicate major divisions, capital letters to indicate the breakdown of each main part, arabic numbers for subdivisions under each capital-letter heading, and lowercase letters for further subdivision under arabic-numbered headings. For example:

I. First main point
  A. First part in breakdown of major division
    1. Subdivision
      a. Subdivision
      b. Subdivision
    2. Subdivision
  B. Second part in breakdown of major division
II. Second main point

After the four degrees of headings have been used, numbers and letters may be repeated in parentheses to indicate further subdivisions. For instance:

a.
  (I)
    (A)
      (1)
        (a)

In most cases, however, it is not necessary to carry an outline beyond three or four degrees of subdivision. By alternating letters and numbers

—or roman and arabic numerals, or capital and lowercase letters—any of the following patterns might be consistently used:

```
I.          or      A.          or      1.
   1.                  1.                  A.
      A.                  a.                  a.
         a.               b.                  b.
         b.            2.                  B.
      B.                  a.                  a.
   2.                     b.                  b.
   3.                  3.                  C.
II.                 B.                  2.
```

In the decimal system of outlining, only arabic numbers and the decimal point are used. The number of degrees may be expanded without limitation. For example:

```
1. First main topic
   1.1 First item in first degree of subdivision
       1.11       First item in second degree of subdivision
       1.12       Second item in second degree of subdivision
       . . .
       1.1 (10)   Tenth item in second degree of subdivision
       1.1 (11)   Eleventh item in second degree of subdivision
                  1.1 (11) 1  First item in third degree of subdivision
                  1.1 (11) 2  Second item in third degree of subdivision
                              1.1 (11) 21  First item in fourth degree
                              1.1 (11) 22  Second item in fourth degree
                                           1.1 (11) 221  First item in
                                                         fifth degree
                                           1.1 (11) 222  Second item in
                                                         fifth degree
   1.2 Second item in first degree of subdivision
2. Second main topic
```

Regardless of the system or pattern used, consistency must be maintained. Each heading begins on a separate line. When it covers more than one line, the second line begins directly under the beginning of the first line. Each subsequent subdivision is indented and all headings of equal rank have the same indention. In the number–letter system, numbers and letters may be consistently followed by a period or the period may consistently be omitted. The topics are usually left unpunctuated, but the outliner may use final punctuation if he does so consistently. In a sentence outline, each division is usually punctuated and capitalized as a sentence. The first letter in the first word or in each word of a topic outline may or may not be capitalized as long as consistency is maintained.

Division

Outlining is a process of division to show the breakdown of a whole into parts. These parts may be further divided and subdivided. Division produces equal and comparable parts. Costs on a research project might be divided, for example, as follows:

Costs
a. Preliminary survey
b. Questionnaire
c. Travel expenses

Each of these costs could be further subdivided:

c. Travel expenses
  (1) Transportation
  (2) Hotel
  (3) Meals

It is very important to remember that when something is divided there must be at least two parts. The division of costs given above could never be:

Costs
a. Preliminary survey

Unless there are at least two aspects of costs to be discussed, the topic should be rephrased:

Cost of preliminary survey

Always, then, in outlining, an "A" calls for a "B," a "1" calls for a "2," and an "a" calls for a "b," etc.

Always	*Never*

I.
  A.
  B.
II.
	I.
	  A.
	II.

Always	*Never*

1.
  a.
  b.
2.
	1.
	  a.
	2.
	  a.

Parallelism

Parallelism deals with relatedness. All points in an outline are related by being expressed in the same grammatical construction and by being given equal rank or importance through division and subdivision. The three outlining principles discussed here, for instance, are parallel in grammatical construction, for they are all nouns—consistency, division, and parallelism. They are of equal importance because they are all principles of outlining. An outline indicates the subordinate position of each point making up a larger whole.

Correct	*Incorrect*
Principles of outlining	A. Principles of outlining
1. Consistency	1. Consistency
2. Division	2. Division
3. Parallelism	B. Parallelism

In the second case, "A" and "B" are not of equal importance.

Correct	*Incorrect*
How to write better letters	How to write better letters
1. Be concise	1. Be concise
2. Be complete	2. Completeness
3. Be courteous	3. Courtesy
4. Be correct	4. Don't be abstract
5. Be concrete	5. Be correct

In the second case, the points are not expressed in the same grammatical construction.

By expressing points in an outline in parallel forms, a simple, logical balance is achieved. When the first main caption is stated as a sentence, all main captions should be in sentence form. When a subdivision of the second degree is expressed in noun form, all subdivisions of that degree should be nouns. When a phrase, such as *Be concise,* is used, all other points of that degree should be phrases. When a participial form is used, all corresponding forms should end in *-ing*.

Correct	*Incorrect*
Writing	Writing
Listening	Listen
Speaking	Speech
Reading	Reading

Consistency in parallelism can be maintained by placing all topics of the same degree of outline division in the same grammatical form, for parallelism indicates the relatedness of topics just as division does and acts to clarify expression.

SUMMARY

The report writer first interprets and organizes his material to make it meaningful to him, then organizes it for presentation to someone else.

The first process results in conclusions, supporting evidence, or solutions to problems; the second results in an outline to be used as a guide in preparing a report. The first requires logical reasoning in thinking through ideas, facts, opinions, and other material. Critical judgment comes into play as we study our material, for we are concerned with rearranging it, reasoning, and finding relationships and meaning in it.

Logic is the study of the structure of reasoning. We apply it in evaluating and selecting our points for consideration, in achieving order and harmony in our thoughts, in sifting through our material, and in insuring the logical rightness of the parts and the whole. Several main patterns of reasoning that will help you see the relationships of data and sharpen your reasoning powers are inductive reasoning, causal relationships, deductive reasoning, and analogy.

In *inductive reasoning,* one moves from particulars, details, instances, or cases to a general conclusion, hypothesis, or principle. After examining a sufficient number of particulars, a common pattern, element, or trend may be found that points to a general conclusion. This is valuable to support ideas and to test the adequacy of an idea or statement. A *cause-and-effect relationship,* in essence, is a form of inductive reasoning. The writer may go from examining a cause to studying its effect, or vice versa. This is helpful in understanding and analyzing problems, in evaluating alternate solutions, and in predicting the effect of the best solution, which must be done before putting a solution into action.

In *deductive reasoning,* one begins with a major premise (which is generally accepted or can be proved), moves to its application in a specific case, and reaches a conclusion in respect to it. The common form of deductive reasoning is the *syllogism,* in which the major premise is an all-inclusive statement, the minor premise is the specific application, and the conclusion is reached from an element or middle term common to both. Syllogisms can be categorical, hypothetical, or disjunctive. Although complete syllogisms aren't often found in general conversation or reports, *enthymemes* are abundant; these are syllogisms in which one of the premises or the conclusion has been omitted and the reader or listener fills in the missing part. The major use of the syllogism is to test the accuracy of our thinking. Definition and classification are two other forms of deduction; both move from the general to the specific.

Analogy is based on the assumption that if two things are alike in several important and known respects, they will be alike in other (unknown) respects. It is useful especially for comparison and contrast, and adds vividness, clarity, and interest for both the writer and, more important, the reader.

Because much of the data presented in reports are statistical in nature, the writer should have command of several statistical devices that are useful in interpreting data and reaching conclusions. Statistics reveal relationships. They may be expressed as simple percentages or as a frequency distribution showing a pattern or trend. *Averages* show central tendencies or trends. The mean is used to show the arithmetic average; the median shows the mid-point; and the mode indicates the highest frequency point, where the most cases occur. The extremes and exceptions should also be considered to find to what extent they affect the central figures.

Sampling, which is a form of probability and induction, is useful in securing quantitative information on behavioral characteristics, opinions, and attitudes. It is especially useful in product, consumer, and public opinion research.

After thinking through data, interpreting them, and reaching conclusions, the writer is ready to outline them for presentation in a report. Here he may use his pattern of reasoning as a basis for organizing inductively or deductively. Three principles apply: consistency, division, and parallelism. The following checklist may be used in outlining.

For consistency:

1. Are either sentences or topics consistently used?
2. Are equal ideas consistently expressed in either general or specific terms?
3. Are indentions uniform?
4. Are letters and numbers alternately and consistently used?
5. Are symbols for subdivision consistently followed either by a period or by none?
6. Is final punctuation used or omitted consistently?
7. Does each heading begin on a separate line?
8. Are second lines directly under first lines?
9. Do headings of equal rank have the same indention?
10. Are capital letters consistently used?

For division:

1. Do all corresponding divisions have equal rank?
2. Do the parts make up a unified whole?
3. Are there always at least two parts wherever there is a division?

For parallelism:

1. Are the ideas parallel?
2. Is parallel grammatical construction followed? For instance, are points of the same degree of subordination all expressed as nouns? or sentences? or past participles?
3. Are either sentences or topics used for the same degree of division?

FURTHER READING

Brown, Leland, *Effective Business Report Writing*, 2nd ed. Englewood Cliffs, N. J.: Prentice-Hall, Inc., 1963.

Chase, Stuart, *Guide to Straight Thinking.* New York: Harper & Row, Publishers, 1956.

Huppé, Bernard F., and Jack Kaminsky, *Logic and Language.* New York: Alfred A. Knopf, Inc., 1957, pp. 110–94.

Lesikar, Raymond V., *Report Writing for Business,* 3rd ed. Homewood, Ill.: Richard D. Irwin, Inc., 1969.

Parker, F. H., and H. B. Veatch, *Logic as a Human Instrument.* New York: Harper & Row, Publishers, 1959.

Shurter, Robert L., J. P. Williamson, and W. G. Broehl, Jr., *Business Research and Report Writing.* New York: McGraw-Hill Book Company, 1969. See especially Chapters 5 and 6.

Sigband, Norman, *Communication for Management.* Glenwood, Ill.: Scott, Foresman & Company, 1969.

QUESTIONS AND PROBLEMS

1. Select from magazine articles, newspapers, books, or speeches a few examples of each reasoning pattern discussed in Chapter 9 (inductive, causal, deductive, and analogical). Examine them for their purpose, method of reasoning, and conclusion.
2. Write a paragraph in which you support a conclusion or thesis statement by each of the four logical reasoning patterns. Some suggested topics are:
   a. ROTC training benefits
   b. Legalizing marijuana and other drugs
   c. Wearing Bermuda shorts to college classes
   d. Lowering the voting age
   e. Saturday classes at your university
   f. State aid to private and parochial schools
   g. Selective Service
   h. Income taxes (federal, state, or city)
3. During the next few days, make a study of the times you use one of the logical reasoning patterns when you are thinking about an idea or a problem or when you are expressing yourself to others. Prepare a short memorandum, indicating the extent to which you used this type of reasoning and under what circumstances. Also include your evaluation of your effectiveness in using it.
4. Over a period of a week, analyze a radio or television news commentator. Classify his statements as being either facts, interpretative opinions, or value judgments. Note the instances in which he used logical reasoning. Present your findings as an oral report to the class or in a memorandum to your instructor.
5. Try your hand at defining some of the following terms:
   a. University
   b. Professional fraternity
   c. On-campus political activity

d. Mature adult
e. Education
f. Student
g. Faculty
h. Political right and left

First make your definition a one-sentence statement; then develop it into a paragraph or two.

You might also try your hand at defining the following terms:

a. Logic
b. Reasoning
c. Plagiarism
d. Business report
e. Communication
f. Tone and style

6. What might be the effect of the following phrases used in a sales promotion?

a. Cheap
b. Bargain
c. Evening shopping hours
d. Advance showing
e. Low credit terms
f. High-quality item

7. Distinguish between the three kinds of averages and their uses in drawing conclusions and interpreting data.
8. Why should the range and the extremes be considered in relation to the average?
9. What determines the validity and reliability of sampling?
10. Explain how you would go about outlining material for a report by using the inductive reasoning pattern or the deductive reasoning pattern.
11. How would you arrange the topics that follow according to a causal relationship?

War:

Making profits
Making a living
Winning the war
Making peace

Prosperity:

Women not content to stay home
Good salaries for the asking
Widespread juvenile delinquency
Children roaming the streets
High wages

12. Confronted with having to organize the following material for an employee handbook, what categories and sequence would you use?

Wages and hours
Recreation
Notice and final pay
Our goal and yours
Savings, insurance, and credit
Vacations
Tax-return help
Health services
Safety
Old-age benefits
Welcome to our company
Military duty
Loans
Educational opportunities
Participation in civic affairs
Citizenship
Fire and flood protection
Your progress
Soliciting
The Company News
Suggestion award plan
Family assistance
Visitors
Unemployment insurance
Reference inquiries
How to get a good start
Lost and found
Hospital care
Confidential work
Legal advice

13. Discuss the three major principles of outlining and how to apply them in preparing a report.
14. Read and outline an article of current interest from one of the business magazines such as *Fortune, Harvard Business Review,* or *Journal of Business.*
15. Suppose that you were doing a bibliography of current materials on business communication. Under what headings would you look in the library card catalog and periodical indexes? Why?
16. Outline the steps in a process such as:

    a. Proofreading
    b. Improving dictation
    c. Thinking creatively
    d. Thinking logically
    e. Learning to type
    f. Writing a business letter
    g. Conducting a customer survey
    h. Investigating for and preparing a report

Chapter Ten

PRESENTING MATERIAL IN REPORTS

For the last three chapters, we have been stressing the investigation and preparation necessary for writing effective business reports. You have analyzed the problem to understand it better, gathered data and created ideas, interpreted and organized the facts and ideas to reach conclusions and solutions, and outlined the material for report presentation. Now you are ready to consider all the facets of writing the report and getting it ready for presentation to someone else. Thus the purpose of this chapter is to help you to improve your writing of the report and to assemble all the report's various parts so that it will be understandable and persuasive, and will motivate action from the reader. Following the suggestions given here should make it easier for you to write the text and to put your report together effectively.

WRITING THE REPORT TEXT

The task of writing the report text will be simplified if the material has been organized and outlined. With a detailed outline as a guide, a report will almost write itself, because it becomes easy to move from one point to the next. Attention can be focused on the facts and on the reader who will absorb them. Since the arrangement has already been worked out, the report can be written rapidly; in fact, any short report can be written in one sitting, as can individual sections of long reports. Getting ideas down in a logical order is important, and sticking to the outline makes it difficult to go off on tangents. Good report writing is achieved by rapid writing based on effective organization. The first draft records facts and ideas within the framework of an outline. At this point, the writer is not concerned with punctuation, spelling, or the mechanics of writing that will be checked during revision. He should strive for an easy flow of related ideas; this is necessary to get the message across. A great deal of attention should be given to the best way to tie the material together and to discuss the facts and ideas.

The writer should keep before him the purpose and the reader: he should measure his ideas against them, keep them in focus, and relate them to each other, to give perspective and shape to the material at hand. Examining ideas from the reader's point of view will make them more meaningful.

When expanding an outline in writing, the writer must think, for thinking is a chain reaction. One idea generates another. The outline suggests the sequence and subject matter; it does not include the thoughts that will occur as points are developed. For this reason, the writer should depart from the outline when his thoughts do—if they are in line with the purpose. He also should sit back and think at times, go over the material, and try to find a fresh approach, a different way of saying something. This naturally slows down writing and is not necessary if enough thinking and planning have been done ahead of time. Most report writers will write the first draft rapidly, applying, partly out of habit, all the principles and techniques of style, tone, and so on, that can be related to the particular problem at hand. Then they revise and rewrite to improve the report before it appears in final form.

Writing the Opening

Logically the report begins with an introduction that presents the subject or problem to the reader and gets his attention. By furnishing the reader with sufficient material concerning the investigation and the problem, the introduction leads him to an easy understanding of the rest of the report. It should thus give him a general view of the report before he is plunged into details. Each introduction must be arranged to suit the situation and the reader, and must set up an orderly path for him to follow. Although few introductions will include all the items in the following list, the items are suggestive of what goes into a good introduction:

1. An explanation of or reference to the authorization of the report
2. The situation giving rise to the report
3. The author's understanding of the problem
4. The author's attitude toward the problem
5. The report's scope and limitations

Introduction

The purpose of this report is to determine whether the establishment of a steel barge fabricating plant in the Lafayette area would prove profitable. There are three objectives:

1. to determine if present and potential production of the area afford a sufficient market for profitable operation

2. to determine the competitive market factors of the area

3. to ascertain if the Lafayette area offers facilities for efficient plant operation

The latest available information was obtained from the United States Department of Labor, the Louisiana Department of Conservation, Public Affairs Research Council of Louisiana, United States Corps of Engineers, Lafayette Chamber of Commerce and Louisiana Department of Highways. From these sources sufficient data were obtained for making the survey complete and conclusions accurate.

The scope of the report has been limited to the three major points considered essential to the solution of the problem:

Present and future market potential

Competitive market factors

Factors conducive to profitable operation

These three main issues are discussed in the report, and it is recommended that the corporation establish a steel barge fabricating plant on the Vermillion River near Lafayette, Louisiana.

Purpose and objectives clearly stated.

Sources acknowledged.

Scope and limitations stated.

General plan of report makes transition to next section.

6. The report's purpose and objectives
7. The basic principles or theories involved
8. The methods used to gather the data
9. The sources of information
10. The procedure used in organizing the material
11. Definitions of the terms
12. A brief summary of the findings or results
13. A brief statement of the main conclusions
14. A brief statement of the chief recommendation
15. The general plan used in developing the solution
16. The general plan of the report

Notice how the introduction above, from a report called "Establishing a Steel Barge Fabrication Plan in the Lafayette, Louisiana, Area," has treated its elements. No words are wasted in informing the reader of what the report is about, for in the very first sentence, its subject and purpose are clearly stated.

The end of the introduction must make an effective transition to the

Conclusions and Recommendations

A national consumer preference mail survey among 9,250 owners of 20- to 30-foot pleasure boats was made to determine if future hulls of Rand boats of this size should be of plank or plywood construction. Based on the respondents' opinions of plywood constructed boats which they have owned and on their consideration of buying a boat with a treated plywood hull, it was found that:

1. The greater the satisfaction the owners have had with plywood, the relatively larger are the positive considerations they give to purchasing such a boat.
2. Present plywood owners favor plywood more than past owners or present non-owners of this type of hull.
3. Owners of all molded plywood hulls are better satisfied with plywood than those who have all sheet plywood hulls, but relatively more of the latter group say they would buy a treated hull.
4. The smaller the present boat is, the relatively greater is the respondent's positive reaction to plywood hulls.
5. Relatively more owners of vee bottom boats favor plywood than owners of round botton boats.
6. Owners of models 1 and 4 indicate a comparatively higher acceptable attitude toward plywood. In contrast, model 5 owners have the relatively least respect for a plywood hull.
7. Rand boat owners have a comparatively less favorable feeling toward plywood hulls than do other boat owners, with the exception of those who have "A" boats and custom built or government boats which are dominantly of plank construction.
8. Gulf and South Pacific residents are relatively more favorable to plywood hulls.
9. Satisfaction with plywood and consideration given to buying it is comparatively greater among those who use their boats for water skiing and lower among commercial users.
10. Relatively more people who believe hull material is an important factor in choosing a boat indicate a negative feeling toward plywood.
11. Middle age owners are relatively more favorable to plywood hulls.

next section of the report. If it ends with an explanation of the general plan of the rest of the report, a logical transition is made. If it ends with a discussion of the procedures used to gather data, then the next section should present the results. A brief synopsis of findings or a statement of major conclusions or recommendations also provides a logical transition.

Boats having all plank hulls have the largest share of the market, followed by "any plywood" hulls. All sheet plywood has the highest market position within the latter group. The plank market is strongest in the Atlantic and South Pacific regions, and among the larger, round bottom, and models 5 and 6 boat owners. Plywood's strongest position is found in the Gulf and North Pacific areas, and among the smaller, vee bottom, and model 4 boat owners. As age of boat increases, relative plywood hull ownership decreases.

Two types of recommendations are submitted:

1. Should immediate gain in sales be sought, future 20- to 30-foot pleasure boat hulls should be of all plank construction. The majority of the boats should have round bottoms.

2. Should long range gains be sought, the smaller boats should have all plywood hulls and vee bottoms. Only models 1 and 4 should be built at first. These should be test marketed in the Gulf area.

Larger-size boats should be built as outlined in the first recommendation. If the second recommendation is followed, it is also suggested that the company undertake educating the public on the advantages of plywood hulls. This could be accomplished by the use of publicity and advertising.

One of the trends today is to begin the introduction with a summary of the conclusions or findings, which immediately interests the reader and leads him to read further in the report. When the report has a separate summary section as part of the preliminary sections, the summary should be omitted from the introduction or relegated to a brief treatment at the end to serve a transitional function.

Another trend is to begin the report with conclusions and recommendations, instead of with an introduction. This practice is especially good when the reader has sufficient knowledge and background to understand them, for it conserves his time and effort. By being placed first in a report, conclusions and recommendations also gain a position of importance and emphasis. The conclusions and recommendations on pages 326–27 were placed first in a report called "Consumer Attitude Toward Plywood Hulls Among Owners of 20- to 30-Foot Pleasure Boats."

Using Subject Headings

The text material of a report is usually divided into sections and subsections. Because subject headings indicate the content of each section and the degree of relationship between different sections, they make the report easy to read. Headings should be descriptive in content and parallel in construction. The instructions on page 328 for typing and spacing different degrees of subject headings are often followed.

```
                    FIRST-DEGREE HEADING

     When it is necessary to have headings of five different
degrees of importance, one generally accepted sequence is
shown here.  Note that the main heading above is centered and
that it is written in all caps.  It may be underscored or not.
Headings of the first three degrees should have two clear
spaces above them, and one below.


                    Second-Degree Heading

     The second degree heading is written in caps and lower
case.  It is underscored only if the main heading has been.


Third-Degree Heading

     The text starts two spaces below this heading, at a stand-
ard indentation.  Note that there are two spaces between this
heading and the last line of the preceding text.


     Fourth-Degree Heading.  This heading is followed by a
period, dash or by a colon.  It is indented with a regular
paragraph indentation.  The text begins on the same line as
the heading.


     The Fifth-Degree Heading is made by underscoring the first
words of the sentence.  This means rearranging the sentence so
that the key word or words are at the sentence beginning.  Note
that each of the key words underlined starts with a capital let-
ter.
```

When only one degree of subordination is needed, a centered heading and a heading beginning flush with the left margin, or at the margin indention, are commonly used. Subject headings may be numbered and lettered as in outlining, or numbers and letters may be omitted. Underscoring may or may not be used as long as consistency is observed throughout the report. Flexibility in the selection and use of subject headings is often desirable, but a certain amount of standardization must be maintained for consistency and readability.

Presenting Supporting Material

Supporting material consists of quotations, visual aids, facts, figures, statistics, and the like, which offer evidence and proof that the statements made are valid and which serve as a basis for analysis, interpretation, and the drawing of conclusions. The writer should question the authority of his sources and the reliability of the supporting evidence, then pass this on to his reader. Using recognized, reliable sources and citing them lends authority to the supporting material being presented.

Quoting should be done with discretion. In most cases frequent and long quotations are not justified in reports. In some instances they may be relegated to a footnote or placed in an appendix. At times, however, a quotation may be relatively concise and particularly apt, or the writer may need the statement of an authority for an idea that is not generally accepted as fact. In such instances quotations should be used and their source cited in a footnote.

Footnoting the sources of figures and facts lends weight and authority to their use. In addition to giving credit for the source of quoted material and authority to a statement, footnotes explain or give additional information, give an appraisal of a source, or provide a cross-reference to material presented in some other part of the text.[1] The following suggestions will be helpful:

1. Place footnotes at the bottom of the page, separated from the text material by a solid line partially or completely across the page.
2. Leave one line space after typing the last line of text material on the page, type the solid line, then leave another line space, indent five to ten spaces from the left margin, and begin the first line of the footnote.
3. Space succeeding lines even with the margin. Single-space each footnote entry, but double-space between entries.
4. Number footnotes consecutively by arabic numbers in an unbroken series throughout the text. Place the reference figure in the text after the passage to which it refers, after all punctuation marks, and slightly above the line, and repeat it at the beginning of the footnote entry without punctuation.
5. To footnote a book, arrange the author's name with given name or initial first, then the title of the book, place of publication, publisher, date, and page reference, as:

   [1]Raymond Lesikar, *Business Communication Theory and Practice* (Homewood, Ill.: Richard D. Irwin, Inc., 1968), p. 38.

6. To footnote an article, arrange the author's name with given name or initials first, then the title of the article, name of the magazine, volume number, date, and page reference, as:

   [2]C. G. Browne, "Understanding Nations Through Communication," *Harvard Business Review*, Vol. XXXIX (January 1970), 46.

   Note that when the volume number is given, the page reference is not preceded by "p." or "pp."

In quoting, anything less than three lines should be written as part of the text and enclosed with quotation marks. It is better to separate material of over three lines from the rest of the text by indenting it equally from the left and right margins and single-spacing it (assuming that the text is double-spaced). In this case no quotation marks are used.

Any statement we make is an assertion of fact that we wish the reader to believe. The statement may assert something directly or indirectly

[1]See also the section on "Footnotes" in Appendix C for correct forms and usage.

observable according to the writer's experience and knowledge, and it will be readily believed if it agrees with the reader's experience and knowledge. Statements may also reflect an opinion or value judgment; for instance:

This explains why the surtax was added to the income tax last year.	(opinion)
We did not make sufficient profits to increase the stockholders' dividends.	(value judgment)

Statements made in reports should be followed with facts and evidence to back them up, so that the reader can distinguish among opinion, fact, and judgment. It is the writer's responsibility to make the distinction easy for the reader so that he will be neither confused nor misled. Facts do not always speak for themselves; often they are facts only by definition, or because they can be verified by numerous opinions or by other facts. In general:

1. A fact claims that something is, was, or will be true.
2. An opinion reflects on the meaning or significance of an action, person, or object.
3. A value judgment claims something about the worth or value of an action, person, or object.
4. A definition urges agreement on a given view to achieve a common understanding.

Claims are often separated into reasoning or evidential elements. Evidence is the body of fact and opinion bearing upon the point in question. Reasoning is the process by which we go from pieces of evidence to new ideas, which we can accept because of the proof presented. Conclusions are supported by reasoning and evidence.

When he knows that the reader will accept a statement without question, the writer can go on to the next assertion. However, when he thinks that the reader will not understand or accept a statement, he should stop and help him along. This means presenting evidence or reasoning or both.

Some forms of support serve to make things clear, to increase the possibility for understanding, and to make an impact on the reader:

1. *Explanation* simply relates what happened or how; it may tell how something works or give the steps in sequence.
2. *Comparison, contrast,* and *analogy* tell how something is like or unlike something similar in nature.
3. *Illustrations* are examples that provide details; they are good for visualizing and for securing an emotional impact or a sense of reality.

Other forms of support serve to prove something, rather than to explain or to make things clear:

1. *Specific instances* support a conclusion arrived at inductively. Used with condensed, abbreviated examples or illustrations, they show that something did take place.
2. *Statistics* are mathematical treatments of examples; they condense specific instances into one or more index numbers that can describe a large amount of data.
3. *Testimony* consists of the statements of people who are considered reliable by the reader. People will recognize and accept testimony by an expert who they know is knowledgeable and perceptive, by a lay person with whom they can relate or identify, or by anyone whose personal testimony agrees with their previous knowledge and experience.

A few forms of support serve both purposes—understanding and proof. Repeating what has been said before gives added emphasis to a statement, and saying the same thing in a different way or in a summary also reinforces the point. Visual aids of all kinds—diagrams, charts, tables, illustrations, etc.—add clarity and proof, as well as attention and interest. "A picture is worth a thousand words" is a trite statement but a true one.

Tying the Facts Together

The outline provides the topics and points to be covered in writing a report. By its major divisions and subdivisions, it also indicates the relationship between topics. In this respect it provides a flow of ideas. The writer can add to the fluency of the flow, however, by adding connecting words, which will help the reader to relate the ideas in his mind to each other:

These words	*indicate*	*these relationships*
more than, rather than		comparison
although, even if		concession
if, in case		condition
so that, to		purpose
after, when, since		time
because, since		cause
so . . . as, such . . . that		result

Linking sentences together by subordinate conjunctions creates a closer relationship of ideas and facts.

Consider presenting an argument where the opposing points are relatively slight or where you do not want to overemphasize them. The structure of your writing might be diagrammed by using connecting words and phrases like this:

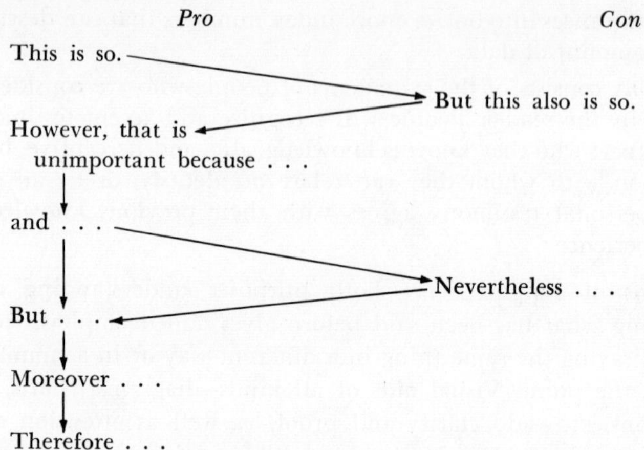

If the opposition is considerable, it may be attacked point by point. The structure of your writing might be diagrammed by using connecting words and phrases like this:

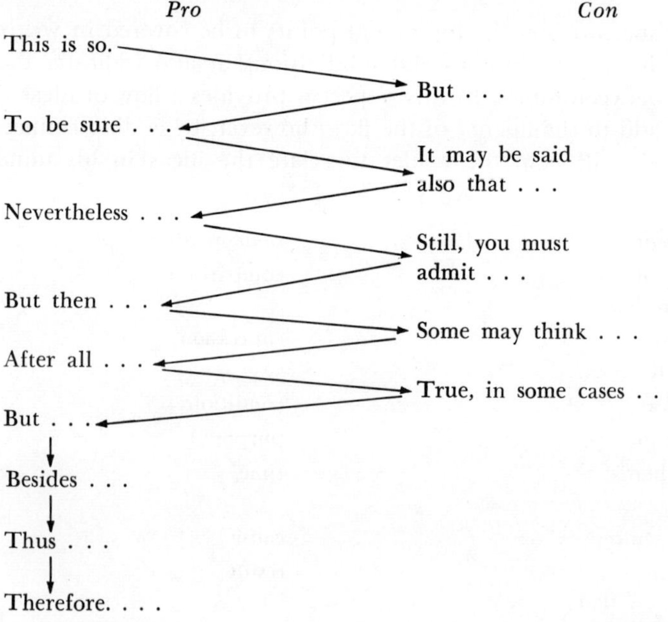

When ideas and facts flow naturally, the reader easily follows and understands what is being said.

Writing the Ending

The report, "Consumer Attitude Toward Plywood Hulls Among Owners of 20- to 30-Foot Pleasure Boats," began with conclusions and recommendations.[2] It ended with the summary on page 334.

The arrangement of the summary at the end of the report and conclusions and recommendations at the beginning could have been reversed. Most reports end with either conclusions and recommendations or summary sections. This will depend in most instances on the relation of the reader to the material in the report, the use he will make of the report, and the report's purpose. An informative report, for example, which does not offer conclusions and recommendations but does present facts and data for the reader's use in increasing his knowledge or as a basis for his decision making, will end with a summary section that brings together the most important and significant facts that were developed in the discussion part of the text. If the reader is not well versed in the subject matter of the report or is not ready for action, it is better to lead him through the introduction and discussion to the conclusions and recommendations at the end of the report. The line of reasoning used by the writer throughout the text of the report prepares him to understand and accept the conclusions and recommendations.

Conclusions are reached through analysis and interpretation of data. They are the result of thinking over the facts and logical reasoning. Sometimes facts are given and analyzed, and a conclusion is reached in the discussion section; then the writer moves on to another set of facts, their analysis, and another conclusion. Under this organizational plan, conclusions are reached along with analysis of the material and would be brought together in a summary of conclusions at the end of the report.

Recommendations pertain to the action that is to be taken as a result of the report. The conclusions support them, and they are aimed toward accomplishing the purpose of the report. If the purpose of the report is to investigate the need for establishing another bakery in a city, the recommendation will state that it should or should not be done and, if the decision is "yes," will give further suggestions for carrying out this action. Recommendations often answer the questions: What is to be done? by whom? when? where? how? The more detailed they are, the easier they are to follow. The more general they are, the more leeway there is for the reader to decide specifically the steps necessary for their implementation. The intended use of the report usually decides whether they will be detailed or general.

[2]See pp. 326–27.

Summary

A national consumer preference mail survey among 9,250 owners of 20- to 30-foot pleasure boats was made to determine, if future hulls of Rand boats of this size should be of plank or plywood construction. From the 2,040 replies, it was found that the greater the satisfaction the owners have had with plywood, the relatively larger are the positive considerations they give to purchasing a boat with a treated plywood hull. About three-fourths of present plywood owners favor plywood. Slightly less than half of past plywood owners believe plywood is at least very satisfactory. About one-third of the non-plywood owners say they would consider purchasing a plywood hull.

Wherever plywood construction presently has its better market position, a more favorable attitude is found toward this type of hull. On the other hand, lower plywood acceptance is among those owners of whom plank hulls have their greater share. The characteristics of these two groups of people are listed in the table below:

Attitude Toward Plywood

Most Favorable	Least Favorable
They own the larger boats.	They own the smaller boats.
Their boats have vee bottoms.	Their boats have round bottoms.
They have model 4 boats.	They have model 5 boats.
Their boats are manufactured by "C."	Their boats are manufactured by "A."
They live in the Gulf area.	They live in the North Atlantic area.

Since 77% of the 20- to 30-foot pleasure boats are of plank construction, two types of recommendations are submitted:

1. For immediate sales gains, build all boats with plank hulls - the majority having round bottoms.

2. For long ranges sales gains

   a. Build smaller boats with all plywood hulls and vee bottoms. Test market models 1 and 4 in the Gulf area.

   b. Build larger boats with all plank hulls - the majority having round bottoms.

   c. Educate the public on plywood hull's advantages.

Since all data obtained from the survey is recorded on IBM cards, any additional tabulations are available.

USING VISUAL AIDS

Visual aids help present effectively numerical, statistical, and factual data through meaningful pictorial symbols. Their purpose is the same as that of the printed word: to communicate information. The present trend toward visual presentation is largely the result of such factors as the movies, television, picture magazines, and comics, which have all made people increasingly receptive to visual material. Supplementary in nature to other material being transmitted, visual aids can be purposefully used to clarify or explain a point, to attract the reader's attention or interest, and to prove a point or to convince. They include such devices of graphic presentation as tabels, charts and graphs, photographs, maps, and diagrams. It behooves the communicator to have sufficient knowledge of different types of aids to be able to select and use the best possible ones to convey his material effectively and to achieve his purpose.

Selection

The selection of appropriate visual aids depends on:

1. The nature and purpose of the communication piece
2. The intended reader
3. The way in which the aid is to be used
4. The nature of the material being presented in the aid

Widely distributed annual reports make use of visual aids to boost the company or its products, and aids are selected that will gain the most popular interest and understanding. However, reports used internally to convince management of the wisdom of taking positive action on a recommendation must assemble visual aids that will prove the action is necessary.

Consideration must be given to the type of reader—to what he wants and to his ability to comprehend charts and tables—for he needs to be able to grasp quickly and accurately the information in the table or chart. Consideration must also be given to what special purpose the aid will accomplish and how it is to be used. Although visual aids draw attention to the material and make it attractive, their real function is to make the material understandable. Specific types of charts will show certain data to advantage; certain other data are better presented in tabular form.

Kinds of Aids

Tables arrange data systematically in columns and rows. A series of related facts or a large number of items may be easily seen and followed when displayed in tabular form. Tables are a logical way of analyzing and summarizing numerical and other statistical data. They show comparisons, trends, and quantities; point up significant facts; and make it easy for the reader to interpret them.

Whenever a table, chart, or other graphic aid is used, it should be introduced into the text of the report and placed as near as is possible to the material with which it is used.

A complete explanation or analysis of each table should be given, including a description of the data and a discussion of the extent to which the figures establish the facts and relate to other data, with full explanations of technical terms and details. When it is appropriate, attention should be called to averages, trends, and tendencies. Extremes should be pointed out, exceptions noted, and conditions explained. The discussion can be organized by considering in sequence the total figures, the significant figure making up the total, and the conclusions.

Note how the significant figures have been made a part of the discussion in the next example, taken from the report on plywood hulls.

Of the 2,040 respondents, 77 percent have boats of all-plank hull construction. Only 11 percent of the boat hulls are made of all plywood; a total of 14 percent contain some plywood.

Construction	No. of Respondents		Percent of Total	
All plank		1,573		77
Any plywood (all or part)		281		14
All sheet plywood	164		8	
All molded plywood	53		3	
Side plywood, bottom plank	36		2	
Side plank, bottom plywood	28		1	
Steel		147		7
Other		35		2
No answer		4		-
Total		2,040		100%

As boat size increases, all-plank construction's share increases with the exception of the 25- to 26-foot class where steel hulls have an unusually high market position of 20 percent, as indicated in Table 16, Hull Material of Present Boat (by Its Length), page 23. The smaller the boat is, the greater is "any plywood" hull ownership.

Most of the points relevant to the discussion of tables also apply to analyses of charts. A chart does not require the detailed interpretation a table does, because it presents less detail and is constructed to convey a complete message in itself. But its relationship to the points mentioned in the text and to other charts and material should be discussed as a part of the text material in the report. All visual aids in a report have a purpose, and to achieve that purpose fully they must add something to the discussion; thus they become an integral part of the report.

Charts represent data by lines, bars, areas, diagrams, graphs, drawings, or photographs. They supplement and emphasize the material in a table; they show relationships; they simplify and clarify; they reinforce the message by emphasizing important points; and they interest and persuade the reader. Although they may have explanatory notes

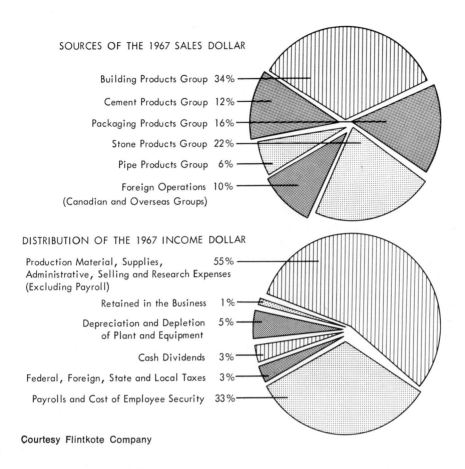

SOURCES OF THE 1967 SALES DOLLAR

Building Products Group 34%

Cement Products Group 12%

Packaging Products Group 16%

Stone Products Group 22%

Pipe Products Group 6%

Foreign Operations 10%
(Canadian and Overseas Groups)

DISTRIBUTION OF THE 1967 INCOME DOLLAR

Production Material, Supplies, Administrative, Selling and Research Expenses (Excluding Payroll) 55%

Retained in the Business 1%

Depreciation and Depletion of Plant and Equipment 5%

Cash Dividends 3%

Federal, Foreign, State and Local Taxes 3%

Payrolls and Cost of Employee Security 33%

Courtesy Flintkote Company

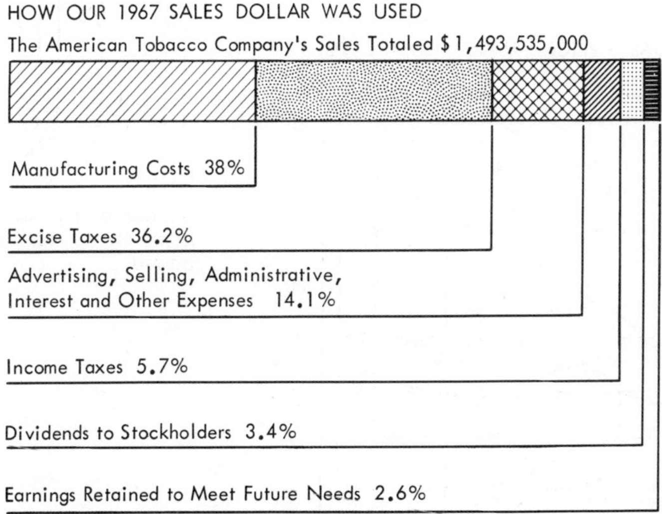

Courtesy American Tobacco Company

Pie charts and single bar charts show portions of the total and comparison of parts of the whole

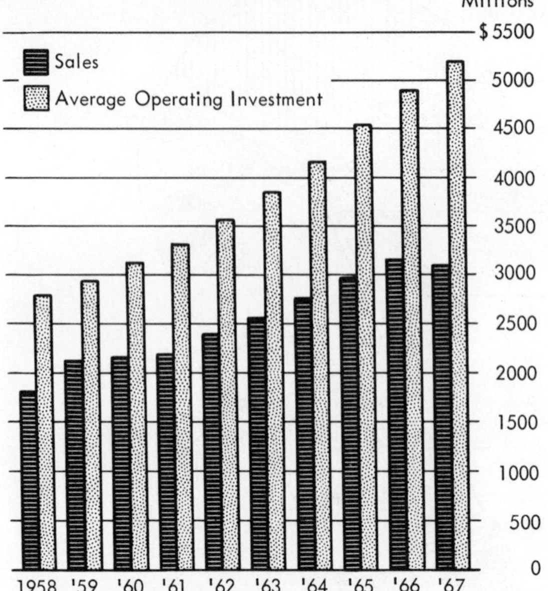

Courtesy E. I. du Pont de Nemours and Company

Columns (vertical bars) grouped for each year compare two items within the same year or other time period

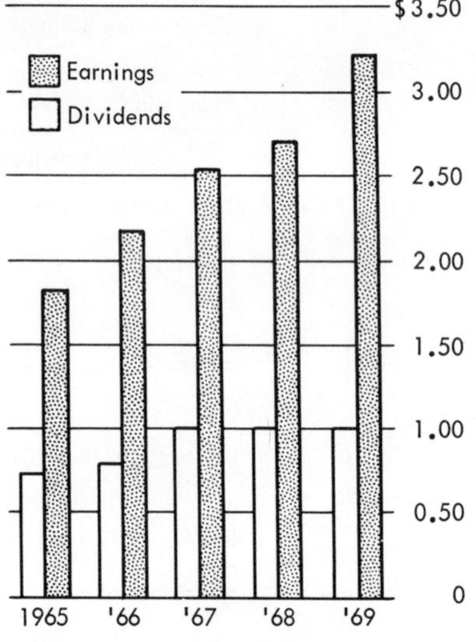

Courtesy Harris-Intertype Corporation

Shaded bars show comparison of two items for a single year or other time period

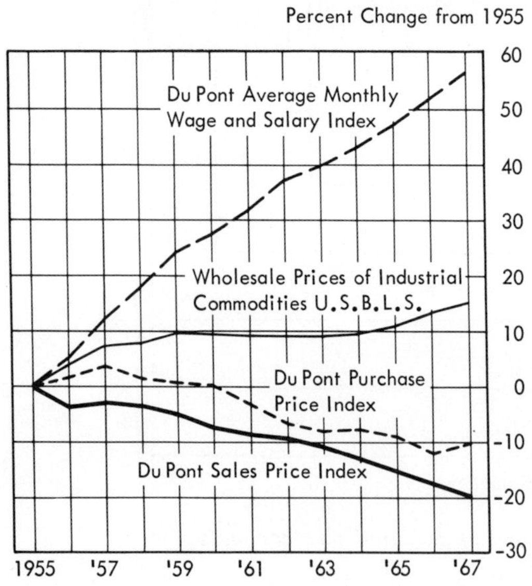

Courtesy E. I. du Pont de Nemours and Company

Several line curves on the same scale compare variables

in accompanying paragraphs to relate their points to the rest of the discussion, charts will often stand alone. *Bar charts* are probably the most popular and decorative type. They are widely used in advertising and promotional material, for they attract the reader's eye. They are very effective for comparing unlike items with a common element or items that are alike in two or three respects. For comparison of items in a series, *line charts* and *curve charts* are appropriate. They depict a continuous process over a time period, showing the data and trends. For comparing the parts of a whole and studying their relationships to each other and to the whole, *circle* or *pie charts* are commonly used. The pie is divided into segments that readily depict their relationships to each other. To show flow, direction, or course, *flow charts* and *organization charts* are used. To provide exact knowledge of an object's appearance, *photographs* are vivid and interesting.

Here are several suggestions for preparing charts:

1. Vary bars and figures in one dimension only to avoid optical illusion.
2. Provide keys and footnote explanations so that the reader will understand.
3. Make the chart simple enough for the reader to comprehend quickly.
4. Create a caption with action words for the chart.
5. Use as few charts as possible to convey the necessary data.
6. Use color to call attention to a figure, trend, or feature, or to add interest.
7. Give an accurate portrayal of the data.

Interpretation and Discussion

Visual aids require explanation and interpretation. Therefore, the writer should discuss the implications of his statistics and give generalizations based on the figures. He should introduce tables, charts, and other types of aids and make them part of the text. He should also give a complete explanation or analysis of each table, including a description of the data and a discussion of the extent to which the figures establish the facts and the way in which they relate to other data, with full explanations of technical terms and details. Consider the total figure and significant figures that reinforce the conclusions. Call attention to averages, trends, and tendencies. Although charts do not call for as full an explanation as tables do, they should still be related to points mentioned in the text. To achieve their purpose, all visual aids must add something to the discussion and become an integral part of the message being communicated.

Here are some suggestions on how to make numerical data, tables, and charts meaningful and purposeful:

1. Spot trends for the reader; tables and graphs do not tell the story by themselves.
2. Use the right average. Remember that the mean is the sum total divided by the number of cases; the median is the midpoint between the upper and lower halves; and the mode is the case that is most common. Quite often the median or the mode will give the reader a clearer picture, for the mean shows what things would be like if everybody got an equal share, and this is rarely true.
3. Point out the range, because averages tell only half the story. Unfortunately, measures that describe spread, such as the standard deviation, don't mean much to the ordinary reader.
4. Point out the exceptions; readers are interested in them.
5. Spare your reader tables if you can by cutting them to a minimum.
6. Use spot tables to highlight significant figures.
7. Round out your figures, as long figures are hard to read. Round them to the nearest whole number, ten, hundred, thousand, million, or billion—whichever tells your story best.
8. Whenever possible, round out figures under 13 that are usually spelled out by the printers. Instead of 84.7 percent, say "five out of six"; instead of 12.5 percent, say "One in eight."
9. Keep your pictorial statistics simple. If they are too complicated, you will defeat your purpose.
10. Explain your symbols; they do not explain themselves.

BUILDING A REPORT FROM ITS POSSIBLE PARTS

The main principle involved in building a report from its possible parts is: *dress a report up or down by adding, subtracting, or combining parts to meet the needs of the situation, purpose, and reader.* In general, the more parts there are, the more formal the report will be. A formal report, for instance, with its text broken into parts and written in a formal style, might have a cover, title page, letter of transmittal, table of contents, summary, text, appendix, and bibliography. On the other hand, an informal short report might have only a memorandum of transmittal, title page, text, and appendix.

Reports are usually either long and formal or short and informal. Written for informal situations, informal, short reports vary in length from one to ten pages. They are often written on a subject of temporary or current interest and speed up the process of keeping someone else informed. The pages may be clipped or stapled, creating a less finished appearance than that of the long, formal report. Memorandums and letter reports are common examples; both are personal forms of reports, whose degree of informality depends upon the relationship between the reader and the writer and on the purpose of the report.

For more formality and in a more complicated situation, the short report can take on some of the aspects of the long, formal report by adding a formal title page, table of contents, or letter of transmittal and by presenting its material in a more formal style.

Formal reports are usually over ten pages in length. Their subjects are given comprehensive treatment, since the problems are involved ones and cover a wide scope. The subject matter is broken down into parts, and formal organization and style are used. Adding more parts dresses up the report and makes it more impressive and important.

Parts of a Report

The possible parts of a report fall into three general classifications—preliminary sections, report text, and supplemental sections. Preliminary sections present reference and informational material that explains and identifies the report and the situation for which it has been prepared. The report text, often referred to as the *body* or *report proper,* presents the facts, their analysis, conclusions, and recommendations. Supplemental sections follow the report proper and include material of a general and secondary interest for the record and for reference purposes.

Although it is conceivable that a long, formal report might contain all the parts mentioned here, this would be rare. The writer should be selective and use only the parts that are appropriate to the situation, the reader, and the purpose or use of the report.

PRELIMINARY SECTIONS:

Cover—Identifies and protects the report. The title, author, and date are sufficient information. Sometimes a printed form is filled out and attached.

Flyleaf—Precedes the title page. Adds a high note of formality.

Title page—Provides complete identification. May include the title, subtitle, and author (his position and address), the name and address of the person or company for whom the report has been prepared, the serial designation, and the date of completion.

Letter of authorization—Establishes the authority and states the terms under which the report is made. Becomes a part of the report *only* if this is desirable as part of the record. Most of the time, authorization is given verbally, or the report rises out of the reporter's work and there is no letter of authorization.

Letter of transmittal—Accompanies the report. Not always a bound part. Used to transmit the report, interest the reader, increase confidence in the report, and point out items of significance. May include a summary of the report. May take the place of an introduction.

Table of contents—Outlines the topics in the report, facilitating reference by giving page numbers for each topic listed. May also list preliminary and supplemental sections of the report.

List of tables or charts—Lists in consecutive order the tables, graphs, or charts used and gives their page numbers.

Summary—Summarizes the content of the report. Used to speed up action so that not everyone will have to read the entire report. When not a separate section, it may be a part of a letter of transmittal, an introduction, or the first section of the report, thus serving transitional or introductory function.

REPORT TEXT:

Introduction—Presents a problem or subject to the reader and gets his attention. Furnishes sufficient background to allow easy understanding of the rest of the report. The trend is to begin the introduction with a summary of conclusion or findings. May contain many of the elements of the problem worked out in the working plan.

Discussion—Presents, interprets, and analyzes information and data. Meanings, ideas, and facts are made clear to the reader. Evaluations are given and significant relationships pointed out. Illustrative and visual material is included. Supporting statements are used for validation. Leads the reader through reasoning processes to reach conclusions and shows him that they are sound.

Conclusion—Shows the result of reasoned analysis and judges the data in the report; serves as a basis for recommendations. May present conclusions and recommendations in the same section or separate sections.

Recommendations—Pertain to the action to be taken as a result of the report. They are supported by conclusions and aimed toward accomplishing the report's purpose. They answer the questions: What is to be done? by whom? where? and how?

SUPPLEMENTAL SECTIONS:

Appendix—Presents supplementary material, which, if placed in the body of the report, might disrupt or delay the reading process. Contains record and reference material such as large tables and charts, sample questionnaires or forms used, extensive quotations and summaries, specifications, mailing lists, glossaries, or letters. Short, simple reports rarely have appendixes, nor do all formal, long reports. The appendix is what the writer wants to make it.

Bibliography—Sometimes included as part of the appendix. When separate, it may precede or follow the appendix. Lists printed sources used in gathering data and writing the report; also includes any interviews that were made. Unless bibliographical research or individual interviews have been used, there can be no bibliography.

Index—Used only with long, extensive, complicated reports. Lists page references to important words, phrases, facts, names, ideas, main divisions, subdivisions, and so on. For short reports and most long reports, the table of contents serves the function of the index.

Dressing a Report Up or Down

By adding, subtracting, or combining parts to meet the needs of the situation, purpose, and reader, a report can be dressed up to make it formal or down to make it informal. Suppose that a report on personnel practices in fifty manufacturing firms is to be dressed up for the director of personnel. The writer can add a title page, table of contents, and summary of findings in front of the text, follow it with an appendix and bibliography, and use a separate letter of transmittal to accompany the report.

To make it less formal, the writer can omit the summary, incorporating it in the letter of transmittal; if the report is short, he can omit the table of contents, making it part of the transmittal letter. Another way of making the report informal would be to use a memorandum of transmittal in place of a letter, omitting the title page. The memorandum can carry out the functions of the title page, transmittal, and summary, leaving the report composed only of the memorandum, text, and appendix (with the bibliography a part of the appendix). The parts of a report are highly flexible and adaptable. The important point is to understand the function of each part in relation to the other parts and to the total effect desired.

A report can also be dressed up or down by adapting the writing style. Impartial, objective treatment of the subject matter is generally more formal than subjective, personal treatment. To be formal in writing, omit personal references and pronouns, and write in the third person. Omit opinions, personal experiences, anecdotes, and the like. Present facts uncolored, show conclusions that are based on the facts, and validate and support the statements. To be informal in writing, add personal references and pronouns, and write in the first and second persons. Include opinions, personal experiences, anecdotes, and the like. Present facts, validate and support them, and draw conclusions, but let some subjectivity in for consideration. Show a friendly attitude toward the

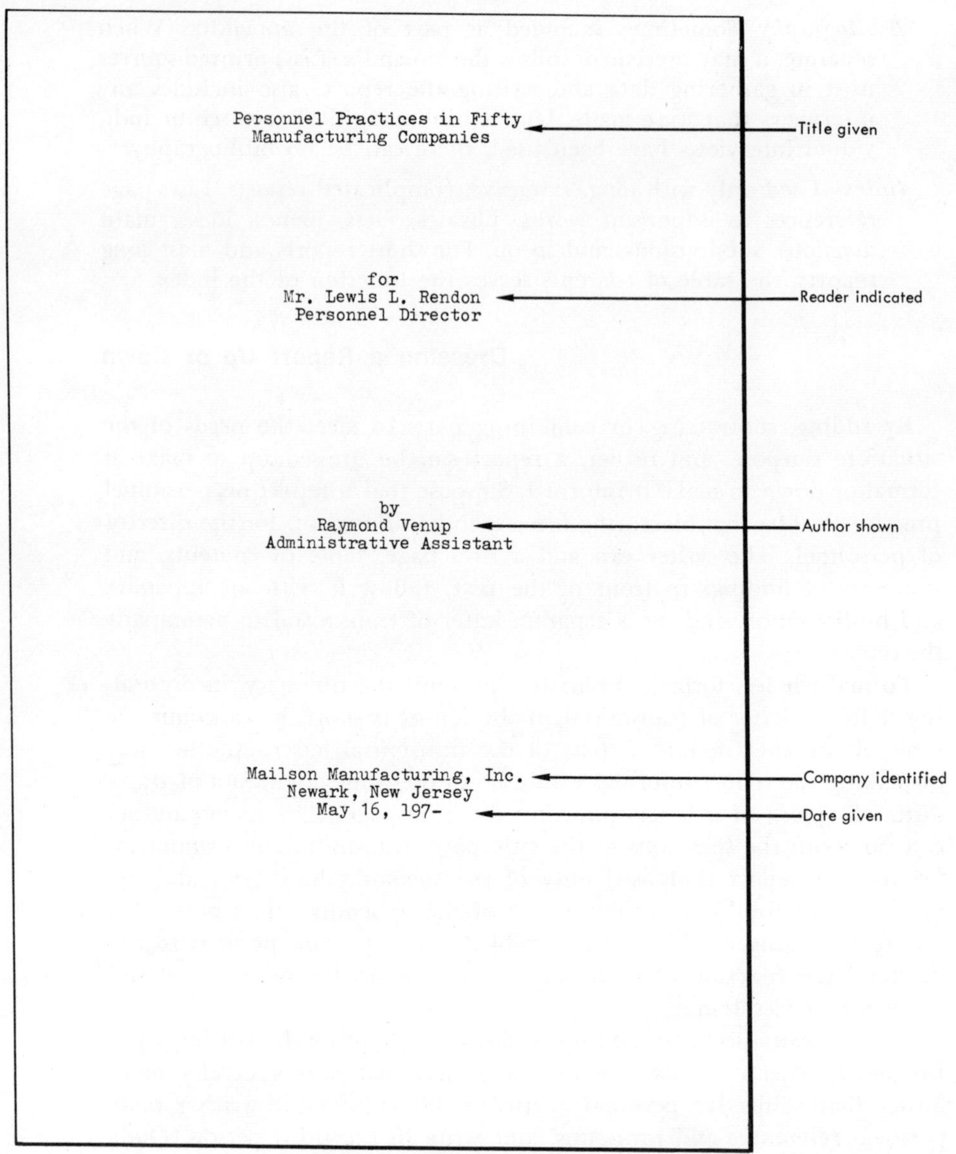
Personnel Practices in Fifty
Manufacturing Companies

for
Mr. Lewis L. Rendon
Personnel Director

by
Raymond Venup
Administrative Assistant

Mailson Manufacturing, Inc.
Newark, New Jersey
May 16, 197-

Formal title page #1. Elements arranged in standard format, centered.

work and the reader. Personalize material for the reader's interest or use.

The arrangement and makeup of separate parts of a report also reflect a degree of formality or informality that should be in keeping with the entire report. A formal title page, for example, would contain complete information and follow a set pattern in its arrangement. An in-

Personnel Practices in Fifty
Manufacturing Companies

for
Mr. Lewis L. Rendon
Personnel Director

by
Raymond Venup
Administrative Assistant

Mailson Manufacturing, Inc.
Newark, New Jersey
May 16, 197-

Formal title page #2. Elements arranged in standard format, using indention and blocking.

formal title page, on the other hand, would not include all the elements, and it could vary the pattern in its arrangement.

The same principles apply to the letter of transmittal and other report parts. The letter is written after the report has been completed and is

for
Mr. Lewis L. Rendon
Personnel Director

Personnel Practices in Fifty
Manufacturing Companies

by
Raymond Venup
Administrative Assistant

Informal title page #1. Variation in typing and spacing.

addressed to the person or group for whom the report has been prepared. Generally a natural, conversational, but dignified tone and style are effective. However, the letter can be written informally and personally whenever the relationship of the reader and writer warrants it. This provides the opportunity to mention personal ideas that would

Mailson Manufacturing, Inc.
Newark, New Jersey

PERSONNEL PRACTICES
IN FIFTY MANUFACTURING COMPANIES

May, 197-
Raymond Venup

Informal title page #2. Variation in typing and spacing.

be out of place in an impersonal report. In some such instances, the letter would be placed first, outside the report, where it could be detached after being read only by its intended reader.

The composition of the letter of transmittal varies from report to report. It may contain any or all of the following elements and any additional appropriate ones:

1. Authorization
2. Scope and limitations
3. History and background
4. Summary of the report
5. Acknowledgments
6. Need for the report
7. Use of the report
8. Conclusions
9. Recommendations
10. Personal opinions

The reader will become interested if you obtain his attention; you can persuade him to accept the report, and he will wish to read further. This may be done by calling his attention to the points that are significant to him.

Note how these points have been taken care of in the following letter to the dean of a business college, which accompanied a report entitled "Proposed Public Relations Program to Attract Black Students to the College of Business."

Dear Dean____________:

Here is the preliminary report on how you might approach the problem of attracting more black students to the College of Business Administration. As you know, we have not completed the preliminary attitude survey (Exhibit 4), so we have relied entirely upon conferences with people on and off campus. Yet I think we have the framework for an effective program which meets the criteria you set:

1. that it be low-keyed in view of the recent campus demonstrations,
2. that it be inexpensive in terms of direct cost and in the time of faculty and administrators,
3. that it not result in a "flash" flood of enrollees, but a steady continuous source of educable black students.

The background of the report is extensive because it is essential that the psychological and sociological variables affecting the program be clearly stated. Disagreement on any one could result in modification of the action program.

I have enjoyed doing this preliminary study for you and look forward to discussing it with you and your staff in the next few days.

Sincerely yours,

Notice, in the letter of transmittal on the opposite page, how the emphasis is placed upon procedures.

The contents page and other parts added to a report can also be informal, formal, or middle-of-the-road. An informal contents page usually lists only the major divisions of the text. Pagination may be set down in various ways; one method is illustrated on page 350. Another good, informal method, easy to type and to read, is listing the divisions, with each followed by a comma and page number. A formal contents page, however, will follow a set pattern (like the formal title page) and will

CHILDREY RESEARCH SERVICE, INC.
7309 Three Chopt Road
Richmond, Virginia

288-7680 288-5316

Richmond Newspapers, Inc.
Richmond, Virginia

Gentlemen:

Submitted herewith are the questionnaires which have been processed among telephone homes in the Richmond metropolitan area. A total of 6,329 calls were attempted, of which 5,173 were effectively completed. We estimate that there are approximately 150,000 dwelling units in the Richmond metropolitan area, of which we reached approximately 3 percent.

The survey was conducted Monday through Friday, January 6-10, 1969. A total of seven experienced interviewers worked on a schedule of two-hour periods for five days--totaling 14 hours of calling each day between 8:00 A.M. and 10:00 P.M. EST. Dialing of numbers was continuous during these hours, utilizing phone numbers previously selected. We understand that these numbers were selected by a random procedure to insure that every telephone home listed in the current (October, 1969) Richmond area telephone directory had an equal opportunity to be selected.

Weather during the period was a little cooler than normal, with temperatures ranging from teens to thirties.

Interviewers were instructed and rehearsed to insure that all calls would be made uniformly and without interview bias. A percentage of the respondents were reinterviewed by a supervisor, verifying that procedures had been followed. The name of the survey sponsor was not known to interviewers or respondents. The basic procedure followed in this survey, we understand, is the one that has been used without variation in all the semiannual surveys of broadcast audiences in metropolitan Richmond that have been conducted since June, 1956. We understand that this is a total of 26 surveys with an aggregate of 119,271 effective calls--equal to about 80 percent of all homes presently in the area.

Sincerely yours,

Virginia V. Childrey
Virginia V. Childrey

Courtesy Richmond Newspapers, Inc.

include preliminary and supplementary sections as well as the divisions of the report text. Note the use of spacing, capitals, and indention in the two sample contents pages on page 350.

Usually there is some form of summary in every report to enable the busy executive to find the significant facts without reading the entire report. The first paragraph of the introduction might be a summary of the findings that is designed to call the reader's attention to them. A brief paragraph in the letter of transmittal may summarize significant points to interest the reader in continuing. As a separate part of the

Informal table of contents

Personnel Practices

Table of Contents

Formal table of contents

report, however, the summary may be from one to five pages long, depending upon the report's length; it completes the preliminary sections used to dress up the report. Copies of the summary section may be made and distributed separately from the report to speed up action. Twelve people may make decisions after reading the summary, while only one or two of them have read the entire report.

The summary should be concisely written and direct and should give pertinent data. The essence of each main division is stated in proportion to its importance. In preparing a summary, read through the report and pick out its main points. Then go back for details, visualizing them in proper perspective. Now you are ready to write. An outline can be as valuable in writing a summary as it is in writing the text. In fact, a sentence outline itself, presented in paragraph form according to the major divisions, would make a good summary.

REVISING AND EDITING

After you have written the report and have dressed it up by adding parts, especially preliminary ones, to make it impressive and useful, you should read it again to find out whether or not it can be further improved in its content, expression, and mechanics. The Royal Bank of Canada in a monthly letter, "Writing a Report," states: "The writer who achieves distinction of expression, conciseness, directness—and, if the nature of his work permits it, dramatic quality, beauty of rhythm, and some adventurousness of phrase and idea—has not done something miraculous. He has worked hard and intelligently." Writing reports calls for hard work, but it can be a very interesting and stimulating job to offer thought-provoking interpretations and ideas and to present solutions to problems.

The report writer uses his ability to think and communicate to make his report practical, complete, concise, clear, intellectually honest, and readable. It must meet the demands of any communication. To fulfill its purpose, it must be written clearly, interestingly, and persuasively.

Not all reports are written, revised, and rewritten. The type of report and its use, the amount of time available, and how well the first draft was prepared determine the amount of revision needed. The individual who normally expresses what he has to say clearly, concisely, and interestingly will have little revision to do. In revision lies the opportunity to make up for any deficiencies of the report or the writer, so that the finished product can accomplish its purpose as quickly as possible. Reports of a routine nature or use and, to some degree, short or informal reports written for only one specific reader, usually within the company organization, do not warrant spending a lot of time on revisions.

They often contain information of temporary use; nevertheless, they must be checked for accuracy of facts, clearness of expression, and overall organization; tested to see whether their purposes are accomplished; and proofread for correction of mechanical errors in form and typing.

Revising a report calls for systematically reading the report several times, checking each time for a different purpose. The reading may be done silently or aloud, to or by someone other than the writer. It is well to check the report's content and organization, clarity of expression and mechanics of style and form, adaptation to the reader, and general readability. The following questions provide a helpful checklist for revising reports.

To check contents:

1. Have the purpose and objectives been attained?
2. Have accuracy and completeness been maintained in:
   a. Background material?
   b. Numerical data?
   c. Quotations?
   d. Supporting evidence?
   e. Explanations?
   f. Scope?
   g. Tables and charts?
   h. Examples?
   i. Facts and figures?
   j. Illustrations?
3. Do major and minor issues stand out in proper perspective?
4. Is there a logical development and flow of ideas?
5. Are the conclusions sound, logical, definite, and clear?
6. Are the recommendations an outgrowth of the conclusions, and are they workable?

To check organization:

1. Does the overall organization present the total picture?
2. Are all the parts related?
3. Is there a logical sequcnce of topics and ideas?
4. Is there general coherence and unity throughout the report?
5. Have appropriate transitions been made?

To check for clearness of expression:

1. Are specific facts and details given?
2. Are short sentences predominant?
3. Is there an average sentence length of 17 to 22 words per sentence?
4. Are sentences varied according to structure, length, and type?
5. Are the words used concrete, familiar, precise, and simple?

To check the mechanics of style and form:

1. Is correct usage followed in spelling, punctuation, and grammar?
2. Does the report conform to a standard form for its type—letter, memorandum, short form, or long form?

3. Are correct typing details of form, margins, spacing, subject headings, and so on followed?
4. Are correct forms used for footnotes, bibliography, and subject headings?
5. Is there consistency of form?

To check readability and adaptation:

1. Has the appropriate level of readability been maintained?
2. Has the proper tone been maintained?
3. Has the reader been told what he needs to know to understand the report?
4. Has the material been adapted to the reader's knowledge and experience?
5. Has his interest been gained through the vocabulary, illustrations, layout, and approach to the problem?
6. Has the reader's need and use for the report been recognized?

The extent to which this checklist is used will depend on the writer's experience and abilities, the type and use of the report, and the amount of time available for revisions. Not all reports are revised, nor should they be. Most reports, however, can be improved by careful revision.

Any printed report should be carefully revised and edited before publication, for it would be foolish to spend money to print ineffective or incorrect writing. Editing is basically the same as revising, for its purpose is to correct and improve the report—to prepare and check the final copy. After being revised, the report is read again before publication. It is checked for accuracy, completeness, and clearness of subject matter, then for overall and sectional organization, and last for correctness in mechanics and form. When this has been done and any changes have been made, the copy is marked for the printer.

Large companies employ editors to polish material for publication or for wide distribution. In some cases, depending upon the need, they merely correct errors and do some final polishing. In other cases, complete rewriting is called for. Publishers also have editors who correct, polish, and mark material for publication. They instruct the printer on the type, size, layout, etc., to follow, so that he can make his plans accordingly.

SUMMARY

The task of writing a report is made easier if the writer has gone through the steps of report investigation and preparation and has outlined his material. Adding the subsidiary parts to the report text improves its effectiveness. Logically the report begins with an introduction, which is used to present the problem or subject to the reader and to get his attention. A report may, however, begin with a summary or with conclusions and recommendations, depending upon the reader's knowledge of and experience with the subject of the report, and upon the purpose and use of the report.

Subject headings are useful to indicate the various topics treated in the report and their relationships. A great deal of flexibility in selecting and using headings is often desirable, but a certain amount of standardization must be maintained for consistency and clearness.

Supporting material, consisting of quotations, facts, figures, tables, statistics, charts, and the like, offers proof and evidence of the validity of the data and serves as a basis for analysis, interpretation, and the drawing of conclusions. Proper footnote citations should be made, and explanations of tables and charts should be given. Forms of support consisting of explanation, comparison or contrast, illustration, and the like make things clear and increase the reader's understanding. Other forms, such as specific instances, statistics, testimony, and the like prove something rather than just explaining. Tying facts together by association of ideas and connecting words helps to create a smooth flow of ideas. Linking sentences together also speeds understanding of the supporting material presented.

Logically, a report that begins with an introduction ends with a summary or with conclusions and recommendations. When the order is reversed, and conclusions and recommendations begin the report, it should end with a summary or with suggestions for implementing the recommendations. This sequence depends, in most instances, on the relationship of the reader to the material in the report and on the use he is likely to make of it.

Visual aids help to present effectively numerical, statistical, and factual data through meaningful pictorial symbols. They inform, clarify, add interest, and convince or prove a point. The selection of aids depends upon the nature and purpose of the report, the reader, and the nature of the data being presented. A variety of charts and tables may be used: formal and informal tables, spot tables, bar charts, line and curve charts, circle charts, graphs, and photographs. They all should be discussed and integrated into the text of the report.

The major principle in building a report from its parts is to dress it up or down by adding, subtracting, or combining parts to meet the needs of the situation, purpose, and reader. There are preliminary sections: the title page, letter of authorization, letter of transmittal, table of contents, and summary. There are text sections: the introduction, discussion, conclusions, and recommendations. There are supplemental sections: the appendix, bibliography, and index. The parts of a report are highly flexible and adaptable. They may be organized and presented informally or formally to suit the occasion. The style of writing also affects the degree of informality or formality in any given report.

The revising process consists of checking through a report and its parts in order to improve it. The extent to which this is done depends upon the ability of the report writer, the immediacy of the situation, and the permanence of the report. Careful revision and editing are demanded in reports or other materials that are to be published. Proofreading for mechanical correctness is always required.

FURTHER READING

Anderson, C. R., F. W. Weeks, and A. G. Saunders, *Business Reports,* 3rd ed. New York: McGraw-Hill Book Company, 1957.

Brown, Leland, *Effective Business Report Writing,* 2nd ed. Englewood Cliffs, N. J.: Prentice-Hall, Inc., 1963.

Lesikar, Raymond V., *Report Writing for Business,* 3rd ed. Homewood, Ill.: Richard D. Irwin, Inc., 1969.

Robinson, David, *Writing Reports for Management Decisions.* Columbus, Ohio: Charles E. Merrill Books, Inc., 1969.

Shurter, Robert L., J. P. Williamson, and W. G. Broehl, Jr., *Business Research and Report Writing.* New York: McGraw-Hill Book Company, 1969.

Sigband, Norman, *Communication for Management.* Glenwood, Ill.: Scott, Foresman & Company, 1969.

QUESTIONS AND PROBLEMS

The best use of the material in this chapter is to apply it to the problems, projects, and cases given at the ends of Chapters 7, 8, and 9. The suggestions, principles, and ideas presented here will aid you greatly in working out the problems selected and assigned earlier, for much of it is reference material to be checked and applied as called for in the report-writing situation. Your goal is to use it to improve your reports and to present them effectively. You can make further use of this material by writing the reports called for in any additional report situations you may have to handle outside this class or on the job after graduation.

Chapter Eleven

APPLYING FOR A JOB AND GETTING IT

One of the biggest problems to confront you will be applying for a job and getting it. Approximately 3,700,000 high school and college students seek employment each May and June, and 1,000,000 of them will be seeking permanent jobs; the others are looking for summer employment to earn money and experience for future education.[1] College graduates are in great demand and are deluged with job offers (which were up 25 to 30 percent in 1969 over 1968), and the pay has never been better.[2] A graduate with a master's degree in Business Administration and a technical bachelor of science degree will receive an average starting salary of $991 a month; an accounting major receives $929.[3] Pay is up significantly for business trainees, public utilities specialists, and sales and marketing personnel.

Basically, obtaining a job means selling your ability and personality to your prospective employer. You must present your qualifications well enough to persuade him that you will make a good employee, take pride in doing your job well, work harmoniously with other employees, and prove to be an asset to the company. To accomplish this objective, three important items cannot be overemphasized: the résumé, the letter of application, and the interview. The purpose of this chapter is to assist you in preparing all three effectively.

[1] *Changing Times,* April 1969, p. 6.

[2] *Ibid.*, p. 4.

[3] *Wall Street Journal,* December 23, 1968, p. 13.

PREPARING YOUR RÉSUMÉ

Preparing your résumé is an important single step toward securing employment, for it presents a complete outline of your qualifications. It accompanies the letter of application and supports the points of emphasis that the letter discusses. In supplying the details of your training and experience, it frees the letter to emphasize your major qualifications.

The résumé can be and usually is adapted to a number of other uses. Used as an enclosure in the letter, it will assist you (through the letter) to get an interview, for it will help convince the employer that you are qualified and will demonstrate your ability to organize and present your qualifications. It will provide the interviewer with data from which he can plan the interview, showing him points of common interest and questions to ask for further information. Once you are hired by the company, the résumé will become part of your personnel file; kept up-to-date, it will be used periodically to reevaluate you for promotion, salary increase, or job placement. It may also serve a public relations function whenever the occasion arises for publicity or news releases about you for company publications or for the public news media. We are concerned here, however, with its use as an enclosure with your letter of application.

Follow These Principles

Application of the principles of communication is certainly necessary for a well-prepared résumé. It must make a favorable first impression through a neat appearance and must include the essentials of understanding—especially clearness, correctness, and completeness. It is important to be creative, so that your résumé will not look and read like others and will reflect something of you and your personality. You should organize your facts in outline form so that they will be readable and persuasive.

At the very outset you might call your résumé by some other name. Call it "Data Sheet," "Personal Record," "Qualifications Record," or something else. This may help it to stand out from a hundred others. The functions of the data presented on the first page are identification and reference. The material on this page can be arranged differently simply by the way you type and space it:

```
                    Qualifications Record

                             of

                                    Michael H. Fomston
                                    1929 Witmore Street
                                    Galveston, Texas
```

or

```
                        Personal Résumé
                              of
                      Michael H. Fomston

School Address:                     Home Address:
     Ball Hall, #109                     1929 Witmore Street
     University of Houston               Galveston, Texas
     Houston, Texas
```

Include here only what is necessary to identify that the paper is a résumé, whose it is, and how that person may be reached. Often, telephone numbers are also included.

Decide on the Content

Before you can hope to sell yourself in a résumé and application letter, you must know what you have to sell. One approach is to make a complete list of information about yourself. Then ask yourself three questions whose answers will determine what to put into the résumé and, for that matter, into the letter of application:

1. What does the job call for?
2. What is the prospective employer looking for?
3. What do I have to offer?

This corresponds basically to what you have been doing all semester by sizing up the situation and the reader for letters and reports.

What are some of the possible bits of information about you that might be used in answering these questions? You might start by brainstorming for ideas and facts, organizing them later under major categories. Or you might start with the categories and then accumulate all the facts. For example, education and experience are major categories. Under education you might include:

1. Schools and years attended
2. Degrees
3. Major and minor courses of study
4. Class rank or grade point average
5. Courses taken in major field
6. Courses in related fields
7. Scholarships or fellowships
8. Honors and awards

9. Foreign languages read or spoken
10. Memberships in fraternities, clubs, etc.
11. Campus activities

Experience might include:

1. Position held
2. Company
3. Dates
4. Duties and responsibilities
5. Part-time or summer employment

Personal data about yourself might include:

1. Address
2. Telephone number
3. Date and place of birth
4. Marital status
5. Draft status
6. Physical makeup—height, weight, etc.
7. Health

Other points of interest would be:

1. Hobbies
2. Percentage of college expenses earned
3. Membership in civic organizations
4. Practical training
5. Military service
6. Job objectives
7. Goals and future plans

Surveys and studies show that personnel directors and prospective employers look for the qualities in the job applicant that he possesses as an individual. They seek modesty, sincerity, and a willingness to learn; knowledge of the job and how he will fit into the company; a mastery of skills and tools combined with a well-rounded education and a desire to work; common sense, intelligence, and integrity; evidence of social development and the ability to get along with others; and the ability to learn and think, to create ideas, to solve problems, and to express himself. What goes on the qualification record sheet and in the letter of application, and what shows up in the personal interview, should all go to demonstrate that the applicant possesses and can utilize these qualities and character traits. Among the virtues that are most wanted are compulsive curiosity, productivity, creativity, and enthusiasm. The content of the résumé will give evidence of these qualities in a factual, supporting way; however, the organization and format that are followed can further demonstrate some of these characteristics.

Organize and Display the Data

Consider your educational qualifications. The prospective employer is interested first in your latest and present status. Therefore, start with the college from which you were graduated and list your schools in reverse chronological order, as:

```
EDUCATION

    University of Tulsa, College of Business Administration,
       1968-1970, BBA degree June, 1970.

    University of Kansas, 1966-1968.

    Emporia High School, Emporia, Kansas, 1962-1966, college
       preparatory curriculum.

    Major:  Accounting           Minor:  Economics
```

Consider your experience. Place your present or most recent job first and list the others in reverse chronological order, as:

```
EXPERIENCE

    Baer Furniture Company, Kansas City, Kansas, As-
         sistant bookkeeper, summers 1969 and 1970.

    Modern Lighting, Inc., Emporia, Kansas, bookkeeping,
         general office, and sales work, summer 1968.
```

If you have held numerous jobs, you might set up headings and arrange the information in a columnar format:

Position	Duties	Company	Dates

Here it is important that you follow the outlining principles of consistency, division, and parallelism, as well as the advertising principles of creative layout to catch the eye and to attract attention.

One organizational decision you must make is whether to give your educational qualifications or your work experience the major emphasis.

This will depend upon your background in each. For a recent college graduate, his greatest contribution is, in most instances, his educational training and personal attributes. For a person who has been out of school a while or who has considerable experience related to the position for which he is applying, experience becomes the bigger contribution of the two. Physical and personal data are minor and should be subordinated along with the identification and reference facts at the beginning or relegated to a later position just before the references.

Look at the two résumés on pages 361–63. They are somewhat conventional in their organization and format, but they both get the job done effectively and show the applicant in a very favorable light. Note how the principles and suggestions given here have been put into practice.

Background - Accomplishments - Experience

of

ALLEN G. JAROSZ

Permanent Address:	School Address:
15112 Payne Court Dearborn, Michigan	701 Pearl Street Ypsilanti, Michigan
Date of birth: May 16, 1947	Sex: Male
Height: 5 ft. 11 in.	Marital status: Single
Weight: 175 lbs.	Physical condition: Good

EDUCATION

Colleges attended:

Eastern Michigan University, Ypsilanti, Michigan, September, 1967, to June, 1969

Henry Ford Community College, Dearborn, Michigan, September, 1965, to June, 1967

Degree received:

Bachelor of Business Administration degree from Eastern Michigan University, June, 1969

Major courses completed in college:

Insurance	Management
Salesmanship	Marketing
Business Communication	Accounting
Human Relations	Statistics

Other educational accomplishments:

Completed An Introduction To Life Underwriting correspondence course by Jefferson National Life Insurance Company, Indianapolis, Indiana, May, 1968

Completed Life Insurance correspondence course by Research and Review, Indianapolis, Indiana, July, 1968

Received Michigan's life underwriting license in July, 1968

EXPERIENCE

Presently underwriting life and health insurance for:

Jefferson National Life Insurance Co., Indianapolis, Indiana; date commissioned: July, 1968

Continental Assurance Company, New York, New York; date commissioned: September, 1968

Prudential Insurance Company, Minneapolis, Minnesota; date commissioned: October, 1968

Other work experience:

Liquor salesman, sold and inventoried liquor, Civic Drug Center, Dearborn, Michigan, June, 1966, to September, 1967

Retail clerk, sold merchandise, J. L. Hudson's, Dearborn, Michigan, June, 1965, to May, 1966

REFERENCES

Mr. James Holland, Holland's Insurance Agency, 6745 Mead, Utica, Michigan
Mr. Paul Mitchell, Cale's General Agency, 18976 Ford Road, Dearborn, Michigan
Mr. D. R. Applebaum, Merril Drugs, 19775 Greenfield, Detroit, Michigan
Dr. W. Oscar Collins, Head, Department of General Business, Eastern Michigan University, Ypsilanti, Michigan
Mr. Richard Ashton, Assistant Professor of Marketing, Eastern Michigan University, Ypsilanti, Michigan

Although the résumés of Allen G. Jarosz and John S. Wholehouse are fairly standard in their content, organization, and form, they differ from each other, and each takes on a personality of its own. We will now consider how to further reflect creative and personal characteristics. Recently a résumé sent to a personnel director contained these headings:

Résumé concerning:
John M. Peterack

How to contact him:

Important physical characteristics:

His educational experience:

His work experience:

People he knows who will recommend him:

This shows a little ingenuity and is somewhat different from the run-of-the-mill résumé.

An interesting qualifications record was done by a former student of mine, in the form of a four-page brochure called "Meet Dick Bennett." It is reproduced by his permission on pages 364–67. The brochure dem-

Personal Résumé

JOHN S. WHOLEHOUSE

Home address:
324 Newton Street
Boston, Massachusetts

Telephone:
333-2232

EDUCATION

Bachelor of Arts, Northeastern University, Boston, Massachusetts. To be granted June 1971. Major in Marketing (B average), minor in Journalism (B average). Emphasis on courses in salesmanship, advertising, product management, and communication.

CAREER OBJECTIVES

Hope to obtain position with direct customer contact which will lead to position in sales management. Prefer working with people and in an organization emphasizing customer service concept.

WORK EXPERIENCE

Salseman (Summer 1970)
Bingham's Storm Door Company, 751 Rochester Street, Boston. Sold storm doors and windows to local home owners. Earned over $1,000 in commissions under supervision of the sales manager.

Sales clerk (During 1969-1970 and 1968-1969 school years)
Campus Men's Shop, 910 University Avenue, Boston. Employed part-time (20 hours per week) as salesman of men's furnishings and sports clothes under supervision of the store owner.

PERSONAL FACTORS

Appearance: 5 feet 9 inches tall, 170 lbs., brown hair and eyes.

Place and date of birth: Born January 1948, Framingham, Massachusetts

Military Status: Member Massachusetts National Guard

Marital Status: Single, free to travel

Hobbies: Participation in swimming, tennis, golf. Reading in general and business publications.

REFERENCES

Dr. George L. Jones
Professor of Marketing
Boston University

Mr. James Dee Ballet
Associate Professor, Journalism
Boston University

Mr. Martin Edwards
Sales Manager
Bingham's Storm Door Co.
751 Rochester Street
Boston, Massachusetts

Mr. Samuel Henricks
Campus Men's Shop
910 University Avenue
Boston, Massachusetts

onstrates creative ability and convinces the recipient that Dick Bennett is well qualified for sales, marketing, or public relations positions, for "He's quite a guy!!!"

Generally instructors try to discourage a student from doing a résumé in the third person and in sentence–paragraph construction. Prospective employers generally don't like them that way, largely because they take

Dynamic...

EDUCATION

EASTERN MICHIGAN UNIVERSITY B.B.A.
(Feb. 1965 - June 1966)
Marketing Major:
Sales Management
Salesmanship
Merchandising
Marketing Research & Analysis
Marketing Management
Marketing Principles
Advertising
Related Courses:
Psychology of Human Relations
Creative Writing
Business Report Writing
Public Speaking
Statistics
Cumulative grade point: 3.60/4.00

UNIVERSITY OF MICHIGAN
(Sept. 1958 - Jan. 1960 & Sept. 1960 - June 1961)
Pre-business curriculum - liberal arts
Cumulative grade point: 2.20/4.00

WESTERN MICHIGAN UNIVERSITY
(Feb. 1960 - June 1960)
Pre-business curriculum - liberal arts
Cumulative grade point: 3.00/4.00

PLYMOUTH HIGH SCHOOL
(Sept. 1954 - June 1958)
College preparatory curriculum
Cumulative grade point: 2.80/4.00

Capable...

POSITION & DATES	COMPANY	JOB DESCRIPTION
Accountant Jan. 1962..	Chevrolet Motor Div., G.M.C. Willow Run Plant Ypsilanti, Michigan	Accounting-clerical: Accounts Payable General Ledger Factory Cost Analysis
Inspector Fall 1961	Chevrolet Motor Div., G.M.C. Spring & Bumper Plant Livonia, Michigan	100% inspection Chrome and raw bumpers, Mono-leaf spring
Machine Operator Fall 1961	Plymouth Stamping Co. Ann Arbor Road Plymouth, Michigan	Operate Punch and Drill Presses
Farm Laborer Summer 1961	Palmer & Sons Plymouth, Michigan	Pick, Pack and Load Sweet Corn
General Repairman Summer 1960	Western Electric Co. Sheldon Road Plymouth, Michigan	Repair and rennovation of coin-operated telephones
Sales Clerk Jr. - Sr. yrs. High School	Davis & Lent Men's Wear South Main Street Plymouth, Michigan	Wait on customers in Mens furnishings and Spurting Goods Depts.

Responsible...

MARITAL STATUS: Married 4 years
MILITARY CLASSIFICATION: 3-A

ACTIVITIES

Chairman:	Social committee, Chi Phi Fraternity, University of Michigan, Spring 1961
Co-Chairman:	Rush committee, Chi Phi Fraternity, University of Michigan, Fall 1960 - Spring 1961
Captain:	Intra-mural swimming team, University of Michigan, Fall 1958 & Fall 1961
President:	Social Fraternity pledge class, University of Michigan, Spring 1959
Representative:	Junior Inter-Fraternity Council, University of Michigan, Spring 1959
Reporter - Newscaster:	WCBN campus radio, University of Michigan, Sept. 1958 - June 1959
Disc-Jockey:	WIDR campus radio, Western Michigan University, Feb. 1960- June 1960
President:	Catholic Youth Council, Plymouth Parish, Sept. 1957 - June 1958
Student Council Representative:	Junior year of High School

REFERENCES

Dr. B. L. Martin	Chairman, Department of Marketing, Eastern Michigan University, Room 106 Welch Hall, Ypsilanti, Michigan
Mr. R. L. Miller	Associate Professor of Markering, Eastern Michigan University, Room 107C Welch Hall, Ypsilanti, Michigan
Mr. L. Brown	Associate Professor of Business Communications, Eastern Michigan University, Room 107A Welch Hall, Ypsilanti, Michigan

Available!!!

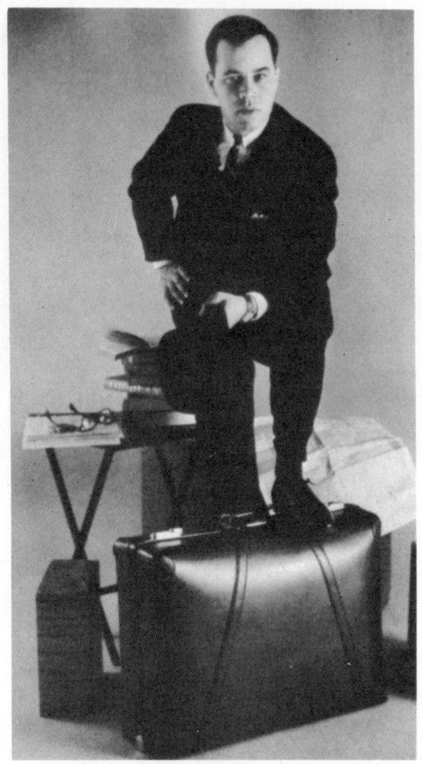

Immediately after June, 1966... no realty or property to divest, prefer beginning in Sales and Sales Promotion for ultimate development for Marketing Manager responsibilities. Will go where the job needs to be done...no geographical preference. Personal references furnished on request.

Richard V. Bennett, Jr.
9905 Westmore Avenue
Livonia, Michigan 48150
Area Code 313..Phone 427-7254

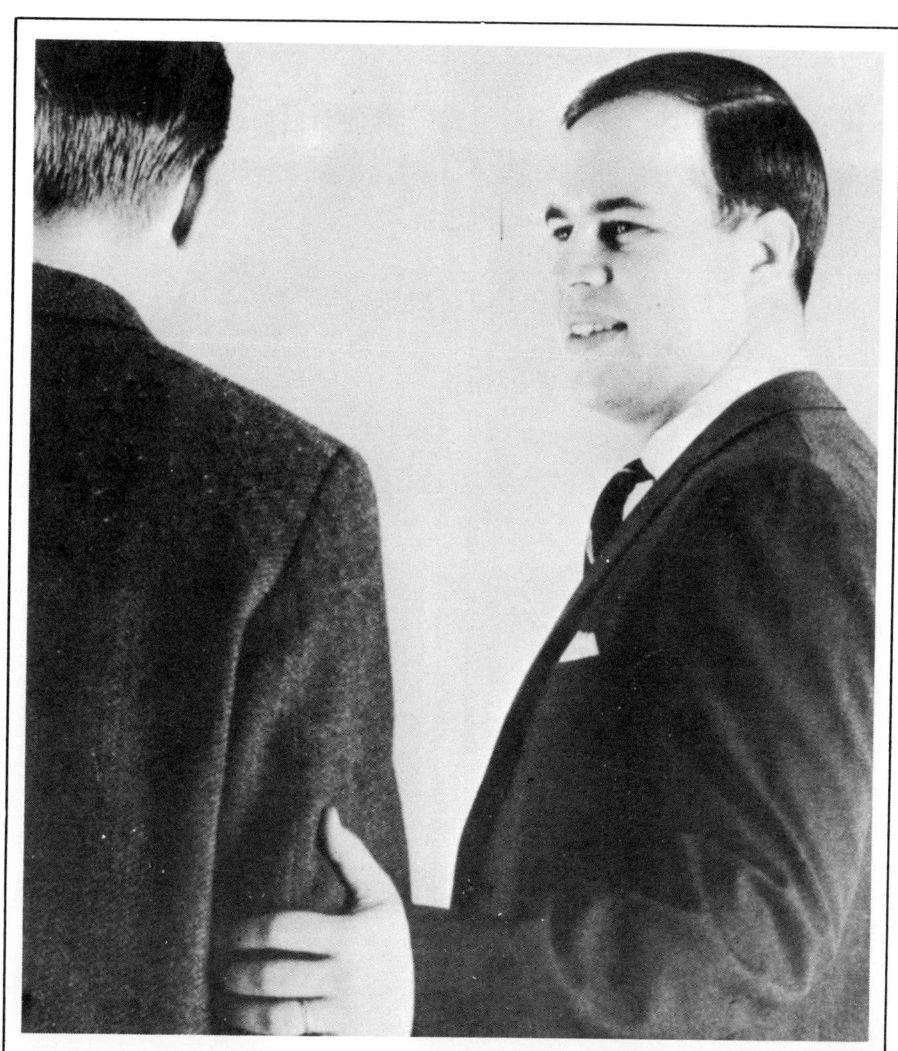

He's quite a guy!!!

longer to read. The one on these two pages, however, captures the reader's eye and holds his interest. Like Dick Bennett's punch line at the end, the opening line encourages the reader to find the answer to the question: "What is Patricia P. Bills really like?"

WHAT IS PATRICIA P. BILLS REALLY LIKE?

She might just be an ordinary housewife living at:

9261 Knolson Avenue
Livonia, Michigan 48150
(Telephone 464-2623)

She might just be an ordinary housewife and an ordinary mother of five.

She might have lived an ordinary routine life during her 13 years of married life.

E X C E P T - -

She has never been satisfied with just the ordinary things in life.

After graduation from Bethesda-Chevy Chase High School in June, 1954, she met and married a U. S. Marine (and everyone knows Marines are not just ordinary).

During the first eight years of marriage she helped her husband obtain his B.S. Degree and Teaching Certificate in History and English (June, 1963; Eastern Michigan University) and several pilot licenses, including two instructor's ratings. During this same eight years she also gave birth to three boys and two girls.

During the next five years she completed work on her own B.B.Ed. degree and received this degree and her teaching certificate in June, 1969, from Eastern Michigan University (majoring in Accounting and Typing).

A N D - -

She worked for five years (from 1953-1958) for the Vicar Camera and Hobby Shop, of Chevy Chase, Maryland, gaining a wide variety of experience in typing, inventory, bookkeeping, photofinishing, and buying and selling of photo and hobby supplies.

She has participated over the years in Girl and Boy Scout activities, Little League activities, and various church activities. She has also bowled in a league for the past four years (carrying a 157 average).

She has lived in Maryland (19 years) and Michigan (12 years) and has traveled nearly every state in the union (as well as Mexico and Canada) with her family during summer vacation trips.

M O R E - -

I N   A D D I T I O N - -

She has also managed to build up a wide variety of extraordinary friends all over the country. Friends such as:

Mr. Carroll B. Sager
7700 Maryknoll Avenue
Bethesda, Maryland 20714

(Owner and manager of the Vicar Camera and Hobby Shop)

Dr. Charles Duncan
College of Business Education
Eastern Michigan University
Ypsilanti, Michigan

(Head of the Department of Business Education at E.M.U.)

Dr. Gary H. Knapp, M.D.
23611 Goddard Road
Taylor, Michigan 48180

(Her personal physician for the past 8 years)

All these friends would be willing to recommend her for any ordinary teaching position; but, remaining true to form, she doesn't want just an ordinary teaching position. She wants one with a challenge; one with extraordinary experiences to offer, which will satisfy her yearning to tackle the extraordinary things in life, because she's not just an ordinary person.

SHE MEETS THE REQUIREMENTS !

(the above friends will verify this)

CAN YOU OFFER THE CHALLENGE ?

Through the years, students have repeatedly asked questions about creating their own résumés and have received answers to assist them. The following list of questions and answers is given in anticipation of questions you might raise when composing your résumé.

Question: How long should a résumé be?

Answer: No set length. Most employers will say, "Make it short, one page if possible." Placement officers in colleges and universities will agree. *But*—the applicants who get interviews are those who give enough information to create an interest, and that takes more than a page—usually one and one-half to two pages. It stands to reason that the more experience and education one has, the more he has to tell. However, do not try to tell everything.

Question: How should the résumé be reproduced?

Answer: Printing, Xeroxing, or other reproduction methods are acceptable. However, the letter that accompanies the résumé should be typed personally. The résumé should give the impression that it is being sent to only a selected few. Do not send carbon copies.

Question: How can I give the résumé wide exposure?

Answer: Distribute it to friends and acquaintances. Mail it with a letter of inquiry or full letter of application to selected companies. Send it to college placement offices and good employment agencies.

Question: Should I include my past salary and the salary I expect now?

Answer: No. Avoid the issue. You can discuss it when it comes up during the interview or later. Even then, be somewhat vague and general. Ask what their salary schedule pays for the job, or give a range according to what most people with your qualifications receive.

Question: What about grades?

Answer: It depends upon what they are and whether the job requires exact and specialized knowledge. For a position as a research chemist, grades would be significant; for a salesman of drug products, they would not. If your grades are average, don't mention them; if they are "B's" and "A's," you might say so.

Question: May I omit references?

Answer: Yes, providing that you write "References available on request" or "References available at the University Placement Center." Be sure to have names and addresses available.

Question: Should I state the reason for terminating my other employments?

Answer: Not always. Do so when it was for advancement or promotion, or for other interests. When it was because of conflict or a problem, don't mention it. This will come out in the interview later. Be prepared then.

Question: Do employers want you to follow the standardized format?

Answer: They want you to cover your qualifications, and they want the résumé to reflect something of you. The format also should be appropriate to the position you seek. You might use standard forms for banking, accounting, and other conservative positions, and more creative ideas for advertising, sales, and public relations.

WRITING YOUR LETTER OF APPLICATION

Your letter of application must overcome competition; out of many applicants for any one position, only a few are called for interviews. A letter showing that its writer has an orderly mind and can present information completely, logically, and persuasively paves the way for that all-important interview. There is no set pattern for a letter of application, since each letter responds to a different problem situation. It behooves the applicant to think over his qualifications and to proceed seriously.

Sell Your Qualifications

Because every application letter is a sales letter, it must follow the principles of all effective sales letters. At the outset it must attract the *attention* of its reader, the prospective employer, and arouse in him an *interest* in your qualifications and in your value as a prospective employee. Your letter must create a *desire* by presenting facts about your qualifications—your education, your experience, and your personal data—that will show that you can do something for the company. You must *convince* your reader that you are the man for the position and that you are sincere and dependable. The *action* sought is the interview. If the letter results in an interview, it has accomplished its job. This means that you have succeeded in selling your qualifications and yourself to your prospective employer. It's up to you to convince him further at the interview, so that you will get the job.

Locate Employers Who Need You

One good way to get job leads is by talking with friends, relatives, and acquaintances. Let as many people as possible know that you are seeking employment and what your qualifications and objectives are. Many times friends or relatives will know of possible openings or opportunities and can give you information about the companies where they work. There are also placement bureaus and employment agencies to assist you. Be sure to register and file your qualifications with your college or university placement center; it serves as a clearing house for company representatives who interview, on campus, graduating seniors and students who are applicants for summer or part-time employment. The Civil Service Commission and state employment agencies, whose services are free, are also good sources for job opportunities. Private employment agencies charge fees, but they know of many opportunities and are in business to place qualified applicants.

You should also look for job opportunities by reading newspapers, trade journals, association and professional journals, and even general news magazines. They not only carry job want ads, but also give news of any planned expansion or development of companies—which would indicate job opportunities. Nothing takes the place of application letters sent directly to companies where you would like to work and that may have suitable openings. The sources for names and information about companies for this purpose are directories, such as those prepared by chambers of commerce, manufacturers' associations, or state industrial commissions. Most libraries will have *Moody's Manuals,* Standard & Poor's *Corporation Records, Thomas' Register,* and other guides that you may also consult.

Decide on Your Approach

There are two situations in which you should write an application letter: when there is a known vacancy in a company, and when you do not know if there is an opening now, but would like to work for the company if there is an opening later. These are called *solicited* and *unsolicited applications.* In solicited applications, you may be asked to apply for a certain position through a want ad, a personal notification, an announcement, or an employment agency. There is a job open and you know quite a bit about its requirements. You know the company (except in a blind ad) and the location. There is competition with other applicants. Perhaps you don't meet all the requirements but have other qualifications to offset your weaknesses. In unsolicited applications, you make the application without knowing whether or not openings are available. You are willing to take a chance. There is less competition among applicants and you are unhampered by the requirements of an advertisement; accordingly, you can give yourself a bigger buildup for the position you want.

The situation determines your approach. It should be quite simple and direct in the solicited situation. Let the reader know where you found out about the opening and what you want. This will get his attention, for it identifies you with the opening. For instance, you might say:

> When I was talking yesterday with Dr. Claude Shell, the head of the Management Department at Eastern Michigan University, he mentioned that you were seeking young college graduates for your management trainee program.

or

> I am very much interested in the position as cost accountant for which you advertised in *The Wall Street Journal,* April 23, 197–.

or

> Please consider my qualifications for the position of administrative secretary that you advertised for in *Today's Secretary,* April 197–.

These illustrations are direct and to the point. They identify you with the position the reader is seeking to fill.

The psychological approach for the unsolicited letter is much more difficult to handle. You must create your own point of contact and justify your writing to this particular individual or company. Think about yourself, the job, and the company before you write. Ask yourself why you selected this firm and what you have to offer your potential employer. Interest and knowledge beget more interest and knowledge. Show a knowledge of the company and an interest in working for it. The reader will in all likelihood reciprocate. He will be impressed by your awareness of what is going on and your interest. For instance, you might say:

> Columbia Records produces pleasurable listening with some of the entertainment industry's most talented artists. Because Columbia Records is dynamic and offers the public the first in entertainment, I would like to become a part of Columbia's "Professional Team."
>
> My objective through college was to prepare myself by majoring in speech and broadcasting and minoring in business administration for representing a recording company in the area of public relations.

or

> Your program of management development has launched many a college graduate on a successful business career in the Detroit area. When you choose trainees from this year's graduating seniors, please consider my qualifications.

or

> "Success in auditing requires more than technical efficiency; it requires the ability to deal with others in cooperation and harmony; it requires initiative and adaptability."
>
> The above is part of a speech given by Mr. Kenneth Paul McKnight as guest speaker at the Accounting Club meeting, University of Illinois, in April. This talk interested me very much in applying for a position as junior accountant in your firm.

In these illustrations, the applicant finds a common ground with the reader; the openings attract his attention and interest and simplify the transition to what follows.

Discuss and Emphasize Your Major Qualifications

Because the résumé has presented all the data about you and your qualifications, you can be selective in the application letter and discuss your major qualifications, using your judgment as to choice and treatment. You will want to match yours with those the job calls for and those the employer is looking for. Talk about any of your college work that is pertinent to the job. Include some of the courses you have studied, why, and how they contributed to your education and will help you on the job. Write directly about what you can do and want to do. Wouldn't you consider an applicant who is enthusiastic, sincere, interested in his work, and adaptable? If you can decide on some of the main points that fit the employer's needs, you can discuss them too.

Convince him with specific details rather than general statements.

Don't say, for instance, "I have leadership ability." Instead, mention offices you have held and work you may have accomplished on committees. Specific discussion is proof by performance. Don't say, "You need a man with ambition." Show that you are ambitious by what you have done and accomplished while a college student, and mention your job objectives and plans for further development.

Discuss your work experience. Can you work with and without supervision? What have you done to indicate that you can get along well with people, think up ideas, reason to conclusions, and express yourself orally and in writing? Examine the following excerpts for the ways in which the applicants discuss their qualifications:

> While working last summer for Anchor Steel Corporation, I gained valuable experience in applying the fundamentals of accounting, such as in checking invoices to see that they agreed with accounts payable, working with company inventory, and completing weekly statements. The accountants were helpful in letting me observe such accounting procedures as journalizing, closing the books, and preparing financial statements.

and

> My duties entailed being responsible for six student salesmen, coordinating WHUR activities with university functions, making budgets for purchasing new equipment, and finally getting the month-end billings out to advertising customers. These complex duties helped me to gain knowledge of the radio station's organizational structure and functioning.

In your discussion of your qualifications you should be sure to make these points:

1. You want the position.
2. Your education fits you for the job.
3. Your experience fits you for the job.
4. Your personal data and background fit you for the job.

Then you are ready to compose the ending to your letter.

Request an Interview

Application letters accompanied by data sheets rarely obtain a job by themselves. However, when they are effective, they will obtain an interview. End your letter with a request for an interview, or at least express a willingness to come in for one. You can adapt the action ending of a sales letter to the application situation:

1. Request action.
2. Make action easy.
3. Motivate for action.

A simple request for an interview might get one—but only if the letter has in its entirety interested, convinced, and motivated the reader so that he wants to interview the applicant. Here you might suggest a time and place and indicate that you are available and interested. But don't be presumptuous or "pushy." For instance, you might write:

> I plan to be visiting in Chicago between semesters and would be glad to arrange a time at your convenience for an interview.

Do not write:

> Between semesters I shall be in Chicago and will come for an interview at 9:30 a.m. Monday.

You might also write:

> I would be pleased to arrange an interview at a time most convenient for you.

or

> I should like an opportunity to start and to advance on my own merits. May I have this opening with J. S. Smith and Sons? May I come for an interview soon after May 29?

Let us now turn to some letters of application, pages 376–77, and consider how the writers have sold their qualifications. The first one accompanied the data sheet on pages 361–62. The letter from Gerard A. Pound has an excellent flow of ideas and development of a central selling point. Both discuss the writer's qualifications, get the reader's attention and interest, and motivate him to grant an interview.

CONDUCTING YOUR INTERVIEW

Even if your résumé and letter of application were effective enough to win you a personal interview, you can't sit back and take the attitude: "I've got it made." Prepare yourself ahead of time, for the interview can make or break your chances for the position. The interview is a meeting of the job prospect and the company representative so that a personal appraisal can be made. It should be enjoyable and pleasant, and you should look forward to it with eagerness.

Prepare Yourself Ahead of Time

One way to prepare yourself is to know something about the company. Do a little research. Find out the history of the company; the locations of its various plants, offices, or stores; information about its products and services; what its growth and development have been; and

15112 Payne Court
Dearborn, Michigan
January 23, 1969

Mr. T. J. Reynolds
American Life Insurance Company
140 Park Street
Detroit, Michigan

Dear Mr. Reynolds:

Your firm, Michigan's only agent-owned company and a very youthful one, has expanded rapidly due to your wise choice of assets. Your company has invested wisely to reach such a large volume in a short period of time. I would like to contribute to your growth in sales and personnel.

While obtaining my Bachelor of Business Administration degree from Eastern Michigan University, I centered my education toward a sales position with a reputable life insurance company such as yours. In pursuing my education I took courses such as General Insurance, Life and Health Insurance, Human Relations, and many salesmanship courses, so I have gained not only knowledge of insurance but have also learned sales technique and how to deal with people. In addition to college courses I have completed two correspondence courses in life insurance during my senior year, which enabled me to receive a Life Underwriting License in the state of Michigan in July 1968.

After receiving my license, I became commissioned with three life insurance companies within a four-month period. Through my sales and correspondence with these companies, I have gained much experience in the sales field as well as in the operation of other companies.

I have prepared myself well for the position of a life underwriting agent, as the enclosed résumé points out. I would like to offer my service to your company so that we may grow together.

I can be in Detroit almost anytime during the latter part of next month, and will be happy to arrange an interview with you at your convenience.

Sincerely yours,

Allen G. Jarosz

enc. personal résumé

how its future prospects and plans look. Learn something about the company's policies, particularly the personnel policies on hiring, fringe benefits, salaries, and promotions. This will give you something to talk about other than yourself and will show your knowledge and interest. It will also enable you to ask questions. There are a number of publications you can check in researching a company:

Annual reports of the company
Careers in Business annual
Moody's Manuals
Fitch Corporation Manuals
MacRae's Blue Book
College Placement Annual

209 Best Hall
Eastern Michigan University
Ypsilanti, Michigan
March 28, 197-

Mr. Bradley J. Lawton
Personnel Director
Star Cutter Company
30460 Grand River Avenue
Farmington, Michigan

Dear Mr. Lawton:

Your program of management development with an eye toward youth has launched many a college graduate to a successful business career. When you choose trainees from this year's graduating seniors, please consider my qualifications.

My years at Eastern Michigan University, besides affording me a hard-earned BBA degree, have instilled in me both a desire to work and the leadership capabilities required for a managerial position.

Although a General Business major, I have been exposed to a good many courses strictly management-oriented, such as Business Policy, Human Relations in Business, and Principles of Management. Aside from these particular courses, my activities in other academic and social areas have helped develop the leadership qualities necessary for a position in management. For two years I was a Resident Advisor at Best Residence Hall where my duties consisted solely of dealing with people. My advisory position placed me in charge of a group of young men whom I not only counseled and disciplined, but also helped to organize their student government and social and athletic endeavors. From this position I learned many things about dealing with people on a group and individual level.

Also, while a member of Delta Sigma Phi, social fraternity, I was Public Relations Director and Rush Chairman. Both positions demanded leadership and social understanding.

Going hand in hand with my college experiences are my summer work experiences. From my association with many types of people and situations at various labor levels, I have gained an insight into the worker's mind and a feeling of empathy for his problems. Gaining an insight into labor's problems could prove invaluable in a managerial position.

The ability to get along with people, coupled with my college and work experiences, furnish me with qualities necessary for your management development program. May I arrange an interview any afternoon after 2 p.m. at your convenience?

Sincerely yours,

Gerard Alan Pound

Dun & Bradstreet *Reference Book*

Standard & Poor's *Corporation Records*

You might also secure information from friends or acquaintances who already work for the company.

Find out what you can about the person who is to interview you. Try to discover some points of common interest or a common background so that you can share your knowledge and experiences. Perhaps you went to the same school or are a member of the same fraternity or other organization. All this will show that you are human, personable, and able to carry on a conversation.

Review your education, experience, and other qualifications. Think of them in terms of the company's needs and the job qualifications. You will want to be prepared to answer any question that might be asked about you and your qualifications.

It seems superfluous to call attention to the need for appropriate dress and cleanliness, which is generally taken for granted; but with today's long-haired students and "anything goes" dress, it is well to be aware that employers still look for clean, appropriately dressed, well-mannered young people.

Men

1. Wear a clean, neat, well-kept suit.
2. Wear a shirt and tie.
3. Have your hair cut and combed.
4. Shave.
5. Shine your shoes.
6. Trim and clean your nails.

Women

1. Use makeup conservatively.
2. Wear sensible shoes.
3. Be conservative in your choice of jewelry.
4. Have neat, combed hair.
5. Wear a dress or suit that is appropriate for the job.

Be Effective During the Interview

Since you have a definite appointment, arrive at the place of the interview a few minutes in advance. Allow enough time so that you won't be late. State your business to the receptionist or secretary briefly and to the point. When you are ushered into the office of the interviewer, be alert and friendly. Greet him by name; identify yourself promptly; and shake hands naturally, firmly, and with warmth. Don't hang up your coat until asked to do so. Remain standing until you are asked to sit. Let the interviewer take the lead; you take your cues from him.

During the interview be alert at all times, and answer questions promptly. When the interviewer gives you the opportunity, you should tell him, honestly and sincerely, why you want to work for the company and why you want to work in this particular capacity. Sell him indirectly on the idea that you are the one for the job. You might call attention to any of your special skills or qualifications that he may have overlooked. You may ask about training courses and opportunities offered by the company. A few interviewers like to ask a general question at the start, like, "Tell me about yourself," or "Why are you interested in this company?" Tell the interviewer that you are seeking a job in a certain company operation and want to progress into a more advanced phase. Show him that you are interested, and be as specific as you can.

Sit up in the chair; be relaxed and a good listener. Look at him directly and smile at appropriate occasions. Most interviews are conducted in a question-and-answer pattern. Your ability to answer intelligently and quickly is of importance. One favorite question is, "What do you intend to be doing ten years from now?" This is to test your ability to plan and think ahead.

Most interviews last around thirty minutes. When your time is almost up, don't continue talking and talk yourself out of a job. Be alert for a sign from the interviewer that the session is almost at an end. Sum up your talk and stop. Thank him for his time and consideration.

The interviewer will rate you on:

1. Your personal appearance
2. Your social characteristics
3. Your business characteristics
4. Your mental ability
5. Your ability to express yourself
6. Your job qualifications

Follow Up the Interview

What you do afterward depends upon what happened during the interview and what decisions were reached by the interviewer and the company. To keep the door open and your name before the employer, you might send a brief typewritten note about your case, as:

2729 Oakwood Avenue
Chicago, Illinois
May 31, 197-

Mr. John L. Franks
Roberts Manufacturing Company
822 North Wabash Avenue
Chicago, Illinois

Dear Mr. Franks:

On May 19, I discussed with you the possibility of a position as junior cost accountant in your company.

I am still interested in working for you and would like to know your decision as soon as possible.

Should you need any additional information, please write or telephone me.

Thank you for your consideration.

Very truly yours,

Mark A. Stephenson

The follow-up should come a week to ten days after the interview. Sometimes a telephone call can be made. Although it is not necessary, a thank-you note is a goodwill gesture. Simply thank the person for his time and effort. Mention that you profited or gained something from the interview, and indicate your further interest in the job.

Suppose that you are sent a job offer following the interview, and you have decided not to accept, for in the meantime you have accepted another offer. How would you reply? Follow the rules for composing a refusal letter. Do not place the negative refusal first in the letter; instead, begin with something favorable or agreeable to find a common ground and create goodwill. Give a reason for the refusal (if there is one other than money). Be constructive and build goodwill in your ending. A brief note similar to the following one might be used:

Dear Mr. Smithson:

Working for you as your executive secretary would be a pleasure.

Since I did not hear from you, however, following the interview ten days ago, I have accepted a position with Roberts and Donalds Manufacturing Company as secretary to their vice-president, Research and Development.

This will likewise be a challenging position for me and should provide me with some interesting experience.

I appreciate your consideration of my qualifications and the interest you showed at the interview. You do have a progressive firm and cooperative employees. I would have enjoyed working with you.

Very truly yours,

Of course, you may accept the job offer. Here follow the basic pattern for a letter of acceptance. Present the good news first, be appreciative, and show your enthusiasm for the job. You might also confirm the offer and state when you will be able to begin work. If you have any need for information or help, it is appropriate to ask for it here.

Dear Mr. Smithson:

I shall be happy to accept your offer to work as executive secretary for $600 per month. After our interview, I have thought how fortunate I would be to be working for such a considerate and thoughtful person as you.

The responsibilities will be very challenging, and I shall put forth every effort to meet the high standards expected.

Since I'll be out of school May 31, I shall be glad to begin work after the following week, Monday, June 10. I am looking forward to putting into practice what I have learned.

Very truly yours,

SUMMARY

Obtaining a job requires that you sell your ability and personality to a prospective employer. It means persuading him that you are the man for the job. Your résumé, your letter of application, and the personal interview will help you to accomplish this objective.

A résumé presents a complete outline of your qualifications and is generally sent along with your letter of application. It gives data on your education, experience, and personal characteristics. The résumé should be arranged so that it will not be like a hundred others. It should reflect your creative ability and your ability to organize and express yourself effectively; in writing it, you must consider what the job requires, what the employer wants to know, and what you have to offer.

The letter of application is a sales letter and as such follows the steps of selling: attract attention; arouse interest; create desire; convince; and motivate action. Letters of application are solicited or unsolicited, depending upon whether or not a known vacancy exists. The situation helps you to determine your approach and opening. In the solicited letter, attract attention by identifying your source of information and your relation to the position. In unsolicited letters, attract the reader's attention by indicating a knowledge and interest in the company. Look for a common ground with the prospective employer.

Make the transition from the opening paragraph to a major qualification, then discuss and emphasize your best points. Use specific details for support and in the place of general statements. Emphasize what you can do. Convince the reader that you are qualified by relating your education, experience, etc., to the job you are seeking. End with a request for an interview and make it easy for him to arrange one.

If your résumé and letter of application are successful, you will be called for an interview. Prepare yourself ahead of time. Inform yourself about the company and the job. Learn something about the interviewer; review your qualifications. Be on time, cordial, and at ease. Let the interviewer set the tone and direct the questions and discussions. Answer his questions honestly and sincerely. When the opportunity arises, you can ask him questions. Be aware of the time and end the interview at a sign from the interviewer. Thank him and leave.

You might follow up the interview with a thank-you note or a letter of inquiry indicating that you are still interested. This should be done a week to ten days after the interview.

The material presented in this chapter should be used for reference when you apply for a summer job or a permanent position near the time of your graduation. Best wishes for success in getting your desired job!

FURTHER READING

Aurner, Robert R., and M. Philip Wolf, *Effective Communication in Business,* 5th ed. Cincinnati: South-Western Publishing Co., 1967. See especially Chapters 12 and 13.

Career booklets on about fifty different careers, New York Life Insurance Company, New York, N. Y.

Damerst, William A., *Resourceful Business Communication.* New York: Harcourt, Brace & World, Inc., 1966. See especially Chapters 19 and 20.

Dawe, Jessamon, and William J. Lord, Jr., *Functional Business Communication.* Englewood Cliffs, N. J.: Prentice-Hall, Inc., 1968. See especially Chapter 5.

Devlin, Frank J., *Business Communication.* Homewood, Ill.: Richard D. Irwin, Inc., 1968. See especially Chapter 15.

"Getting the Right Job." Cleveland, Ohio: The Glidden Paint Company, 1950.

"How to Get the Job." Chicago: Economic Institute, 1950.

Menning, J. H., and C. W. Wilkinson, *Communicating Through Letters and Reports,* 4th ed. Homewood, Ill.: Richard D. Irwin, Inc., 1967. See especially Chapters 11 and 12.

Wells, Walter, *Communication in Business.* Belmont, Calif.: Wadsworth Publishing Company, Inc., 1968. See especially Chapter 12.

"Your Future Is What You Make It." New York: National Association of Manufacturers, 1950.

"Your Job Interview." New York: New York Life Insurance Company.

QUESTIONS AND PROBLEMS

1. If your library does not have the booklets listed under Further Reading, send for them from the companies, and after discussing them in class, place them in your school library. "Your Job Interview" is reprinted in the Damerst text.
2. Invite the placement officer of your college to speak before your class. He might distribute and discuss the data sheet required by his office, or speak about the company recruiters who interview students on campus —their likes and dislikes, what they look for in applicants, etc.
3. Invite a personnel representative from a company to speak to the class, or formulate a panel of three company representatives. You might have them speak on the résumé, application letter, or interview. Their ideas and comments should supplement the suggestions in your text.
4. Collect and evaluate a number of application letters and data sheets. Pick out what is effective and what is weak. Perhaps your instructor will assign a memorandum report on your conclusions or form a student panel for oral presentation in class. Several of the better letters might be displayed on a bulletin board.

5. Read and discuss surveys or reports on what employers want in letters of application. Two surveys were made by Dr. Charles E. Peck, University of Washington, Seattle, and were published as articles:

   "The Follow-up Letter in Job Presentation," *The ABWA Bulletin*, The American Business Writing Association, March 1963, pp. 22–30.
   "Qualities Employers Look for in a College Graduate," *Collegiate News and Views*, December 1958, pp. 13–16.

6. Conduct a survey of personnel directors or other hiring or interviewing officials in companies in your area for "what they look for in considering a college graduate." Present your findings in a written or oral report.

7. In writing application letters, some sound advice to follow is to relate your courses and educational facts, experiences, and activities to the job for which you are applying, with the emphasis on what you can do. The following isolated sentences violate this suggestion. Point out why they are weak and rewrite them:
   a. I believe my background has supplemented the principles acquired in my courses of study.
   b. Courses in industrial corporate management and personnel administration have given me a basic understanding of administrative problems.
   c. I shall appreciate an interview at any date that suits your convenience.
   d. This does show that I have come into contact with many types of work and the situations that arise in each type.
   e. I have studied courses in accounting, industrial management, and economics.
   f. I would like to have you consider my application for this job.
   g. I feel that I fulfill the necessary requirements for the job.
   h. I am industrious, reliable, and honest.
   i. I am a veteran of the Vietnam conflict.

8. Here are some blundering sentences taken from actual application letters. Why are they blundering? Rewrite them.
   a. I once had a stenographic position and which I held five years.
   b. I am a Democrat, but I have no objection to changing my politics.
   c. I am meticulous about my appearance and scrupulously honest.
   d. I was popular on the campus.
   e. Soliciting a brief interview, I beg to remain . . .
   f. A party told me that there is a splendid vacancy.
   g. I have been versatile enough to change positions often.
   h. I want to get married next June.
   i. Your business will thrive if you employ me.
   j. I don't want to take up too much of your time, seeing that you are a busy man, with a thousand and one tasks for every minute in the day, like most other executives.
   k. I can see you next Friday at twelve o'clock.
   l. Won't you please give me a position?
   m. I shall expect $800 a month.

n. I am seeking a position as a salesman. I was a member of the Philological Society in college.
o. I don't know what I'm worth.
p. The reason why I am writing is because I read your ad.
q. Professor A. T. Grant, of Fairmont University, wants me to ask you for a position.
r. I have never been late for work. I don't use tobacco or intoxicants. I am willing to work overtime.
s. I didn't do well in college, but, then, I didn't try.
t. I should like a position as stenographer. I took the commercial course in high school and was elected May Queen in my senior year.

9. Assume that the spring semester is well under way and you want to seek a job for the summer. Write the application letter and data sheet you would send out. This may be an answer to an advertisement in the paper or an unsolicited prospecting letter to a firm for which you would like to work.
10. Assume that you are nearing graduation and write an unsolicited application letter and data sheet. Assume that you have completed your courses by the time you write. You might even date the letter and data sheet to that time. Apply for the position and type of work you are or will be interested in and qualified for at that time.
11. Assume the roles of both a prospective employer and an applicant during an interview. Conduct the interview. A data sheet can be used as a basis for the questioning.

Chapter Twelve

AN OVERVIEW: TOWARD A BROADER PERSPECTIVE

At the beginning of this book its purposes were set forth, and you were asked to take stock of your goals and objectives in studying business communication. The book has tried to increase your skills in several ways:

1. It has sought primarily to help you develop communicative power as a basis for your further professional development.
2. It has presented the basic elements, principles, and practices underlying all business communication.
3. It has considered not only skills and techniques, but also ways of thinking and of understanding others in order to communicate effectively with them.
4. Particular attention was given to the thinking and creative processes involved in writing letters, memorandums, and reports.

Through your confrontation with communicating situations and the practice you have had in writing various pieces of communication, you should have improved your skills and abilities in communicating and increased your understanding of human relations and communicating situations. This book should have thus stimulated you to think creatively, logically, and critically, and helped you to express yourself clearly, interestingly, and persuasively.

Now that you have come to the last chapter, it would be worthwhile to take stock of the objectives you set forth at the beginning of the book and to think back over what you have accomplished.

WHAT HAVE YOU ACCOMPLISHED?

The following checklist should call attention to whether or not you have accomplished the goals you established for yourself at the beginning of this book:

	Fully	To some degree	Not at all
1. Do I understand the communication process, its importance, and its role in a business enterprise?	_____	_____	_____
2. Have I learned and am I able to apply the principles of communication?	_____	_____	_____
3. Have I developed the power to inform and persuade others through language?	_____	_____	_____
4. Do I understand human nature and the role of communication in human relations?	_____	_____	_____
5. Have I developed skill in handling communication problems through writing letters and reports?	_____	_____	_____
6. Have I developed the ability to gather, organize, and evaluate facts and ideas, to reach conclusions and recommendations?	_____	_____	_____
7. Do I understand and am I able to use form, style, and tone in writing effectively, especially business letters and reports?	_____	_____	_____

This brings us to the purpose of this chapter in relation to the book and to you. Its goals are to lead you toward a broader perspective of an area of business communication you might have forgotten while increasing your writing skills from day to day; and to help you analyze your own abilities and their development so that you can answer the question—"Where do we go from here?"

COMMUNICATION AS A TOOL OF MANAGEMENT

A manager gets things done through people; he plans for action to accomplish results; he makes decisions and solves problems; and he influences the behavior and attitudes of others. No matter how sound his ideas may be or how well reasoned his decisions, they can be effective only when they are communicated to others and achieve a desired action or reaction. It is for this reason that communication has become the most valuable tool management can possess, and that the responsibility for maintaining an environment conducive to communicating and to keeping communication lines or channels open rests in the hands of management.

Management not only communicates with others but also, as indicated in the following figure, becomes the receiver of communication. It is only through the give-and-take of a two-way flow of communication that management can effectively manage.

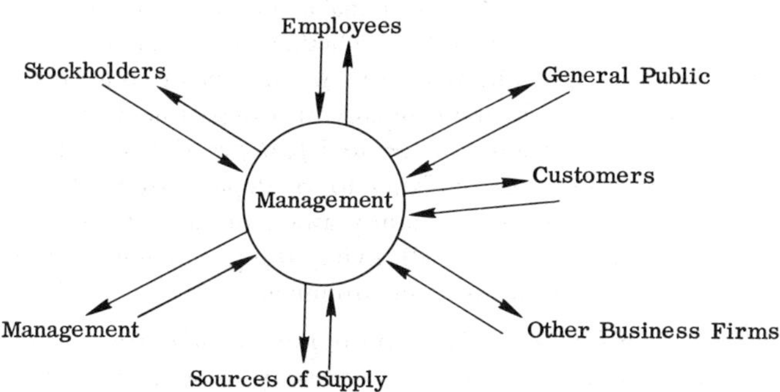

Recognizing the importance of communication and its relation to management, the American Management Association conducts executive communication courses in strategic cities throughout the United States and, in other seminars and courses for management, deals with communication as an important aspect of management. In these sessions, the AMA helps executives to improve their skills as managers by improving their skills of communication—with their superiors, subordinates, and associates. The AMA maintains that how well one manages may depend in large part upon how well one communicates through attitudes and actions as well as words, and it has set forth the following "Ten Commandments for Good Communication":

1. *Seek to clarify your ideas before communicating.*
   The more systematically we analyze the problem or idea to be communicated, the clearer it becomes. This is the first step toward effective communication. Many communications fail because of inadequate planning. Good planning must consider the goals and attitudes of those who will receive the communication and those who will be affected by it.
2. *Examine the true purpose of each communication.*
   Before you communicate, ask yourself what you *really* want to accomplish with your message—obtain information, initiate action, change another person's attitude? Identify your most important goal and then adapt your language, tone, and total approach to serve that

specific objective. Don't try to accomplish too much with each communication. The sharper the focus of your message the greater its chances of success.

3. *Consider the total physical and human setting whenever you communicate.*
Meaning and intent are conveyed by more than words alone. Many other factors influence the overall impact of a communication, and the manager must be sensitive to the total setting in which he communicates. Consider, for example, your sense of *timing*—i.e., the circumstances under which you make an announcement or render a decision; the *physical setting*—whether you communicate in private, for example, or otherwise; the *social climate* that pervades work relationships within the company or a department and sets the tone of its communications; *custom and past practice*—the degree to which your communication conforms to, or departs from, the expectations of your audience. Be constantly aware of the total setting in which you communicate. Like all living things, communication must be capable of adapting to its environment.

4. *Consult with others, where appropriate, in planning communications.*
Frequently it is desirable or necessary to seek the participation of others in planning a communication or developing the facts on which to base it. Such consultation often helps to lend additional insight and objectivity to your message. Moreover, those who have helped you plan your communication will give it their active support.

5. *Be mindful, while you communicate, of the overtones as well as the basic content of your message.*
Your tone of voice, your expression, your apparent receptiveness to the responses of others—all have tremendous impact on those you wish to reach. Frequently overlooked, the subtleties of communication often affect a listener's reaction to a message even more than its basic content. Similarly, your choice of language—particularly your awareness of the fine shades of meaning and emotion in the words you use—predetermines in large part the reactions of your listeners.

6. *Take the opportunity, when it arises, to convey something of help or value to the receiver.*
Consideration of the other person's interests and needs—the habit of trying to look at things from his point of view—will frequently point up opportunities to convey something of immediate benefit or long-range value to him. People on the job are most responsive to the manager whose messages take their own interests into account.

7. *Follow up your communication.*
Our best efforts at communication may be wasted, and we may never know whether we have succeeded in expressing our true meaning and intent, if we do not follow up to see how well we have put our message across. This you can do by asking questions, by encouraging the receiver to express his reactions, by follow-up contacts, by subsequent review of performance. Make certain that every important

communication has a "feedback" so that complete understanding and appropriate action result.

8. *Communicate for tomorrow as well as today.*
   While communications may be aimed primarily at meeting the demands of an immediate situation, they must be planned with the past in mind if they are to maintain consistency in the receiver's view; but, most important of all, they must be consistent with long-range interests and goals. For example, it is not easy to communicate frankly on such matters as poor performance or the shortcomings of a loyal subordinate—but postponing disagreeable communications makes them more difficult in the long run and is actually unfair to your subordinates and your company.
9. *Be sure your actions support your communications.*
   In the final analysis, the most persuasive kind of communication is not what you *say* but what you *do*. When a man's actions or attitudes contradict his words, we tend to discount what he has said. For every manager this means that good supervisory practices—such as clear assignment of responsibility and authority, fair rewards for effort, and sound policy enforcement—serve to communicate more than all the gifts of oratory.
10. *Last, but by no means least: Seek not only to be understood but to understand—be a good listener.*
    When we start talking we often cease to listen—in that larger sense of being attuned to the other person's unspoken reactions and attitudes. Even more serious is the fact that we are all guilty, at times, of inattentiveness when others are attempting to communicate to us. Listening is one of the most important, most difficult—and most neglected—skills in communication. It demands that we concentrate not only on the explicit meanings another person is expressing, but on the implicit meanings, unspoken words, and undertones that may be far more significant. Thus we must learn to listen with the inner ear if we are to know the inner man.[1]

The head of every company wants his organization to function efficiently. Both management and employees must work together toward common interests. Development of loyalties, favorable attitudes, respect, and cooperation is essential for efficient operation and for making profits. Informed personnel contribute to the accomplishment of these goals. Customer and public relations are also essential for the life of the firm, and communication is helpful in building goodwill and selling the company and its products. As mentioned in an earlier chapter, communication functions in three areas:

1. Employee communication
2. Intramanagement communication
3. Customer and public communication

[1]© 1955 by the American Management Association, Inc. Reprinted by permission of the publisher.

To have effective communication, a company must have a definite policy concerning the way it will treat and communicate with the employees and management in the organization and with others outside the firm.

ESTABLISHING A COMMUNICATION POLICY

A policy is a general statement of principles. It presents guidelines with which managers can make decisions and solve the problems that arise in carrying out the functions of management. It also sets the boundaries or limits within which choices and effective decisions may be made. Look at the following statement of an oil corporation's policy on employee and management communication:

I. *Need for a Policy*

Employee attitudes and resulting performances are improved when employees are well informed about company affairs and how they affect them as individuals, and when all levels of management create and maintain a receptive climate for the upward transmission of employee ideas, suggestions, and opinions.

A policy is needed to guide managers in establishing throughout the corporation the climate and the channels necessary to maintain a consistent, two-way flow of effective communication—communication that will not depend on varying interpretations by managers of its desirability or on other extraneous factors.

II. *Statement of Policy*

It is an established Policy of Acme Oil Corporation:

A. To promote a better understanding that the personal objectives of employees are closely related to the success of the company, by actively providing employees with timely, direct, pertinent, and appropriate information on:

1. Objectives, plans, and operations of the Corporation,
2. Developments affecting our business and its employees, and
3. Other matters of interest or concern to employees, including the basic economics of how private business enterprise operates in a free society.

B. To place on line management the responsibility to maintain, at local level, active and regular employee and management communication programs.

C. To communicate directly by corporate and line publications and to supplement them appropriately by other oral and written media; e.g., management clubs, meetings, bulletin boards, employee letters, etc.

D. To insure that, whenever practicable, employees first learn of important matters that affect them and their jobs through internal channels rather than through external sources.

E. To regard employee ideas, opinions, and suggestions for improving operations as an important corporate asset; to provide a uniform upward communication program—including specifically the establishment of a uniformly administered, formal corporate suggestion plan that will provide awards to employees for usable suggestions.

III. *Delegation of Responsibilities*

A. *Staff, Office, Group, Division, and Plant Heads*:
Establish and maintain effective communication programs for employees under their respective direction.

B. *Personnel Office*:

1. Provide interpretation of this Policy, and develop procedures and technical instructions to implement this Policy.
2. Review communication programs for their adequacy, and report periodically to local and corporate management.
3. Provide communication services to Plants, Divisions, and Staffs.
4. Establish oral and written media as necessary to create or encourage an effective, two-way flow of pertinent, direct communication among all employees or special groups of employees.

It is readily apparent that Acme's policy on internal communication arose out of need, objectives, and problems that occurred. The focal point was to examine goals and objectives, beliefs and philosophy, principles and their application—all in terms of decisions to be made in the process of communicating. This policy is directly responsive to many of the communication needs identified in management communication surveys.

Seeking to point up weaknesses in the company and to find areas where improvements could be made, West Penn Power Company, Greensburg, Pennsylvania, had a management survey made that pointed out opportunities for changes, several relating specifically to communication. A communication policy was formulated to help the supervisory group develop more skill in communicating within itself and with nonsupervisory employees—working toward overall job performance and efficiency. Conferences were held on two topics:

1. Keeping people informed on matters affecting their jobs
2. Keeping people informed on their personal progress on the job

Prior to the conferences the company distributed background material to be used in discussing communication. The outline that follows indicates the thinking that went on prior to establishing a communication policy and points out numerous features that belong in almost any communication policy.

Outline of Background Material for Conference Discussions

I. West Penn policy on communication
II. Nature and importance of keeping people informed
  A. Reasons for communicating
    1.
    2.
    3.
  B. Elements of communication
  C. Communication as a two-way process
III. Ways and means of communicating (media)
  A. Face to face
  B. In writing
  C. By implication
IV. Roadblocks to communication
  A. Boss-consciousness (status)
  B. Selfish interests
  C. Lack of sincerity
  D. Differences in experience
  E. Language problems
  F. Tendency to evaluate
  G. Other barriers
V. Doing a better job of keeping people informed
VI. The payoff

West Penn met three requirements of good management by the way it went about establishing a communication policy: people were informed; they contributed ideas; and they actively participated. West Penn also recognized some of the barriers to communication and how they might be overcome. For any program of communication to be effective in a given company, there must exist an understanding of communication barriers and how to eliminate them, overcome them, or prevent their happening. In fact, many barriers will never arise if management is alert to what it is doing and to efficient ways of using the communication process for getting things done through people.

OVERCOMING COMMUNICATION BARRIERS

Communication barriers fall into several categories: organizational, linguistic, psychological, and managerial. An ineffective flow of communication between management and workers is basically the result of the organizational structure of the plant. Language difficulties can exist between well-educated and poorly educated people, or if people do not say what they mean, or if they do not have consideration for the receiver. Psychological barriers show themselves in the climate of the plant and in faulty interpersonal relations. Managerial barriers consist of bad policy or lack of policy, lack of common purpose, and failure to listen and to follow through. With the proper desire and effort, management can effect remedies.

Organizational Barriers

Organizational barriers arise when responsibilities and lines of authority are not clearly defined and announced. Often management fails to use the most expeditious communication channels in the company. Daily meetings of a plant manager with his staff might be desirable at times, but when overcommunication results, the meetings lose their effectiveness. Having too many levels or echelons of management can cause delays in communicating and provide chances for distortion of the original message. When management fails to emphasize and encourage a three-way flow of communication—upward, downward, and lateral—lack of communication results and the job is not done well. Decentralization may create barriers in large companies spread out geographically. In some cases, pressure on supervisory personnel to get a job done allows little time for communicating with workers—or for listening to what they have to say.

Within a company, there should be unity of command. Lateral communication helps in integrating and coordinating work. Everyone should recognize a common goal and work toward it. Work toward making a profit, but also have the interests of the employees at heart and secure their cooperation. Mr. Lynn A. Townsend, while president of Chrysler Corporation, gave his views on effective internal communication in a speech to the International Council of Industrial Editors. His advice included eight requirements:

1. Recognize internal communication as an essential tool of good management.
2. Inform employees concerning their mutual interest in company success.
3. Actively support the corporate communication effort.
4. Put great emphasis on communication planning and measurement.
5. Establish a good climate for communication.
6. Invest in professional talent and communication programming.
7. Recognize your responsibility to *listen* as well as to speak.
8. Recognize the desire of employees to help their company, and the power of communication to tap this great potential.

It is true that these aren't just suggestions for overcoming organizational barriers, for they also help in overcoming managerial and psychological barriers or preventing them from rising. But then, management *is* the organization.

Managerial Barriers

An atmosphere of warmth and friendliness should prevail in a company. The environment set by management for creating ideas and solving problems is also conducive to effective communication. People need to feel free of conflict and pressures. They need to be able to think, talk, and express themselves. An unrestricted flow of communication allows an exchange of ideas, cross-fertilization, and the stimulation that produces free expression.

There must be mutual confidence and understanding between management and employees. Although they may have different backgrounds, objectives, ambitions, and motivations, they should have a common purpose and should be willing to listen to and understand opposing points of view. Openmindedness should prevail. Fears, prejudices, and jealousies among employees will disappear when management is listening and is sincere in its attitudes toward the individuals making up the firm. When management has shown insincerity, failed to keep its promises, failed to follow through after an employee attitude survey, or failed in some other way to take an indicated action, it has erected a barrier not only to communication but also to good employee relations.

Managerial barriers are the fault of management; no one else is to blame, for they are the people in charge. Barriers consist largely of bad company policies or a lack of policies, and of a failure to test the effectiveness of the communication. Both faults are often shown by shortsighted employers, reflecting unfriendly feelings toward the company's employees and toward people outside the firm. One initial barrier caused by poor policy is the lack of provision for two- or three-way communication. Management men in these instances feel that they should send questions and orders down to workers and receive reports and answers from them, and that two-way communication should go no further. They do not believe that employees should have any voice in the workings of the firm or be allowed to make suggestions, and they think employees should not bother them with their problems. Management men thus forget that concerning themselves with employees is one of the jobs of managing.

Show an interest in the other person. Before presenting your (management's) point of view, try to understand the other person's (the employee's) thoughts, feelings, and frame of reference. Once you do this you may change your approach or your point of view. Think what would happen in a labor–management dispute if it were handled in such a way that labor could state management's point of view and management could state labor's. This would mean that understanding had taken place. Once this communication was established, a reasonable outcome could result.

Psychological Barriers

Employees have four basic psychological needs: the need for a feeling of security, the hope of an opportunity for advancement, the desire to be treated as a human being, and the realization of doing something useful. The employee wants the peace of mind that results from the knowledge that his pay will enable him to live comfortably, that his job will continue, and that he will be taken care of after retirement. He also wants to advance himself. He thinks, "What good is it to work hard if I'm not going to receive some benefit from it?" Fair play enters into this attitude, since proper credit and recognition must be given. Everyone wants to be treated as a human being. This is especially important to workers, because they are under the authority of management and can easily feel inferior. Part of this human treatment consists of listening to the employee and making him feel that he belongs and is appreciated, that he is necessary to the company. When an employee feels important and useful, he will do well and will be happy.

Management can do much to eliminate psychological barriers by satisfying these basic desires of employees. For instance, instead of merely making statements, explain to the employees why no layoff or reduction in hours is expected. This will help to give them job security.

Psychologically, subordinates are reluctant to admit to supervisors that a job is not going according to plan. They know the boss likes to hear that things are going well, so often they do not give him the true state of affairs. Sometimes the subordinate avoids asking questions because he feels that he will be criticized for not already knowing the answers. A foreman asks an employee, "Do you understand what to do?" The answer, more times than not, will be "yes." But often he does not really understand. The question, "What are you to do next?" would give an answer that would let the foreman know how well the employee has really understood the order.

Supervisors sometimes do not share their information with employees because they do not want to lose their sense of superiority. In reality, sharing information would give them the superior status of "being in the know." If a supervisor is to benefit from upward communication of ideas, he must not ask only for those ideas, but also display a sincere interest in his subordinates as individuals and demonstrate an honest regard for their ideas and well-being. Appeal to their special needs and interests. They will feel better and be more cooperative if they see their job made easier, more important, or more secure.

Linguistic Barriers

Problems of language are present in oral and written reports, letters, memorandums, and interpersonal, face-to-face communication. It is important to pick the right word in terms of the receiver of the message. The words *vision* and *sight* may be quite comparable in some respects, but they are different when applied to a lady. The same may be said about *kitten* and *cat*.

A college-trained production manager who is explaining something to a foreman or giving him an instruction should use expressions within the foreman's high-school level of comprehension. Likewise, the foreman should talk in terms that a semi-skilled machine operator with an eighth-grade education can understand. The proper frame of reference should be used, so that both the communicator and receiver will understand the same meaning. Faulty definitions and ambiguous language should be avoided. Select words because their meanings are within the experience of the receiver. Frequently, the person who is the target for a given communication cannot think about the message objectively because of his tendency to evaluate the words in terms of his own experience, viewpoint, or emotions. As a consequence of this evaluation, the receiver's mind is partially blocked to the message and it never gets across. An example of this might be the case of the person in the audience who says, "Here we go again—more of that freedom stuff. I'm sick and tired of it."

As another example, suppose that one of the girls in your office has been spending more and more time away from her desk talking with the other girls. Her work is suffering and she is interfering with the work of the others. You ask her into your office for a private conversation about the matter. In your discussion you come to grips with the problem.

She reacts with the remark, "But, Mr. Jones, the fan on the wall over my desk blows on me and I've had just one cold after another." You could say, "Sally, the fan is ten feet over the top of your head, and if a breath of air comes anywhere near your desk, you should consider yourself lucky." If this is the way you "evaluate" Sally's statement about the fan, countering with the facts of the case as you see them, the interview will probably never get on to the real reasons for Sally's conduct. She may even walk out in a huff. It is far better if you simply say, "Is that so?"—making no evaluation, but encouraging Sally to go on.

Listen with an aim to understanding. This requires strenuous self-discipline. One way to cultivate the habit of listening with understanding is to begin by trying to restate the other person's point of view in your own words to his satisfaction before you proceed with your own contribution to the discussion. Many of the suggestions in Chapter 3 will also help you in overcoming linguistic barriers.

TESTING THE EFFECTIVENESS OF COMMUNICATION

Communication is effective when the receiver understands what is being transmitted and responds to it favorably or takes the action called for. A department store might keep a check on the effectiveness of its direct mail promotional pieces by recording the purchases resulting from the advertisement and their amounts. An employee who reads on the company bulletin board a request for men to play in the plant's softball league takes the action called for when he signs up for the team. Similarly, a reader of a magazine subscription letter may renew his subscription by sending in a check; or a customer may pay his bill on receipt of a monthly statement.The firm in each case knows that its letter has been effective, for the action called for was taken. In each of these instances the communicator has a means of checking up on the recipient: He looks for the resulting action.

Feedback

Feedback is a measure of the effectiveness of communication; it is the procedure set up for gauging success. Feedback moves from the receiver back to the transmitter, so that the sender can compare what he receives with what he sent out as a message. A student's examination paper is a simple example of feedback; it shows his instructor what he received and retained. To a speaker, the nods and attentiveness of his audience indicate how well he is getting his ideas across. A foreman gives a suggestion to one of his men, who acknowledges it and starts to do what he was asked. In marketing, research is a means of securing feedback from consumer to manufacturer. The advertiser uses the feedback procedure, for example, to learn popular opinion about himself and his products. This knowledge is useful in formulating advertisements and in manufacturing new products or changing old ones. This type of measurement has opened up the important new field of motivation research for marketing, advertising, and sales. The conception and design of compact cars in the last few years has come about largely because of a number of consumer studies whose results were communicated to the manufacturers.

Surveys may be used to gather information concerning the uses of a product, consumer approval of changes, brand preferences, and the potential market and testing of a product—all useful in putting products on the market, appraising attitudes toward the products, and distributing the products. Finding out the attitudes of the public toward a company, product, or individual, and educating them in the direction of a favorable opinion or approval, is an important aspect of public relations work. The attitude of a group or person can be obtained from questionnaires or interviews. After this knowledge is obtained, it can be used as a basis for mutual understanding and harmony among the various publics with which a firm deals. For management, information obtained from questionnaires and interviews provides data for making decisions and establishing policies necessary to run the business. Knowing the attitudes, feelings, and opinions of employees also helps management to build mutual understanding among departments and individuals. Learning whether or not employees understand management and how well they understand each other provides a guide for testing the effectiveness of employee communication.

The National Association of Manufacturers advocates the use of a questionnaire as a self-estimate of progress in developing understanding with employees. By answering and then analyzing the results of such a questionnaire, a company can have a fairly good understanding of what is being done to make employee communication effective in the company. This understanding will tell whether or not the audience is being reached and will point up weaknesses in the existing communication program, thus indicating possible steps toward improvement.

A SELF-ESTIMATE OF PROGRESS IN DEVELOPING UNDERSTANDING WITH EMPLOYEES

EMPLOYEE COMMUNICATIONS AS A WAY OF LIFE IN INDUSTRY[2]

1. Does the company have a program of communications with employees, clearly identified as such? Yes________ No________
2. If yes___
   a. Has one individual been assigned the responsibility for the overall planning of the program? Yes________ No________
   b. Does the president take an active part in the program? Yes________ No________
   c. Have any attempts been made to evaluate the effectiveness of the program? Yes________ No________
3. With regard to the role of supervisors in the communications program—
   a. Are they given advance information about the company's plans and progress? Yes________ No________
   b. Are they trained to transmit information to employees and answer their questions? Yes________ No________
   c. Do they have a specific method for keeping superiors regularly informed about employee thinking and rumors? Yes________ No________
   d. Do supervisors meet regularly with employees for discussion?
      (1) In groups? Yes________ No________
      (2) Individually? Yes________ No________

[2]National Association of Manufacturers (leaflet), Industrial Relations Division, September 1952. Leaflet reprinted by permission.

4. Are employees given information about—
   a. Background and philosophy of company operations?
   Yes________ No________
   b. The use of company products—where, by whom, and for what?
   Yes________ No________
   c. The way wages are determined? Yes________ No________

5. Do employees hear frequently about—
(Check areas in which information is provided)
________ operating problems
________ material shortages, if any
________ customer complaints
________ the "breakeven" point
________ sales outlook
________ the role of stockholders
________ value of advertising
________ costs of doing business
________ the company's financial situation
________ the significance of productivity
________ the driving force of competition

6. Do employees understand—
(Check areas in which information is provided)
________ the function of executives
________ your philosophy of employee relations
________ problems of financing the business
________ the essentiality of profits
________ the meaning of job security
________ the importance of their individual jobs

7. Are broader issues of our economic system discussed with employees?
(Check areas in which information is provided)

		Regularly	*Occasionally*	*Never*
________	the burden of taxes	_____	_____	_____
________	government spending	_____	_____	_____
________	our essential freedoms	_____	_____	_____
________	the interdependence of big and small business	_____	_____	_____
________	machines make jobs	_____	_____	_____
________	national labor policy	_____	_____	_____
________	the reasons for high standard of living	_____	_____	_____
________	the causes of inflation	_____	_____	_____

8. Does management use any of the following channels to ascertain employee views?
________ conferences with foremen
________ employee suggestion plans
________ exit interviews
________ employee audits or opinion polls

9. Does the top officer of the company–

	Regularly	Occasionally	Never
a. talk with employees in a group	____	____	____
b. write letters to employees	____	____	____
c. meet socially with employees	____	____	____
d. visit informally with employees in walking through the plant	____	____	____

10. If there is a union in your plant, has its place in the communications program been determined? For example, has consideration been given to–

    ______ utilizing the union as an avenue of communication, both up and down?

    ______ giving the union copies (or advance notice) of communications distributed to employees?

    ______ educating union spokesmen on basic economics and company problems in day-to-day discussions and contracts?

Listening

Through listening in day-to-day contacts and in casual conversation, a progressive management can learn what employees are thinking and how they feel. As a link in the company's communication program, management must develop the ability to receive messages as well as the ability to send them. Listening is a part of the responsibility of a receiver. Harold P. Zelko and Harold J. O'Brien, professors of speech and management-communication consultants, offer the following suggestions for the receiver:

1. *Attune yourself to the sender.* An attitude of waiting to be sold or convinced may keep you in the dark. You must have a positive attitude of wanting to learn or understand.
2. *Try to receive, no matter how poorly a message may be sent.* Although a poorly organized talk, a rambling speech, a disjointed conversation make listening difficult, try to understand.
3. *Evaluate and analyze as you receive.* People normally send what they want you to hear or what they believe you want to hear.
4. *Receive objectively.* People tend to select senders who offer compliments or make life pleasant. This discourages the sender who has valuable though unpleasant information. Try to see the message from the sender's point of view.
5. *Be ready to receive at all times.* Keep the receiving set turned on.
6. *Take appropriate action on what you receive.* Receiving implies action.[3]

Successful business executives and leaders use listening to test the effectiveness of their communications and to build good human rela-

[3]Harold P. Zelko and Harold J. O'Brien, *Management–Employee Communication in Action* (Cleveland, Ohio: Howard Allen, Inc., 1957), p. 152.

tions. Listening encourages others to express themselves freely, and an atmosphere of friendly give-and-take in a company keeps the flow of communication open. As Wesley Wiksell states, "Listening is more than the process of hearing. It involves a receptive attitude. One must concentrate actively to understand and interpret what is being said. Finally one must remember and apply what one has heard."[4] He further maintains that understanding comes through listening, and that face-to-face communication cannot exist without reciprocation. Accordingly, he states that one must recognize the obstacles within himself and his environment that keep him from listening.[5] Once aware of barriers to listening, you can analyze yourself, find the causes, and take steps to remove them, change them, or adjust to them.

Why don't we listen? Professor David Berlo of Michigan State University, in his film series, *Effective Communication,* gives five reasons:

1. We're too busy passing messages around.
2. We're too wrapped up in ourselves.
3. We want to avoid trouble.
4. We feel threatened or insecure.
5. We're sloppy observers.

You can probably recall in your experiences instances in which each of these causes has occurred. Yet it is easy to listen to others, for everything a person says or does tells something about him. Everyone wants someone to listen to him—to pay attention. Then what can you do? Be aware of the people around you. Observe what they are saying and doing. Relate this to your own frame of reference and apply it to making your decisions and solving your problems.

There is no doubt about it. Measuring the effectiveness of communication by means of feedback, listening, and observing is an important step in the total communication process in any personal or business situation.

WHERE DO WE GO FROM HERE?

You began this chapter by reviewing your objectives and analyzing what you have accomplished through this text and through the work you have done this semester. Communication is a continuing process that began for you when you were born and that will be a part of you all your life. This book has sought to help you to become a more effective communicator as both a sender and a receiver. Where you go from here depends upon you. The analysis of your skills, abilities, and progress

[4]Wesley Wiksell, *Do They Understand You?* (New York: The Macmillan Company, 1960), p. 86.

[5]*Ibid.*, p. 99.

that you made at the beginning of this chapter will serve as a basis for determining your need for further improvement and professional development. Remember always to look for a better way to do things and to express yourself. Communication is the key to mutual understanding in interactions among people. There is no better way of stating the principle than to say: *Do and say unto others as you would have them do and say unto you.*

SUMMARY

Communication is one of the most valuable tools that management has. Management can manage effectively only through give-and-take in the flow of communication. A definite communication policy helps build an effective communication program. The internal communication policy at Acme Oil Corporation was developed out of need, objectives, and problems that occurred. The procedure and ideas followed by West Penn Power Company are worth following in formulating a communication policy. West Penn tried to build into its policy provisions for eliminating or reducing barriers to communication, as well as for obtaining the cooperation and participation of its people.

Communication barriers may be by nature either organizational, managerial, psychological, or linguistic. It is management's responsibility to recognize and overcome them, and to see that conditions giving rise to barriers do not continue.

Communication is effective when the receiver understands what is being transmitted and responds to it or takes the action called for. Its effectiveness can be measured by feedback and by listening. Motivation research, public opinion polls, and employee surveys are used to provide feedback information to tell company management how well its messages are getting across. Listening keeps one informed and aware of whether he is being understood. The effective communicator is one who is also an effective receiver. He becomes attuned to the other person, listens, and receives messages that help him in turn when he is the sender. This alertness is the key to mutual understanding.

FURTHER READING

Baker, Helen, "Community-Wide Understanding of Industrial Relations Policies." New York: National Industrial Conference Board.

Campbell, James H., and Hal W. Hepler, eds., *Dimensions in Communication,* rev. ed. Belmont, Calif.: Wadsworth Publishing Company, Inc., 1970.

Gentle, Edgar C., Jr., ed., *Data Communications in Business.* New York: American Telephone and Telegraph Company, 1965.

Haney, William V., *Communication and Organizational Behavior,* rev. ed. Homewood, Ill.: Richard D. Irwin, Inc., 1967.

Mussman, William, "Communication Within the Management Group." New York: National Industrial Conference Board, Personnel Policy Series 80.

Robinson, Edward J., *Communication and Public Relations.* Columbus, Ohio: Charles E. Merrill Books, Inc., 1966.

Rogers, Carl, and F. J. Roethlisberger, "Barriers and Gateways to Communication," *Harvard Business Review,* Vol. XXXVII, July 1959, 46–52.

Scholz, William, *Communication in the Business Organization.* Englewood Cliffs, N. J.: Prentice-Hall, Inc., 1962.

Sigband, Norman B., *Communication for Management.* Glenwood, Ill.: Scott, Foresman & Company, 1969.

Thayer, Lee O., *Administrative Communication.* Homewood, Ill.: Richard D. Irwin, Inc., 1961.

——, *Communication and Communication Systems.* Homewood, Ill.: Richard D. Irwin, Inc., 1968.

——, ed., *Communication–Spectrum '7: Proceedings of the 15th Annual Conference of the National Society for the Study of Communication.* Lawrence, Kan.: Allen Press, Inc., 1968.

Wiksell, Wesley, *Do They Understand You?* New York: The Macmillan Company, 1960.

QUESTIONS AND PROBLEMS

1. The "Ten Commandments for Good Communication" as set forth by the American Management Association (pages 387–89) are geared mainly to face-to-face and small-group communication. Discuss how they can apply to written communication.
2. Discuss the possible barriers to communication and how to overcome them.
3. Assume the management and supervisory position in West Penn Power Company and hold a conference discussing the outline topics (page 392) from the company's background material for establishing a communication policy.
4. After discussing the topics in the outline mentioned above, write a statement of communication policy. This could be presented as an oral report before management (the class) or as a written report for their approval.
5. Find out what the communication policy is in a particular company and evaluate it. In a report, present suggestions for improving the policy.
6. Discuss the advantages and disadvantages of various methods for testing the effectiveness of communication.

7. Using the survey questionnaire recommended by the National Association of Manufacturers (pages 398–400), make a survey of employee communications in a particular company. Analyze your findings to determine suggestions for improvement.
8. What can management do to improve its listening skill? What can you do to develop yours?
9. What can you do to further improve and develop your communicative effectiveness?
10. What should be your professional attitude and concept of communication in business?

Appendix A

HINTS FOR IMPROVING YOUR DICTATION

With good communication skills and with some effort and practice, you can become good at dictation. The dictator and transcriber must work together to reduce the cost of written messages by saving time and to improve written communications by making them as understandable and effective as possible. Good dictation practices pertain to planning and organizing, dictating, and transcribing. They must also take into account the human, working relationship between the boss and secretary.

PLANNING AND ORGANIZING

Planning begins with analyzing the situation and making decisions on the information at hand. You are either initiating correspondence or answering someone else's letter. (This also applies to dictating memorandums or other short messages.) When answering a letter or memorandum, begin by analyzing it to determine what questions need answering or what information is sought.

1. Arrive at a purpose and determine what is necessary to accomplish it.
2. Know what you are going to say and say it. Assemble all the information called for. Make a study of previous correspondence if it will be useful. Place marginal notes in the letter you are answering, underline phrases or sentences to remind you what to say, or jot down notes on a separate sheet.

3. Organize your thoughts. Outline them or merely number them to indicate the sequence in which you will use them.
4. Assemble several dictation jobs together to save your dictating time and that of your secretary. This practice will also enable her to handle them in order of importance or timeliness.
5. Set aside a regular time and place for dictating: a time when fewer telephone calls are coming in, there is less traffic in and out of the office, and neither you nor your secretary is tired.

GIVING DICTATION

In dictating a letter, apply the principles of any effective communication and be thoughtful of your secretary. You work together for common goals: efficient office operation, improved written correspondence, etc.

1. Respect and be loyal to your secretary. Be aware of her as an individual, learn her likes and dislikes, and know her schedule and work habits.
2. Apply the principles of good letter-writing: clarity, courtesy, completeness, conciseness, and correctness. Pay special attention to psychological principles: empathy, creativity, and persuasiveness. (See Chapters 4, 5, and 6 for a full discussion of these principles.)
3. Visualize your reader. See him in your mind as sitting across from you; then dictate in the simple language you would use in conversing with him. Be yourself when you dictate and talk naturally, following your outline and notes.
4. Dictate preliminary instructions, then the body of the letter and the closing items.
5. Dictate clearly. Your vocal inflections will indicate normal punctuation. For speed and accuracy, however, say "period" or "paragraph" when called for and indicate special punctuation.
6. Spell out proper names, places, and technical terms that your secretary may not know.
7. Speak distinctly and take your time. Don't mumble or meander, but talk directly. Transmit the message, letting the obvious remain unsaid.
8. Dictate in thought groups. Put words together in phrases, clauses, and short sentences.
9. Ask your secretary to read the letter back so that you can evaluate it and check its content, style, tone, and impression on the reader. Make changes when improvement will result.

10. Provide your secretary with the letter you are answering and any relevant materials that may assist her. She can file them afterward.

DICTATING TO A MACHINE

Because the transcriber can slow down a dictating machine and play back sections, you can speak more directly when dictating to a machine.

1. Begin by identifying yourself and what you want done. Give full detailed instructions.
2. You will need to give names, addresses, and the like if they are not known or available to the transcriber. Spell names that might be misunderstood or misspelled by the transcriber.
3. You can give your secretary corrections, instructions, or reminders on the machine. Talk to her in a friendly, courteous manner, but be sure that she can distinguish between what she is to type and what is meant for her. In making a correction, say "correction," then dictate the corrected form. In giving an instruction, say "operator" or "secretary," then dictate the instruction.
4. Be sure to speak clearly, because the transcriber cannot ask you to repeat, and because in this means of communication, you cannot enlist the aid of facial expression or feedback.
5. Indicate the end of each dictated message (there can be several on the same tape) by saying "end of letter" or "end of memo."

TAKING DICTATION AND TRANSCRIBING

The secretary who takes dictation and transcribes has had training to develop her skills in taking shorthand notes and in transcribing from both machines and notes. The suggestions here simply point up a few hints to keep in mind.

1. Pay close attention to correctness in spelling, punctuation, expression of numbers, underscoring, verb and subject agreement, and possessives. These are generally the trouble spots where errors most frequently occur. The key is to listen attentively. Ask questions when you are not sure, and look up spellings before transcribing.
2. Read through each letter or message prior to transcribing it. This practice will familiarize you with the material and accordingly will increase your accuracy, rhythm, and speed in typing. Making every effort to understand the meaning in each message dictated will also help you to read back your notes and make you a more helpful secretary.

3. Estimate the size of the letter from the number and length of the paragraphs. This will help you to set margins and place the letter attractively on the page.
4. Mark punctuation and write out difficult words in longhand above your shorthand notes as aids in transcribing. Also make notes of difficult words when listening to dictated tape or records as an aid in transcribing.
5. Be careful to type insertions in their proper places and to make corrections when they are needed.
6. Show consideration for your boss. Earn his respect and loyalty through your work.

Appendix B

IMPROVING YOUR TELEPHONING TECHNIQUES

With the advent of all-number dialing, direct long distance dialing, lower rates for businesses making numerous calls, and increased telephone services, the telephone is being used more than ever for obtaining facts, giving information, selling, ordering, making complaints, etc. Add to these factors the ever-increasing high cost of correspondence, and you will begin to understand that the telephone is accomplishing many of the tasks that business letters have done traditionally through the years.

To accomplish these objectives courteously and efficiently, you should know how to use the telephone properly, apply good manners, and present messages clearly and convincingly.

PLANNING AND MAKING CALLS

Just as in any other communicating situation, your planning begins with analyzing the situation and making necessary decisions on the information that is known and assumptions that have been made.

1. Have a *purpose* to accomplish. This may be to give directions or information, to obtain information or data, to order, persuade, complain, or adjust. Make notes on what you plan to say and the order in which you will say it. Organizing a telephone message is much like organizing a letter. You may follow the "yes," "no," or psychological patterns for your sequence of points. It is essen-

tial to be concise, complete, direct, and courteous. Identify yourself and state your purpose and message.

2. Have the *correct name and telephone number.* Frequently called telephone numbers should be listed in a personal number booklet or desk-top list. Numbers may be obtained from the telephone directory, special listings, stationery letterheads, or the directory assistance operator.
3. Decide on the *timing* of your call. Consider the differences in time zones on some long distance calls and the likelihood that the called person will be available.

   Also consider whether the call will tie up your line when an important call is expected or during a busy time for the usual incoming calls.
4. Decide on the *type of call* required: local, long distance, collect, station-to-station, or person-to-person.
5. To make *local calls:*
   a. Dial the number listed for the person you are calling.
   b. Dial the number listed for directory assistance, when needed.
   c. Dial "operator" for help in making a call.
6. To make *long distance calls:*
   a. With direct-distance dialing, dial station-to-station calls to numbers that have up to seven digits or two letters and five numerals.
   b. To call within your area code, dial the number for the long distance operator as listed in the telephone directory, then the telephone number. (Do not dial the area code.)
   c. To call outside your area code, dial the number for the long distance operator, then the distant area code and the telephone number.
   d. To reach long distance directory assistance, dial the long distance operator's number, then the area code you wish plus 555-1212. Tell the operator the city or town and the name or place you want.
   e. For help in making calls, dial "operator."
   f. For person-to-person calls, dial "operator" and tell her you wish to make a person-to-person call. Tell her the specific name and extension if you know it.
   g. For collect calls, dial, then tell the operator you are making a collect call.
   h. For conference calls, dial and tell the operator you wish to make a conference call. Give her the names and places.
7. To make *emergency calls,* keep a list of emergency numbers

readily available or listed in the front of your telephone directory (fire, police, medical aid, etc.), or dial "operator" in any emergency and say, "I want to report a fire . . ." or "I want a policeman at. . . ." Tell the operator the location where help is needed.

ANSWERING THE TELEPHONE

1. Identify yourself at once. After the customary "Hello" or "Good morning," give the name of your company, the department, and your name; for instance:

    XYZ Company, Purchasing Department, Lee Allan Jones speaking

    or

    Dr. Smithson's office, Miss Gallodon, secretary, speaking.

2. Keep the caller informed:

    I'll check the shipping date for you, if you wish to hold the line.

    or

    I'm sorry, Mr. Baker is not in. May I take a message?

    or

    Just a moment. Mr. Jones will be with you.

    Listen attentively with appropriate remarks such as "yes," "I'll tell him," "I understand," etc.

3. Take down information. Have paper, pencil, and message forms by the telephone ready for use, so that there will be no delay. Make sure that the appropriate person gets the message.
4. Handle any difficulties that may arise. When it is necessary to leave the line, explain the reason appropriately to the caller. Do not let the caller hold the line more than one minute without letting him know that you are trying to get the information or person. Remember, he can't see you. When transferring a call, notify the caller. When promising a "call-back," establish time limits.
5. Take care of complaints by remaining calm and friendly, for calmness breeds calmness. Let the caller "blow off steam," while you listen without interrupting. Because the caller is not interested in who is to blame, avoid blaming anyone. Simply tell him what happened. You may express regret and agree with the caller that "the situation should not have occurred." Inform the complainant of any corrective action that is planned. Make and fulfill commitments. Allow the caller to hang up first. This allows him to mention any last-minute thought he might have.
6. Say what you have to say and stop. End with "Goodbye," which is the customary way of indicating that the conversation is over.

DEVELOPING PLEASANT MANNERS

The impressions we make when we use the telephone add to our success as much as personal contacts do. You can develop a pleasing and effective telephone manner by following these rules:

1. Have a cheerful and considerate attitude toward each call.
2. Express courtesy and thoughtfulness by the tone of your voice. This will create goodwill and make friends.
3. Picture the person at the other end of the line as being across from you. Talk to and with him, not at him.
4. Use a moderate and lively tone in your voice to show your alertness and interest.
5. Show a personal interest and attention to what is being said.
6. Be sincere in what you say.
7. Indicate a spirit of helpfulness appropriate to the occasion by giving information, granting a request, arranging an investigation, suggesting alternatives, explaining reasons, taking action, etc.

UTILIZING YOUR VOICE

Variety and flexibility in your voice can help to convey your attitude. These qualities can be attained through pitch, inflection, and emphasis. Some common do's and don'ts follow:

Do:	*Do not:*
1. *Speak distinctly.* Pronounce your words carefully. Give proper formation to each sound. Open your mouth; move your lips.	1. Mouth your words or mumble, run words together, or talk with something in your mouth.
2. *Speak directly.* Talk into the transmitter with your lips close to the mouthpiece.	2. Shout or talk in a loud voice.
3. *Take your time.* Speak neither too fast nor too slowly.	3. Speak hurriedly.
4. *Make your voice interesting.* Make your voice pleasant, cheerful, cordial, and friendly.	4. Make your voice flat, mechanical, indifferent, or expressionless.
5. *Be interested and helpful.* Give attention to what is said and show a desire to help.	5. Be inattentive, flat, weary, listless, or repelling.

Remember that your voice carries the whole load, for the caller cannot see you.

ACCOMPLISHING CLARITY AND CONCISENESS

Clarity and conciseness are essential to understanding and action. To achieve this, follow these rules:

1. Organize your thoughts before speaking.
2. Select words that are short, simple, descriptive, and appropriate to the occasion and person.
3. Use complete sentences, generally of no more than seventeen words.
4. Use concise statements that are directly related to the purpose of the call.
5. Avoid speech mannerisms.
6. Refrain from interruptions.

Appendix C

REFERENCE REMINDERS

On the following pages are presented rules of grammar, punctuation, and the mechanics of manuscript preparation. They do not take the place of a complete handbook of English. Instead, they will serve as a review if you wish to brush up on principles and as a reference guide to check particular questions. Only the rules that are commonly needed by college undergraduate students are included. In using these reminders, recognize that they reflect custom and usual practice. Although they are not final rules in every case, and although many good communicators have violated some of them whenever the situation demanded it, they will aid you in writing clearly and correctly. Topics are presented in alphabetical order.

ABBREVIATIONS

1. In general, avoid abbreviations in formal writing.
2. Use acceptable standard abbreviations in some personal, informal writing.
3. Use abbreviations when the company uses them as part of its firm name:

   Co.—Company Inc.—Incorporated
   Bros.—Brothers Ltd.—Limited

4. Use title abbreviations when followed by the name of the person:

   Mr. Messrs. Dr.
   Mrs. Mmes. St. (Saint)

5. Use title abbreviations after proper names:

Jr.	M.D.	D.D.	M.A.
Sr.	Ph.D.	LL.D.	M.B.A.

6. In footnote and bibliographical entries, use abbreviations for words designating parts when they are followed by numbers:

   Bk. I (plural, Bks.)—Book I
   Chap. 2 (plural, Chaps.) —Chapter 2
   Col. 2 (plural, Cols.)—Column 2
   2nd ed. (plural, eds.)—Second edition
   Fig. 2 (plural, Figs.)—Figure 2
   l. 9 (plural, ll.)—line 9
   p. 7 (plural, pp.)—page 7
   pp. 7f.—page 7 and the page following
   pp. 7ff.—page 7 and the pages following
   pp. 5–7—pages 5 to 7 inclusive
   sec. 9 (plural, secs.)—section 9
   Vol. III (plural, Vols.)—Volume III
   cf.—compare
   ed. (plural, eds.)—editor

7. Capitalize abbreviations when the word or words represented would ordinarily be capitalized or when a capitalized form has become established practice.
8. In general, use a period after an abbreviation or each part that represents a single word. Common exceptions include chemical symbols and names of government agencies.

AGREEMENT

1. Make every verb agree with its subject in person:

   I go, you go, he goes.

2. Make every verb agree with its subject in number:
   a. Do not be confused by nouns or pronouns between the subject and verb, as:

      Your shipment of paper towels is on its way.

   b. Use a singular verb for compound subjects joined by *or* or *nor,* as:

      Neither the sales manager nor the personnel director intends to go to the convention.

      When one subject is singular and one plural, make the verb agree with the nearer, as:

      Neither the sales manager nor the salesmen are going.

c. Use a singular verb with words such as *each, either, neither, anyone, somebody, someone, everybody, everyone, no one,* and *nobody.* (*None* or *any* may be singular or plural, according to the meaning of the sentence.)

d. Use a plural verb for subjects joined by *and,* as:

The director of personnel and the new sales manager are to be at the conference in my office.

e. Use a singular verb for collective nouns when they refer to the collection as a whole, as:

The committee has approved the suggestion to purchase a new movie projector.

f. Use a plural verb for collective nouns when they refer to the individuals of the group separately, as:

A large number of incoming freshmen are expected to enroll in business courses.

3. Make every pronoun agree with its antecedent in person and gender. (Lack of agreement causes a shift in person.)
4. Make every pronoun agree with its antecedent in number:
   a. Use a singular pronoun to refer to such antecedents as *person, man, one, anyone, somebody, everyone, each,* and *kind.*
   b. Use a plural pronoun to refer to two or more antecedents connected by *and.*
   c. Use a singular pronoun to refer to two or more singular antecedents connected by *or* or *nor.* When one is singular and one plural, make the pronoun agree with the nearer of the two.
   d. Use either a singular or plural pronoun for referring to a collective noun, depending upon whether or not the collective noun is considered singular or plural in its meaning.

APOSTROPHE

1. Use an apostrophe to show possession as follows:
   a. To indicate the possessive case of singular and plural nouns that do not end in *s,* and of indefinite pronouns, add the apostrophe and *s.*
   b. When the plural ends in *s,* add only the apostrophe.
   c. When the singular ends in *s,* add the apostrophe and *s* unless the second *s* makes pronunciation difficult.
2. Use the apostrophe to indicate omissions in contracted words or numerals:

can't o'clock class of '60

(Remember that the apostrophe in *it's* makes it mean *it is,* the contraction. Don't confuse it with the possessive form, *its,* without the apostrophe, as in *its paws.*)

3. Use the apostrophe and *s* to form the plurals of letters, figures, and words referred to as words:

   three A's; 2's; if's

4. Use the apostrophe and *s* to form the possessive of the noun preceding a gerund:

   The secretary's typing the report well made a good impression on her boss.

BIBLIOGRAPHIES

1. Attach a bibliography as a list of sources of information used in gathering data and writing:
   a. To support the fact that authoritative sources were used
   b. To acknowledge or give credit for sources used
   c. To help others pursue the subject further
2. Place the bibliography at the end of the text. It may appear before or after the appendix or as part of the appendix material.
3. Classify entries in a bibliography according to types of publication and sources of information or according to subject matter.
4. Arrange entries in alphabetical order within each classified section of the bibliography by authors' last names, or by titles when the authors are not known.
5. Arrange elements in bibliographical references according to a set pattern (use block or hanging indention consistently):
   a. For a book entry, follow either of these arrangements, but be consistent:

      (Informal) Robinson, David M., *Writing Reports for Management Decisions,* Charles E. Merrill Publishing Co., Columbus, Ohio, 1969.

      (Formal) Robinson, David M., *Writing Reports for Management Decisions.* Columbus, Ohio: Charles E. Merrill Publishing Co., 1969.

   b. For an article entry, be consistent in following one of these arrangements:

      Spataro, Lucien, "Management of Communications," *The Journal of Business Communication,* Vol. VI (Summer 1969), 15–19.

      Spataro, Lucien, "Management of Communications," *The Journal of Business Communication,* VI: 15–19, Summer 1969.

c. For a newspaper entry:

The New York Times, May 16, 197–, p. 10.

d. For a personal interview entry:

Personal interview, Mr. Henry Jonson, Personnel Director, Union Oil Company, Houston, Tex., May 21, 197–.

e. For a personal letter entry:

Personal letter from Mr. Mark Hodgers, President, Dawson Manufacturing Company, Indianapolis, Ind., June 10, 197–.

6. Consult a good reference manual like the *Chicago Manual of Style* or Kate L. Turabian's *A Manual for Writers of Term Papers, Theses, and Dissertations* (based on the *Chicago Manual*) for entry forms less commonly used than those given here. You may also refer to the *U. S. Government Printing Office Manual* or the *PMLA Style Manual.*
7. Single-space bibliographical entries, with a double space between entries.
8. Either use an indention of five to ten spaces at the beginning of each entry, block each entry with no indention, or use hanging indention.
9. You may or may not cite the total number of pages when the entire book is being cited. When only part of the reference has been consulted, indicate the pages of the chapter or section used.

BINDING

1. Bind reports on either the left or the top. Make adjustments of ½ to 1 inch accordingly in the margins.
2. You may bind reports with either staples or wire stitching, gummed tape, paper fasteners, or spiral bindings.
3. Place reports in either two- or three-ring notebooks, plastic covers, or manila folders.

BOXING AND RULING MATERIAL

1. For emphasis, set off facts and figures by lines or a decorative border.
2. Leave a white space, as in advertising, around the material to be emphasized.
3. For easy reading of tables, draw lines between groups of items and between columns.
4. Rule tables of more than three columns at the top and bottom, or enclose them by also ruling the sides.

CAPITALIZATION

1. Capitalize all proper names and their derivatives and abbreviations. Include:
    a. Specific persons or places
    b. Organizations of all kinds
    c. Races, citizens, and languages
    d. Days of the week, months, and special days
    e. Historical periods and events
    f. Words pertaining to deity or personifications
    g. Sections of the country when used as nouns
2. Capitalize titles preceding names or any words used as parts of a proper name.
3. Capitalize every word in the titles of books, magazines, articles, and newspapers except *a, an, the,* and internal prepositions and conjunctions.
4. Capitalize the main words in names of schools, colleges, associations, and business firms.
5. Do not capitalize fields of study unless they are a part of a specific course title.
6. Capitalize the first word of every sentence or line of poetry, including quoted sentences, questions, and complete statements inserted in sentences.
7. Capitalize the pronoun *I* and the interjection *O*.

CHARTS

1. Use charts to represent data by lines, bars, areas, or graphs.
2. Use charts:
    a. To supplement, emphasize, and support
    b. To show relationships between data
    c. To simplify and clarify
    d. To reinforce by emphasizing major points
    e. To interest and persuade the reader
3. Portray data accurately.
4. Create a caption with action words.
5. Provide keys and explanations for understanding.
6. Make charts simple enough to be comprehended at a glance.

COLON

1. Use a colon after an introductory word, phrase, or statement to call attention to what follows:

    The idea was simply this: Harold was not mature enough to drive.

2. Use a colon to separate two main clauses when the second explains or amplifies the first:

   Parallel ideas should be expressed in parallel grammatical structure: an infinitive phrase should be paralleled by infinitives, not by a gerund, and so on.

COMMA

1. Use a comma to separate main clauses connected by one of the coordinating conjunctions (*and, but, or, nor,* and *for*), as:

   You have maintained an average checking account balance of $500 during the past year, but you have not added to your savings account.

   The comma may be omitted when the clauses are short.

2. Use a comma to set off introductory phrases or clauses, as:

   Although it was difficult to maintain order at the meeting, the chairman did a commendable job at presiding.

   The comma may be omitted when the introductory phrase is short and there is no danger of confusion.

3. Use a comma to set off items in a series. (Some writers omit the comma before the conjunction unless it is required for clarity.)

   Delivery dates for coffee, leather, cotton, and wool have been set.

4. Use a comma to separate coordinate adjectives (equal in value) that modify the same noun, as:

   Stately, plump Buck Mulligan came from the stairhead.

5. Use commas to set off nonrestrictive clauses and other parenthetical elements. A nonrestrictive clause is used as an aside with an otherwise complete assertion and is set off by commas, as:

   Mr. Smith's report, which I read this morning, recommended changes in the company's vacation policy.

   A restrictive clause is one that adds meaning or identification to an otherwise incomplete assertion and is *not* set off by commas, as:

   The report that I read this morning is the one recommending changes in the company's vacation policy.

   Note that *which* should be used only with the nonrestrictive clause.

6. Use commas to set off appositives, geographical names, items in dates and addresses, and parenthetical expressions:

   Mr. Henry Smith, director of personnel of Jones Manufacturing Company, is a friend of mine.

   The work for which he sent in specifications, however, has not been finished.

7. Set off by commas words of direct address:

   It is your book, John, and you must decide whether to lend it or not.

DASH

Use a dash (formed by typing two hyphens in succession) to mark a sudden break in thought, to give emphasis in setting off parenthetical elements, or to set off a summary. In some uses the dash is beginning to supplant the colon, but it is in danger of being too broadly used.

> To make the boat we shall need—let's see, what shall we need?
>
> For the picnic, we will have to buy a supply of paper goods—cups, plates, forks, and spoons.

EXCLAMATION POINT

Use the exclamation point to express strong feeling or emphasis at the end of either a complete sentence or a fragmentary thought.

FOOTNOTES

1. Use footnotes to give credit for the source of quoted material in the text, to lend authority to a statement not generally accepted, to explain or give additional information, to give an appraisal of a source, or to provide a cross-reference to material presented in some other part of the text.
2. Place footnotes at the bottom of the page, separated from the text material by a solid line across part or all of the page.
   a. Single-space after typing the last line of text material on a page, type the solid line, then double-space, indent five to ten spaces from the left margin, and begin the first line of the footnote.
   b. Space succeeding lines even with the margin. Single-space each entry. Double-space between entries.
3. Number footnotes consecutively by Arabic numerals in an unbroken series throughout the text material. Place the reference figure in the text after the passage to which it refers, after all punctuation marks, and slightly above the line. Type the reference figure in the footnote at the beginning of the entry, one-half space above the line, and without punctuation. If footnotes are relatively few, asterisks, single and double, may be used, but they are awkward to use in typing if more than two notes will appear on a page. If the piece is divided into sections or chapters, the numbering of notes can begin again with each new division.
4. To footnote a book, arrange the author's name with his given name or initials first, then the title of the book, place of publication, publisher, date of publication, and page reference.
   a. Punctuate this arrangement as follows:

      [1]Loyce Adams, *Managerial Psychology* (Boston: The Christopher Publishing House, 1965), p. 38.

b. Or use a simplified entry, as:

[2]Norman Sigband, *Communication for Management,* Scott, Foresman, 1969, p. 109.

c. Or when a bibliography accompanies the work, use a short form, as:

[3]Adams, *Managerial Psychology,* p. 38.

d. For a book with two or three authors, write the names, as:

[4]William Strunk, Jr., and E. B. White
[5]C. R. Anderson, A. G. Saunders, and F. W. Weeks

e. For a book with more than three authors, write the first name and *et al.* for the other names.

5. To footnote an article, arrange the author's name with his given name or initials first, then the title of the article, name of the magazine, volume number, date, and page reference, as:

[6]T. G. Brown, "Communication Means Understanding," *Personnel Administration,* Vol. XXI (January 1970), 14.
[7]T. G. Brown, "Communication Means Understanding," *Personnel Administration,* Vol. XXI, January, 1970, 14.
[8]T. G. Brown, "Communication Means Understanding," *Personnel Administration,* XXI: 14. January, 1970.

6. For a newspaper item, give the name of the paper, date, and page reference, as:

[9]*Chicago Tribune,* January 21, 1970, p. 5.

7. After the first full form has been given, do not repeat it for a successive reference to the particular work, but use one of the appropriate short footnote forms:

a. Use *ibid.* (for the Latin *ibidem,* meaning *in the same place*) when the reference is to the same work without an intervening footnote. If it refers to a different page, cite the page number.

[10]*Ibid.,* p. 23.

b. Use the author's name and *op. cit.* (for the Latin *opus citatus,* meaning *work cited*) when there are intervening footnotes and it is necessary to refer to a previous entry for a reference.

[11]Shurter, *op. cit.,* p. 56.

c. Use *loc. cit.* (for the Latin *locus citatus,* meaning *place cited*) when the reference is to the same page in a previous book reference or to the same article or part of a work previously footnoted:

[12]Zirkle, *loc. cit.,* p. 125.

Do not use a short-form abbreviation, however, when one or more pages intervene between the footnote and its antecedent. For the reader's convenience, use the short form described in number 4c above.

8. Use Roman numerals (capitals) in footnotes when referring to a volume, book, part, or division:

   Vol. I   Bk. II   Pt. III

9. Use Roman numerals (lower case—i, ii, iii, iv, etc.) to refer to introductory or prefatory pages in a book and Arabic numbers for designating pages, lines, and chapter references:

   pp. 10–15   p. 5   l. 3   Chap. 2

10. Always consult a good reference manual for entry forms less commonly used than those given here. (Kate L. Turabian's *A Manual for Writers of Term Papers, Theses, and Dissertations,* the *Chicago Manual of Style,* and the *Publications Modern Language Association Style Manual* are good ones.)

HYPHEN

1. Use hyphens in compound words; when in doubt always consult the dictionary.
2. Use hyphens to join two or more words forming a compound adjective that precedes a noun:

   These are up-to-the-minute models.
   They lived on a well-paved street.
   She wore a yellowish-green dress.

3. Use hyphens with compound numbers from twenty-one to ninety-nine.
4. Use hyphens with the prefixes *ex-, self-,* and *all-* and the suffix adjective *-elect:*

   ex-mayor; self-educated; all-American; governor-elect

ITALICS (see UNDERLINING)

MARGINS

1. Maintain uniform standard margins on each page throughout a given piece of writing.
2. For reports and letters use the same width margins, varying them from one to two inches, on each of the four sides of the typewritten page. For letters, the final effect should be that of type within a frame of white space.
3. You may instead leave top and bottom margins the same, preferably 1¼ inches, with the left margin wider than the right, preferably 1¼ inches on the left and ¾ inch on the right.
4. Leave an extra margin on the left or top for material that is to be bound.
5. Avoid very ragged margins on the right.

NUMBERS

1. Use figures for numbers 10 and over, but fully spell out those under 10.
2. Spell out all numbers beginning a sentence or recast the sentence.
3. Treat alike all numbers referring to similar things.
4. Use figures for dates and sums of money.
5. Use figures for street numbers, pages of a book, decimals and percentages, dimensions, distances, weights and measures, expressions of time used with A.M. and P.M., temperatures, and market quotations.
6. Use figures when setting up tables or handling statistics.
7. Use figures for numbers composed of units and fractions, but spell out fractions standing alone.
8. In sums of money involving whole dollars, omit the decimal point and following ciphers:

   He paid $5 for the leather notebook and $20.50 for the briefcase.

9. Set off with a comma or commas numbers of four or more figures, except for page numbers and street numbers:

   25,000 1440 Broadway pp. 1520–1736

PAGINATION

1. Number the pages (other than page 1) of a business letter and letter report, as:

   Mr. James Wilson 2 January 10, 197–

   or

   Mr. James Wilson
   January 10, 197–
   page 2

2. Number the pages of a memorandum report, as:

   Mail Distribution 2 January 10, 197–

   or

   Mail Distribution
   January 10, 197–
   page 2

3. Number the pages of a short or long formal report, as:

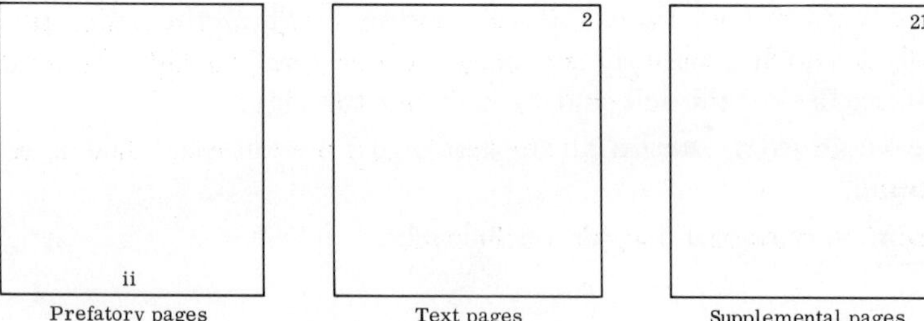

Prefatory pages Text pages Supplemental pages

Page numbers may also be centered consistently at the top of a page except on display pages.

4. Number pages of other pieces of writing, such as term papers, theses, and articles, by simply placing the page number at the top center of the page or in the upper right-hand corner.

PARAGRAPH STRUCTURE

1. Construct each paragraph so that it will reflect unity and coherence.
   a. Write each sentence in the paragraph so that it will contribute to the main idea of the paragraph.
   b. Express each sentence so that it is related to the ones before and after it. Use transitional words and phrases to relate the flow of ideas.
   c. Express the main idea of the paragraph in a topic sentence, which can be either stated or implied.
2. Develop each paragraph adequately and logically by details, illustration or example, definition, narration, explanation, or argumentation.
3. Avoid excessively long paragraphs. Use short opening and closing paragraphs.
4. Provide good transition between paragraphs.
5. Vary the length and structure of paragraphs.

PERIOD

1. Use a period after every complete declarative sentence and after an abbreviation.
2. For a demand or request expressed as a question for the sake of courtesy, use a period instead of a question mark, as:

   Will you please let me know as soon as possible so that I can make reservations.

QUESTION MARK

1. Use a question mark after every complete sentence that asks a question.
2. At the end of a question within a sentence, use the same mark of punctuation it would have if it stood alone, as:

   After asking his secretary, "What are the preferable dates for your vacation?" he resumed his dictating.

QUOTATION MARKS

1. Use quotation marks to set off all direct quotations.
2. Use quotation marks to set off titles of magazine articles and of subdivisions and chapters of books.

3. When punctuating quotations, place commas and periods inside the final quotation marks and colons and semicolons outside. Place other punctuation marks inside or outside, depending upon their application to the quoted material.

QUOTATIONS

1. Quote with discretion: use quotations where the statement is relatively concise and particularly apt, or where the idea is not a generally accepted fact.
2. Incorporate quotations of fewer than four lines in the written text and enclose them in double quotation marks.
3. Indent quotations consisting of more than four lines from both margins and single-space them, omitting the quotation marks.
4. Set off quotations in footnotes from the text of the note and enclose them in quotation marks.
5. Reproduce direct quotations exactly—the content, capitalization, spelling, and punctuation should be the same as in the original material.
6. Interpolate the Latin *sic,* enclosed in brackets, within the body of a direct quotation to indicate that an error is part of the quoted material, and not the author's. Also set off any remarks other than the quoted material by brackets [ ].

   Winston tastes good like [*sic*] a cigarette should [taste].
7. Use ellipses (. . .) to designate omission of any portion of a quotation. When a complete paragraph of prose or a full line of poetry is omitted, type a row of dots (. . . . .) all the way across the quotation.

   Oh say, can you see, . . . / What so proudly we hailed . . . ?
8. To set off a quotation within a quotation, use single quotation marks.

SEMICOLON

1. Use a semicolon to separate two main clauses not connected by *and, but, or, nor,* or *for* (the coordinating conjunctions).
2. Use a semicolon to separate two main clauses connected by a conjunctive adverb, such as:

accordingly	similarly
consequently	so
however	therefore
in fact	thus
nevertheless	yet

3. Use a semicolon to separate coordinate elements which themselves contain commas:

   The credit manager called a meeting of the collection manager, the correspondence clerks, the public relations director, and the sales manager; but the hour set, inconvenient for some, resulted in poor attendance.

SENTENCE STRUCTURE

1. Write each sentence so that it will present a complete thought.
   a. Avoid putting two or more unrelated thoughts in the same sentence.
   b. Avoid breaking ideas into short, choppy sentences.
   c. Keep related parts of the sentence together, and avoid dangling modifiers.
2. Construct sentences with proper attention to unity, subordination, coherence, and emphasis.
   a. Put the main idea of a sentence in an independent clause and less important ideas in subordinate clauses.
   b. Combine short sentences into longer ones by subordinating the less important ideas.
   c. Arrange a sentence to give emphasis to the important idea by placing it at the beginning or end, or by placing a word or phrase out of its natural order.
   d. Make sure that conjunctions and prepositions express the exact relationships between clauses, phrases, and words.
   e. Avoid long, rambling sentences with too many qualifying clauses and phrases.
   f. Avoid putting words between *to* and the verb form of an infinitive unless a natural expression cannot be achieved any other way.
   g. Place adverbs such as *only, almost,* and *merely* close to the words they modify.
   h. Place modifiers so that they will be logically and naturally connected with the words they modify.
3. Vary sentences to avoid monotony for the reader.
   a. Change the basic pattern by placing a clause or phrase ahead of the main subject and verb.
   b. Vary the length of sentences.
   c. Vary the kinds of sentences by using simple, compound, and complex sentences.
   d. Use your own words instead of worn-out expressions that have lost cleverness and force through overuse.

4. Construct sentences for most letters and reports with an average seventeen-word length, for ease in reading.

SPACING

1. Single- or double-space material, depending upon its length and use.
   a. Single-space reports that consist of fewer than three pages; double-space those that are longer.
   b. Single-space business letters, letter reports, memorandums, and short bulletins.
2. In single-spaced material, double-space between paragraphs.
3. In double-spaced material, indent five to ten spaces at the beginning of each paragraph, and double-space between paragraphs. (Occasionally you may consistently block the paragraphs and triple-space between them.)
4. For emphasis, leave more space around the material.

SPELLING[1]

1. Constantly use the dictionary to find the correct spelling of words.
2. Look carefully at the arrangement of letters in words.
3. Keep a list of words you misspell and concentrate on learning, through practice, to spell them correctly.
4. Be aware of your pronunciation as it compares with the correct pronunciation of a word. Learning to pronounce a word correctly may help you learn to spell it correctly.
5. Carefully proofread all written and typed work.
6. Review and apply the rules of spelling as given in any good handbook of English.

SUBJECT HEADINGS[2]

1. You may use subject headings to indicate the division of material in reports, articles, and other types of communication.
   a. Use them to indicate the content of each division and subdivision.
   b. Use them to indicate the degree of relationship between different sections.
2. Make headings descriptive in content and parallel in construction.

[1]See also pp. 144–45.

[2]See also pp. 327–28 for further suggestions on typing and spacing subject headings.

SYLLABICATION

1. To keep the right-hand margin as even as possible, thus producing a neatly typed page, divide words at the ends of lines according to their syllabic division.
2. Divide hyphenated words at the hyphen and nowhere else.
3. Do not divide words of one syllable.
4. Do not divide words of only four or five letters.
5. Keep prefixes and suffixes intact.
6. Avoid divisions that leave one or two letters on a line, as:

   a-mong, prov-en, according-ly
7. Do not divide the last word in a paragraph or on a page.
8. Do not divide initials, names, numbers, abbreviations, or titles.
9. Always consult the dictionary when in doubt.

TABULATION[3]

1. Present systematized material or figures in tables.
2. Display a short and simple group of figures as a paragraph inset.
3. Place tables in either the text material or an appendix, depending upon their purpose and use.
   a. For reference, place them in an appendix.
   b. For analysis, place them in the text.
4. Place tables as close as possible to the discussion point with which they are used.
5. Number tables consecutively.
   a. Use either Roman or Arabic numerals, but be consistent.
   b. Use a separate numbering system for tables and charts or other types of visual aids.
   c. Center the table number above the title at the top of the table.
6. Construct tables so that the contents can be easily followed and readily understood.
   a. Place the title above the table.
   b. Make column headings concise and descriptive.
   c. Let each column heading apply only to material in that particular column, naming the item and the unit of measurement in which it is expressed.
   d. Use footnotes for supplemental information, placing them at the bottom of the table.

[3]See also pp. 335–36.

e. Cite the source of the data at the bottom of the table. (Sometimes this may be done beneath the title caption.)
f. Avoid a crowded effect in typing and spacing tables. Use plenty of white space for display purposes.
g. Rule tables of over three columns.

TENSE

1. Use the form of the verb that correctly shows its time relationship.
   a. To express present time, use the present tense.
   b. To express actions that take place habitually or ideas that are true, use the present tense.
   c. To express action completed in the past, use the past tense.
   d. To express an action or condition that will take place in the future, use the future tense.
2. Make infinitives, participles, and verbs in subordinate clauses agree in tense with the verb in the main clause.
3. Use *shall* and *will* interchangeably except for the more formal types of writing.
   a. To express simple futurity, use *shall* in the first person and *will* in the second and third persons.
   b. To express determination, willingness, desire, or promise, use *will* in the first person and *shall* in the second and third persons.
4. To express obligation, use *should* in all three persons.
5. To express habitual action, use *would* in all three persons.
6. Put infinitives in the present tense unless they represent action prior to that of the governing verb.

UNDERLINING

1. In typed material, underline titles and words that are usually printed in italics:

   Titles of books, works of art, and music
   Titles of periodicals
   Footnote reference abbreviations
   Foreign words and phrases (consult a dictionary to learn which words have become part of the English language)

2. Underline written material for emphasis, as:

   Subject headings and subheads
   Words and phrases containing important facts or figures

3. Use either a single, solid line or a broken line under each individual word:

   <u>A Manual for Writers of Dissertations</u>

   <u>A</u> <u>Manual</u> <u>for</u> <u>Writers</u> <u>of</u> <u>Dissertations</u>

VOICE

1. Use the active voice of verbs (somebody or something does something) when a direct, personalized style is appropriate for the purpose and reader.
2. Use the active voice of verbs to gain emphasis.
3. Use the passive voice of verbs (the subject is acted upon) when an impersonal, indirect style suits the subject matter and reader.
4. Use the passive voice for suggestions, instructions, and recommendations when an impersonal style is appropriate.
5. Avoid shifting from the active to passive voice or from the passive to active voice.

INDEX

A

B

C

G

H

I

J

K

L

M

N

O

P

Q

R

S

T

U

V

W

Y

Z